Extending and Modifying LAMMPS

Writing Your Own Source Code

A pragmatic guide to extending LAMMPS as per custom simulation requirements

Dr. Shafat Mubin

Jichen Li

BIRMINGHAM—MUMBAI

Extending and Modifying LAMMPS
Writing Your Own Source Code

Group Product Manager: Aaron Lazar
Senior Editor: Rohit Singh
Content Development Editor: Rosal Colaco
Technical Editor: Pradeep Sahu
Copy Editor: Safis Editing
Project Coordinator: Deeksha Thakkar
Proofreader: Safis Editing
Indexer: Rekha Nair
Production Designer: Aparna Bhagat

First published: January 2021

Production reference: 1220121

Published by Packt Publishing Ltd.
Livery Place
35 Livery Street
Birmingham
B3 2PB, UK.

ISBN 978-1-80056-226-4

www.packt.com

All praise is to Allah, the most merciful, the most gracious.

– Dr. Shafat Mubin

To all the people who make the world better.

– Jichen Li

Packt.com

Subscribe to our online digital library for full access to over 7,000 books and videos, as well as industry leading tools to help you plan your personal development and advance your career. For more information, please visit our website.

Why subscribe?

- Spend less time learning and more time coding with practical eBooks and Videos from over 4,000 industry professionals

- Improve your learning with Skill Plans built especially for you

- Get a free eBook or video every month

- Fully searchable for easy access to vital information

- Copy and paste, print, and bookmark content

Did you know that Packt offers eBook versions of every book published, with PDF and ePub files available? You can upgrade to the eBook version at packt.com and as a print book customer, you are entitled to a discount on the eBook copy. Get in touch with us at customercare@packtpub.com for more details.

At www.packt.com, you can also read a collection of free technical articles, sign up for a range of free newsletters, and receive exclusive discounts and offers on Packt books and eBooks.

Foreword

Many users of LAMMPS think of it as a tool that provides various features; they likely never look at the source code itself, which is a perfectly fine way to use it. But if you want LAMMPS to do something a little different than what it already does, or you have an idea for something completely new that LAMMPS could do, and you either don't know where to start or want a big-picture view of how to go about it, then this book is for you.

It gives a gentle introduction to how the LAMMPS source code is structured, how to find the code that corresponds to specific features of a LAMMPS input script so you can see how it works, and how to modify or write new code to implement new options or new commands that you want to add to LAMMPS. Most importantly, in my view, it gives some concrete and non-trivial examples of features in different categories (what LAMMPS calls *styles*) that could be added in the code.

If you follow the step-by-step explanations and instructions provided in this book, you will have a sound understanding of how to do the preceding activities yourself for some new idea you care about in your own research. In fact, about 95% of the LAMMPS source code are styles, which the developers or users added to the code in the same manner and for the same reasons. They wanted to alter an existing model, formulate a new one, or measure a new property, so that LAMMPS could be used to tackle a new problem.

Finally, if you follow the methodologies explained in this book and write some new code for LAMMPS that you think will be useful to others, I hope you will consider submitting it on the LAMMPS GitHub site for possible inclusion in the distribution. That is how many features in current LAMMPS came to be. And it is how its user community continues to help the code grow and become a more useful tool.

Dr. Steven Plimpton

Lead developer of LAMMPS

Contributors

About the authors

Dr. Shafat Mubin (PhD in physics, Penn State) is an assistant professor of physics at Valdosta State University. Since his graduate student days, he has worked with molecular simulations primarily using LAMMPS and has investigated a variety of simulation systems employing a wide array of techniques. He possesses extensive experience in writing custom routines and extending the LAMMPS source code and hosts his own website to instruct and demonstrate how to do so to other users. At present, he is engaged in computational physics research, including molecular simulations, and endeavors to train undergraduate students in computational techniques to help them better prepare for careers in physics.

I want to thank the people who have supported me, especially Farhana.

Jichen Li (graduated from Qingdao University of Science and Technology) is now studying for his master's degree at the University of Science and Technology of China. He has used LAMMPS to conduct molecular simulations to explore the relationship between polymer microstructure and macro mechanical and rheological properties. He has developed several modeling and post-processing frameworks for LAMMPS and possesses a thorough understanding of its program architecture. He is dedicated to community learning and contributes to the community through his website, where he has written several columns and tutorials for LAMMPS beginners. At present, he is working on trans-scale simulation and the combination of deep learning and simulation.

I would like to thank my parents for their encouragement, Peiyuan Wang, for his support, and my tutor, Jianhui Song, who led me to the field of molecular dynamics.

About the reviewers

Jie Peng is a postdoc from the School of Material Science at Purdue University, US. He has great experience in the area of physics and material engineering. He graduated from the Shanghai Jiao Tong University (China) with a bachelor's and a master's degree, and obtained his PhD from the University of Maryland (US) in May 2019. He likes working in interdisciplinary areas where he can see the fundamental science behind materials' behavior while being able to exploit his knowledge to make use of these materials. He studies the least amount of energy that is transferred in materials – electrons and phonons. The goal is to understand the law of energy transfer at the nanoscale, at which most modern devices operate – cell phones, computers, and so on.

Shih-Hsien Liu is a postdoctoral research associate at the Center for Molecular Biophysics of Oak Ridge National Laboratory. He is a research professional with a chemical engineering background and has experience in physical and computational chemistry for biological applications. His research interests include drug discovery, bioenergy, nanoscience, and molecular dynamics. He obtained his PhD in computational chemistry from the Pennsylvania State University in 2017, an M.S. in materials chemistry from National Taiwan University in 2010, and a B.S.E. in chemical engineering from National Taiwan University in 2008.

Packt is searching for authors like you

If you're interested in becoming an author for Packt, please visit `authors.packtpub.com` and apply today. We have worked with thousands of developers and tech professionals, just like you, to help them share their insight with the global tech community. You can make a general application, apply for a specific hot topic that we are recruiting an author for, or submit your own idea.

Table of Contents

Preface

Section 1: Getting Started with LAMMPS

1

MD Theory and Simulation Practices

Technical requirements	4	Implementing MD simulation practices	11
Introducing MD theory	4	Pair-potential cutoff	11
Understanding the dynamics of point particles	4	Periodic boundary conditions	11
Performing iterative updates using the Velocity Verlet algorithm	6	Neighbor lists	14
		Processor communication	15
Understanding rotational motion	8	Summary	17
Examining temperature and velocity distribution of particles	9	Questions	17

2

LAMMPS Syntax and Source Code Hierarchy

Technical requirements	20	Reviewing the source code hierarchy	23
Introducing the LAMMPS input script structure	20	Summary	25
Introducing the source code repository	22	Further reading	25
		Questions	25

Section 2: Understanding the Source Code Structure

3

Source Code Structure and Stages of Execution

Technical requirements	30	verlet.cpp	36
Introducing parent and child classes	30	min.cpp	41
fix.cpp and fix.h	30	Role of pointers class	42
pair.cpp and pair.h	32	Parsing input script commands by input.cpp	43
compute.cpp and compute.h	35	Summary	44
Stages of executing the simulation	36	Further reading	45
		Questions	45

4

Accessing Information by Variables, Arrays, and Methods

Technical requirements	48	Accessing physical constants	55
Accessing atom properties during simulation runs	48	Reading parameters from the input script	57
Mapping atom indices	51	Incorporating new data types	62
Requesting a neighbor list	52	Summary	64
		Questions	64

5

Understanding Pair Styles

Technical requirements	66	PairMorse::coeff()	70
Reviewing the general structure of pair styles	66	PairMorse::init_one()	71
		PairMorse::compute()	72
Reviewing the Morse potential	67	PairMorse::single()	74
PairMorse::allocate()	68	Reviewing the table potential	75
PairMorse::settings()	69	PairTable::settings()	76

PairTable::coeff()   78
PairTable::compute()   79

Reviewing the DPD potential   80
PairDPD::settings()   82

PairDPD::compute()   83

Summary   85
Questions   86

6
Understanding Computes

Technical requirements   88
**Reviewing the general structure
of computes   88**
Reviewing the compute KE class 89
ComputeKE::ComputeKE()   90
ComputeKE::init()   90
ComputeKE::compute_scalar()   91

**Reviewing the compute group/
group class   93**
ComputeGroupGroup::Compute
GroupGroup()   93
ComputeGroupGroup::init() and init_list() 95
ComputeGroupGroup::pair_
contribution()   95
ComputeGroupGroup::compute_

scalar() and
compute_vector()   97

Reviewing the compute RDF class98
ComputeRDF::ComputeRDF()   100
ComputeRDF::init() and init_list()   102
ComputeRDF::init_norm()   103
ComputeRDF::compute_array()   104

**Reviewing the compute heat
flux class   107**
ComputeHeatFlux::ComputeHeatFlux() 109
ComputeHeatFlux::init()   110
ComputeHeatFlux::compute_vector()   110

Summary   114
Questions   115

7
Understanding Fixes

Technical requirements   118
**Exploring the general structure
of fixes   118**
**Reviewing the Fix AddForce
class   118**
FixAddForce::FixAddForce()   119
FixAddForce::init()   120
FixAddForce::setmask()   122
FixAddForce::post_force()   123

Studying the Fix NVE class   125
FixNVE::initial_integrate()   127
FixNVE::final_integrate()   128

Studying the Fix NH class   129
Studying the Fix Print class   134
FixPrint::FixPrint()   134
FixPrint::end_of_step()   136

Reviewing the Fix Orient/FCC
class   137
FixOrientFCC::FixOrientFCC()   141
FixOrientFCC::find_best_ref()   142
FixOrientFCC::post_force()   143

Analyzing the Fix Wall and Fix
Wall/LJ126 classes   144

Fix wall/lj126   146
Exploring the Fix Rigid class   148
FixRigid::initial_integrate()   152
FixRigid::set_xv()   153
FixRigid::final_integrate()   154
Summary   155
Questions   156

8
Exploring Supporting Classes

Technical requirements   158
Discovering the Group class   158
Exploring the Variable class   161
Studying the Error class   164
Error::all()   165
Error::one()   166
Error::warning() and message()   166

Reviewing the Memory class   167
Discussing the Angle and angle/
harmonic classes   173
The Angle class   176
The angle/harmonic class   176
Summary   180
Questions   181

Section 3: Modifying the Source Code

9
Modifying Pair Potentials

Technical requirements   186
Writing a harmonic potential   186
Changing class names   187
Changing variables and equations   189
Parsing input parameters for Pair
Harmonic   192
Trial run (in.Test_PairHarmonic)   193

Writing a height-dependent
pair potential   196
Changing the header file, pair_table.h   199
Parsing input parameters for Pair

TableZ   200
Implementing height-dependence   202
Trial run (in.Test_PairTableZ)   206

Writing a friction-based pair
style   209
Modifying the compute() method   210
Trial run (in.Test_PairCundallStrack)   214

Summary   218
Questions   219

10
Modifying Force Applications

Technical requirements 222

Writing a fix to apply a 2D
spring force 222

Theory (2D spring force) 222

Modifying the header
file – addforceXY.h 223

Modifying the constructor in
fix_addforceXY.cpp 224

Modifying the init() method in
fix_addforceXY.cpp 225

Modifying the post_force() method in
fix_addforceXY.cpp 227

Trial run (in.Test_FixAddforceXY) 229

Writing a fix to apply an active
force 231

Theory (active force on bonded atoms) 232

Modifying the header
file – fix_activeforce.h 233

Modifying the constructor in
fix_activeforce.cpp 234

Modifying the post_force() method in
fix_activeforce.cpp 235

Trial run (in.Test_ActiveForce) 240

Writing a fix to apply a custom
wall force 243

Theory (expanded Lennard–Jones
wall force) 244

Modifying the header file 244

Modifying the constructor in
fix_wall_region.cpp 245

Modifying the init() method in
fix_wall_region.cpp 246

Adding the lj126Expanded() method 247

Modifying the post_force() method 248

Trial run (in.Test_WallRegion) 249

Writing a fix to apply a
bond-boost potential 252

Theory (the bond-boost method) 253

Modifying the header
file – fix_addboost.h 254

Modifying the constructor in
fix_addboost.cpp 256

Modifying the init() method in
fix_addboost.cpp 257

Modifying the post_force() method in
fix_addboost.cpp 258

Trial run (in.Test_FixAddboost) 260

Summary 265

Questions 266

11
Modifying Thermostats

Technical requirements 268

Writing a fix to apply the
Andersen thermostat 268

Theory – Andersen thermostat 268

Modifying the header
file – fix_temp_andersen.h 269

Modifying the constructor in
fix_temp_andersen.cpp 270

Modifying the end_of_step() method of
fix_temp_andersen.cpp 271

Trial run – in.Test_Andersen 273

Writing a fix to apply a non-linear temperature increment 277

Theory – Exponential temperature increment 277
Modifying the fix_nh.h header file 278
Modifying the constructor in fix_nh.cpp 279
Modifying the init() method in fix_nh.cpp 281
Modifying the compute_temp_target() method in fix_nh.cpp 282
Modifying the compute_scalar() method in fix_nh.cpp 284
Trial run – in.Test_Addboost 285

Writing a fix to print output at evaporation 289

Theory – Evaporation region 289
Modifying the header file – fix_printEvaporate.h 290
Modifying the constructor and init() methods in fix_printEvaporate.cpp 290
Modifying the end_of_step() method in fix_printEvaporate.cpp 292
Trial run – in.Test_PrintEvaporate 293

Summary 296
Questions 296

Appendix A
Building LAMMPS with CMake

Technical requirements 297
Prerequisites for working with LAMMPS 298
Downloading the source code 298
Installing the dependencies 298
Downloading MPICH 299

Building LAMMPS 299
Including packages in the build 300
Including modified codes 301
Building with CMake 301

Compiling LAMMPS in Windows 304
Downloading Git for Windows 304
Downloading the source code 304
Downloading CMake for Windows 305
Downloading Microsoft MPI 306
Downloading Code::Blocks 306

Developing LAMMPS 306
Building with Make 311

Further reading 312

Appendix B
Debugging Programs

Technical requirements 313
What is debugging? 314
Prerequisites 314
Method 1 – Debugging with GDB 317

Method 2 – Debugging with VSCode 319
Insight into sbmask() 321
Further reading 324

Appendix C
Getting Familiar with MPI

Technical requirements	326	MPI receive message	328
What is MPI?	326	MPI message	328
MPI initialization	326	MPI in LAMMPS	329
MPI finalization	326	Example of evaluating π	333
MPI current process ID	327	Data exchange between owned	
MPI (number of processes)	327	atoms and ghost atoms	336
MPI send message	327		

Appendix D
Compatibility with Version 29Oct20

Technical requirements	340	parameters	341
Translating Fix Widom into the		Incompatibility 2 – Atom class	341
3Mar20 version	340	Incompatibility 3 – Function signatures	
Incompatibility 1 – Parsing input		in group.cpp	343

Assessments

Other Books You May Enjoy

Index

Preface

LAMMPS is one of the most widely used tools for running simulations for research in molecular dynamics. While the tool itself is fairly easy to use, more often than not, you'll need to customize it to meet your specific simulation requirements.

Extending and Modifying LAMMPS bridges this learning gap and helps you achieve this by writing custom code to add new features to LAMMPS source code. Written by ardent supporters of LAMMPS, this practical guide will enable you to extend the capabilities of LAMMPS with the help of step-by-step explanations of essential concepts, practical examples, and self-assessment questions.

Filled with real-world examples, this book teaches you how to find your way around the LAMMPS source code and shows you, in a pragmatic and easily digestible way, how to modify the code to achieve custom simulations for your work.

This LAMMPS book provides a hands-on approach to implementing associated methodologies that will get you up and running and productive in no time. You'll begin with a short introduction to the internal mechanisms of LAMMPS and gradually transition to an overview of the source code along with a tutorial on modifying it.

You'll also learn how to identify how LAMMPS input script commands are executed within the source code and understand the architecture of the source code. You'll learn how to modify the source code to implement custom features in LAMMPS, relate source code elements to simulated quantities, and explore pair styles and computes within LAMMPS. You'll also learn how to create various custom fixes to control your simulation using pre-defined criteria.

As you advance, you'll learn about the structure, syntax, and organization of LAMMPS source code, and will be able to write your own source code extensions to LAMMPS that implement features beyond the ones available in standard downloadable versions. You'll understand how to work with custom solutions for applications on force, thermostats, and pair potentials.

By the end of this source code book, you'll have learned how to how to add your own extensions and modifications to the LAMMPS source code that can implement features that suit your simulation requirements.

Who this book is for

This book is for students, faculty members, and researchers who are currently using LAMMPS or considering switching to LAMMPS, have a basic knowledge of how to use LAMMPS, and are looking to extend LAMMPS source code for research purposes. This book is not a tutorial on using LAMMPS or writing LAMMPS scripts, and it is assumed that the reader is comfortable with basic LAMMPS syntax. The book is geared toward users with little to no experience in source code editing. Familiarity with C++ programming is helpful but not necessary.

What this book covers

Chapter 1, MD Theory and Simulation Practices, briefly introduces fundamental concepts of molecular dynamics, common techniques, and features that will be addressed later in the book to provide a link between theory and simulation.

Chapter 2, LAMMPS Syntax and Source Code Repository, introduces LAMMPS input script and the execution of MD simulation features through LAMMPS commands and an introduction to the repository of standard LAMMPS code.

Chapter 3, Source Code Structure and Stages of Execution, introduces the LAMMPS source code format and the sequence of execution followed in a LAMMPS script.

Chapter 4, Accessing Information by Variables, Arrays, and Methods, describes the elements that store information and perform calculations during a simulation run.

Chapter 5, Understanding Pair Styles, describes and dissects selected pair styles.

Chapter 6, Understanding Computes, describes and dissects selected computes.

Chapter 7, Understanding Fixes, describes and dissects selected fixes.

Chapter 8, Exploring Supporting Classes, describes and dissects other additional LAMMPS features.

Chapter 9, Modifying Pair Potentials, discusses the implementation of custom pair styles.

Chapter 10, Modifying Force Applications, discusses the implementation of custom fix styles to apply forces based on pre-defined criteria.

Chapter 11, Modifying Thermostats, discusses the implementation of custom fix styles associated with temperature control.

Appendix A, Building LAMMPS with CMake, introduces LAMMPS compilation using CMake in Linux and Windows.

Appendix B, Debugging with GDB and Visual Studio Code, introduces debugging tools with applications on understanding bit operations.

Appendix C, Getting Familiar with MPI, introduces MPI parallel processing.

Appendix D, Compatibility with Version 29Oct20, discusses source code differences between stable versions **3Mar20** and **29Oct20**.

Assessments, contains the answers to all the questions from this book.

To get the most out of this book

Software required	OS requirements
LAMMPS stable version 3Mar20	Windows, macOS X, and Linux (any)
A text editor (such as Gedit, Notepad++)	
Linux Terminal	

If you are using the digital version of this book, we advise you to type the code yourself or access the code via the GitHub repository (link available in the next section). Doing so will help you avoid any potential errors related to the copying and pasting of code.

Also, we advise that you download the LAMMPS stable version **3Mar20** *and have the corresponding files open when viewing the code discussions provided in the book.*

Download the example code files

You can download the example code files for this book from GitHub at `https://github.com/PacktPublishing/Extending-and-Modifying-LAMMPS-Writing-Your-Own-Source-Code`. In case there's an update to the code, it will be updated on the existing GitHub repository.

We also have other code bundles from our rich catalog of books and videos available at `https://github.com/PacktPublishing/`. Check them out!

Download the color images

We also provide a PDF file that has color images of the screenshots/diagrams used in this book. You can download it here: `https://static.packt-cdn.com/downloads/9781800562264_ColorImages.pdf`.

Conventions used

There are a number of text conventions used throughout this book.

`Code in text`: Indicates code words in text, database table names, folder names, filenames, file extensions, pathnames, dummy URLs, user input, and Twitter handles. Here is an example: "In the `single()` method, the `scalingZ` variable is calculated and used to scale the potential before it is returned."

A block of code is set as follows:

```
units metal
dimension 3
boundary p p p
atom_style        atomic
atom_modify map array
```

When we wish to draw your attention to a particular part of a code block, the relevant lines or items are set in bold:

```
pair_style   tableZ linear 10000
pair_coeff   1 1   Table_Potential.table V_Table 12.0 17.0 1.0
-0.04 10.0
compute TABLE_PE G1 group/group G2
variable TABLE_PE equal c_TABLE_PE
```

Bold: Indicates a new term, an important word, or words that you see onscreen. For example, words in menus or dialog boxes appear in the text like this. Here is an example: "As you can see, the atoms will cross **R_EVAP** sequentially and the `Fix PrintEvaporate` command will be able to register these crossings by printing to file."

Tips or important notes
Appear like this.

Get in touch

Feedback from our readers is always welcome.

General feedback: If you have questions about any aspect of this book, mention the book title in the subject of your message and email us at customercare@packtpub.com.

Errata: Although we have taken every care to ensure the accuracy of our content, mistakes do happen. If you have found a mistake in this book, we would be grateful if you would report this to us. Please visit www.packtpub.com/support/errata, selecting your book, clicking on the Errata Submission Form link, and entering the details.

Piracy: If you come across any illegal copies of our works in any form on the Internet, we would be grateful if you would provide us with the location address or website name. Please contact us at copyright@packt.com with a link to the material.

If you are interested in becoming an author: If there is a topic that you have expertise in and you are interested in either writing or contributing to a book, please visit authors.packtpub.com.

Reviews

Please leave a review. Once you have read and used this book, why not leave a review on the site that you purchased it from? Potential readers can then see and use your unbiased opinion to make purchase decisions, we at Packt can understand what you think about our products, and our authors can see your feedback on their book. Thank you!

For more information about Packt, please visit packt.com.

Section 1: Getting Started with LAMMPS

A LAMMPS input script performs molecular dynamics simulations according to the input commands provided. *But what happens behind the scenes as each command is parsed and executed? How are these commands processed and how are relevant calculations invoked within the source code?*

This section introduces you to molecular dynamics theory and standard simulation practices that are implemented in LAMMPS, along with the corresponding syntax. The theory and practices will be revisited in later sections when the LAMMPS source code is analyzed.

This section comprises the following chapters:

- *Chapter 1, MD Theory and Simulation Practices*
- *Chapter 2, LAMMPS Syntax and Source Code Repository*

1
MD Theory and Simulation Practices

This chapter introduces the theory behind **molecular dynamics (MD)** and some common simulation practices. Starting from **Newton's laws**, we outline the physics behind the dynamics of point particles and rigid bodies, discuss iterative updating and the relevance of temperature, and end by listing computational practices.

In this chapter, we will cover the follow topics:

- Introducing MD theory
- Understanding the dynamics of point particles
- Performing iterative updates using the Velocity Verlet algorithm
- Understanding rotational motion
- Examining temperature and velocity distribution of particles
- Implementing MD simulation practices including cutoff, periodic boundaries, and neighbor lists

By the end of this chapter, you will have grasped an understanding of the theoretical fundamentals implemented in MD software.

Technical requirements

You can find the full source code used in this book here: https://github.com/PacktPublishing/Extending-and-Modifying-LAMMPS-Writing-Your-Own-Source-Code

Introducing MD theory

MD is based on simulating individual particle trajectories over a desired time period to analyze the time evolution of an entire system of particles in a solid, liquid, or gaseous state. Each particle (usually an atom) is allowed to traverse in space as determined by Newton's laws of classical dynamics, where the atomic positions, velocities, and accelerations at one point in time are used to calculate the corresponding kinematics quantities at a different point in time. This process is repeated over a sufficiently long-time interval for every atom in a system, and the final configuration of the atoms indicates the time evolution of the system over the said time interval.

Typical MD simulations are limited to the study of atomistic systems consisting of atoms in the range of 10^2 to 10^6, occupying a simulation box with a length in the order of nanometers, over a regular timescale of nanoseconds. MD simulations of such microscopic systems are relevant when the systems are able to represent the time evolution of corresponding macroscopic systems.

The theory behind MD is described briefly in the following sections. For a more detailed understanding, you are advised to refer to the dedicated literature on MD theory (*Computer Simulation of Liquids* by Michael P. Allen and Dominic J. Tildesley, and *Understanding Molecular Simulation* by Daan Frenkel and Berend Smit).

Understanding the dynamics of point particles

The trajectory $\vec{r}(t) = (x(t), y(t), z(t))$ of a point particle over time t is calculated from its mass m and net force $\overrightarrow{F_{net}}$ using Newton's equation, as illustrated here:

$$\overrightarrow{F_{net}} = m\ddot{\vec{r}}(t)$$

$\overrightarrow{F_{net}}$ is determined from the sum of all forces acting on the particle. In a system of interacting particles, the force $\vec{F}$ acting between one pair of particles can be determined from the gradient of the potential energy function $V(\Delta x, \Delta y, \Delta z)$. Here, $(\Delta x, \Delta y, \Delta z)$ is the displacement vector that points *to* the particle for which we are calculating $\vec{F}$ (using the following equation) and originates *from* the other particle in the pair (shown in *Figure 1.1*):

$$\vec{F} = -\nabla V(\Delta x, \Delta y, \Delta z)$$

This gives us the three components of $\vec{F} = (F_x, F_y, F_z)$. The (x) force component is given as follows:

$$F_x = -\frac{dV}{dr} \cdot \frac{\Delta x}{r}$$

The (y) force component is calculated by the following formula:

$$F_y = -\frac{dV}{dr} \cdot \frac{\Delta y}{r}$$

The (z) force component is given by the following formula:

$$F_z = -\frac{dV}{dr} \cdot \frac{\Delta z}{r}$$

Here, $r = |(\Delta x, \Delta y, \Delta z)|$ is the distance between the pair of particles. By Newton's third law, it follows that the force components acting on the other particle in the pair have the same magnitudes, with the opposite sign.

The following diagram illustrates this concept, using two particles interacting via a **12-6 Lennard-Jones potential** of the form $V(x) = 4\varepsilon\left[\left(\frac{\sigma}{x}\right)^{12} - \left(\frac{\sigma}{x}\right)^{6}\right]$, where ε represents the well depth and σ represents the position at which the potential is zero:

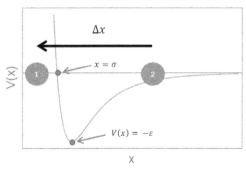

Figure 1.1 – Two particles in 1D interact via a Lennard-Jones potential $V(x) = 4\varepsilon\left[\left(\frac{\sigma}{x}\right)^{12} - \left(\frac{\sigma}{x}\right)^{6}\right]$

In this diagram, if we want to calculate the force from particle **2** (located at $x = |\Delta x|$) acting on particle **1** (located at $x = 0$), then we use $F_{x1} = -\dfrac{dV}{dx} \dfrac{(-|\Delta x|)}{|\Delta x|}$. Subsequently, the reaction force acting on particle **2** is given by $F_{x2} = -\dfrac{dV}{dx} \dfrac{(|\Delta x|)}{|\Delta x|}$.

Since potential energy functions are commonly expressed as functions of r, the expressions we saw earlier make it more convenient to calculate the force components. The sum of forces acting on a single particle by its interaction with all particles in the system gives the net force, as illustrated here:

$$\overrightarrow{F_{net}} = \sum_{all\ pairs} \vec{F} = -\sum_{all\ pairs} \nabla V$$

Altogether, we obtain three equations to solve for $x(t)$, $y(t)$, and $z(t)$. The $x(t)$ equation is given as follows:

$$\ddot{x}(t) = -\frac{1}{m} \sum_{all\ pairs} \left(\frac{dV}{dr} \cdot \frac{x}{r} \right)$$

The $y(t)$ equation is given by the following formula:

$$\ddot{y}(t) = -\frac{1}{m} \sum_{all\ pairs} \left(\frac{dV}{dr} \cdot \frac{y}{r} \right)$$

The $z(t)$ equation is given by the following formula:

$$\ddot{z}(t) = -\frac{1}{m} \sum_{all\ pairs} \left(\frac{dV}{dr} \cdot \frac{z}{r} \right)$$

These values are used to generate the complete trajectory of the particle over a desired time interval. This process is repeated for all particles in the system to yield the complete system time evolution in the same time interval.

Performing iterative updates using the Velocity Verlet algorithm

As particles move in a system over time, the separation $\vec{r}$ between each pair of particles changes accordingly, resulting in a change of the derivatives described in the previous section—that is, the force becomes time-dependent. Therefore, the trajectory is updated over a small increment of time called the *timestep* (Δt), and by iteratively updating the trajectory over a large number of timesteps, a complete trajectory can be obtained.

The purpose of keeping the timestep small is to ensure that the particles do not undergo drastic changes in position and therefore conserve energy in the system. For atomic masses, especially in the presence of forces from molecular bonds, angles, and dihedrals, a timestep of approximately 1 *femtosecond* is typically employed.

An advantage of using a small timestep is that the net force $\overrightarrow{F_{net}}$ acting on a particle can be approximated to remain constant in the duration of the timestep. Therefore, the equations of motion that iteratively update the trajectory at timestep increments become the following:

$$x(t + \Delta t) = x(t) + v_x(t)\Delta t + \frac{1}{2}\frac{F_{net,x}(t)}{m}\Delta t^2$$

$$y(t + \Delta t) = y(t) + v_y(t)\Delta t + \frac{1}{2}\frac{F_{net,y}(t)}{m}\Delta t^2$$

$$z(t + \Delta t) = z(t) + v_z(t)\Delta t + \frac{1}{2}\frac{F_{net,z}(t)}{m}\Delta t^2$$

Here, $\left(v_x(t), v_y(t), v_z(t)\right)$ represents the velocity vector of the particle, and its components are iteratively updated by the following:

$$v_x(t + \Delta t) = v_x(t) + \frac{1}{2}\left[\frac{F_{net,x}(t)}{m} + \frac{F_{net,x}(t + \Delta t)}{m}\right]\Delta t$$

$$v_y(t + \Delta t) = v_y(t) + \frac{1}{2}\left[\frac{F_{net,y}(t)}{m} + \frac{F_{net,y}(t + \Delta t)}{m}\right]\Delta t$$

$$v_z(t + \Delta t) = v_z(t) + \frac{1}{2}\left[\frac{F_{net,z}(t)}{m} + \frac{F_{net,z}(t + \Delta t)}{m}\right]\Delta t$$

Here, the terms within the [ ] represent the average acceleration in each dimension, calculated using the accelerations at time t and the following iteration, $(t + \Delta t)$. This is known as the **Velocity Verlet algorithm**, which considerably reduces errors over a long simulation period as compared to algorithms that use the acceleration at a single point in time (for example, the **Euler algorithm**). Furthermore, the Velocity Verlet algorithm is able to conserve energy and momentum within rounding errors with a sufficiently small timestep, unlike the Euler algorithm, which can lead to an indefinite increase in energy over time.

In effect, the position and velocity of each particle are tabulated at each iteration, as illustrated in the following table:

t	Particle 1		Particle 2		...
	$\vec{r}$	$\vec{v}$	$\vec{r}$	$\vec{v}$	

Table 1.1 – Table showing sequence of iterative update of position and velocity vectors of each particle

This table shows the sequence of iterative update of point particles that undergo a linear motion without any rotational component. In the case of a non-point object such as a rigid body, both linear and rotational motion must be incorporated for a proper treatment of its dynamics. Similar to linear motion, rotational motion of rigid bodies can be iteratively updated using a similar algorithm, as discussed next.

Understanding rotational motion

Rigid bodies are often used to represent molecules with inactive vibrational degrees of freedom. In a rigid body, the locations of all constituent atoms are frozen with respect to the rigid-body coordinates. The intramolecular forces from *bonds, angles, dihedrals,* and *impropers* are assumed not to create any distortion of the rigid body. Therefore, for the purposes of MD, all intramolecular forces in a rigid body can be disregarded. Any force exerted on any constituent atom in a rigid body acts on the entire rigid body. In addition to changing its linear velocity, this force can create a torque on the rigid body and change its angular momentum and angular velocity. The total force on a rigid body $\overrightarrow{F_{tot}}$ composed of N particles is calculated using the following formula:

$$\overrightarrow{F_{tot}} = \sum_{i=1}^{N} (\vec{F_i})$$

Using the displacement vector $\vec{r_i} = (x_i, y_i, z_i)$ of particle i measured from the center of mass of the rigid body as the origin, the torque $\vec{\tau}$ of the rigid body is calculated by the following formula:

$$\vec{\tau} = \sum_{i=1}^{N} (\vec{r_i} \times \vec{F_i}) = \sum_{i=1}^{N} (y_i F_{zi} - z_i F_{yi} , z_i F_{xi} - x_i F_{zi} , x_i F_{yi} - y_i F_{xi})$$

The angular momentum $\vec{L}$ of the rigid body is obtained from the time-integration of τ using the Velocity Verlet algorithm, as follows:

$$\vec{L}(t + \Delta t) = \vec{L}(t) + \frac{1}{2}[\vec{\tau}(t) + \vec{\tau}(t + \Delta t)]\Delta t$$

The angular velocity $\vec{\omega}$ of the rigid body is obtained by a two-step procedure from $\vec{L}$ using an intermediate step at a *half-timestep* $\left(t + \frac{1}{2}\Delta t\right)$ and a second step at a *full-timestep* $(t + \Delta t)$, which will be described in more detail when analyzing the dynamics of rigid bodies in *Chapter 7, Understanding Fixes*. The procedure is illustrated here:

$$I\,\vec{\omega}\left(t + \frac{1}{2}\Delta t\right) = \vec{L}\left(t + \frac{1}{2}\Delta t\right)$$

$$I\,\vec{\omega}(t + \Delta t) = \vec{L}(t + \Delta t)$$

Here, I is the moment of inertia tensor of the rigid body.

For a system of point particles or rigid bodies, the average kinetic energy and the average speed or angular speed are determined by the system temperature. Therefore, controlling the temperature adequately is often essential when simulating a molecular system. The next section discusses the features of a molecular simulation determined by the temperature.

Examining temperature and velocity distribution of particles

A system at thermal equilibrium at a constant temperature T is characterized by its **Maxwell-Boltzmann velocity distribution**. According to this distribution, the probability distribution $f(v_i)$ of velocities in a single direction i (which can be x, y, z) of a system of particles of mass m each is given by the **Gaussian function**, illustrated here in *Figure 1.2*:

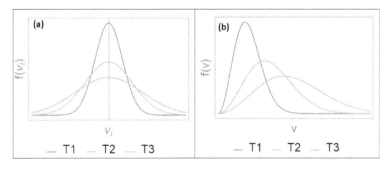

Figure 1.2 – The Maxwell-Boltzmann velocity distributions (left) and speed distributions (right)

The preceding graph is plotted for the same system at three different temperatures **T3 > T2 > T1**.

The corresponding functional form that depends on the mass and temperature is shown here:

$$f(v_i) = \sqrt{\frac{m}{2\pi k_B T}} \exp\left(-\frac{mv_i^2}{2k_B T}\right)$$

Here, k_B is the Boltzmann constant. This distribution has a mean of $\mu = 0$ and a standard deviation of $\sigma = \sqrt{\frac{k_B T}{m}}$. The shape of the Gaussian curve is determined by the ratio of m/T.

The velocity distribution of the velocity vector $\left(v_x, v_y, v_z\right)$ is given by the following formula:

$$f\left(v_x, v_y, v_z\right) = f(v_x)f(v_y)f(v_z) = \left(\frac{m}{2\pi k_B T}\right)^{\frac{3}{2}} \exp\left[-\frac{m\left(v_x^2 + v_y^2 + v_z^2\right)}{2k_B T}\right]$$

In spherical coordinates, this distribution can be written in terms of the speed v, as follows:

$$f(v) = \sqrt{\frac{2}{\pi}} \left(\frac{m}{k_B T}\right)^{3/2} v^2 \exp\left[-\frac{mv^2}{2k_B T}\right]$$

This is the Maxwell-Boltzmann *speed* distribution, also known as a **Rayleigh distribution**. The shape of the speed distribution changes with temperature, as shown in *Figure 1.2*, and the peak speed increases with temperature. The velocity distributions are wider at higher temperatures, and the speed distributions show larger peak speeds at higher temperatures. An algorithm that controls temperature in a molecular simulation must account for the preceding features regarding particle velocities.

So far, concepts that dictate the operation of an MD simulation have been discussed. These concepts are implemented in a computational environment through codes that will be discussed in later chapters. In the next section, we will discuss related computational concepts that are commonly encountered in MD simulations and that are prevalently used to enhance simulation performance.

Implementing MD simulation practices

In order to implement MD simulations that are computationally efficient and model realistic atomic systems, a number of standard simulation practices are employed. A user is likely to find these practices employed in typical **Large-scale Atomic/Molecular Massively Parallel Simulator (LAMMPS)** scripts and it is therefore helpful to be familiar with these concepts before delving into the LAMMPS source code. In this section, we will briefly discuss some of these practices (details are available in the MD textbooks referred to in the *Introducing MD theory* section).

Pair-potential cutoff

If it is desired that a potential reaches exactly zero at the cutoff, an offset (V_{offset}) can be employed by calculating the potential $V(r)$ at the cutoff $r = r_{cut}$, that is $V_{offset} = V(r_{cut})$. This offset can then be subtracted from the original potential to guarantee a zero value at the cutoff, that is $V(r) \rightarrow V(r) - V_{offset}$. Altogether, the potential with the offset changes the value of the system potential, but does not alter the forces because V_{offset} is a constant term that produces zero force contribution upon differentiating.

Most pair-potential functions are defined to asymptotically approach zero potential—for example, the Lennard-Jones function approaches zero as the *inverse-sixth* power of separation. For particles located far from each other, it implies that there exists some small but non-zero potential between them, which may be negligible in a simulation context but still adds numerical computation overhead.

Therefore, a common practice is to employ a cutoff distance for pair potentials, beyond which the interaction is assumed to be zero. The cutoff is chosen at a separation where the potential value is sufficiently small so as not to create significant errors by discounting interaction with neighbors located beyond the cutoff. During a simulation run, only the neighbors located within the cutoff radius of a particle are considered for force or potential calculations, thereby reducing computation time.

Periodic boundary conditions

Simulated systems often consist of a small cell that is representative of a larger system—for example, *nanocrystal* representation of a metal lattice. In such systems, it can often be assumed that the entire system is made up of many replications of the simulation box. In 1912, Born and von Karman came up with the implementation of **periodic boundary conditions** that can simulate a continuous replicated system starting from a simulation box.

Each wall (that is, boundary) of the simulation box is assumed to be adjacent to an identical simulation box containing identical atoms at identical positions. In effect, each wall of the box leads to a replica of the simulation box, containing images of the same atoms as in the simulation box. At every iteration, as the atom positions in the simulation box are updated, the image atoms in the replicas are accordingly updated. The following diagram shows this simulation box:

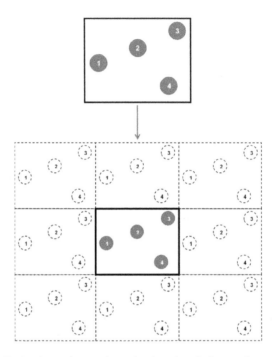

Figure 1.3 – A 2D simulation box without (top) and with (bottom) periodic boundaries

In this diagram, we see the following:

- *Top*: A snapshot of a 2D simulation box consisting of four particles (indexed from **1** to **4**) without periodic boundaries.

- *Bottom*: The same simulation box with periodic boundaries in all directions produces 8 replicas (26 replicas in 3D) containing image atoms (*dashed circles*). At every iteration, all replicas are identically updated by replicating the particles in the central simulation box.

This way, enclosing wall boundaries are eliminated, and any atom that exits the simulation box by passing through a wall will automatically re-enter through the opposite wall, thus conserving the number of atoms and modeling continuous motion of atoms. Furthermore, the atoms in the simulation box are permitted to interact with the image atoms located in the replicas, ensuring that atoms located near to the walls are not considered as fringe atoms with few neighbors only because of their remoteness from the box center.

In *Figure 1.3*, in the absence of periodic boundaries, particle **3** at the top-right corner is observed to be located far from particles **1** and **4**, and would undergo reduced or zero interactions with these particles. By contrast, when periodic boundaries are implemented, particle **3** is located considerably closer to images of particles **1** and **4**.

Subsequently, particle **3** is able to interact with other particles located in all directions around itself as if it were contained in a continuous, unbounded simulation box. At the same time, consistency of interaction requires that particle **3** interacts with either an image or with the original particle in the simulation box, but not both together, and it is accomplished by setting the side lengths of the simulation box to be at least double the pair-potential cutoff distance between atoms. This requirement is known as the **minimum image convention**, which guarantees that pair-potential interactions are not double-counted.

Long-range electrostatic potentials decay considerably slower than many other interactions (as inverse of the separation) and would therefore require disproportionately long cutoffs and correspondingly large simulation boxes to model with a traditional pair potential. To circumvent this problem, electrostatic interactions with image atoms are summed up by an Ewald summation (or a related particle-mesh method) that divides the calculation to a *real-space component* and a *reciprocal-space component*. This way, a cutoff is not required, but periodic boundaries are necessary to ensure sum convergence.

When an atom exits a simulation box and its image enters from the opposite side of the box, the atom coordinates can extend beyond the simulation box coordinates. This is accounted for using the concept of *wrapped* and *unwrapped coordinates*, where unwrapped coordinates represent the unadjusted atom coordinates and wrapped coordinates represent the coordinates adjusted by resetting to the coordinates of the re-entry wall.

In LAMMPS, trajectory output files may include an **image flag** to keep track of wrapped and unwrapped coordinates. When an atom exits the simulation box along the positive direction in any dimension, the image flag corresponding to this axis would increment by one. Accordingly, the image flag decrements by one if the atom exits along the negative direction. Thus, the image flag of an atom multiplied by the corresponding simulation box side length can be used to convert from wrapped to unwrapped coordinates.

Neighbor lists

An atom only interacts with its neighbors located within a cutoff radius, and these neighbors are identified by calculating their distances from the atom in consideration. For a system of N atoms, this could lead to calculating the distance between each of the $\frac{1}{2}(N^2 - N)$ pairs of atoms. To reduce the computation overhead, for every atom a subset of neighbors is selected into a **neighbor list** (suggested by Verlet in 1967), and only these short-listed neighbors are used to calculate the interactions with the atom.

At the beginning of a simulation, a neighbor list is built for every interacting atom in the system by tagging all its neighboring atoms that lie within its cutoff or within a short buffer width, known as the **skin width** (shown in *Figure 1.4*). If the atoms are not traveling at extreme speeds, only the atoms located within the cutoff or the skin (that is, the neighbor-list members) at a certain iteration can be expected to lie inside the cutoff radius in the next iteration, and it can be expected that no atom previously located outside the skin will be able to cross inside the cutoff radius in the space of one iteration.

This way, the neighbor list excludes atoms that are located sufficiently far by reusing information from the preceding iteration, and this therefore reduces computation time in calculating neighbor distances. The process is illustrated in the following diagram:

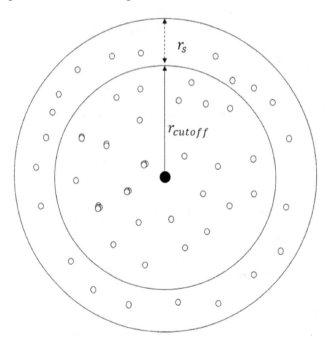

Figure 1.4 – Illustration of the radial cutoff distance r_{cutoff} and the skin width r_s of a central atom (black dot)

At any timestep, the atoms that are located inside r_s are included in the neighbor list of the central atom, whereas only the atoms located inside r_{cutoff} interact with the central atom. At the next iteration, only the atoms tagged in the neighbor list are considered when identifying atoms that can interact with the central atom, and the neighbor list may be rebuilt depending on the displacements of the atoms.

Generally, the neighbor lists do not have to be rebuilt at every iteration, and the interval between rebuilding can be defined by the user. Also, a common practice is to rebuild only when an atom has traveled more than half the skin width since the previous neighbor-list build. It also implies that a larger skin width requires less frequent neighbor-list builds, at the cost of including a greater number of neighbors per list at every iteration.

The skin width can be specified independently of the cutoff distance and is generally chosen according to timestep and expected particle velocities. At the lower limit, the skin width should be double the maximum displacement expected of a particle in an iteration. In LAMMPS, if an atom is able to cross the skin width in one iteration, the associated neighbor lists experience a **dangerous build** whereby the loss of the atom can lead to errors in force calculations and violation of energy conservation. If a dangerous build is detected, the neighbor list needs to be rebuilt to rectify this.

When a neighbor list is used to calculate the interaction force between a pair of atoms, the two atoms in the pair can be assigned equal and opposite forces by Newton's third law. This equivalency can be enabled using a *full-neighbor list*, whereas it can be disabled by using a *half-neighbor list*. While a full-neighbor list reduces computation cost, half-neighbor lists may be preferred in simulations where equal and opposite forces are not applicable.

Processor communication

Modern parallel computers have two main forms: **shared-memory** machines, where multiple processors (often called **cores**) access the same memory; and **distributed-memory** machines, where a processor (often called a **node**) cannot access the memory designated to another processor. Modern high-performance computing facilities are all based on a hybrid architecture. A node consists of multiple cores, and many nodes combine to form a supercomputer. This architecture also leads to an issue of distributing the workload and allocating tasks between nodes and cores.

In the context of MD, one strategy that addresses the task allocation problem is **spatial decomposition**, which divides the simulation box into equal sections and assigns atoms located in each section to a different core, as shown here:

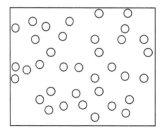 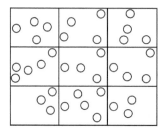

Figure 1.5 – (Left) A single processing core calculating the trajectory of every atom in the simulation box. (Right) The simulation box is divided into domains, and the atoms in each domain are assigned to a different core

The domains in the preceding diagram are spatially decomposed by volume. Copies of atoms, known as *ghost atoms*, are exchanged between processors to account for interactions between atoms located on different cores. Each core calculates the interactions of atoms assigned to it in parallel and thereby increases the overall simulation speed.

To account for interactions between atoms located on different cores, each core builds its domain with a shell that accommodates particles located at the edges of a domain, and exchanges copies of particles (known as ghost atoms) with other cores, as illustrated in the following diagram:

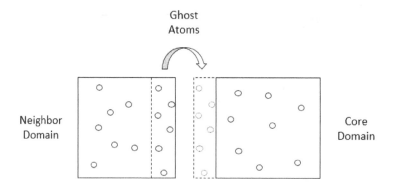

Figure 1.6 – A core domain showing its shell (dashed box) and ghost atoms shared with a neighboring domain

There are two stages of communication between cores involved, detailed here:

- In the first stage, the shell exchanges the ghost-atom coordinates with neighboring cores to register the particles that can interact with the particles contained in the domain. The ghost atoms in these shells are essentially images of atoms in other domains.

- In the second stage, the updated atom positions at the following iteration are used to determine whether any atom has moved to a different domain, and if so, the atom coordinates and kinematics information are communicated to the appropriate cores. After this step, the particles in the shell are deleted from the memory.

This parallel mechanism demonstrates that communication time between cores multiplies as the number of cores increases. Due to memory and bandwidth limits, parallelization cannot achieve the ideal optimization of N/P, where N is the number of atoms and P is the number of processors, and leads to a sub-linear speedup. Therefore, for a given simulation system an increasing number of cores eventually reduces efficiency, and there exists an optimum number of cores that delivers the best performance.

Summary

The basics of MD and common MD simulation practices have been laid out in this chapter to help elucidate the physics and mathematics implemented in MD codes. When the LAMMPS source code is discussed in later chapters, the concepts discussed here will be referenced and explicated in terms of the source code.

In the next chapter, you will be introduced to LAMMPS input script and the execution of MD simulation features through LAMMPS commands, and the repository of standard LAMMPS codes.

Questions

1. Using a simulation box having periodic boundaries in all directions, how can a metal slab consisting of a few layers be generated such that the slab extends indefinitely in the xy-plane but accommodates a long vacuum above and below the slab?

2. How should the optimum skin width compare between a solid at a low temperature versus a gas at a high temperature?

3. In a large simulation box containing a uniform density of solute and solvent molecules, how would the pair-potential energy of a solute molecule at the center of the box change with periodic or non-periodic boundaries (assuming that the pair-potential cutoff is shorter than half of any of the simulation box side lengths)?

4. Given a uniform-metal nanocrystal, how can subdomains and ghost atoms be established?

2
LAMMPS Syntax and Source Code Hierarchy

In this chapter, we will outline the LAMMPS input script structure and connect script commands with the source code operating in the background. The source code repository is introduced, followed by the class hierarchy that is responsible for setting up the simulation framework and parsing commands, and it culminates in a brief overview of several top-level classes.

We will cover the following topics:

- Introducing the structure of a typical LAMMPS input script
- Introducing the repository of source code files
- Reviewing the source code hierarchy
- Functions of selected top-level classes

The end goal of this chapter is to explain how the source code lays out the simulation foundations, which will help you better understand the process of modifying or extending LAMMPS.

Technical requirements

To execute the instructions in this chapter, we only need a text editor (for example, **Notepad++, Gedit**)

You can find the full source code used in this chapter here: `https://github.com/PacktPublishing/Extending-and-Modifying-LAMMPS-Writing-Your-Own-Source-Code`.

Introducing the LAMMPS input script structure

LAMMPS offers built-in features to construct MD simulations using its own scripting syntax. An inventory of LAMMPS script syntax is available on the LAMMPS website (`www.lammps.sandia.gov`). The input script is executed line by line from beginning to end. A typical input script consists of the following parts:

- **Initialization Settings**
- **System Definitions**
- **Simulation Settings**
- **Simulation Execution**

A sample input script may look like the one shown here:

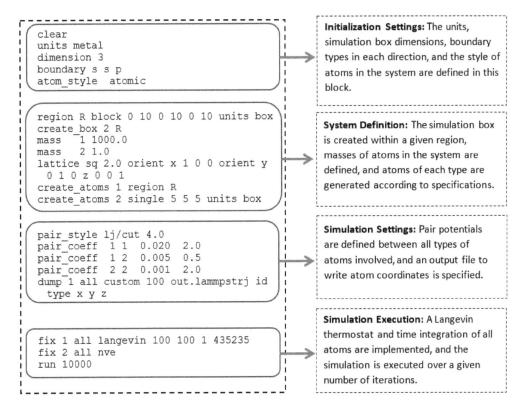

Figure 2.1 – A sample input script of LAMMPS

An input script such as this sets up an MD simulation by specifying the simulation box size and boundaries, creating atoms, defining the pair potentials between atoms, applying a thermostat, and finally executing the simulation. The command lines starting with `pair` define pair potentials, and the lines starting with `fix` perform a multitude of operations on the system, including thermostat and time integration. A large number of MD features are implemented via the `pair` and `fix` commands, both of which will be discussed in detail later in *Chapter 5, Understanding Pair Styles*, and *Chapter 7, Understanding Fixes*.

At each line, the command script is scanned by the LAMMPS executable and the corresponding source code is executed. The source codes controlling the entire operation are introduced in the next section.

Introducing the source code repository

After downloading and unzipping LAMMPS (visit `https://lammps.sandia.gov/doc/Install_tarball.html` for instructions), the source code can be accessed from the `src` folder, shown as follows:

Figure 2.2 – A screenshot of the src folder showing .cpp and .h source files in pairs, and a list of packages separated into folders

The source files are mostly arranged in pairs of **C++** and header files with the extensions `.cpp` and `.h`, respectively, which together are responsible for performing a given role in the simulation.

When a LAMMPS executable is compiled, the source files are built into it, along with any optional package. The folders titled in all uppercase letters in *Figure 2.2* contain optional packages that can be built into the LAMMPS executable if specified. Once compiled successfully, the executable is capable of recognizing LAMMPS input script commands and calling the appropriate source code files that have been installed.

When a LAMMPS script is executed, the top-level classes in the source code first instantiate LAMMPS and set up the simulation by allocating memory, parsing input script lines, partitioning processors, instantiating an integrating class, and constructing neighbor lists. It allows the rest of the input script to be executed, including pair and fix commands, and to finish by printing screen outputs. The top-level classes and the source code hierarchy are discussed in the next section.

Reviewing the source code hierarchy

The topmost-level class in the source code hierarchy is `lammps.cpp` (and `lammps.h`), which initiates LAMMPS by accommodating an instance of LAMMPS. In doing so, `lammps.cpp` allocates fundamental classes that are accessible throughout the code, as shown in the following screenshot:

```
84  /* ----------------------------------------------------------------------
85       start up LAMMPS
86       allocate fundamental classes (memory, error, universe, input)
87       parse input switches
88       initialize communicators, screen & logfile output
89       input is allocated at end after MPI info is setup
90  ------------------------------------------------------------------------- */
91
92  LAMMPS::LAMMPS(int narg, char **arg, MPI_Comm communicator) :
93     memory(NULL), error(NULL), universe(NULL), input(NULL), atom(NULL),
94     update(NULL), neighbor(NULL), comm(NULL), domain(NULL), force(NULL),
95     modify(NULL), group(NULL), output(NULL), timer(NULL), kokkos(NULL),
96     atomKK(NULL), memoryKK(NULL), python(NULL), citeme(NULL)
```

Figure 2.3 – Code snippet from lammps.cpp

This instantiation is invoked by the `main.cpp` file, which also conveys the input script to this instance of LAMMPS for subsequent execution, as shown in the following screenshot:

```
53    try {
54       LAMMPS *lammps = new LAMMPS(argc,argv,MPI_COMM_WORLD);
55       lammps->input->file();
56       delete lammps;
57    } catch(LAMMPSAbortException & ae) {
58       MPI_Abort(ae.universe, 1);
59    } catch(LAMMPSException & e) {
60       MPI_Finalize();
61       exit(1);
62    }
63  #else
64       LAMMPS *lammps = new LAMMPS(argc,argv,MPI_COMM_WORLD);
65       lammps->input->file();
66       delete lammps;
```

Figure 2.4 – Code snippet from main.cpp

The rest of the simulation setup is performed by several other top-level classes, some of which are described here in brief:

- `memory.cpp`: Creates and destroys multi-dimensional arrays
- `error.cpp`: Prints errors and warning messages and aborts simulation
- `universe.cpp`: Creates and initializes partitions to divide and assign simulation domains to different cores
- `input.cpp`: Parses and executes commands in LAMMPS input script
- `finish.cpp`: Prints output to screen at the completion of a simulation
- `atom.cpp` and `atom_vec.cpp`: Store and allocate arrays that contain atomic information, such as position, force, and molecule index
- `update.cpp`: Instantiates an integrator; contains physical constants in various units and provides access to the timestep
- `neighbor.cpp`, `neigh_list.cpp`, and `neigh_request.cpp`: Construct neighbor lists and store lists for all atoms; allow particular categories of neighbor lists to be invoked when required
- `group.cpp`: Assigns atoms to groups, and controls and computes properties of these groups
- `force.cpp`: Sets up the platform to calculate bonded and non-bonded forces by creating and validating pair, bond, angle, dihedral, and many more classes
- `modify.cpp`: Sets up the platform to apply fixes and computes by creating and validating lists of `fix` and `compute` classes
- `output.cpp`: Sets up classes and memory to write outputs to file or display on screen

In addition, there are parent classes, known as `styles`, that hold a large number of child classes (for example, *fix style*, *pair style*, and *compute style*). These parent classes and their child classes are most relevant when implementing MD features, especially in the simulation settings and simulation execution stages in a LAMMPS script where these classes are called.

> **Important Note:**
> For more information on the source code repository and hierarchy, please refer to `https://lammps.sandia.gov/doc/`.

While the top-level classes generally do not need to be modified for end user purposes, the child style classes can be readily modified to implement custom MD features. These classes will be discussed in detail in the following chapters.

Summary

The LAMMPS source code hierarchy has been presented in this chapter to illustrate the roles performed by various top-level classes in setting up the simulation groundwork. Furthermore, we mentioned three styles that are more pertinent when custom features need to be incorporated into LAMMPS, and these styles will be explored in depth.

The next chapter will guide you through the structure of the source code files and the stages of execution that the source code undergoes within each iteration of the timestep.

Further reading

- LAMMPS Developer Guide – Source Files and Class Topology: `https://lammps.sandia.gov/doc/Developer_org.html`

Questions

1. In the `src` folder, what files do the folders titled in uppercase letters contain?

2. Which is the topmost-level class in the source code hierarchy?

Section 2: Understanding the Source Code Structure

The LAMMPS source code controls the flow of information and performs required calculations during a MD simulation run. Given the vast extent of the source code, *how can we understand the functions of the various components?*

In this section, you will learn how to understand the various components of the source code that run in the background when LAMMPS commands are executed. Emphasis is placed on the internal mechanisms that function during the execution of pair styles, computes, and fixes.

This section comprises the following chapters:

- *Chapter 3, Source Code Structure and Stages of Execution*
- *Chapter 4, Accessing Information by Variables, Arrays, and Methods*
- *Chapter 5, Understanding Pair Styles*
- *Chapter 6, Understanding Computes*
- *Chapter 7, Understanding Fixes*
- *Chapter 8, Exploring Supporting Classes*

3
Source Code Structure and Stages of Execution

Continuing from the previous chapter, this chapter will further illustrate the source code hierarchy by describing parent and child classes in the source code. The various methods used in some of these classes will also be discussed. To complete the picture, the flow of control from top-level classes to the code termination stage will be explained using the sequence of execution of methods as determined by the integrator.

This chapter is intended to complete your understanding of the source code hierarchy and flow, which will help you to identify code sections that need modifications when implementing custom features.

We will cover the following topics:

- Parent and child classes in the source code
- The stages of executing the simulation within each timestep
- The role played by `pointers.h`
- Parsing input script commands by `input.cpp`

Technical requirements

To execute the instructions in this chapter, you just need a text editor (for example, **Notepad++** or **Gedit**).

You can find the full source code used in this chapter here: `https://github.com/PacktPublishing/Extending-and-Modifying-LAMMPS-Writing-Your-Own-Source-Code`

This is the link to download LAMMPS: `https://lammps.sandia.gov/doc/Install.html`. This is the LAMMPS GitHub link (`https://github.com/lammps/lammps`), where the source code can be found as well.

Introducing parent and child classes

As mentioned in *Chapter 2, LAMMPS Syntax and Source Code Hierarchy*, certain styles are given in the source code that can support child classes. These styles serve as parent classes and their child classes inherit their methods, thereby ensuring a degree of uniformity in the child classes that makes classification and syntax synthesis more streamlined. In this section, we will describe some of these parent classes and some of the inherited methods in their child classes.

fix.cpp and fix.h

These are the parent classes of all fixes used in LAMMPS. Among other purposes, they read the first three arguments common to all fixes (fix ID, group ID, and fix style) and sets up energy or virial computations. The following screenshot shows the code snippet from `fix.cpp` that invokes an instance of LAMMPS and reads the three common arguments:

```
33   Fix::Fix(LAMMPS *lmp, int /*narg*/, char **arg) :
34     Pointers(lmp),
35     id(NULL), style(NULL), extlist(NULL), vector_atom(NULL), array_atom(NULL),
36     vector_local(NULL), array_local(NULL), eatom(NULL), vatom(NULL)
37   {
38     instance_me = instance_total++;
39
40     // fix ID, group, and style
41     // ID must be all alphanumeric chars or underscores
42
43     int n = strlen(arg[0]) + 1;
44     id = new char[n];
45     strcpy(id,arg[0]);
46
47     for (int i = 0; i < n-1; i++)
48       if (!isalnum(id[i]) && id[i] != '_')
49         error->all(FLERR,"Fix ID must be alphanumeric or underscore characters");
50
51     igroup = group->find(arg[1]);
52     if (igroup == -1) error->all(FLERR,"Could not find fix group ID");
53     groupbit = group->bitmask[igroup];
```

Figure 3.1 - Code snippet from fix.cpp

All fixes inherit these three arguments from fix.cpp, along with the methods that set up computations. A typical fix child class that inherits from the fix.cpp parent contains the following lines (extracted from fix_addforce.cpp):

```
38    FixAddForce::FixAddForce(LAMMPS *lmp, int narg, char **arg) :
39      Fix(lmp, narg, arg),
```

Figure 3.2 – fixaddforce.cpp inheriting from fix.cpp

This child fix class inherits the three arguments from its parent class and reads the arguments specific to itself afterward. Similarly, fix.h stores a list of variables shared by all fix child classes, as shown:

```
21  class Fix : protected Pointers {
22    public:
23      static int instance_total;     // # of Fix classes ever instantiated
24
25      char *id,*style;
26      int igroup,groupbit;
27
28      int restart_global;            // 1 if Fix saves global state, 0 if not
29      int restart_peratom;           // 1 if Fix saves peratom state, 0 if not
30      int restart_file;              // 1 if Fix writes own restart file, 0 if not
31      int force_reneighbor;          // 1 if Fix forces reneighboring, 0 if not
32
33      int box_change_size;           // 1 if Fix changes box size, 0 if not
34      int box_change_shape;          // 1 if Fix changes box shape, 0 if not
35      int box_change_domain;         // 1 if Fix changes proc sub-domains, 0 if not
36
37      bigint next_reneighbor;        // next timestep to force a reneighboring
38      int thermo_energy;             // 1 if fix_modify enabled ThEng, 0 if not
39      int thermo_virial;             // 1 if fix_modify enabled ThVir, 0 if not
40      int nevery;                    // how often to call an end_of_step fix
41      int rigid_flag;                // 1 if Fix integrates rigid bodies, 0 if not
42      int peatom_flag;               // 1 if Fix contributes per-atom eng, 0 if not
43      int virial_flag;               // 1 if Fix contributes to virial, 0 if not
44      int no_change_box;             // 1 if cannot swap ortho <-> triclinic
```

Figure 3.3 - Code snippet from fix.h

Child fix header classes inherit these variables by including fix.h:

```
#include "fix.h"
```

This way, all child fixes share common syntax and variables, such as id, igroup, and style to store fix ID, group ID, and fix style, respectively.

For example, a `fix` command is entered in the LAMMPS input script:

```
fix F1 all nvt temp 100 100 0.1
```

The quantities are parsed as described:

- `fix`: This is the type of command, registered by `input.cpp`.
- `F1`: This is the name of fix, parsed by `fix.cpp`.
- `all`: This is the group name, parsed by `fix.cpp`.
- `nvt`: This is the style of fix, parsed by `fix.cpp`.
- `temp, 100, 100, 0.1`: These are the keywords specific to the fix, parsed by the fix child class.

pair.cpp and pair.h

These parent classes initialize all pair styles by validating that all pair coefficients have been specified, applying mixing rules when required, determining cutoff, requesting neighbor lists, and setting up computations. The following screenshots show some of the code segments from `pair.cpp` that execute these tasks. First, let's see the pair coefficient assignment:

```
230    // I,I coeffs must be set
231    // init_one() will check if I,J is set explicitly or inferred by mixing
232
233    if (!allocated) error->all(FLERR,"All pair coeffs are not set");
234
235    for (i = 1; i <= atom->ntypes; i++)
236      if (setflag[i][i] == 0) error->all(FLERR,"All pair coeffs are not set");
```

Figure 3.4 - Code snippets from pair.cpp showing code for pair coefficient assignment

Next, here's a screenshot of mixing coefficients:

```
664   /* --------------------------------------------------------------------
665       mixing of pair potential prefactors (epsilon)
666   -------------------------------------------------------------------- */
667
668   double Pair::mix_energy(double eps1, double eps2, double sig1, double sig2)
669   {
670     if (mix_flag == GEOMETRIC)
671       return sqrt(eps1*eps2);
672     else if (mix_flag == ARITHMETIC)
673       return sqrt(eps1*eps2);
674     else if (mix_flag == SIXTHPOWER)
675       return (2.0 * sqrt(eps1*eps2) *
676         pow(sig1,3.0) * pow(sig2,3.0) / (pow(sig1,6.0) + pow(sig2,6.0)));
677     else return 0.0;
678   }
679
680   /* --------------------------------------------------------------------
681       mixing of pair potential distances (sigma, cutoff)
682   -------------------------------------------------------------------- */
683
684   double Pair::mix_distance(double sig1, double sig2)
685   {
686     if (mix_flag == GEOMETRIC)
687       return sqrt(sig1*sig2);
688     else if (mix_flag == ARITHMETIC)
689       return (0.5 * (sig1+sig2));
690     else if (mix_flag == SIXTHPOWER)
691       return pow((0.5 * (pow(sig1,6.0) + pow(sig2,6.0))),1.0/6.0);
692     else return 0.0;
693   }
```

Figure 3.5 - Code snippets from pair.cpp showing code for mixing coefficients

Finally, we'll see code for requesting the default neighbor list:

```
294   /* ----------------------------------------------------
295       init specific to a pair style
296       specific pair style can override this function
297        if needs its own error checks
298        if needs another kind of neighbor list
299       request default neighbor list = half list
300   ---------------------------------------------------- */
301
302   void Pair::init_style()
303   {
304     neighbor->request(this,instance_me);
305   }
```

Figure 3.6 - Code snippets from pair.cpp showing code for requesting the default neighbor list

By including `pair.h`, child pair classes can inherit variables, classes, and methods used for implementing pair potentials between atoms and computing relevant quantities, including the following:

- `cutforce`: This is the maximum cutoff distance for all atom pairs.

- `cutsq`: This is the pointer that stores the square of the cutoff for each atom pair.

- `list`: This is the pointer to the neighbor list used in most pair potential calculations.

- `compute`: This is the method to compute forces between atom pairs.

- `single`: This is the method to calculate pair interaction energy.

The pair coefficients and cutoff, after both the `pair_style` and `pair_coeff` commands in the input script, are read from the child pair classes instead of the parent class.

When multiple types of potentials need to be implemented using a `pair_style hybrid` command, `pair_hybrid.cpp` creates a different pair style for each style specified and maps each atom pair to the correct pair style, as shown in the following screenshots. First, we will have a look at the snippet to show pair style creation:

```
427    int ilo,ihi,jlo,jhi;
428    force->bounds(FLERR,arg[0],atom->ntypes,ilo,ihi);
429    force->bounds(FLERR,arg[1],atom->ntypes,jlo,jhi);
430
431    // 3rd arg = pair sub-style name
432    // 4th arg = pair sub-style index if name used multiple times
433    // allow for "none" as valid sub-style name
434
435    int multflag;
436    int m;
437
438    for (m = 0; m < nstyles; m++) {
439      multflag = 0;
440      if (strcmp(arg[2],keywords[m]) == 0) {
441        if (multiple[m]) {
442          multflag = 1;
443          if (narg < 4) error->all(FLERR,"Incorrect args for pair
       coefficients");
444          if (!isdigit(arg[3][0]))
445            error->all(FLERR,"Incorrect args for pair coefficients");
446          int index = force->inumeric(FLERR,arg[3]);
447          if (index == multiple[m]) break;
448          else continue;
449        } else break;
450      }
451    }
```

Figure 3.7 - Code snippets from pair_hybrid.cpp showing pair style creation

And next, we will see the pair style mapping:

```
482    // set setflag and which type pairs map to which sub-style
483    // if sub-style is none: set hybrid setflag, wipe out map
484    // else: set hybrid setflag & map only if substyle setflag is set
485    //       previous mappings are wiped out
486
487    int count = 0;
488    for (int i = ilo; i <= ihi; i++) {
489      for (int j = MAX(jlo,i); j <= jhi; j++) {
490        if (none) {
491          setflag[i][j] = 1;
492          nmap[i][j] = 0;
493          count++;
494        } else if (styles[m]->setflag[i][j]) {
495          setflag[i][j] = 1;
496          nmap[i][j] = 1;
497          map[i][j][0] = m;
498          count++;
499        }
500      }
501    }
```

Figure 3.8 - Code snippets from pair_hybrid.cpp showing pair style mapping

When pair potentials are superimposed by using the `pair_style hybrid/overlay` command, `pair_hybrid_overlay.cpp` carries out similar tasks along with the option of mapping multiple pair potentials for the same atom pairs.

compute.cpp and compute.h

The parent classes for all computes read the first three arguments, similar to fix classes, and allows the child classes to read the remaining arguments, as shown in the following screenshot:

```
37   Compute::Compute(LAMMPS *lmp, int narg, char **arg) :
38     Pointers(lmp),
39     id(NULL), style(NULL),
40     vector(NULL), array(NULL), vector_atom(NULL),
41     array_atom(NULL), vector_local(NULL), array_local(NULL), extlist(NULL),
42     tlist(NULL), vbiasall(NULL)
43   {
44     instance_me = instance_total++;
45
46     if (narg < 3) error->all(FLERR,"Illegal compute command");
47
48     // compute ID, group, and style
49     // ID must be all alphanumeric chars or underscores
50
51     int n = strlen(arg[0]) + 1;
52     id = new char[n];
53     strcpy(id,arg[0]);
54
55     for (int i = 0; i < n-1; i++)
56       if (!isalnum(id[i]) && id[i] != '_')
57         error->all(FLERR,
58                    "Compute ID must be alphanumeric or underscore characters");
59
60     igroup = group->find(arg[1]);
61     if (igroup == -1) error->all(FLERR,"Could not find compute group ID");
62     groupbit = group->bitmask[igroup];
```

Figure 3.9 - Code snippet from compute.cpp

This way, all child computes share the `id`, `igroup`, and `style` variables to store the fix ID, group ID, and compute style, respectively. Similarly, child classes inherit variables from `compute.h`, including `scalar` and `vector`, which are used as outputs of typical computes.

Each `.cpp` file corresponding to a class contains several methods that perform different functions at different stages of the simulation. The sequence of executing methods in the correct order is carried out by an integrator, such as the `Verlet` class in `verlet.cpp`. The `Verlet` class is a child class of `integrate.cpp`, which in turn is initiated by the top-level class, `update.cpp`. In the next section, we describe the control of flow determined by `verlet.cpp`.

Stages of executing the simulation

A LAMMPS simulation is executed by iterating over timesteps (for example, **velocity Verlet integration**) or through algorithms that do not perform timestepping (for example, **minimization**). Next, we will describe the Verlet integration scheme as implemented in `verlet.cpp` and then briefly outline the minimization scheme implemented in `min.cpp`.

verlet.cpp

The `verlet.cpp` class implements timestepping through a series of methods that are executed in a pre-defined order. At the beginning of a timestep, the following methods in `verlet.cpp` are called:

- `init()`: This method checks whether fixes are defined in the input script and sets up flags for arrays, shown as follows:

```
41  /* ------------------------------------------------------------------
42     initialization before run
43  ------------------------------------------------------------------ */
44
45  void Verlet::init()
46  {
47    Integrate::init();
48
49    // warn if no fixes
50
51    if (modify->nfix == 0 && comm->me == 0)
52      error->warning(FLERR,"No fixes defined, atoms won't move");
53
54    // virial_style:
55    // 1 if computed explicitly by pair->compute via sum over pair interactions
56    // 2 if computed implicitly by pair->virial_fdotr_compute via sum over ghosts
57
58    if (force->newton_pair) virial_style = 2;
59    else virial_style = 1;
60
61    // setup lists of computes for global and per-atom PE and pressure
62
63    ev_setup();
64
65    // detect if fix omp is present for clearing force arrays
```

Figure 3.10 – Code snippet from verlet.ccp showing the init() method

- `force_clear()`: This method clears forces on all atoms to store combined forces during the course of the timestep:

```
362  /* ------------------------------------------------------------------
363     clear force on own & ghost atoms
364     clear other arrays as needed
365  ------------------------------------------------------------------ */
366
367  void Verlet::force_clear()
368  {
369    size_t nbytes;
370
371    if (external_force_clear) return;
372
373    // clear force on all particles
374    // if either newton flag is set, also include ghosts
375    // when using threads always clear all forces.
376
377    int nlocal = atom->nlocal;
378
379    if (neighbor->includegroup == 0) {
380      nbytes = sizeof(double) * nlocal;
381      if (force->newton) nbytes += sizeof(double) * atom->nghost;
382
383      if (nbytes) {
384        memset(&atom->f[0][0],0,3*nbytes);
385        if (torqueflag) memset(&atom->torque[0][0],0,3*nbytes);
386        if (extraflag) atom->avec->force_clear(0,nbytes);
387      }
388
389    // neighbor includegroup flag is set
390    // clear force only on initial nfirst particles
391    // if either newton flag is set, also include ghosts
392
393    } else {
394      nbytes = sizeof(double) * atom->nfirst;
395
396      if (nbytes) {
397        memset(&atom->f[0][0],0,3*nbytes);
398        if (torqueflag) memset(&atom->torque[0][0],0,3*nbytes);
399        if (extraflag) atom->avec->force_clear(0,nbytes);
400      }
```

Figure 3.11 - Code snippet from verlet.ccp showing the force_clear() method

- setup(): This method sets up domains with ghost atoms and builds neighbor lists; then computes forces as required to perform position and velocity updates in the velocity Verlet algorithm:

```
81  /* -----------------------------------------------------------------
82     setup before run
83  ------------------------------------------------------------------ */
84
85  void Verlet::setup(int flag)
86  {
87    if (comm->me == 0 && screen) {
88      fprintf(screen,"Setting up Verlet run ...\n");
89      if (flag) {
90        fprintf(screen,"  Unit style     : %s\n",update->unit_style);
91        fprintf(screen,"  Current step    : " BIGINT_FORMAT "\n",update->ntimestep);
92        fprintf(screen,"  Time step      : %g\n",update->dt);
93        timer->print_timeout(screen);
94      }
95    }
96
97    if (lmp->kokkos)
98      error->all(FLERR,"KOKKOS package requires run_style verlet/kk");
99
100   update->setupflag = 1;
101
102   // setup domain, communication and neighboring
103   // acquire ghosts
104   // build neighbor lists
105
106   atom->setup();
107   modify->setup_pre_exchange();
108   if (triclinic) domain->x2lamda(atom->nlocal);
109   domain->pbc();
110   domain->reset_box();
111   comm->setup();
112   if (neighbor->style) neighbor->setup_bins();
113   comm->exchange();
114   if (atom->sortfreq > 0) atom->sort();
115   comm->borders();
116   if (triclinic) domain->lamda2x(atom->nlocal+atom->nghost);
117   domain->image_check();
```

Figure 3.12 - Code snippet from verlet.ccp showing the setup() method

The rest of the steps in the timestep are conducted by the run() method. This method invokes other sequence-control methods in a predefined order, which in turn invoke fixes at the corresponding points within the same timestep. The following screenshot from the run() method shows the sequence of execution:

```
216  /* ------------------------------------------------------------
217      run for N steps
218  ------------------------------------------------------------ */
219
220  void Verlet::run(int n)
221  {
222    bigint ntimestep;
223    int nflag,sortflag;
224
225    int n_post_integrate = modify->n_post_integrate;
226    int n_pre_exchange = modify->n_pre_exchange;
227    int n_pre_neighbor = modify->n_pre_neighbor;
228    int n_post_neighbor = modify->n_post_neighbor;
229    int n_pre_force = modify->n_pre_force;
230    int n_pre_reverse = modify->n_pre_reverse;
231    int n_post_force = modify->n_post_force;
232    int n_end_of_step = modify->n_end_of_step;
233
234    if (atom->sortfreq > 0) sortflag = 1;
235    else sortflag = 0;
236
237    for (int i = 0; i < n; i++) {
238      if (timer->check_timeout(i)) {
239        update->nsteps = i;
240        break;
241      }
242
243      ntimestep = ++update->ntimestep;
244      ev_set(ntimestep);
245
246      // initial time integration
247
248      timer->stamp();
249      modify->initial_integrate(vflag);
250      if (n_post_integrate) modify->post_integrate();
251      timer->stamp(Timer::MODIFY);
252
253      // regular communication vs neighbor list rebuild
254
255      nflag = neighbor->decide();
```

Figure 3.13 - Code snippet showing run() from verlet.cpp

Here is a table that shows us a list of some of these methods in chronological order:

Method	Description
`initial_integrate()`	Performs the first-half of the velocity Verlet algorithm and is called by fixes that update atom coordinates and velocities, for example, `fix nve`, `fix nvt`, and `fix npt`
`post_integrate()`	Performs an intermediate step before rebuilding neighbor lists and communicating ghost atoms, used in `fix wall/reflect`, to shift atom coordinates and switch velocity direction upon colliding with a wall
`decide()`	Determines whether the neighbor list needs to be rebuilt for the current timestep
`forward_comm()`	Exchanges ghost atom coordinates if the neighbor list need not be rebuilt
`pre_exchange()`	Inserts or deletes atoms before rebuilding the neighbor list, used by `fix deposit` and `fix gcmc`
`pbc()`	When rebuilding neighbor lists, it applies periodic boundary conditions and remaps atoms back into the simulation box if they have moved outside
`exchange()` and `borders()`	Allocates atoms to new processors based on migration from one subdomain to another, and identifies and communicates ghost atom information to neighboring processors
`pre_neighbor()`	Rebuilds some data structures used by fixes after atoms have been assigned to different processors
`build()`	Builds neighbor lists involving all owned and ghost atoms of processors
`compute()`	Calculates pair potentials, bonded interaction potentials, and electrostatic potentials
`reverse_comm()`	Reads forces on ghost atoms and finds net force acting on owned atoms of each processor
`post_force()`	Accounts for external forces other than bonded and non-bonded forces, such as those applied by `fix addforce`, and adds them to the force vectors for each atom
`final_integrate()`	Performs the second half of the velocity Verlet algorithm that updates velocity using the current force and the force at the following timestep, as used in fixes that integrate over time, for example, `fix nve`, `fix nvt`, and `fix npt`
`end_of_step()`	Carries out tasks at the end of a timestep that do not influence the dynamics of the system, for example, `fix print`
`write()`	Outputs quantities updated at the end of the timestep to screen, log files, dump files, and restart files as specified

Table 3.1 – Table showing a list of methods

Every fix is assigned a sequence-control method to determine its order of execution, as will be described in *Chapter 7, Understanding Fixes*. The modify.cpp class stores all fixes and calls these methods at the appropriate points in the timestep, thereby facilitating the execution of all fixes in the specified order. The list of methods is imported from modify.h into verlet.cpp. The screenshot from modify.h shows a list of these methods in the order of execution:

```
50    Modify(class LAMMPS *);
51    virtual ~Modify();
52    virtual void init();
53    virtual void setup(int);
54    virtual void setup_pre_exchange();
55    virtual void setup_pre_neighbor();
56    virtual void setup_post_neighbor();
57    virtual void setup_pre_force(int);
58    virtual void setup_pre_reverse(int, int);
59    virtual void initial_integrate(int);
60    virtual void post_integrate();
61    virtual void pre_exchange();
62    virtual void pre_neighbor();
63    virtual void post_neighbor();
64    virtual void pre_force(int);
65    virtual void pre_reverse(int,int);
66    virtual void post_force(int);
67    virtual void final_integrate();
68    virtual void end_of_step();
69    virtual double thermo_energy();
70    virtual void thermo_energy_atom(int, double *);
71    virtual void post_run();
72    virtual void create_attribute(int);
```

Figure 3.14 - Code snippet showing methods from modify.h

When writing a custom fix, the exact location of executing the fix can be specified by incorporating one or more of the preceding methods in the fix.

min.cpp

The min.cpp class, which is also initiated by update.cpp, uses a non-timestepping algorithm to perform minimization. Similar to a timestepping algorithm, force computations, neighbor list builds, and atom designation to processors are performed. However, different fix class sequence-control methods are called: min_pre_exchange(), min_pre_force(), and min_post_force(). Fixes that incorporate these methods can be called during minimization.

So far, we have covered the source code hierarchy and the control flow dictated during timestepping or non-timestepping procedures that call different classes in the source code (please see the LAMMPS manual at `https://lammps.sandia.gov/doc/Developer.html` for more information). These classes are able to share information through the `Pointers` class (`pointers.h`), which contains pointers to the pointers listed in `lammps.h`, as is elaborated next.

Role of pointers class

The `pointers.h` file facilitated information transfer between classes by creating pointers to all important quantities listed in `lammps.h`. All classes inherit from `pointers.h` and are able to access these variables. The following screenshot illustrates the pointers created:

```
48  class Pointers {
49    public:
50      Pointers(LAMMPS *ptr) :
51        lmp(ptr),
52        memory(ptr->memory),
53        error(ptr->error),
54        universe(ptr->universe),
55        input(ptr->input),
56        atom(ptr->atom),
57        update(ptr->update),
58        neighbor(ptr->neighbor),
59        comm(ptr->comm),
60        domain(ptr->domain),
61        force(ptr->force),
62        modify(ptr->modify),
63        group(ptr->group),
64        output(ptr->output),
65        timer(ptr->timer),
66        world(ptr->world),
67        infile(ptr->infile),
68        screen(ptr->screen),
69        logfile(ptr->logfile),
70        atomKK(ptr->atomKK),
71        memoryKK(ptr->memoryKK),
72        python(ptr->python) {}
73      virtual ~Pointers() {}
```

```
75    protected:
76      LAMMPS *lmp;
77      Memory *&memory;
78      Error *&error;
79      Universe *&universe;
80      Input *&input;
81
82      Atom *&atom;
83      Update *&update;
84      Neighbor *&neighbor;
85      Comm *&comm;
86      Domain *&domain;
87      Force *&force;
88      Modify *&modify;
89      Group *&group;
90      Output *&output;
91      Timer *&timer;
92
93      MPI_Comm &world;
94      FILE *&infile;
95      FILE *&screen;
96      FILE *&logfile;
97
98      class AtomKokkos *&atomKK;
99      class MemoryKokkos *&memoryKK;
100     class Python *&python;
101   };
```

Figure 3.15 - Code snippets from pointers.h showing (left) pointers to classes
and (right) pointers to pointers in lammps.h

The pointers to different classes are created, as well as pointers to pointers listed in `lammps.h`, indicated by `*&` at the front. This way, variables from `lammps.h` can be accessed from other classes directly by declaring proper pointers, as will be explained in later chapters.

In the next section of this chapter, we will describe how input script commands are parsed using a pre-defined list of permitted commands in `input.cpp`.

Parsing input script commands by input.cpp

In this section, the parsing of input script commands is described as handled by the `execute_command()` method in `input.cpp`, along with the steps followed after each command.

The `execute_command()` method in `input.cpp` is responsible for parsing the first word of each line of the input script. This method contains a list of permitted commands that are compared with the first word of each line. An error is returned if there is no match, and pre-defined methods in `input.cpp` are called for each match. This method is called within the `file()` method and the `one()` method in `input.cpp` to facilitate parsing and execution.

The following screenshot shows the `execute_command()` method:

```
775        process a single parsed command
776        return 0 if successful, -1 if did not recognize command
777     ------------------------------------------------------------------
778
779    int Input::execute_command()
780    {
781        int flag = 1;
782
783        if (!strcmp(command,"clear")) clear();
784        else if (!strcmp(command,"echo")) echo();
785        else if (!strcmp(command,"if")) ifthenelse();
786        else if (!strcmp(command,"include")) include();
787        else if (!strcmp(command,"jump")) jump();
788        else if (!strcmp(command,"label")) label();
789        else if (!strcmp(command,"log")) log();
790        else if (!strcmp(command,"next")) next_command();
791        else if (!strcmp(command,"partition")) partition();
792        else if (!strcmp(command,"print")) print();
793        else if (!strcmp(command,"python")) python();
794        else if (!strcmp(command,"quit")) quit();
795        else if (!strcmp(command,"shell")) shell();
796        else if (!strcmp(command,"variable")) variable_command();
797
798        else if (!strcmp(command,"angle_coeff")) angle_coeff();
799        else if (!strcmp(command,"angle_style")) angle_style();
800        else if (!strcmp(command,"atom_modify")) atom_modify();
801        else if (!strcmp(command,"atom_style")) atom_style();
802        else if (!strcmp(command,"bond_coeff")) bond_coeff();
803        else if (!strcmp(command,"bond_style")) bond_style();
804        else if (!strcmp(command,"bond_write")) bond_write();
805        else if (!strcmp(command,"boundary")) boundary();
806        else if (!strcmp(command,"box")) box();
807        else if (!strcmp(command,"comm_modify")) comm_modify();
808        else if (!strcmp(command,"comm_style")) comm_style();
809        else if (!strcmp(command,"compute")) compute();
810        else if (!strcmp(command,"compute_modify")) compute_modify();
811        else if (!strcmp(command,"dielectric")) dielectric();
812        else if (!strcmp(command,"dihedral_coeff")) dihedral_coeff();
813        else if (!strcmp(command,"dihedral_style")) dihedral_style();
814        else if (!strcmp(command,"dimension")) dimension();
815        else if (!strcmp(command,"dump")) dump();
816        else if (!strcmp(command,"dump_modify")) dump_modify();
```

Figure 3.16 – The execute_command() method in input.cpp containing
a list of permitted input script commands

As you can see, in the preceding screenshot, the command variable represents the first word of the line being parsed, and it is compared with the list of permitted commands. For example, if the word clear is matched (*line 783*), the clear() method in input.cpp will be invoked, as shown in the following screenshot:

```
890   void Input::clear()
891 ▢{
892      if (narg > 0) error->all(FLERR,"Illegal clear command");
893      lmp->destroy();
894      lmp->create();
895      lmp->post_create();
896   }
```

Figure 3.17 – The clear() method in input.cpp

As you can see, the clear() method is self-contained and effectively deletes previous instances of LAMMPS and presents a fresh platform to continue.

Similarly, if the word lattice is matched (*line 824*), the lattice() method in input.cpp is invoked, as shown in the next screenshot:

```
1647   void Input::lattice()
1648 ▢{
1649      domain->set_lattice(narg,arg);
1650   }
```

Figure 3.18 – The lattice() method in input.cpp

As you can see, in the lattice() method, the domain->set_lattice() method is invoked, which opens domain.cpp for further execution.

Methods are invoked for other commands including fix and pair_style, and often, external classes are called to continue the simulation. Adding new permitted commands in the input script will require modifying this method to reflect these changes.

Summary

In this chapter, the parent classes for fixes, pair potentials, and computes were introduced and their inheritance to child classes was outlined. The methods used to control the flow of execution were explained as well. These concepts will be beneficial when writing custom features, especially when establishing the sequence of execution.

Having covered the source code framework, in the next chapter, we will explore the different variables, methods, and arrays that represent physical quantities in MD simulations, such as the position, velocity, and force of atoms, which need to be implemented correctly to represent physical aspects of an MD model.

Further reading

- LAMMPS Developer Guide – How a timestep works:
  `https://lammps.sandia.gov/doc/Developer_flow.html`

- LAMMPS Developer Guide – LAMMPS Class:
  `https://lammps.sandia.gov/doc/Classes_lammps.html`

Questions

1. What quantities are represented by the `id`, `igroup`, and `style` variables in `fix.cpp`?

2. Which method in `pair.h` returns the pair potential between atoms?

3. Which methods in `verlet.cpp` perform the two halves of the velocity Verlet algorithm?

4

Accessing Information by Variables, Arrays, and Methods

In this chapter, we will describe how to access physical quantities, such as the position, velocity, and force of an atom, which are relevant to MD simulations, using internal LAMMPS variables and methods. These methods and variables are coded into the classes (which are located in the `src` folder) described in the previous chapters.

We will cover the following topics:

- Accessing atom properties
- Mapping local and global atom indices
- Requesting a neighbor list

- Accessing physical constants
- Reading input parameters from the input script

By the end of this chapter, you will know how to use these handles to access essential simulation data, such as the system status and particle properties, as well as how to use the proper methods to negotiate common simulation scenarios encountered in MD.

Technical requirements

To execute the instructions in this chapter, you just need a text editor (for example, **Notepad++** or **Gedit**).

You can find the full source code used in this chapter here: `https://github.com/PacktPublishing/Extending-and-Modifying-LAMMPS-Writing-Your-Own-Source-Code`

This is the link to download LAMMPS: `https://lammps.sandia.gov/doc/Install.html`. The LAMMPS GitHub link is `https://github.com/lammps/lammps`, where the source code can be found as well.

Accessing atom properties during simulation runs

In this section, we will learn how to access the properties of atoms during a simulation run using the `Atom` class.

The `Atom` class represented in `atom.cpp` and `atom.h` provides access to various atom properties, including the atom type, molecular ID, position, velocity, and force. These quantities are listed in the `atom.h` header file, as follows:

```
32    int nlocal,nghost;           // # of owned and ghost atoms on this proc
33    int nmax;                    // max # of owned+ghost in arrays on this proc
34    int tag_enable;              // 0/1 if atom ID tags are defined
35    int molecular;               // 0 = atomic, 1 = standard molecular system,
36                                 // 2 = molecule template system
37    bigint nellipsoids;          // number of ellipsoids
38    bigint nlines;               // number of lines
39    bigint ntris;                // number of triangles
40    bigint nbodies;              // number of bodies
41
42    bigint nbonds,nangles,ndihedrals,nimpropers;
43    int ntypes,nbondtypes,nangletypes,ndihedraltypes,nimpropertypes;
44    int bond_per_atom,angle_per_atom,dihedral_per_atom,improper_per_atom;
45    int extra_bond_per_atom,extra_angle_per_atom;
46    int extra_dihedral_per_atom,extra_improper_per_atom;
47
48    int firstgroup;              // store atoms in this group first, -1 if unset
49    int nfirst;                  // # of atoms in first group on this proc
50    char *firstgroupname;        // group-ID to store first, NULL if unset
51
52    // per-atom arrays
53    // customize by adding new array
54
55    tagint *tag;
56    int *type,*mask;
57    imageint *image;
58    double **x,**v,**f;
```

Figure 4.1 – A code snippet from atom.h

These quantities can be accessed from other classes by importing this header file into their .cpp files:

```
#include "atom.h"
```

Variables can be declared to read these quantities by using arrow operators that point to quantities in atom.h. For example, as you can see in the preceding screenshot, to access the position of an atom defined by x in atom.h (*line 58*), we use the following line:

```
double **x = atom->x;
```

Here, ** indicates that x is stored as a 2D array, where one dimension represents the atom index and the other represents the three x, y, and z coordinates. To access the three coordinates of an atom with index i and to store them as x1, y1, and z1 variables, we can type the following:

```
double x1 = x[i][0];
double y1 = x[i][1];
double z1 = x[i][2];
```

While per-atom vector quantities such as the position, velocity, and force are stored in 2D arrays, per-atom scalar quantities such as atom types and molecule types are stored in 1D arrays. Additionally, global quantities such as the number of atom types in a system are stored as single variables. The following points present an inventory of selected quantities from atom.h:

- `double **x = atom->x`: This returns the position of an atom as *x[i][w]*, where *i* represents the atom index, and w=0,1,2 represents the x, y, and z coordinates, respectively.

- `double **v = atom->v`: This returns the velocity of an atom as *v[i][w]*, where *i* represents the atom index, and w=0,1,2 represents the x, y, and z components, respectively.

- `double **f = atom->f`: This returns the total force acting of an atom as *f[i][w]*, where *i* represents the atom index, and w=0,1,2 represents the x, y, and z components, respectively.

- `int *type = atom->type`: This returns the atom type of an atom as *type[i]*, where *i* represents the atom index; the value returned corresponds to the atom type designated during initialization in the input script or supporting data file.

- `tagint *molecule = atom->molecule`: This returns the molecule ID of an atom as *molecule[i]*, where *i* represents the atom index. This command is useful for identifying atoms that belong to the same molecule.

- `bigint natoms = atom->natoms`: This returns the total number of atoms in a system.

- `int nlocal = atom->nlocal`: This returns the number of owned atoms belonging to the core that executes this line. When multiple cores are employed, each core is only able to manipulate atoms or ghost atoms contained in its domain.

- `int molecular = atom->molecular`: This returns the type of atom style used in the input script, where the output values of 0,1,2 are used to represent an atomic system, a molecular system, and a molecular template system, respectively.

- `int *num_bond = atom->num_bond`: This returns the number of bonds of an atom as *num_bond[i]*, where *i* represents the atom index.
- `tagint **bond_atom = atom->bond_atom`: This returns the index of the bonded atom as *bond_atom[i][j]*, where *i* represents the atom index, and *j* represents the bond index. The output value is the index of the atom bonded to atom *i* at its bond with index, *j*. Additionally, the output atom index corresponds to the global atom ID designated in the input script and data file instead of the local atom index.

The ID of an atom can be described by a local index or a global index that needs to be handled properly when writing code. This concept is described in more detail in the next section.

Mapping atom indices

The atom ID specified in an input script or a data file read by an input script is considered a **global** atom ID, whereas a different **local** atom index is used by individual cores that range from 0 to `(nlocal-1)` of the processor.

As explained in *Chapter 1, MD Theory and Simulation Practices*, each core in a multi-core system is assigned a certain number of *owned* atoms for which it performs calculations. When accessing information using the Atom class, as described previously, the local index must be used as input and the individual core uses this index to calculate the required output.

We use the following commands to convert from a global to a local index and vice versa:

- Converting from global index G to local index L:

```
int L = atom->map(G);
```

- Converting from local index L to global index G:

```
tagint *tag = atom->tag;
int G = tag[L];
```

The `atom->map()` function returns `-1` if the input atom ID is not present.

In this section, we learned about various atom properties and the various quantities used to access them, along with the codes to convert between global indices and local indices.

During an MD simulation, a **neighbor list** is often required to account for the interactions of an atom with its neighbors, and hence it has to be incorporated within the same class that reads atom properties. In the next section, we will describe how to call a neighbor list and identify neighbors.

Requesting a neighbor list

In this section, we will learn how to initialize and access a neighbor list for individual atoms.

The neighbor list is controlled by the `NeighList` class represented by `neigh_list.cpp` and `neigh_list.h`. When a neighbor list is requested, the system neighbor list is generated by `neighbour.cpp`, and access to various elements of the neighbor list is facilitated by the `Neighlist` class.

In the case of pair styles, the neighbor list is created in `pair.h` and is inherited by the child pair classes; this is depicted as follows:

```
100    class NeighList *list;        // standard neighbor list used by most pairs
101    class NeighList *listhalf;    // half list used by some pairs
102    class NeighList *listfull;    // full list used by some pairs
```

Figure 4.2 – Code snippet from pair.h

A neighbor list is requested by the `Pair:init_style()` method, as shown in *Figure 3.6* from *Chapter 3*, *Source Code Structure and Stages of Execution*. A full, or a half, neighbor list can be requested as required. In the case of fixes, the `fix.h` parent class does not request a neighbor list, so individual child fix classes need to request it when required. In the following screenshot, we show the neighbor list request implemented in `fix_orient_fcc.cpp` (which is located in the `src/MISC` folder):

```
211    void FixOrientFCC::init()
212    {
213      if (strstr(update->integrate_style,"respa")) {
214        ilevel_respa = ((Respa *) update->integrate)->nlevels-1;
215        if (respa_level >= 0) ilevel_respa = MIN(respa_level,ilevel_respa);
216      }
217
218      // need a full neighbor list
219      // perpetual list, built whenever re-neighboring occurs
220
221      int irequest = neighbor->request(this,instance_me);
222      neighbor->requests[irequest]->pair = 0;
223      neighbor->requests[irequest]->fix = 1;
224      neighbor->requests[irequest]->half = 0;
225      neighbor->requests[irequest]->full = 1;
226    }
227
228    /* -------------------------------------------------------- */
229
230    void FixOrientFCC::init_list(int /*id*/, NeighList *ptr)
231    {
232      list = ptr;
233    }
```

Figure 4.3 – Code snippet from fix_orient_fcc.cpp showing the init() and init_list() methods

As you can see in the preceding screenshot, on *line 221*, the init () method shows the request, and *lines 222* to *225* specify a full neighbor list applicable to a fix, as opposed to a half neighbor list applicable to a pair style. Then, an init_list () method needs to be introduced to get hold of the neighbor list pointer, with a placeholder named list.

Once the pointer has been obtained, the following neighbor list elements are commonly accessed:

- int inum = list->inum: This returns the number of atoms for which neighbor lists have been determined.

- int *ilist = list->ilist: This returns the local indices of atoms as ilist[ii], where ii is the index of the same atom designated between 0 and (inum-1) according to its position in the neighbor list array.

- int *numneigh = list->numneigh: This returns the number of neighbors of each atom as numneigh[i], where *i* is the local atom index.

- int **firstneigh = list->firstneigh: This returns the local index of the neighboring atom as firstneigh[i][j], where *i* represents the central atom local index, and j represents the neighboring atom index. The j index is not the local atom index but is designated between 0 and (numneigh[i]-1), that is, according to its position in the neighbor list. The output value is the local atom index of the neighboring atom, j, of the central atom, i.

The following diagram illustrates the aforementioned architecture of the neighbor list and their quantities:

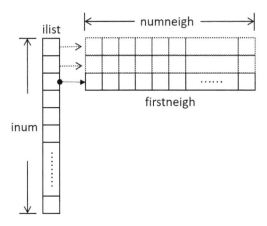

Figure 4.4 – Architecture of the neighbor list showing the inum, ilist, numneigh, and firstneigh quantities

As you can see in the preceding diagram, when considering all of the owned atoms in a core and calculating their interactions with the atoms in their neighbor lists, a common strategy is to loop over all the central atoms, `inum`, for which neighbor lists exist and to iteratively loop over the neighbors of each of these central atoms.

In the first loop over `inum` (with index `ii`), the local atom index (`i`) of each central atom is extracted (`i = ilist[ii]`), the number of neighbors for the atom (`jnum`) is retrieved (`jnum = numneigh[i]`), and an array of neighbors (`jlist`) is created (`jlist = firstneigh[i]`).

A second loop (with index `jj`) located inside the first loop traverses over all neighbors `jnum` of atom `i`, and extracts the local atom index (`j`) of each neighbor (`j = jlist[jj]`). In effect, `jlist[jj]` returns the same output as `firstneigh[i][jj]`.

The following code lines illustrate this process:

`for (int ii = 0; ii < inum; ii++) {`	1st loop: over all central atoms `ii`
`  int i = ilist[ii];`	Extracts local atom index `i` of central atom
`  int jnum = numneigh[i];`	Retrieves number of neighbors of atom `i`
`  int *jlist = firstneigh[i];`	Creates array of neighbors of atom `i`
`  for (int jj = 0; jj < jnum; jj++) {`	2nd loop: over all neighbors `jj` of atom `i`
`    int j = jlist[jj];`	Extracts local atom index `j` of neighbor `jj`
`    ...`	
`  }`	
`}`	

Figure 4.5 – Typical code that accesses neighbor lists (left) with annotations (right)

As you can see, in this way, all atoms with neighbor lists are accounted for and their neighbors are identified. Additionally, their atom indices can be used to access atom properties, such as atom positions to calculate the separation between a central atom and each of its neighbors.

In this section, we learned about the structure of neighbor lists and how to call them inside pair styles and fix styles.

Other than dynamic simulation features, LAMMPS provides access to a repository of physical constants commonly used in atomic simulations. These constants are hardcoded in the source code, and we will describe them in the next section.

Accessing physical constants

Physical constants in different units used in LAMMPS (for example, SI, "real", and "metal") are available using arrow operators from force.h. A list of these constants is shown in the following screenshot:

```
25       double boltz;                    // Boltzmann constant (eng/degree-K)
26       double hplanck;                  // Planck's constant (energy-time)
27       double mvv2e;                    // conversion of mv^2 to energy
28       double ftm2v;                    // conversion of ft/m to velocity
29       double mv2d;                     // conversion of mass/volume to density
30       double nktv2p;                   // conversion of NkT/V to pressure
31       double qqr2e;                    // conversion of q^2/r to energy
32       double qe2f;                     // conversion of qE to force
33       double vxmu2f;                   // conversion of vx dynamic-visc to force
34       double xxt2kmu;                  // conversion of xx/t to kinematic-visc
35       double dielectric;               // dielectric constant
36       double qqrd2e;                   // q^2/r to energy w/ dielectric constant
37       double e_mass;                   // electron mass
38       double hhmrr2e;                  // conversion of (hbar)^2/(mr^2) to energy
39       double mvh2r;                    // conversion of mv/hbar to distance
40                                        // hbar = h/(2*pi)
41       double angstrom;                 // 1 angstrom in native units
42       double femtosecond;              // 1 femtosecond in native units
43       double qelectron;                // 1 electron charge abs() in native units
```

Figure 4.6 – Screenshot from force.h showing the variables used to implement physical constants

As you can see in the preceding screenshot, `force.h` only contains the variables names that represent the various physical constants. The numeric values of these constants are provided in `update.cpp`, which imports `force.h` and assigns values to these variables in the `Update::set_units()` method, as shown in the following screenshot:

```cpp
118    void Update::set_units(const char *style)
119    {
120        // physical constants from:
121        // http://physics.nist.gov/cuu/Constants/Table/allascii.txt
122        // using thermochemical calorie = 4.184 J
123
124        if (strcmp(style,"lj") == 0) {
125            force->boltz = 1.0;
126            force->hplanck = 1.0;
127            force->mvv2e = 1.0;
128            force->ftm2v = 1.0;
129            force->mv2d = 1.0;
130            force->nktv2p = 1.0;
131            force->qqr2e = 1.0;
132            force->qe2f = 1.0;
133            force->vxmu2f = 1.0;
134            force->xxt2kmu = 1.0;
135            force->e_mass = 0.0;      // not yet set
136            force->hhmrr2e = 0.0;
137            force->mvh2r = 0.0;
138            force->angstrom = 1.0;
139            force->femtosecond = 1.0;
140            force->qelectron = 1.0;
141
142            dt = 0.005;
143            neighbor->skin = 0.3;
144
145        } else if (strcmp(style,"real") == 0) {
146            force->boltz = 0.0019872067;
147            force->hplanck = 95.306976368;
148            force->mvv2e = 48.88821291 * 48.88821291;
149            force->ftm2v = 1.0 / 48.88821291 / 48.88821291;
150            force->mv2d = 1.0 / 0.602214129;
151            force->nktv2p = 68568.415;
152            force->qqr2e = 332.06371;     // see also force->qqr2d_lammps_real
153            force->qe2f = 23.060549;
154            force->vxmu2f = 1.4393264316e4;
155            force->xxt2kmu = 0.1;
156            force->e_mass = 1.0/1836.1527556560675;
157            force->hhmrr2e = 0.0957018663603261;
158            force->mvh2r = 1.5339009481951;
159            force->angstrom = 1.0;
160            force->femtosecond = 1.0;
```

Figure 4.7 – Code snippet from update.cpp that assigns numeric values
to variables representing physical constants

The constants in the correct unit are retrieved by the `Update::set_units()` method when they are accessed from other classes. For example, the following code lines return the Boltzmann constant to a `boltz` variable:

```
#include "force.h"
double boltz = force->boltz;
```

The unit does not need to be specified in the class and will be automatically determined by the units used in the LAMMPS input script.

So far, we have discussed accessing quantities generated by the source code. Next, we will discuss parsing parameters entered in the LAMMPS input script using various methods offered in the `force.cpp` class.

Reading parameters from the input script

In this section, we will learn about parsing parameters entered by a user in the LAMMPS input script. In *Chapter 3*, *Source Code Structure and Stages of Execution*, the role of `input.cpp` in parsing the first words of input script commands was discussed. In this section, we will discuss the methods responsible for parsing user-entered quantities associated with various commands.

User-entered parameters associated with various styles, such as numeric pair coefficient values in pair styles and force values in fixes, are parsed from the LAMMPS input script by the corresponding classes or their parent classes.

> **Important Note:**
>
> These methods are located in `force.cpp` in the LAMMPS stable version, **3Mar20**, whereas they have been moved to `utils.cpp` in the stable version, **29Oct20**. Please refer to *Appendix D* for more information about version compatibility.

The parsing of these quantities is performed by the `force.cpp` class through several methods that are discussed next:

- Here is a screenshot of the `Force::numeric()` method, which reads floating-point numbers from an input script:

```
929   /*  -------------------------------------------------------------------
930       read a floating point value from a string
931       generate an error if not a legitimate floating point value
932       called by various commands to check validity of their arguments
933   -------------------------------------------------------------------
934
935   double Force::numeric(const char *file, int line, char *str)
936   {
937     int n = 0;
938
939     if (str) n = strlen(str);
940     if (n == 0)
941       error->all(file,line,"Expected floating point parameter instead of"
942                  " NULL or empty string in input script or data file");
943
944     for (int i = 0; i < n; i++) {
945       if (isdigit(str[i])) continue;
946       if (str[i] == '-' || str[i] == '+' || str[i] == '.') continue;
947       if (str[i] == 'e' || str[i] == 'E') continue;
948       char msg[256];
949       snprintf(msg,256,"Expected floating point parameter instead of "
950                  "'%s' in input script or data file",str);
951       error->all(file,line,msg);
952     }
953
954     return atof(str);
```

Figure 4.8 – A code snippet from force.cpp showing the numeric() method

As you can see in the preceding screenshot, when the `Force::numeric()` method reads an input string of text, it returns an error if there is a null or empty input (*line 940*) and validates that the string contains only digits and the +, -, ., e, and E symbols (*lines 945 to 951*). Once validated, the string is parsed as a floating-point number (*line 954*).

- Similarly, the Force::inumeric() method reads integers from manually entered text:

```
957  /* --------------------------------------------------------------------
958       read an integer value from a string
959       generate an error if not a legitimate integer value
960       called by various commands to check validity of their arguments
961     --------------------------------------------------------------------
962
963  int Force::inumeric(const char *file, int line, char *str)
964  {
965    int n = 0;
966
967    if (str) n = strlen(str);
968    if (n == 0)
969      error->all(file,line,"Expected integer parameter instead of "
970                        "NULL or empty string in input script or data file");
971
972    for (int i = 0; i < n; i++) {
973      if (isdigit(str[i]) || str[i] == '-' || str[i] == '+') continue;
974      char msg[256];
975      snprintf(msg,256,"Expected integer parameter instead of "
976                      "'%s' in input script or data file",str);
977      error->all(file,line,msg);
978    }
979
980    return atoi(str);
981  }
```

Figure 4.9 – A code snippet from force.cpp showing the inumeric() method

This method follows a similar set of rules as Force::numeric(), except that it only permits the + and - symbols in the input string (*lines 973 to 977*). The validated string is returned as an integer (*line 980*).

- Other methods include Force::bnumeric() and Force::tnumeric(), which read big integers (such as the number of atoms in a system) and tag integers (such as atom and molecule IDs), respectively; this is described in more detail in lmptype.h. When reading atom types that must be constrained to integers between 1 and the number of types of atoms specified, the Force::bounds() method can be used to validate the input string:

```
861  /* ------------------------------------------------------------------
862     compute bounds implied by numeric str with a possible wildcard asterik
863     1 = lower bound, nmax = upper bound
864     5 possibilities:
865       (1) i = i to i, (2) * = nmin to nmax,
866       (3) i* = i to nmax, (4) *j = nmin to j, (5) i*j = i to j
867     return nlo,nhi
868  ------------------------------------------------------------------- */
869
870  void Force::bounds(const char *file, int line, char *str,
871                     int nmax, int &nlo, int &nhi, int nmin)
872  {
873    char *ptr = strchr(str,'*');
874
875    if (ptr == NULL) {
876      nlo = nhi = atoi(str);
877    } else if (strlen(str) == 1) {
878      nlo = nmin;
879      nhi = nmax;
880    } else if (ptr == str) {
881      nlo = nmin;
882      nhi = atoi(ptr+1);
883    } else if (strlen(ptr+1) == 0) {
884      nlo = atoi(str);
885      nhi = nmax;
886    } else {
887      nlo = atoi(str);
888      nhi = atoi(ptr+1);
889    }
890
891    if (nlo < nmin || nhi > nmax || nlo > nhi)
892      error->all(file,line,"Numeric index is out of bounds");
893  }
```

Figure 4.10 – A code snippet from force.cpp showing the bounds() method

This method accommodates the use of an * symbol when defining atom types in pair styles (*lines 873 to 889*), as described in the LAMMPS manual (https://lammps.sandia.gov/doc/). The correct lower and upper bounds of the atom types are returned as nlo and nhi integers, and an error is generated if the atom types violate the permitted ranges, or if the first atom type is larger than the second atom type (*line 891 to 892*).

> **Important Note:**
>
> The `force->` methods are used in LAMMPS version **3Mar20**, while `utils::` methods are used in version **29Oct20**. Please refer to *Appendix D* for a detailed discussion.

- The following excerpt from `pair_morse.cpp` shows some of the preceding methods being used to read parameters from the input script regarding *pair style Morse* (the Morse pair style and its arguments will be described in more detail when we analyze pair styles in *Chapter 5, Understanding Pair Styles*):

```
183    int ilo,ihi,jlo,jhi;
184    force->bounds(FLERR,arg[0],atom->ntypes,ilo,ihi);
185    force->bounds(FLERR,arg[1],atom->ntypes,jlo,jhi);
186
187    double d0_one = force->numeric(FLERR,arg[2]);
188    double alpha_one = force->numeric(FLERR,arg[3]);
189    double r0_one = force->numeric(FLERR,arg[4]);
```

Figure 4.11 – A code snippet from pair_morse.cpp showing input parameters as parsed by methods from force.cpp

As you can see in the preceding screenshot, *lines 184* to *185* use the `force->bound()` method to read the atom types that have this pair style implemented between them. In the arguments of the `force->bounds()` method, `arg[0]` and `arg[1]` refer to the first and second atom types entered in the input script.

Lines 187 to *189* use the `force->numeric()` method to read the floating-point parameters, `d0_one`, `alpha_one`, and `r0_one`, from the three consecutive parameters entered after the atom types. The `FLERR` flag, which is used as the first argument in these methods, is defined in `pointers.h` (*line 34*):

```
#define FLERR __FILE__,__LINE__
```

This flag combines the filename and the line number into a single argument, and it accounts for the first two arguments required in each of these methods.

When executing a style where a user-entered value is expected (for example, a pair style or a fix), the relevant source code employs an appropriate method to parse these values from their correct locations in the input script line. This process will be illustrated in more detail in the chapters that follow when such styles are analyzed.

In this section, we learned about the methods used to parse input script parameters. These methods will be frequently encountered when we cover classes that require input from the LAMMPS script (for example, pair styles, computes, and fixes).

In the next section, we will outline the process of incorporating new data types in LAMMPS, used to expand the functionalities offered in parsing and processing inputs.

Incorporating new data types

When a certain data type does not exist in the standard **C++** repository, it can be created and incorporated in the LAMMPS source code by defining it appropriately in `lmptype.h`. For example, the `tagint` data type described earlier in `tagint **bond_atom = atom->bond_atom` is a variation of the `int` data type. This `tagint` data type has been defined in `lmptype.h`, as shown in the following screenshot:

```
77   #ifdef LAMMPS_SMALLBIG
78
79     typedef int smallint;
80     typedef int imageint;
81     typedef int tagint;
82     typedef int64_t bigint;

109  #ifdef LAMMPS_BIGBIG
110
111    typedef int smallint;
112    typedef int64_t imageint;
113    typedef int64_t tagint;
114    typedef int64_t bigint;
```

Figure 4.12 – Code snippet from lmptype.h showing the declaration of the tagint and bigint data types

As you can see, the built-in `typedef` function in C++ can be used to declare new data types with custom properties in `lmptype.h`, and these data types can be accessed in the rest of the source code.

Generally, `int` is a 4-byte (32-bit) data type by default, which means it can accommodate a 10-digit number up to 2^{31}. Sometimes, if a simulation system has to accommodate a larger number, we can use `typedef` to alias the `int` (32 bit) and `int64_t` (64 bit) data types to `tagint` and `bigint` data types using macros in `lmptype.h`.

As seen in *Figure 4.12*, the `LAMMPS_SMALLBIG` definition (*line 77*) declares the `smallint`, `imageint`, and `tagint` data types as of the `int` type, whereas it declares the `bigint` data type as of the `int64_t` type (*lines 79 to 82*). Similarly, the `LAMMPS_BIGBIG` definition (*line 109*) declares `smallint` as of the `int` type and `imageint`, `tagint`, and `bigint` as of the `int64_t` type (*lines 111 to 114*).

The desired definition can be selected using the `-DLAMMPS-SIZES=value` or `LMP_INC = -DLAMMPS_SMALLBIG` options in CMake and Make, respectively, during compilation (see details in *Appendix A, Building LAMMPS with CMake*).

The following table lists the ranges accommodated by the LAMMPS_BIGBIG, LAMMPS_SMALLBIG, and LAMMPS_SMALLSMALL definitions selected during compilation (*lines 109, 77*, and *140*):

Definition	LAMMPS_BIGBIG	LAMMPS_SMALLBIG	LAMMPS_SMALLSMALL
Total atom count accommodated	$2^{63} = 9.223 \times 10^{18}$	$2^{63} = 9.223 \times 10^{18}$	$2^{31} = 2.147 \times 10^{9}$
Total number of timesteps accommodated	$2^{63} = 9.223 \times 10^{18}$	$2^{63} = 9.223 \times 10^{18}$	$2^{31} = 2.147 \times 10^{9}$
Atom ID values accommodated	$2^{63} = 9.223 \times 10^{18}$	$2^{31} = 2.147 \times 10^{9}$	$2^{31} = 2.147 \times 10^{9}$
Image flag values accommodated	-2^{20} to $(2^{20} - 1)$	-2^{9} to $(2^{9} - 1)$	-2^{9} to $(2^{9} - 1)$

Table 4.1 – List of ranges of number of atoms, number of timesteps, atom IDs, and image flag values accommodated by the available definitions in lmptype.h

The image flag value keeps track of the multiple of the simulation box length traveled by an atom through the periodic boundary in each dimension (see *Chapter 1, MD Theory and Simulation Practices*). To account for the three *(x, y, z)* dimensions, the number of available bits are shared equally by the three dimensions.

Therefore, if 32 bits are available (as in LAMMPS_SMALLBIG and LAMMPS_SMALLSMALL), each dimension is assigned 10 bits, which effectively allows a range of 2^{10} integers, spanning from -2^{9} to $(2^{9} - 1)$. Similarly, for LAMMPS_BIGBIG, the available 64 bits are divided into shares of 21 bits in each dimension that span a range of integers from -2^{20} to $(2^{20} - 1)$.

A more detailed discussion is available in the LAMMPS manual (https://lammps.sandia.gov/doc/Library_utility.html).

In this section, the declaration of custom data types and the ranges spanned by various definitions have been explained. In the context of accessing information in the source code, the topics described in this section will help users understand the associated limitations.

Summary

In this chapter, we have described the different ways in which to access relevant pieces of MD information during a simulation run using built-in methods, which will be useful to users when writing custom codes. We have not provided an exhaustive list of quantities that can be accessed, and as we analyze styles in detail in the following chapters, we will encounter other variables and methods that will be explained as they are encountered.

In the next chapter, we will employ the concepts covered so far to analyze sample pair styles to gain a hands-on understanding of how these styles read, calculate, and generate outputs. Since most new features added to LAMMPS are created by modifying existing features, this overview of existing styles will be particularly helpful when implementing new LAMMPS features.

Questions

1. What do the `*` and `**` symbols preceding variable names imply regarding their memory allocation?

2. What information is contained in the `firstneigh` array that is commonly created during neighbor list requests?

3. When should the `force->inumeric()` method be used instead of the `force->numeric()` method to parse input from a script?

5
Understanding Pair Styles

In this chapter, we will delve into some of the pair styles implemented in LAMMPS and analyze their source code to understand the roles performed by different sections of the code. Pair styles implement pair potentials between atoms according to the equations introduced in *Chapter 1*, *MD Theory and Simulation Practices*. In this chapter, we will look at how the mathematical operations involved are executed by pair style source code.

We will cover the following topics:

- Reviewing the general structure of pair styles
- Reviewing the Morse potential
- Reviewing the table potential
- Reviewing the DPD potential

At the end of this chapter, you will have explored the inner mechanism of several sample pair styles with the aid of the material presented in the previous chapters and will be prepared to make changes to existing pair styles to implement custom pair potentials in LAMMPS.

Technical requirements

To execute the instructions in this chapter, you just need a text editor (for example, **Notepad++** or **Gedit**).

You can find the full source code used in this chapter here: https://github.com/PacktPublishing/Extending-and-Modifying-LAMMPS-Writing-Your-Own-Source-Code

Reviewing the general structure of pair styles

As described in *Chapter 3*, *Source Code Structure and Stages of Execution*, each individual pair style inherits from pair.cpp and pair.h, including the init() method.

In this section, we briefly cover the methods commonly used in the child pair style classes that are inherited from the pair.cpp and pair.h classes.

The parent classes take care of validating pair coefficient assignments, mixing parameters, determining cutoff, requesting neighbor lists, and setting up computations. Some of the methods and variables are also inherited from pair.h. Hybrid styles are accommodated by the pair_hybrid.cpp and pair_hybrid_overlay.cpp classes.

The child pair style classes commonly contain the following methods:

- allocate() allocates memory to arrays used to calculate pair interaction forces.
- settings() reads and processes global pair potential parameters entered after the pair_style command in the LAMMPS input script.
- coeff() reads and processes local pair potential parameters entered after the pair_coeff command in the LAMMPS input script.
- init_one() assigns pairwise coefficients for all atom types.
- compute() calculates pairwise forces and potential between atom types.
- single() returns the pairwise potential to be used by other classes during the simulation run.

In the following sections, we will illustrate how the aforementioned methods are implemented in selected pair styles provided in the LAMMPS repository.

Reviewing the Morse potential

In this section, we analyze the Morse potential implemented by the `pair_morse.cpp` and `pair_morse.h` classes.

The Morse potential (V_{Morse}) is used to represent the covalent character of bonds and consists of a repulsive and an attractive part with a potential minimum in between. The functional form of the Morse potential is given by the following:

$$V_{Morse}(r) = D_0 \left[e^{-2\alpha(r-r_0)} - 2e^{-\alpha(r-r_0)} \right]$$

From the preceding equation, D_0 represents the depth of the Morse potential well, α determines the curvature of the well, and r_0 represents the equilibrium distance. In a LAMMPS input script, the Morse pair potential is implemented using the following commands:

```
pair_style   morse GLOBAL_CUTOFF
pair_coeff        TYPE1    TYPE2      D0   ALPHA   R0   LOCAL_CUTOFF
```

From the preceding code, `D0`, `ALPHA`, `R0` are the three Morse parameters described, and the `GLOBAL_CUTOFF` and `LOCAL_CUTOFF` parameters are the cutoffs used for all atom pairs or specified atom pairs, respectively (described in detail in the LAMMPS manual: `https://lammps.sandia.gov/doc/pair_morse.html`). The `TYPE1` and `TYPE2` parameters specify the pair of atom types that interact via the Morse potential.

In the following sections, we will illustrate how `pair_morse.cpp` and `pair_morse.h` facilitate the processing required to parse and implement the Morse potential in an MD simulation.

PairMorse::allocate()

When implementing pair style Morse, the required arrays are created by the `allocate()` method, shown as follows:

```
129  /* ----------------------------------------------------------
130        allocate all arrays
131     ----------------------------------------------------------
132
133  void PairMorse::allocate()
134  {
135      allocated = 1;
136      int n = atom->ntypes;
137
138      memory->create(setflag,n+1,n+1,"pair:setflag");
139      for (int i = 1; i <= n; i++)
140        for (int j = i; j <= n; j++)
141          setflag[i][j] = 0;
142
143      memory->create(cutsq,n+1,n+1,"pair:cutsq");
144
145      memory->create(cut,n+1,n+1,"pair:cut");
146      memory->create(d0,n+1,n+1,"pair:d0");
147      memory->create(alpha,n+1,n+1,"pair:alpha");
148      memory->create(r0,n+1,n+1,"pair:r0");
149      memory->create(morse1,n+1,n+1,"pair:morse1");
150      memory->create(offset,n+1,n+1,"pair:offset");
151  }
```

Figure 5.1 - Code snippet from pair_morse.cpp showing the allocate() method

As you can see from the preceding screenshot, the number of atom types is stored on *line 136* as n, and several 2D arrays of dimensions, (n+1) * (n+1), are created using the `memory->create()` function.

Each row and column starts at an index equal to 0 and continues to index n to represent all atom types in the rows and columns. *Lines 138* to *141* insert zeros to populate the 2D `setflag` array (see `pair.cpp` in *Chapter 3, Source Code Structure and Stages of Execution*), which checks whether pair styles have been declared between every pair of atom types.

You can see in *line 139* that populating the array starts at index i = 1 to correspond to atom types that also start from an index of 1 (while index i = 0 is excluded). Similar 2D arrays are created in *lines 143* to *150* to represent the square of the cutoff (`cutsq`), the cutoff (`cut`), D_0 (d0), α (alpha), r_0 (r0), a constant based on D_0 and α (morse1), and the offset that shifts the potential to zero at the cutoff (`offset`) for every pair of atom types. These arrays will be populated by other methods and used to calculate the pair interactions.

Now let's move on to the next method.

PairMorse::settings()

This method reads the quantities entered in the LAMMPS input script after the `pair_style morse` command, which, in this case, is only the global cutoff. The following screenshot illustrates the `settings()` method:

```
153  /* ----------------------------------------------------------------
154       global settings
155  ----------------------------------------------------------------- */
156
157  void PairMorse::settings(int narg, char **arg)
158  {
159      if (narg != 1) error->all(FLERR,"Illegal pair_style command");
160
161      cut_global = force->numeric(FLERR,arg[0]);
162
163      // reset cutoffs that have been explicitly set
164
165      if (allocated) {
166          int i,j;
167          for (i = 1; i <= atom->ntypes; i++)
168              for (j = i; j <= atom->ntypes; j++)
169                  if (setflag[i][j]) cut[i][j] = cut_global;
170      }
171  }
```

Figure 5.2 - Code snippet from pair_morse.cpp showing the settings() method

As you can see in the preceding screenshot, *line 159* checks whether there is exactly one parameter present in the LAMMPS input script after the `pair_style morse` command as specified in the LAMMPS manual and returns an error message if not.

Then, *line 161* reads this `arg[0]` parameter as a floating-point number using the `force->numeric()` method and stores it as the `cut_global` variable that has been declared in `pair_morse.h`. In *lines 165* to *170*, the cutoffs for all atom types (`cut[i][j]`) that have been allocated earlier are set to this global cutoff. Note that the `i` index traverses over all atom types 1 through n, but the `j` index traverses from `i` through n, implying that only half the array elements in the 2D array cut are populated. The rest will be populated by the `pair_coeff()` method described next.

PairMorse::coeff()

This method reads the quantities entered in the LAMMPS input script following the `pair_coeff` command. The following screenshot shows the `coeff()` method:

```cpp
173   /* ----------------------------------------------------------------
174      set coeffs for one or more type pairs
175   ---------------------------------------------------------------- */
176
177   void PairMorse::coeff(int narg, char **arg)
178   {
179     if (narg < 5 || narg > 6)
180       error->all(FLERR,"Incorrect args for pair coefficients");
181     if (!allocated) allocate();
182
183     int ilo,ihi,jlo,jhi;
184     force->bounds(FLERR,arg[0],atom->ntypes,ilo,ihi);
185     force->bounds(FLERR,arg[1],atom->ntypes,jlo,jhi);
186
187     double d0_one = force->numeric(FLERR,arg[2]);
188     double alpha_one = force->numeric(FLERR,arg[3]);
189     double r0_one = force->numeric(FLERR,arg[4]);
190
191     double cut_one = cut_global;
192     if (narg == 6) cut_one = force->numeric(FLERR,arg[5]);
193
194     int count = 0;
195     for (int i = ilo; i <= ihi; i++) {
196       for (int j = MAX(jlo,i); j <= jhi; j++) {
197         d0[i][j] = d0_one;
198         alpha[i][j] = alpha_one;
199         r0[i][j] = r0_one;
200         cut[i][j] = cut_one;
201         setflag[i][j] = 1;
202         count++;
203       }
204     }
205
206     if (count == 0) error->all(FLERR,"Incorrect args for pair coefficients");
207   }
```

Figure 5.3 - Code snippet from pair_morse.cpp showing the coeff() method

As you can see from the preceding screenshot, *lines 179* to *180* allows 5 or 6 parameters after the `pair_coeff` command in the LAMMPS input script. *Lines 183* to *185* read the atom type pairs, on which this potential applies, using the `force->bounds()` method and assigns the range of specified atom types to the variables, `ilo`, `ihi`, `jlo`, and `jhi`.

Lines 187 to *189* store the third, fourth, and fifth parameters as floating-point values of D_0, α, and r_0, respectively. *Lines 191 to 192* set the global cutoff as the default cutoff unless a sixth parameter is entered that overwrites the cutoff for the specified atom type pairs. The 2D arrays, `d0`, `alpha`, `r0`, and `cut`, corresponding to these quantities are updated in *lines 194* to *204*, along with changing the `setflag` elements to 1 for these atom type pairs. Only half of these arrays are populated and the rest will be populated in `PairMorse:init_one()`. The `count` integer is used to keep a tally of the number of atom type pairs for which these parameters are assigned, and *line 206* returns an error if no pair is counted.

PairMorse::init_one()

This method reads in two atom types as arguments and validates that pair coefficients are defined for them. It also defines the quantity stored in the morse1 array, calculates the offset required to shift the potential value to zero at the cutoff distance, and populates arrays by copying from one set of atom types to its mirror set of atom types.

The following screenshot demonstrates the init_one() function:

```
210  /* ----------------------------------------------------------------
211      init for one type pair i,j and corresponding j,i
212  ----------------------------------------------------------------- */
213
214  double PairMorse::init_one(int i, int j)
215  {
216      if (setflag[i][j] == 0) error->all(FLERR,"All pair coeffs are not set");
217
218      morse1[i][j] = 2.0*d0[i][j]*alpha[i][j];
219
220      if (offset_flag) {
221          double alpha_dr = -alpha[i][j] * (cut[i][j] - r0[i][j]);
222          offset[i][j] = d0[i][j] * (exp(2.0*alpha_dr) - 2.0*exp(alpha_dr));
223      } else offset[i][j] = 0.0;
224
225      d0[j][i] = d0[i][j];
226      alpha[j][i] = alpha[i][j];
227      r0[j][i] = r0[i][j];
228      morse1[j][i] = morse1[i][j];
229      offset[j][i] = offset[i][j];
230
231      return cut[i][j];
232  }
```

Figure 5.4 - Code snippet from pair_morse.cpp showing the init_one() method

As you can see, after *line 216* validates whether the i and j atom types entered as arguments have pair coefficients assigned for their interaction, *line 218* defines a morse1 quantity as $2\alpha D_0$ for convenience of computation that will be employed later.

Lines 220 to *223* calculate the potential at the cutoff, that is, $V_{Morse}(r_{cut})$, and store it as the offset that can be added to shift the potential function to exactly zero at the cutoff. If the LAMMPS input script does not implement any offset in the potential, the offset array is filled with zeros. Then, in *lines 225* to *229*, the arrays that have been partially populated by PairMorse::coeff() are fully populated by copying elements for every atom pair (i, j) to its mirror pair (j, i).

PairMorse::compute()

After having populated all array elements for all atom pairs, the pairwise forces and potential between these atoms are calculated in this method. The following screenshot shows us the compute() method:

```
77      // loop over neighbors of my atoms
78
79      for (ii = 0; ii < inum; ii++) {
80        i = ilist[ii];
81        xtmp = x[i][0];
82        ytmp = x[i][1];
83        ztmp = x[i][2];
84        itype = type[i];
85        jlist = firstneigh[i];
86        jnum = numneigh[i];
87
88        for (jj = 0; jj < jnum; jj++) {
89          j = jlist[jj];
90          factor_lj = special_lj[sbmask(j)];
91          j &= NEIGHMASK;
92
93          delx = xtmp - x[j][0];
94          dely = ytmp - x[j][1];
95          delz = ztmp - x[j][2];
96          rsq = delx*delx + dely*dely + delz*delz;
97          jtype = type[j];
98
99          if (rsq < cutsq[itype][jtype]) {
100           r = sqrt(rsq);
101           dr = r - r0[itype][jtype];
102           dexp = exp(-alpha[itype][jtype] * dr);
103           fpair = factor_lj * morse1[itype][jtype] * (dexp*dexp - dexp) / r;
104
105           f[i][0] += delx*fpair;
106           f[i][1] += dely*fpair;
107           f[i][2] += delz*fpair;
108           if (newton_pair || j < nlocal) {
109             f[j][0] -= delx*fpair;
110             f[j][1] -= dely*fpair;
111             f[j][2] -= delz*fpair;
112           }
```

Figure 5.5 - Code snippet from pair_morse.cpp showing the compute() method

As you can see, *lines 79* to *89* loop over all central atoms with the local index, i , and then over all their neighboring atoms with local index, j, as described in *Chapter 4, Accessing Information by Variables, Arrays, and Methods*. *Line 90* checks for special bonds between the i and j atoms, and the `factor_lj` variable accounts for weights assigned to special bonds in the LAMMPS input script. This check is performed by bitwise comparison using the `sbmask()` function, which will be explained in *Appendix B, Debugging with GDB and Visual Studio Code*. If a special bond is specified, then `factor_lj` is set equal to the weight of the bond; otherwise, it is set equal to 1.

Lines 93 to *95* calculate the displacement vector components ($\Delta x, \Delta y, \Delta z$) from the j atom to the i atom, and *line 96* calculates the square of the distance between these atoms, $rsq = (\Delta x)^2 + (\Delta y)^2 + (\Delta z)^2$. The distance, r, itself is not calculated unless necessary to circumvent the computational overhead associated with the square root calculation. On *line 99*, rsq is compared with the square of the cutoff between these two atoms to determine whether the atoms are located within the cutoff. If so, r is explicitly calculated in *line 100* and the force between the two atoms is calculated next.

As explained in *Chapter 1, MD Theory and Simulation Practices*, the pairwise force depends on the gradient of the pairwise potential, which is $V_{Morse}(r)$, in this case.

First, we calculate the following quantity:

$$\frac{dV_{Morse}}{dr} = -2\alpha D_0 \left[e^{-2\alpha(r-r_0)} - e^{-\alpha(r-r_0)} \right]$$

Then, the (**x**, **y**, **z**) force components can be calculated. The (**x**) force component is given by the following:

$$F_x = -\frac{dV}{dr} \cdot \frac{\Delta x}{r} = 2\alpha D_0 \left[e^{-2\alpha(r-r_0)} - e^{-\alpha(r-r_0)} \right] \frac{\Delta x}{r}$$

The (**y**) force component is calculated by this:

$$F_y = -\frac{dV}{dr} \cdot \frac{\Delta y}{r} = 2\alpha D_0 \left[e^{-2\alpha(r-r_0)} - e^{-\alpha(r-r_0)} \right] \frac{\Delta y}{r}$$

The (**z**) force component is given by the following:

$$F_z = -\frac{dV}{dr} \cdot \frac{\Delta z}{r} = 2\alpha D_0 \left[e^{-2\alpha(r-r_0)} - e^{-\alpha(r-r_0)} \right] \frac{\Delta z}{r}$$

In the source code (*Figure 5.5*), *lines 101* to *102* define the variables, $dr = r - r_0$ and $dexp = e^{-\alpha(r-r_0)}$, and *line 103* defines the fpair variable in terms of factor_lj, morse1, and dexp. Upon substituting for morse1 (see the *PairMorse::init_one()* section) in here, fpair turns out to be as follows:

$$\text{fpair} = \text{factor\_lj} * 2\alpha D_0 \left[e^{-2\alpha(r-r_0)} - e^{-\alpha(r-r_0)} \right] \frac{1}{r}$$

By multiplying fpair with displacement vector components ($\Delta x, \Delta y, \Delta z$), the corresponding force components scaled by factor_lj are calculated in *lines 105* to *107*. These forces are assigned to the i atom in the force array elements, f[i][0], f[i][1], and f[i][2] (the f array has been defined in *line 66*). The reaction force components acting in opposite directions are assigned to the j atom in *lines 108* to *112*, provided that Newton pairs are activated.

This method can also calculate the energy of interaction between atoms with the offset included and with a scaling of factor_lj if requested (*lines 114* to *118*).

PairMorse::single()

The energy of interaction is often required by other classes, such as computes(), when running MD simulation. It can be calculated and accessed using the single() method, shown as follows:

```
337  double PairMorse::single(int /*i*/, int /*j*/, int itype, int jtype, double rsq,
338                           double /*factor_coul*/, double factor_lj,
339                           double &fforce)
340  {
341      double r,dr,dexp,phi;
342
343      r = sqrt(rsq);
344      dr = r - r0[itype][jtype];
345      dexp = exp(-alpha[itype][jtype] * dr);
346      fforce = factor_lj * morse1[itype][jtype] * (dexp*dexp - dexp) / r;
347
348      phi = d0[itype][jtype] * (dexp*dexp - 2.0*dexp) - offset[itype][jtype];
349      return factor_lj*phi;
350  }
```

Figure 5.6 - Code snippet from pair_morse.cpp showing the single() method

As you can see, the input arguments are used to define the same variables, `dr`, `dexp`, and `fforce` (which is equivalent to `fpair`) described earlier for the atom types, `itype` and `jtype`, entered. Then, in *lines 348 to 349*, the energy is returned as the `phi` variable calculated from the potential function $V_{Morse}(r)$ and its offset and scaling factor, `factor_lj`.

Other pair styles such as the **Lennard-Jones potential** (`pair_lj_cut.cpp`), **Buckingham potential** (`pair_buck.cpp`), and non-long ranged **Coulomb potential** (`pair_coul_cut.cpp`) employ a similar algorithm with different implementations of the potential and force functions. When writing custom pair styles that implement position-dependent potentials, it is recommended to choose one of the existing pair potentials such as `pair_morse.cpp` and modify the relevant sections.

In this section, we learned about the source code responsible for implementing the Morse potential in an MD simulation.

In the next section, we will analyze a table potential that interpolates forces and potentials from a table instead of calculating with a function.

Reviewing the table potential

In this section, we will learn about the various methods that implement the pair table potential.

The table pair potential described by `pair_table.cpp` and `pair_table.h` reads a file containing potential and force values tabulated for a list of data points corresponding to separations between atoms. When the force or potential at a particular separation is required, one or more of the data points in the file closest to the required separation are used to interpolate the force and potential.

The following LAMMPS inputs script commands are used to implement this pair style:

```
pair_style table TABLE_STYLE N KEYWORD
pair_coeff  TYPE1 TYPE2   FILE_NAME   VARIABLE   CUTOFFs
```

From the preceding code, `TABLE_STYLE` has to be one of the styles mentioned in the LAMMPS manual (`LINEAR`, `LOOKUP`, `SPLINE`, or `BITMAP`), and `N` is the number of data points and `KEYWORD` is an optional entry for long-range solvers described in the manual.

In the next line, TYPE1 and TYPE2 represent the atom types that interact with this potential, FILE_NAME is the name of the file containing the data points, VARIABLE is the keyword in the file used to identify the beginning of the file, and CUTOFF has been explained already. The data file format is provided in the LAMMPS manual (https://lammps.sandia.gov/doc/pair_table.html), shown as follows:

```
# DATE: 2020-06-10  UNITS: real  CONTRIBUTOR: ... (header line)
# Morse potential for Fe    (one or more comment or blank lines)

MORSE_FE                    (keyword is first text on line)
N 500 R 1.0 10.0            (N, R, RSQ, BITMAP, FPRIME parameters)
                            (blank)
1 1.0 25.5 102.34           (index, r, energy, force)
2 1.02 23.4 98.5

...

500 10.0 0.001 0.003
```

Figure 5.7 - The table potential data file format from the LAMMPS manual

As you can see, the keyword in the data file must be the same as VARIABLE from the input script, and the four columns represent the index, separation (r), potential, and force used for interpolation.

Having outlined the input script syntax and the data file format, we analyze various methods in pair_table.cpp, in the following sections, that process this pair style, starting with parsing of the global coefficients by PairTable::settings().

PairTable::settings()

This method reads the global coefficients entered after the pair_style table command. The following screenshot shows us the settings() method:

```
210  /* -------------------------------------------------------------------
211       global settings
212  ----------------------------------------------------------------- */
213
214  void PairTable::settings(int narg, char **arg)
215  {
216    if (narg < 2) error->all(FLERR,"Illegal pair_style command");
217
218    // new settings
219
220    if (strcmp(arg[0],"lookup") == 0) tabstyle = LOOKUP;
221    else if (strcmp(arg[0],"linear") == 0) tabstyle = LINEAR;
222    else if (strcmp(arg[0],"spline") == 0) tabstyle = SPLINE;
223    else if (strcmp(arg[0],"bitmap") == 0) tabstyle = BITMAP;
224    else error->all(FLERR,"Unknown table style in pair_style command");
225
226    tablength = force->inumeric(FLERR,arg[1]);
227    if (tablength < 2) error->all(FLERR,"Illegal number of pair table entries");
228
229    // optional keywords
230    // assert the tabulation is compatible with a specific long-range solver
231
232    int iarg = 2;
233    while (iarg < narg) {
234      if (strcmp(arg[iarg],"ewald") == 0) ewaldflag = 1;
235      else if (strcmp(arg[iarg],"pppm") == 0) pppmflag = 1;
236      else if (strcmp(arg[iarg],"msm") == 0) msmflag = 1;
237      else if (strcmp(arg[iarg],"dispersion") == 0) dispersionflag = 1;
238      else if (strcmp(arg[iarg],"tip4p") == 0) tip4pflag = 1;
239      else error->all(FLERR,"Illegal pair_style command");
240      iarg++;
241    }
```

Figure 5.8 - Code snippet from pair_table.cpp showing the settings() method

As you can see, this method allows two or more global coefficients (*line 216*). The table style variable, tabstyle (*lines 220 to 224*), is assigned an integer to correspond to one of the permitted table styles, which are enumerated in pair_table.h (*line 43*):

```
enum{LOOKUP,LINEAR,SPLINE,BITMAP};
```

Line 226 to *227* reads the number of data points (tablength) and requires at least two lines of data. *Lines 232 to 241* implement long-range interactions if specified in the LAMMPS input script.

PairTable::coeff()

This method reads the local coefficients entered for each pair of atom types. The next screenshot exemplifies the `coeff()` method:

```
259  /* ----------------------------------------------------------------------------
260      set coeffs for one or more type pairs
261     ---------------------------------------------------------------------------- */
262
263   void PairTable::coeff(int narg, char **arg)
264   {
265     if (narg != 4 && narg != 5) error->all(FLERR,"Illegal pair_coeff command");
266     if (!allocated) allocate();
267
268     int ilo,ihi,jlo,jhi;
269     force->bounds(FLERR,arg[0],atom->ntypes,ilo,ihi);
270     force->bounds(FLERR,arg[1],atom->ntypes,jlo,jhi);
271
272     int me;
273     MPI_Comm_rank(world,&me);
274     tables = (Table *)
275       memory->srealloc(tables,(ntables+1)*sizeof(Table),"pair:tables");
276     Table *tb = &tables[ntables];
277     null_table(tb);
278     if (me == 0) read_table(tb,arg[2],arg[3]);
279     bcast_table(tb);
280
281     // set table cutoff
282
283     if (narg == 5) tb->cut = force->numeric(FLERR,arg[4]);
284     else if (tb->rflag) tb->cut = tb->rhi;
285     else tb->cut = tb->rfile[tb->ninput-1];
```

Figure 5.9 - Code snippet from pair_table.cpp showing the coeff() method

As you can see, the `coeff()` method allows exactly 4 or 5 parameters (*line 265*) and reads the first two parameters as atom types (*lines 269 to 270*). *Lines 272 to 279* read the filename and the variable name used to identify the table, using the `read_table()` method located inside the same class.

The `read_table()` method takes the filename and the variable name as arguments, opens this file and loops through its lines to locate the variable name and to extract inputs from the *parameters* line (refer *Figure 5.7*) using the `param_extract()` method. When completed, the r variable and energy and force values are calculated or prepared to be read from the file depending on input parameters.

Afterward (*line 320*), the `coeff()` method calls the `compute_table()` method that calculates the table inner bound (`rinner`), table outer bound (`cut`), the square of the spacing between table data points (`delta`), and the inverse of the spacing (`invdelta`).

Here, `invdelta` is the reciprocal of `delta`, and it is calculated once and stored as a variable to circumvent repeated computation that adds overload associated with the division operation. In the same `compute_table()` method, the force and energy values are stored in 1D arrays, f and e respectively. The value obtained for force is divided by r before storing in the f array since it will facilitate calculation of the x, y, z components of the force in the `compute()` method, discussed next.

PairTable::compute()

This method calculates the separation between an atom and each of its neighbors as explained earlier and stores the square of the separation as `rsq`. Using this `rsq` value, the table entry index that gives the `r` value closest to this separation without exceeding it is determined as an integer, `itable`.

The following screenshot shows the part of the code that determines `itable`:

```
114    if (rsq < cutsq[itype][jtype]) {
115      tb = &tables[tabindex[itype][jtype]];
116      if (rsq < tb->innersq) {
117        sprintf(estr,"Pair distance < table inner cutoff: "
118                "ijtype %d %d dist %g",itype,jtype,sqrt(rsq));
119        error->one(FLERR,estr);
120      }
121
122      if (tabstyle == LOOKUP) {
123        itable = static_cast<int> ((rsq - tb->innersq) * tb->invdelta);
124        if (itable >= tlm1) {
125          sprintf(estr,"Pair distance > table outer cutoff: "
126                  "ijtype %d %d dist %g",itype,jtype,sqrt(rsq));
127          error->one(FLERR,estr);
128        }
129        fpair = factor_lj * tb->f[itable];
130      } else if (tabstyle == LINEAR) {
131        itable = static_cast<int> ((rsq - tb->innersq) * tb->invdelta);
132        if (itable >= tlm1) {
133          sprintf(estr,"Pair distance > table outer cutoff: "
134                  "ijtype %d %d dist %g",itype,jtype,sqrt(rsq));
135          error->one(FLERR,estr);
136        }
137        fraction = (rsq - tb->rsq[itable]) * tb->invdelta;
138        value = tb->f[itable] + fraction*tb->df[itable];
139        fpair = factor_lj * value;
140      } else if (tabstyle == SPLINE) {
141        itable = static_cast<int> ((rsq - tb->innersq) * tb->invdelta);
142        if (itable >= tlm1) {
143          sprintf(estr,"Pair distance > table outer cutoff: "
144                  "ijtype %d %d dist %g",itype,jtype,sqrt(rsq));
145          error->one(FLERR,estr);
146        }
147        b = (rsq - tb->rsq[itable]) * tb->invdelta;
148        a = 1.0 - b;
149        value = a * tb->f[itable] + b * tb->f[itable+1] +
150          ((a*a*a-a)*tb->f2[itable] + (b*b*b-b)*tb->f2[itable+1]) *
151          tb->deltasq6;
152        fpair = factor_lj * value;
153      } else {
```

Figure 5.10 - Code snippet from pair_table.cpp showing the compute() method

As you can see, the force computation depends on the `tabstyle` variable that indicates one of the LOOKUP, LINEAR, SPLINE, or BITMAP styles:

- For the LOOKUP style (*line 129*), force is directly read from the `itable` entry of the f array, that is, `f[itable]`.

- For the LINEAR style (*lines 137* to *138*), the fractional distance between the `r` values at the index, `itable` and (`itable+1`), is stored as the `fraction` variable and is used to linearly interpolate between the f values at the same two indices, using the `df` array that contains the differences between every two consecutive f values in the table (see *line 676*).

- For the `SPLINE` style (*lines 147 to 151*), the fractional distance is calculated as for the `LINEAR` style but is fed into a cubic function (*line 149*) to calculate the force.

- For the `BITMAP` style (*lines 153 to 159*), the algorithm described in the manual is performed, using bits to identify the relevant table as `itable` and to interpolate accordingly.

The force determined is stored as `fpair` and multiplied by the displacement vector components ($\Delta x, \Delta y, \Delta z$) to obtain the force components (*lines 162 to 168*). The corresponding energies are calculated in *lines 171 to 181*:

In this section, we learned about the methods used to implement the pair table potential, namely, the `settings()`, `coeff()`, and `compute()` methods.

In the next section, we analyze the pair style DPD that applies pairwise, drag, and stochastic forces.

Reviewing the DPD potential

In this section, we look at the DPD potential and its implementation via the `pair_dpd.cpp` and `pair_dpd.h` classes.

Dissipative Particle Dynamics (DPD) involves a pairwise conservative force coupled with a dissipative force and a stochastic force acting on two particles that are used to represent larger molecules or clusters. The atomistic details of the molecules or clusters are eliminated or minimized by coarse-graining to facilitate simulation over a longer time scale compared to conventional MD. This technique is particularly useful when simulating fluids, where the particles represent molecules or fluid blocks instead of atoms. The dissipative and stochastic forces can be used to model fluid drag forces and collision forces respectively.

When implementing DPD potential, force from the pairwise potential accounts for part of the pairwise force, whereas the dissipative force needs to be calculated using the relative particle velocities and the random force necessarily has to follow a Gaussian distribution. Altogether, the DPD force acting on an `i` particle is given by a sum of three pairwise-additive forces (F^C, F^D, F^R) with a neighboring particle, `j`, that lies within a fixed cutoff distance (r_c):

$$\vec{f} = \left(F_{ij}^C + F_{ij}^D + F_{ij}^R \right) \hat{r}_{ij}$$

The unit vector, $\hat{r}_{ij} = \dfrac{\vec{r}_i - \vec{r}_j}{|\vec{r}_i - \vec{r}_j|}$, points from particle j toward particle i. The conservative force (F_{ij}^C) that represents the chemical properties of the particles provides a soft, linear repulsion with a maximum magnitude of A:

$$F_{ij}^C = A\left(1 - \frac{|\vec{r}_{ij}|}{r_c}\right)$$

The dissipative force (F_{ij}^D) that depends on the velocity difference of the two particles, $\vec{v}_{ij} = \vec{v}_i - \vec{v}_j$, and the drag coefficient, γ, is given by the following:

$$F_{ij}^D = -\gamma_{ij}\left(1 - \frac{|\vec{r}_{ij}|}{r_c}\right)^2 (\hat{r}_{ij} \cdot \vec{v}_{ij})$$

The values of the dissipative force and the random force (F_{ij}^R) are related by the **fluctuation dissipation theorem**, and the statistical values are in accordance with the system temperature (T) distributed over a Gaussian distribution. Using a Gaussian random number, α, with a mean of zero and a variance of 1, F_{ij}^R is given by the following equation:

$$F_{ij}^R = \alpha\sqrt{2k_B T\gamma_{ij}}\left(1 - \frac{|\vec{r}_{ij}|}{r_c}\right)(\Delta t)^{-1/2}$$

From the preceding equation, Δt is the timestep and k_B is the Boltzmann constant.

In the LAMMPS input script, the following commands implement the DPD potential:

```
pair_style dpd   TEMPERATURE   GLOBAL_CUTOFF      SEED
pair_coeff       TYPE1   TYPE2    A   GAMMA    LOCAL_CUTOFF
```

From the preceding code, the TEMPERATURE parameter is self-explanatory and the A and GAMMA parameters represent the quantities A and γ, respectively, described earlier. The GLOBAL_CUTOFF and LOCAL_CUTOFF parameters are the cutoffs used for all atom pairs or specified atom pairs respectively (described in detail in the LAMMPS manual: https://lammps.sandia.gov/doc/pair_dpd.html). The TYPE1 and TYPE2 parameters specify the pair of atom types that interact via the DPD potential. The SEED parameter is an integer used to generate a Gaussian distribution of random numbers, explained in the settings() method.

PairDPD::settings()

This method reads the global input parameters for the DPD potential and initializes a random number generator. The following screenshot shows the `PairDPD::settings()` method:

```
185   /* ----------------------------------------------------------------
186       global settings
187   ----------------------------------------------------------------- */
188
189   void PairDPD::settings(int narg, char **arg)
190   {
191     if (narg != 3) error->all(FLERR,"Illegal pair_style command");
192
193     temperature = force->numeric(FLERR,arg[0]);
194     cut_global = force->numeric(FLERR,arg[1]);
195     seed = force->inumeric(FLERR,arg[2]);
196
197     // initialize Marsaglia RNG with processor-unique seed
198
199     if (seed <= 0) error->all(FLERR,"Illegal pair_style command");
200     delete random;
201     random = new RanMars(lmp,seed + comm->me);
202
203     // reset cutoffs that have been explicitly set
204
205     if (allocated) {
206       int i,j;
207       for (i = 1; i <= atom->ntypes; i++)
208         for (j = i; j <= atom->ntypes; j++)
209           if (setflag[i][j]) cut[i][j] = cut_global;
210     }
211   }
```

Figure 5.11 - Code snippet from pair_dpd.cpp showing the settings() method

As you can see, *lines 193* to *195* read the global parameters, TEMPERATURE and GLOBAL_CUTOFF, as floating-point numbers and the SEED parameter as an integer. In *line 201*, SEED is then used to create the `random` class (declared in `pair_dpd.h`) that calls the **Marsaglia** random number generator coded in the `random_mars.cpp` class (the `random_mars.h` header file has been imported in *line 27*).

The **Marsaglia** random number generator takes an integer argument and processes it to generate a sequence of random numbers. SEED is added to the processor rank assigned to each core among the multicores used (accessed by comm->me) so that a different integer is fed into each core. The random class will be used to generate random numbers in the desired distribution as explained in the next section.

PairDPD::compute()

This method computes the forces involved in DPD pair interactions. After establishing the neighbors of each i particle, it loops over these j neighbors and computes the three force contributions (F^C, F^D, F^R). The following screenshot shows us the PairDPD::compute() method:

```
113    if (rsq < cutsq[itype][jtype]) {
114      r = sqrt(rsq);
115      if (r < EPSILON) continue;      // r can be 0.0 in DPD systems
116      rinv = 1.0/r;
117      delvx = vxtmp - v[j][0];
118      delvy = vytmp - v[j][1];
119      delvz = vztmp - v[j][2];
120      dot = delx*delvx + dely*delvy + delz*delvz;
121      wd = 1.0 - r/cut[itype][jtype];
122      randnum = random->gaussian();
123
124      // conservative force = a0 * wd
125      // drag force = -gamma * wd^2 * (delx dot delv) / r
126      // random force = sigma * wd * rnd * dtinvsqrt;
127
128      fpair = a0[itype][jtype]*wd;
129      fpair -= gamma[itype][jtype]*wd*wd*dot*rinv;
130      fpair += sigma[itype][jtype]*wd*randnum*dtinvsqrt;
131      fpair *= factor_dpd*rinv;
132
133      f[i][0] += delx*fpair;
134      f[i][1] += dely*fpair;
135      f[i][2] += delz*fpair;
136      if (newton_pair || j < nlocal) {
137        f[j][0] -= delx*fpair;
138        f[j][1] -= dely*fpair;
139        f[j][2] -= delz*fpair;
140      }
141
142      if (eflag) {
143        // unshifted eng of conservative term:
144        // evdwl = -a0[itype][jtype]*r * (1.0-0.5*r/cut[itype][jtype]);
145        // eng shifted to 0.0 at cutoff
146        evdwl = 0.5*a0[itype][jtype]*cut[itype][jtype] * wd*wd;
147        evdwl *= factor_dpd;
148      }
```

Figure 5.12 - Code snippet from pair_dpd.cpp showing the compute() method

As you can see, for the neighbors located inside the cutoff, the r separation (*line 114*) and the reciprocal separation, `rinv` (*line 116*), are calculated, followed by the (x, y, z) components of $\vec{v}_{ij}$ (*lines 117* to *120*), where the v array contains the particle velocities declared in *line 75* and the variables (`vxtemp`, `vytemp`, `vztemp`) represent the velocity components of particle, i (*lines 95* to *97*).

Line 120 stores the dot product $(\vec{r}_{ij} \cdot \vec{v}_{ij})$ as the variable, `dot`, which needs to be divided by the r separation to obtain the quantity $(\hat{r}_{ij} \cdot \vec{v}_{ij})$ as required in F^D. *Line 121* defines a variable, `wd`, to use as a shorthand notation for the quantity $\left(1 - \frac{|\vec{r}_{ij}|}{r_c}\right)$. The `randnum` variable is defined in *line 122* to represent α by storing a random number drawn from a Gaussian distribution of mean zero and variance 1 using the `random->gaussian()` method (defined in `random_mars.cpp`).

Having defined the variables, F^C is computed in *line 128* and stored as the variable, `fpair`. In *line 129*, the `rinv` quantity is incorporated to divide `dot` by r while computing F^D, and the result is tallied to `fpair`. Before calculating F^R, the 2D array, `sigma`, is defined in *line 273* inside `PairDPD::init_one()` to store the quantity, $\sqrt{2k_B T \gamma_{ij}}$:

```
sigma[i][j] = sqrt(2.0*force->boltz*temperature*gamma[i][j]);
```

Also, the `dtinvsqrt` variable is defined on *line 81* to store the quantity, $(\Delta t)^{-\frac{1}{2}}$:

```
double dtinvsqrt = 1.0/sqrt(update->dt);
```

On *line 130*, these quantities are multiplied with `randnum` and `wd` to obtain F^R and the result is tallied to `fpair`. Finally, on *line 131*, the `fpair` variable containing contributions from F^C, F^D, and F^R is scaled by the `factor_dpd` quantity to account for any special bonds (*line 104*) and multiplied by `rinv` to facilitate (x, y, z) force component calculations. At this stage, `fpair` effectively equals the following:

$$\text{fpair} = \text{factor\_dpd} * \left(F_{ij}^C + F_{ij}^D + F_{ij}^R\right)\frac{1}{r_{ij}}$$

The (x, y, z) components of `fpair` are assigned to the appropriate array elements of the force array, `f`, in *lines 133* to *139* (see *Figure 5.12*).

The potential $V_{DPD}(r)$ of a DPD potential is calculated only from the conservative force, F^C:

$$V_{DPD}(r) = -\int_0^r F^C(r)\, dr = -\int_0^r A\left(1 - \frac{r}{r_c}\right) dr = \frac{1}{2} A r_c \left(1 - \frac{r}{r_c}\right)^2$$

This potential is computed in *lines 142* to *148* and in the `PairDPD::single()` method and is scaled to accommodate special bonds if required.

In this section, we learned the mechanism behind the DPD pair potential, including the force and potential calculations performed by the `compute()` method.

Summary

In this chapter, some of the existing LAMMPS pair styles have been analyzed to demonstrate the roles played by various methods in performing the required calculations and exchanging information. Other variants of potentials implemented in LAMMPS include the many-body (that is, non-pairwise) **Stillinger-Weber** (**SW**) potential and the `Pair List` option that assigns pair coefficients to individual atom pairs instead of atom type pairs.

Position-dependent potentials are implemented using a functional form in the `compute()` method or can be implemented in a tabulated form read by the pair style. Non-conservative forces can also be implemented alongside by defining the appropriate force functions.

You can now use the lessons and skills learned from this chapter to modify the appropriate methods in a pair potential to customize it per your simulation requirements.

In the next chapter, we will analyze selected compute styles to illustrate the inner mechanism of the code as it has been done in this chapter.

Questions

1. Which methods are used to read global and local coefficients in pair styles?

2. Why does the `fpair` variable always have the force function multiplied with the reciprocal of the separation?

3. What is the primary purpose served by the `single()` method?

6
Understanding Computes

In the previous chapter, we explored some of the pair styles implemented in LAMMPS.

In this chapter, we will analyze some computes and gain a similar understanding of their source code. Computes return various quantities from the simulation run, and learning to understand the code that is responsible for the associated calculations is essential if we wish to write new computes for custom purposes.

We will cover the following topics in this chapter:

- Reviewing the general structure of computes
- Reviewing the compute KE class
- Reviewing the compute group/group class
- Reviewing the compute RDF class
- Reviewing the compute heat flux class

By the end of this chapter, you will understand the inner mechanism of selected computes and be able to make further modifications to the LAMMPS source code.

Technical requirements

To execute the instructions in this chapter, you just need a text editor (for example, **Notepad++** or **Gedit**).

You can find the full source code used in this chapter here: `https://github.com/PacktPublishing/Extending-and-Modifying-LAMMPS-Writing-Your-Own-Source-Code`

This is the link to download LAMMPS: `https://lammps.sandia.gov/doc/Install.html`. The LAMMPS GitHub link is `https://github.com/lammps/lammps`, where the source code can be found as well.

Reviewing the general structure of computes

In this section, we will briefly cover some of the methods most commonly used in compute child classes.

Similar to pair styles, individual computes inherit from the parent `Compute` class described by `compute.cpp` and `compute.h` classes. These parent classes read the first three arguments (compute ID, group ID, and compute style) from the LAMMPS input script. The following screenshot shows some of the variables and arrays from `compute.h` that are inherited:

```
21  class Compute : protected Pointers {
22    public:
23      static int instance_total;      // # of Compute classes ever instantiated
24
25      char *id,*style;
26      int igroup,groupbit;
27
28      double scalar;                  // computed global scalar
29      double *vector;                 // computed global vector
30      double **array;                 // computed global array
31      double *vector_atom;            // computed per-atom vector
32      double **array_atom;            // computed per-atom array
33      double *vector_local;           // computed local vector
34      double **array_local;           // computed local array
35
36      int scalar_flag;                // 0/1 if compute_scalar() function exists
37      int vector_flag;                // 0/1 if compute_vector() function exists
38      int array_flag;                 // 0/1 if compute_array() function exists
39      int size_vector;                // length of global vector
40      int size_array_rows;            // rows in global array
41      int size_array_cols;            // columns in global array
42      int size_vector_variable;       // 1 if vec length is unknown in advance
43      int size_array_rows_variable;   // 1 if array rows is unknown in advance
44
45      int peratom_flag;               // 0/1 if compute_peratom() function exists
46      int size_peratom_cols;          // 0 = vector, N = columns in peratom array
47
48      int local_flag;                 // 0/1 if compute_local() function exists
49      int size_local_rows;            // rows in local vector or array
50      int size_local_cols;            // 0 = vector, N = columns in local array
51
52      int extscalar;                  // 0/1 if global scalar is intensive/extensive
53      int extvector;                  // 0/1/-1 if global vector is all int/ext/extlist
54      int *extlist;                   // list of 0/1 int/ext for each vec component
55      int extarray;                   // 0/1 if global array is all intensive/extensive
```

Figure 6.1 – Code snippet from compute.h

The child compute classes may contain one or more of the following methods:

- The `init()` method sets up the class and performs preliminary validation checks.
- The `init_list()` method sets up neighbor lists or pointers to neighboring lists.
- The `compute_scalar()` method computes a scalar quantity generally used as an output.
- The `compute_vector()` method computes a vector quantity generally used as an output.

> **Important Note:**
> Given the broad range of applications for which computes are used, many other methods can be implemented in individual computes.

Next, we will review a few select computes to illustrate the code working behind these computes.

Reviewing the compute KE class

In this section, we'll study the methods implemented in the `compute  KE` class, which calculates *kinetic* energy of a group of atoms.

The **kinetic energy (KE)** of an atom of mass m and linear velocity (v_x, v_y, v_z) is calculated using the following equation:

$$KE = \frac{1}{2}m(v_x^2 + v_y^2 + v_z^2)$$

The `compute_ke.cpp` class can be used to calculate the kinetic energy of a specified group of atoms. In a LAMMPS input script, the corresponding syntax is as follows:

```
compute   COMPUTE_ID   GROUP_ID   ke
```

As you can see, the COMPUTE_ID parameter is the unique ID of the compute defined, while the GROUP_ID parameter is the ID of the group of atoms that the compute acts on. This is described in detail in the LAMMPS manual (https://lammps.sandia.gov/doc/compute_ke.html). First, we will look at the constructor method, `ComputeKE::ComputeKE()`, of this class.

ComputeKE::ComputeKE()

This constructor method inherits from the `Compute` parent class (*line 26*) and checks the number of arguments, as shown in the following screenshot:

```
25    ComputeKE::ComputeKE(LAMMPS *lmp, int narg, char **arg) :
26        Compute(lmp, narg, arg)
27    {
28        if (narg != 3) error->all(FLERR,"Illegal compute ke command");
29
30        scalar_flag = 1;
31        extscalar = 1;
32    }
```

Figure 6.2 – Code snippet from compute_ke.cpp showing the constructor

For this compute, exactly three arguments (compute ID, group ID, and compute style) are permitted (*line 28*), which are all read in `compute.cpp`. Since KE is returned as a scalar quantity, the `scalar_flag` and `extscalar` variables are activated in *lines 30* and *31*.

Next, we will look at the `init()` method.

ComputeKE::init()

The `init()` method serves to initialize this compute KE class and defines a conversion factor (`pfactor`) that converts into the correct unit of energy, as described in *Chapter 4, Accessing Information by Variables, Arrays, and Methods*. This method is shown in the following screenshot:

```
36    void ComputeKE::init()
37    {
38        pfactor = 0.5 * force->mvv2e;
39    }
```

Figure 6.3 – Code snippet from compute_ke.cpp showing the init() method

The bulk of the KE computation is performed by the `compute_scalar()` method, discussed next.

ComputeKE::compute_scalar()

This method computes the KE of every atom in the group specified and finds the sum over all atoms, as shown in the following screenshot:

```cpp
43    double ComputeKE::compute_scalar()
44    {
45      invoked_scalar = update->ntimestep;
46
47      double **v = atom->v;
48      double *rmass = atom->rmass;
49      double *mass = atom->mass;
50      int *mask = atom->mask;
51      int *type = atom->type;
52      int nlocal = atom->nlocal;
53
54      double ke = 0.0;
55
56      if (rmass) {
57        for (int i = 0; i < nlocal; i++)
58          if (mask[i] & groupbit)
59            ke += rmass[i] * (v[i][0]*v[i][0] + v[i][1]*v[i][1] + v[i][2]*v[i][2]);
60      } else {
61        for (int i = 0; i < nlocal; i++)
62          if (mask[i] & groupbit)
63            ke += mass[type[i]] *
64              (v[i][0]*v[i][0] + v[i][1]*v[i][1] + v[i][2]*v[i][2]);
65      }
66
67      MPI_Allreduce(&ke,&scalar,1,MPI_DOUBLE,MPI_SUM,world);
68      scalar *= pfactor;
69      return scalar;
70    }
```

Figure 6.4 – Code snippet from compute_ke.cpp showing the compute_scalar() method

As you can see, *line 56* checks if the per-atom mass (rmass) is activated, which would assign individual masses to individual atoms. The code loops over all the atoms in the core (*line 57*), identifies the atoms belonging to the specified group (*line 58*), and calculates and appends the KE of each atom using its rmass value and its velocity (*line 59*).

If the mass of each atom is defined according to its atom type, the same procedure is followed (*lines 60 to 65*), with the exception of using the mass of the atom type in the KE calculation (*line 63*).

The `ke` variable stores the combined KE of all the atoms in the core, and the sum of KE over all the cores is computed using the `MPI_Allreduce()` method (*line 67*), which accepts the following arguments:

- `&ke`: This is the variable that passes the local sum in the core as input.
- `&scalar`: This is the variable that stores the global output from all cores combined.
- `1`: This is the size of the input and output arrays.
- `MPI_DOUBLE`: This represents the data type of the input and output quantities.
- `MPI_SUM`: This is the operation type (that is, summation) to be executed.
- `world`: This represents the cores over which the operation is performed.

The **Message Passing Interface** (**MPI**) is an attribute of the compiler (not exclusive to LAMMPS) that allows information exchange between cores. More information about MPI is available in *Appendix C, Getting Familiar with MPI*. The relevant header file can be imported into `compute_ke.cpp` with the following library:

```
#include <mpi.h>
```

Apart from finding the sum, the `MPI_Allreduce()` method allows a number of reduction operations, including finding maximum, minimum, and product of quantities, to be calculated over multiple cores.

Finally, the global sum of KE obtained from the `MPI_Allreduce()` method and stored as the `scalar` variable (which has been inherited from `compute.h`, as seen in *Figure 6.1*) is converted into the proper units by multiplying it by the conversion factor, `pfactor` (*line 68*), and returning it (*line 69*).

In this section, we analyzed a relatively short compute style that returns a scalar quantity.

In the next section, we will look at a compute that calculates the interaction energies and forces between two groups of atoms.

Reviewing the compute group/group class

In this section, we will analyze a more elaborate compute that employs a larger number of methods.

The interaction energy and the forces between two groups of atoms can be obtained using `compute group/group` and are implemented by the `compute_group_group.cpp` and `compute_group_group.h` classes. The LAMMPS input script command to implement this compute is as follows:

```
compute   COMPUTE_ID   G1   group/group   G2
```

The `COMPUTE_ID` parameter is the unique ID of the compute, while the `G1` and `G2` parameters are the IDs of the groups of atoms that the compute acts on (see manual: `https://lammps.sandia.gov/doc/compute_group_group.html`). The optional parameter keywords listed in the manual can be entered after these parameters to specify other options, such as the interaction type (*pair potential* or *electrostatic*) and molecule ID (same or different). The constructor method accommodates these optional parameters, as we'll see in the following sections.

ComputeGroupGroup::ComputeGroupGroup()

This constructor takes in a minimum of four arguments (*line 50*), of which three are read by `compute.cpp`. The scalar and vector output types are specified (*lines 52 to 55*) to accommodate energy and force outputs, respectively.

Lines 57 to *59* read the fourth argument from the input script command and store it as a `group2` string to represent the second group of atoms. Then, the corresponding group ID is located as a `jgroup` variable (*line 61*), and an error is generated if the group does not exist (*lines 62 to 63*). On *line 64*, the bitwise representation of the group is generated as `jgroupbit`, which is used to identify atoms belonging to this group (please see Appendix B, Debugging Programs, for more information about bitwise representations).

The following screenshot shows the ComputeGroupGroup() constructor:

```
46   ComputeGroupGroup::ComputeGroupGroup(LAMMPS *lmp, int narg, char **arg) :
47     Compute(lmp, narg, arg),
48     group2(NULL)
49   {
50     if (narg < 4) error->all(FLERR,"Illegal compute group/group command");
51
52     scalar_flag = vector_flag = 1;
53     size_vector = 3;
54     extscalar = 1;
55     extvector = 1;
56
57     int n = strlen(arg[3]) + 1;
58     group2 = new char[n];
59     strcpy(group2,arg[3]);
60
61     jgroup = group->find(group2);
62     if (jgroup == -1)
63       error->all(FLERR,"Compute group/group group ID does not exist");
64     jgroupbit = group->bitmask[jgroup];
65
66     pairflag = 1;
67     kspaceflag = 0;
68     boundaryflag = 1;
69     molflag = OFF;
70
71     int iarg = 4;
72     while (iarg < narg) {
73       if (strcmp(arg[iarg],"pair") == 0) {
74         if (iarg+2 > narg)
75           error->all(FLERR,"Illegal compute group/group command");
76         if (strcmp(arg[iarg+1],"yes") == 0) pairflag = 1;
77         else if (strcmp(arg[iarg+1],"no") == 0) pairflag = 0;
78         else error->all(FLERR,"Illegal compute group/group command");
79         iarg += 2;
80       } else if (strcmp(arg[iarg],"kspace") == 0) {
81         if (iarg+2 > narg)
82           error->all(FLERR,"Illegal compute group/group command");
83         if (strcmp(arg[iarg+1],"yes") == 0) kspaceflag = 1;
84         else if (strcmp(arg[iarg+1],"no") == 0) kspaceflag = 0;
85         else error->all(FLERR,"Illegal compute group/group command");
86         iarg += 2;
```

Figure 6.5 – Code snippet from compute_group_group.cpp showing the constructor method

The default settings of this compute with regards to the optional keywords, as described in the LAMMPS manual (that is, pair = yes, kspace = no, boundary = yes, and molecule = off), are facilitated by flag values 0 or 1 in *lines 66 to 69*. Any optional keyword is accommodated by *lines 71 to 105*, which loop over all the arguments to look for permitted keywords and adjust the flag values as required.

Once the parameters have been parsed, the init () method performs some error checks and requests a neighbor list, if required.

ComputeGroupGroup::init() and init_list()

The init () method checks whether pair styles and electrostatic interactions exist between the groups specified (if they are enabled) and also initiates the corresponding pair and kspace objects (*lines 122 to 144*). A neighbor list is requested (*lines 167 to 172*) if pair style interaction needs to be calculated, as shown in the following screenshot:

```
167    if (pairflag) {
168        int irequest = neighbor->request(this,instance_me);
169        neighbor->requests[irequest]->pair = 0;
170        neighbor->requests[irequest]->compute = 1;
171        neighbor->requests[irequest]->occasional = 1;
172    }
```

Figure 6.6 – Code snippet from compute_group_group.cpp showing the init() method

The init_list () method provides access to pointers to the neighbor list using the list pointer defined in compute_group_group.h, as shown in the following screenshot:

```
177    void ComputeGroupGroup::init_list(int /*id*/, NeighList *ptr)
178    {
179        list = ptr;
180    }
```

Figure 6.7 – Code snippet from compute_group_group.cpp showing the init_list() method

Having created access to a neighbor list, we will now look at the pair_contribution () method, which calculates the pairwise energy and forces.

ComputeGroupGroup::pair_contribution()

This method is invoked if the pair flag is enabled and the pair potential between the two groups needs to be calculated. First, the neighbor list is built (*lines 230 to 235*), and then the code loops over all the atoms, i, belonging to the first group (G1) and their neighbors, j.

Only the neighbors, j, belonging to the second group (G2) are selected (*lines 261 to 271*). In accordance with the molecule keyword, the molecule IDs are checked in *lines 275 to 281* to determine if each atom, j, belongs to the same molecule as atom i. The following screenshot shows the computations of energy and force:

```
283         delx = xtmp - x[j][0];
284         dely = ytmp - x[j][1];
285         delz = ztmp - x[j][2];
286         rsq = delx*delx + dely*dely + delz*delz;
287         jtype = type[j];
288
289         if (rsq < cutsq[itype][jtype]) {
290            eng = pair->single(i,j,itype,jtype,rsq,factor_coul,factor_lj,fpair);
291
292            // energy only computed once so tally full amount
293            // force tally is jgroup acting on igroup
294
295            if (newton_pair || j < nlocal) {
296               one[0] += eng;
297               if (ij_flag) {
298                  one[1] += delx*fpair;
299                  one[2] += dely*fpair;
300                  one[3] += delz*fpair;
301               }
302               if (ji_flag) {
303                  one[1] -= delx*fpair;
304                  one[2] -= dely*fpair;
305                  one[3] -= delz*fpair;
306               }
```

Figure 6.8 – Code snippet from compute_group_group.cpp showing the pair_contribution() method

The energy and force of pair potential interaction between i and j is computed by invoking the single() method in the corresponding pair style (*line 290*) and tallied into the first element of the 1D array, one (*line 296*). The force components acting on i are tallied in the next three elements of the one array (one[1], one[2], one[3]) in *lines 297 to 306*. The array elements are summed over all cores (*line 324*), as follows:

```
MPI_Allreduce(one,all,4,MPI_DOUBLE,MPI_SUM,world);
```

The sum of energies is tallied in the scalar variable (*line 325*) and updated if the electrostatic energies need to be incorporated in the kspace_contribution() method (*line 346* and *line 363*). The sum of each force component is stored in the 1D vector array (*line 326*). Both scalar and vector are inherited from the compute.h class.

The calculations performed by this method are invoked by the compute_scalar() and compute_vector() methods, as required by the compute.

ComputeGroupGroup::compute_scalar() and compute_vector()

The compute_scalar() method invokes the pair_contribution() and kspace_contribution() methods to obtain the pair and electrostatic energies. The compute_vector() method invokes the same methods to obtain the force components. Both these methods are depicted in the following screenshot:

```cpp
184    double ComputeGroupGroup::compute_scalar()
185    {
186      invoked_scalar = invoked_vector = update->ntimestep;
187
188      scalar = 0.0;
189      vector[0] = vector[1] = vector[2] = 0.0;
190
191      if (pairflag) pair_contribution();
192      if (kspaceflag) kspace_contribution();
193
194      return scalar;
195    }
196
197    /* ------------------------------------------------------
198
199    void ComputeGroupGroup::compute_vector()
200    {
201      invoked_scalar = invoked_vector = update->ntimestep;
202
203      scalar = 0.0;
204      vector[0] = vector[1] = vector[2] = 0.0;
205
206      if (pairflag) pair_contribution();
207      if (kspaceflag) kspace_contribution();
208    }
```

Figure 6.9 – Code snippet from compute_group_group.cpp showing the compute_scalar() and compute_vector() methods

In this section, we analyzed some of the methods that constitute compute group/group and return the energy and force of interaction between two groups of atoms.

In the next section, we'll look at compute RDF.

Reviewing the compute RDF class

In this section, we will look at the source code for the `compute_rdf.cpp` and `compute_rdf.h` classes, which govern the `compute RDF` class.

The `compute RDF` class calculates the **radial distribution function (RDF)** of a group of atoms and returns the normalized numbers of neighbors, sorted into bins that have a uniform radial width (Δr) and that extend from zero to a specified cutoff distance. The output is returned as a 1D array that can be used to plot an RDF histogram. For each atom, the value of its RDF ($g(r)$) at a distance, r, is calculated by taking the ratio of the number of its neighboring atoms (N), which are located in the distance range (r, $r + \Delta r$) from the atom, to the number of atoms that would have been located in the same range if the atom distribution were uniform.

To derive this function, we must divide the periphery space of a central atom into shells of width dr that each occupy a volume of dV_{shell}:

$$dn(r) = \rho g(r) dV_{shell}$$

From the preceding equation, $dn(r)$ represents the number of neighbors in a shell with radius r and width dr, while dV_{shell} is the volume of this shell, which in 3D is approximated by the following equation:

$$dV_{shell} = \frac{4}{3}\pi(r + dr)^3 - \frac{4}{3}\pi r^3 \simeq 4\pi r^2 dr$$

The quantity, ρ, represents the system's atom density, which is calculated by the following equation:

$$\rho = \frac{\text{Number of Neighboring Atoms in Simulation Box}}{\text{Volume of Simulation Box}}$$

Hence, the RDF can be solved using the following equation:

$$g(r) = \frac{dn(r)}{4\pi r^2 dr \rho}$$

Altogether, when a discrete bin width, Δr, is implemented, the RDF in 3D converts into the following:

$$g(r) = \frac{N(r, r + \Delta r)}{4\pi r^2 (\Delta r)\rho} = \frac{N(r, r + \Delta r)}{\frac{4\pi}{3}[(r + \Delta r)^3 - r^3]\rho}$$

The system, g(r), is calculated by averaging individual g(r) values over all the atoms in the system.

In 2D, the equation for g(r) changes in the denominator:

$$g(r) = \frac{N(r, r + \Delta r)}{2\pi r (\Delta r)\sigma} = \frac{N(r, r + \Delta r)}{\pi[(r + \Delta r)^2 - r^2]\sigma}$$

The system density, σ, is calculated over the unit area:

$$\sigma = \frac{\text{number of neighboring atoms in simulation box}}{\text{area of simulation box}}$$

The LAMMPS inputs script command for implementing the compute RDF is as follows:

```
compute  COMPUTE_ID  GROUP  rdf  NBIN
```

As you can see, the COMPUTE_ID parameter is the unique ID of the compute, while the GROUP parameter is the ID of the group of atoms that the compute acts on (see manual: https://lammps.sandia.gov/doc/compute_rdf.html). The NBIN integer is the number of bins for which the g(r) will be calculated. The optional keywords listed in the manual can be entered after these parameters to specify atom type pairs (multiple times) and a user-defined cutoff. The constructor method accommodates these optional parameters, as we will see in the following sections.

ComputeRDF::ComputeRDF()

The following screenshot shows the `ComputeRDF()` constructor method:

```
47     if (narg < 4) error->all(FLERR,"Illegal compute rdf command");
48
49     array_flag = 1;
50     extarray = 0;
51
52     nbin = force->inumeric(FLERR,arg[3]);
53     if (nbin < 1) error->all(FLERR,"Illegal compute rdf command");
54
55     // optional args
56     // nargpair = # of pairwise args, starting at iarg = 4
57
58     cutflag = 0;
59
60     int iarg;
61     for (iarg = 4; iarg < narg; iarg++)
62       if (strcmp(arg[iarg],"cutoff") == 0) break;
63
64     int nargpair = iarg - 4;
65
66     while (iarg < narg) {
67       if (strcmp(arg[iarg],"cutoff") == 0) {
68         if (iarg+2 > narg) error->all(FLERR,"Illegal compute rdf command");
69         cutoff_user = force->numeric(FLERR,arg[iarg+1]);
70         if (cutoff_user <= 0.0) cutflag = 0;
71         else cutflag = 1;
72         iarg += 2;
73       } else error->all(FLERR,"Illegal compute rdf command");
74     }
75
76     // pairwise args
77
78     if (nargpair == 0) npairs = 1;
79     else {
80       if (nargpair % 2) error->all(FLERR,"Illegal compute rdf command");
81       npairs = nargpair/2;
82     }
83
84     size_array_rows = nbin;
85     size_array_cols = 1 + 2*npairs;
```

Figure 6.10 – Code snippet from compute_rdf.cpp showing the constructor method

As you can see, the method accepts a minimum of four input parameters (*line 47*) and activates an array flag to generate output (*line 49 to 50*). The number of bins is read in *line 52* and stored as an integer, `nbin`.

To keep count of any additional arguments that are entered, the `nargpair` variable must be introduced and reset to zero at the fourth argument (*line 64*). While looping over the additional parameters (*lines 66 to 74*), any user-defined cutoff is identified using the `strcmp()` method (*line 67*), which locates the `cutoff` keyword. The corresponding numeric value following this keyword is read by the `force->numeric()` method (*line 69*). If no cutoff is provided, the longest pairwise cutoff defined in the system is used by default (see the `init()` method).

The `npairs` variable is introduced in `compute_rdf.h` (*line 38*) to keep count of the number of atom type pairs specified by the optional input parameters. In the constructor, `npairs` is given a default value of `1` if no additional atom type pairs are entered (*line 78*). For any additional atom type pairs that are entered, the `npairs` variable equals the number of pairs entered (*line 81*), while ensuring that an even number of atom types are entered (*line 80*).

Lines 84 and *85* define the size of the 2D global array (inherited from `compute.h`), which possesses `nbin` number of rows and (`1+2*npairs`) columns to accommodate the bin coordinates, *g(r)* values, and the coordination numbers (described in the LAMMPS manual) to deliver the output.

Lines 88 to *89* initialize two new structures – a 3D array called `rdfpair` and a 2D array called `nrdpair`. Any optional atom type pairs entered are parsed in *lines 98 to 107*. In order to deal with wildcard atom type pairs entered in the input script, the `force->bounds` method is used (*lines 101 to 102*), which can assign the lower and upper bounds of atom types to the `ilo, ihi, jlo`, and `jhi` variables. For example, if there are five atom types in the system and the pair types that have been entered is "`* 4`", then we get `ilo=1, ihi=4`, and `jlo=jhi=4`.

In *lines 109* to *120*, the parsed atom type pairs are stored in the `nrdfpair` and `rdfpair` arrays, which we declared earlier in *lines 88* to *89*. The 2D `nrdfpair` array records the number of atom type pairs for which the RDF should be calculated, while the 3D `rdfpair` array adds an extra dimension to indicate the index of the atom type pair. The array itself records the `npair` value that corresponds to the atom type pair that's been parsed. These two structures help prevent repeated calculations and save computation time in the `compute_array()` method.

In the rest of the constructor method, memory is allocated (*lines 122* to *124*) for the 2D global array (`array`) to generate the final output and the 2D `hist` and `histall` arrays to accommodate the *g(r)* values until the output is ready. These arrays are deallocated in the destructor method (*lines 144* to *146*), along with any other arrays defined in `compute_rdf.h`.

Next, we will look at the `init()` and `init_list()` methods.

ComputeRDF::init() and init_list()

The `init()` method calculates the cutoff and the skin width while determining the bin width from this cutoff, as shown in the following screenshot:

```
155   void ComputeRDF::init()
156   {
157
158     if (!force->pair && !cutflag)
159       error->all(FLERR,"Compute rdf requires a pair style be defined "
160                        "or cutoff specified");
161
162     if (cutflag) {
163       double skin = neighbor->skin;
164       mycutneigh = cutoff_user + skin;
165
166       double cutghost;              // as computed by Neighbor and Comm
167       if (force->pair)
168         cutghost = MAX(force->pair->cutforce+skin,comm->cutghostuser);
169       else
170         cutghost = comm->cutghostuser;
171
172       if (mycutneigh > cutghost)
173         error->all(FLERR,"Compute rdf cutoff exceeds ghost atom range - "
174                          "use comm_modify cutoff command");
175       if (force->pair && mycutneigh < force->pair->cutforce + skin)
176         if (comm->me == 0)
177           error->warning(FLERR,"Compute rdf cutoff less than neighbor cutoff - "
178                                "forcing a needless neighbor list build");
179
180       delr = cutoff_user / nbin;
181     } else delr = force->pair->cutforce / nbin;
182
183     delrinv = 1.0/delr;
184
185     // set 1st column of output array to bin coords
186
187     for (int i = 0; i < nbin; i++)
188       array[i][0] = (i+0.5) * delr;
```

Figure 6.11 – Code snippet from compute_rdf.cpp showing the init() method

As you can see, *lines 162* to *180* calculate the cutoff that can be applied to ghost atoms when a user-defined cutoff is provided, before performing a check to reduce the frequency of rebuilding neighbor lists (*lines 175* to *177*). Then, the bin width, `delr`, is obtained by dividing the cutoff by `nbin`. If a user-defined cutoff is not provided (*line 181*), the cutoff is set to the maximum cutoff distance defined among all implemented pair styles (accessed by `force->pair->cutforce`). The reciprocal bin width (`delrinv`) is calculated in *line 183* to reduce any computational overhead associated with the division operator afterward.

In *lines 187* to *188*, the first column of array is populated with the midpoints of the bins. The neighbor list is requested at the end of this method (*lines 205* to *212*). The init_ list() method provides access to pointers to the neighbor list in the same way as what happens in the compute group/group class.

ComputeRDF::init_norm()

The init_norm() method calculates the normalizing factor used in the *g(r)* calculation. Here, the number of atoms of each type present in the group is determined and used to calculate the normalizing factor when computing the RDF. The following screenshot shows this method:

```
224   void ComputeRDF::init_norm()
225   {
226     int i,j,m;
227
228     // count atoms of each type that are also in group
229
230     const int nlocal = atom->nlocal;
231     const int ntypes = atom->ntypes;
232     const int * const mask = atom->mask;
233     const int * const type = atom->type;
234
235     for (i = 1; i <= ntypes; i++) typecount[i] = 0;
236     for (i = 0; i < nlocal; i++)
237       if (mask[i] & groupbit) typecount[type[i]]++;
238
239     // icount = # of I atoms participating in I,J pairs for each histogram
240     // jcount = # of J atoms participating in I,J pairs for each histogram
241     // duplicates = # of atoms in both groups I and J for each histogram
242
243     for (m = 0; m < npairs; m++) {
244       icount[m] = 0;
245       for (i = ilo[m]; i <= ihi[m]; i++) icount[m] += typecount[i];
246       jcount[m] = 0;
247       for (i = jlo[m]; i <= jhi[m]; i++) jcount[m] += typecount[i];
248       duplicates[m] = 0;
249       for (i = ilo[m]; i <= ihi[m]; i++)
250         for (j = jlo[m]; j <= jhi[m]; j++)
251           if (i == j) duplicates[m] += typecount[i];
252     }
253
254     int *scratch = new int[npairs];
255     MPI_Allreduce(icount,scratch,npairs,MPI_INT,MPI_SUM,world);
256     for (i = 0; i < npairs; i++) icount[i] = scratch[i];
257     MPI_Allreduce(jcount,scratch,npairs,MPI_INT,MPI_SUM,world);
258     for (i = 0; i < npairs; i++) jcount[i] = scratch[i];
259     MPI_Allreduce(duplicates,scratch,npairs,MPI_INT,MPI_SUM,world);
260     for (i = 0; i < npairs; i++) duplicates[i] = scratch[i];
261     delete [] scratch;
262   }
```

Figure 6.12 – Code snippet from compute_rdf.cpp showing the init_norm() method

The number of atoms (of each type) in the group is counted (*lines 235 to 237*). In *lines 243 to 252*, the number of atoms (of each type) used to calculate the RDF is determined. If the default number of atom type pairs is used (npairs = 1), then the index, m = 0, and all atom types in the system are used in the RDF calculation.

Index i (*line 245*) and index j (*line 247*) loop over all the atom types to count the number of atoms to be used in the calculation before storing these as variables; that is, icount[m] and jcount[m] (see *lines 95 to 107* in the constructor method). The number of duplicate atoms that appear in both groups are also counted as duplicates[m]. If optional atom types are entered, then the range of indices, i and j, cover the specified atom types only, and icount[m] and jcount[m] equal the number of atoms of these types only.

The icount, jcount, and duplicates arrays are updated to include atoms from all cores by the MPI_Allreduce() methods in *lines 254 to 261*. The array elements are used in the compute_array() method to calculate and normalize the RDF, as explained in the next section.

ComputeRDF::compute_array()

The compute_array() method calculates the RDF and the coordination number of the specified group and atom types. First, the neighbor list is employed to loop over all the atoms in the core and calculate the distance, r, between every central atom and each of its neighbors (*line 347*). The bin index (ibin) for this r is determined by rounding to the largest integer that's less than the product of r and the reciprocal bin width (delrinv) in *line 348*, which is as follows:

```
ibin = static_cast<int> (r*delrinv);
```

The corresponding bin in the 2D hist array is incremented by 1 to tally this neighbor (*line 353*):

```
hist[m][ibin] += 1.0;
```

In the hist array, the first index (m) identifies the atom type pair for which the neighbor is counted, while the second index (ibin) represents the bin into which the neighbor is tallied. The hist arrays are summed over all the cores (*line 366*) and the results are stored in the 2D histall array.

This way, the `histall` array contains the number of atoms in each bin summed over all the central atoms in the entire simulation box; that is, $\sum_{i=1}^{icount[m]} N_i(r, r + \Delta r)$, sorted into separate rows corresponding to the atom type pair specified. If no additional atom type pair is provided, `histall` consists of a single row corresponding to all atom types.

The final part of the RDF calculation involves proper normalization and is shown in the following screenshot:

```
375    if (domain->dimension == 3) {
376      constant = 4.0*MY_PI / (3.0*domain->xprd*domain->yprd*domain->zprd);
377
378      for (m = 0; m < npairs; m++) {
379        normfac = (icount[m] > 0) ? static_cast<double>(jcount[m])
380               - static_cast<double>(duplicates[m])/icount[m] : 0.0;
381        ncoord = 0.0;
382        for (ibin = 0; ibin < nbin; ibin++) {
383          rlower = ibin*delr;
384          rupper = (ibin+1)*delr;
385          vfrac = constant * (rupper*rupper*rupper - rlower*rlower*rlower);
386          if (vfrac * normfac != 0.0)
387            gr = histall[m][ibin] / (vfrac * normfac * icount[m]);
388          else gr = 0.0;
389          if (icount[m] != 0)
390            ncoord += gr * vfrac * normfac;
391          array[ibin][1+2*m] = gr;
392          array[ibin][2+2*m] = ncoord;
393        }
394      }
395
396    } else {
397      constant = MY_PI / (domain->xprd*domain->yprd);
398
399      for (m = 0; m < npairs; m++) {
400        ncoord = 0.0;
401        normfac = (icount[m] > 0) ? static_cast<double>(jcount[m])
402               - static_cast<double>(duplicates[m])/icount[m] : 0.0;
403        for (ibin = 0; ibin < nbin; ibin++) {
404          rlower = ibin*delr;
405          rupper = (ibin+1)*delr;
406          vfrac = constant * (rupper*rupper - rlower*rlower);
407          if (vfrac * normfac != 0.0)
408            gr = histall[m][ibin] / (vfrac * normfac * icount[m]);
409          else gr = 0.0;
410          if (icount[m] != 0)
411            ncoord += gr * vfrac * normfac;
412          array[ibin][1+2*m] = gr;
413          array[ibin][2+2*m] = ncoord;
414        }
415      }
```

Figure 6.13 – Code snippet from compute_rdf.cpp showing the compute_array() method

As you can see, *g(r)* for a 3D system is calculated in *lines 375* to *394*. The quantity, $\frac{4\pi}{3V}$, is defined in *line 376* as the `constant` variable, where *V* is the volume of the simulation box. Then, for each atom type pair (`m`), a normalization factor (`normfac`) is calculated in *lines 379* to *380* by subtracting the number of duplicates (`duplicate[m]`) from the number of neighbors counted (`jcount[m]`) for all bins.

The code then loops over each bin (*lines 382 to 393*) and calculates the following quantities:

- rlower: The lower bound of the bin (r)

- rupper: The upper bound of the bin (r+Δr)

- vfrac: The volume fraction occupied by the bin $\frac{4\pi}{3V}[(r + \Delta r)^3 - r^3]$

The g(r) of the system is then calculated in *line 387*, like so:

$$g(r) = \frac{\sum_{i=1}^{icount[m]} N_i(r, r + \Delta r)}{\frac{4\pi}{3V}[(r + \Delta r)^3 - r^3] * normfac * icount[m]}$$

The $\frac{normfac}{V}$ ratio represents the density (ρ) of the neighboring atoms, while the $\frac{\sum_{i=1}^{icount[m]} N_i(r, r + \Delta r)}{icount[m]}$ ratio represents the average, $N(r, r + \Delta r)$, over all participating atoms.

Therefore, this expression represents the average g(r) of the system in 3D:

$$g(r) = \frac{N_{avg}(r, r + \Delta r)}{\frac{4\pi}{3}[(r + \Delta r)^3 - r^3]\rho}$$

The g(r) can also be calculated for a 2D system in *lines 396 to 416*. Now, the constant variable (*line 397*) is defined as $\frac{\pi}{A}$, where A is the area of the simulation box, and subsequently the vfrac variable (*line 406*) equals $\frac{\pi}{A}[(r + \Delta r)^2 - r^2]$. Here, the g(r) of the system is as follows (*line 408*):

$$g(r) = \frac{\sum_{i=1}^{icount[m]} N_i(r, r + \Delta r)}{\frac{\pi}{A}[(r + \Delta r)^2 - r^2] * normfac * icount[m]}$$

Similar to the 3D case, the $\frac{normfac}{A}$ ratio represents the density (σ) of the neighboring atoms, and the expression for the average g(r) of the system in 2D is obtained by using the following equation:

$$g(r) = \frac{N_{avg}(r, r + \Delta r)}{\pi[(r + \Delta r)^2 - r^2]\sigma}$$

For both the 3D and the 2D systems, the average g(r) of the system is calculated for different values of r by looping over every bin. The corresponding coordination numbers are calculated (*lines 390 and 411*) using the values of g(r).

The results are stored in the corresponding columns of `array` (*lines 391* to *392*, and *lines 412* to *413*) to generate output in the format described in the LAMMPS manual (that is, the bin midpoint in the first column, *g(r)* values in the next column, the coordination number in the third column, and repeating the *g(r)* and coordination numbers in successive columns for any additional atom type pairs).

It should be noted that `compute RDF` calculates the average *g(r)* and the coordination number for a simulation snapshot at a single timestep. To find the time-average of these quantities over a desired number of iterations, the `fix ave/time` command needs to be used in the LAMMPS input script, as outlined in the LAMMPS manual.

In this section, we covered `compute RDF`, which makes extensive use of 2D arrays to generate 2D output via rows and columns of numeric values. In the next section, we'll review `compute heat flux` as our final example.

Reviewing the compute heat flux class

In this section, we will study the source code for the `compute heat flux` class, which is contained in `compute_heat_flux.cpp` and `compute_heat_flux.h`.

The `compute heat flux` class accepts the per-atom kinetic energy, per-atom potential energy, and per-atom stress to calculate the heat flow (J). This can be calculated as follows:

$$ J = \frac{1}{V} \left[\sum_i e_i \vec{v}_i - \sum_i S_i \vec{v}_i \right] $$

In this equation, e_i represents the sum of kinetic and potential energies of atom i, $\vec{v}_i$ represents the velocity vector (v_{xi}, v_{yi}, v_{zi}) of atom i, S_i represents the stress tensor of atom i, and V represents the volume occupied by the atoms in consideration. The summation of $e_i \vec{v}_i$ is the convective part of the heat flux, while the summation of $S_i \vec{v}_i$ is the virial part of the heat flux.

Therefore, this compute needs to read the kinetic energy, potential energy, and stress of atoms dynamically, and this is facilitated by feeding these quantities as other computes. So, effectively, `compute heat flux` accepts three other computes as input parameters that are evaluated every iteration to update the required quantities.

The stress tensor (S) of an atom is represented in terms of its components, s_{ij}, as follows:

$$S = \begin{bmatrix} s_{xx} & s_{xy} & s_{xz} \\ s_{yx} & s_{yy} & s_{yz} \\ s_{zx} & s_{zy} & s_{zz} \end{bmatrix}$$

Accordingly, the tensor product, $S\vec{v}$, is calculated as follows:

$$S\vec{v} = \begin{bmatrix} s_{xx} & s_{xy} & s_{xz} \\ s_{yx} & s_{yy} & s_{yz} \\ s_{zx} & s_{zy} & s_{zz} \end{bmatrix} \begin{bmatrix} v_x \\ v_y \\ v_z \end{bmatrix} = \begin{bmatrix} s_{xx}v_x + s_{xy}v_y + s_{xz}v_z \\ s_{yx}v_x + s_{yy}v_y + s_{yz}v_z \\ s_{zx}v_x + s_{zy}v_y + s_{zz}v_z \end{bmatrix}$$

The tensor, S, is symmetric along its diagonal (that is, $s_{xy} = s_{yx}, s_{xz} = s_{zx}, s_{yz} = s_{zy}$) if it is returned by compute stress/atom, though it can be asymmetric if is returned by compute centroid/stress/atom. In the case of a symmetric S, there are six unique elements that are stored in LAMMPS as a six-element 1D array ($s_{xx}, s_{yy}, s_{zz}, s_{xy}, s_{xz}, s_{yz}$).

In the case of an asymmetric S, the components are stored in a nine-element 1D array ($s_{xx}, s_{yy}, s_{zz}, s_{xy}, s_{xz}, s_{yz}, s_{yx}, s_{zx}, s_{zy}$). In compute_heat_flux.cpp, the components are accessed from these arrays when calculating the tensor product, $S\vec{v}$, in the heat flow, J, as will be demonstrated in this section.

The LAMMPS inputs script command used to implement compute heat flux is as follows:

```
compute   COMPUTE_ID   GROUP   heat/flux   KE   PE   STRESS
```

In the preceding code, the COMPUTE_ID parameter is the unique ID of the compute, while the GROUP parameter is the ID of the group of atoms that the compute acts on (see manual: https://lammps.sandia.gov/doc/compute_heat_flux.html). The KE, PE, and STRESS computes calculate the per-atom kinetic energy, per-atom potential energy, and per-atom stress that are used in the computation of heat flux, respectively. These computes should apply to the atoms in GROUP.

In the header file, compute_heat_flux.h, 1D character arrays are declared to parse the compute names that are entered (*line 35*):

```
char *id_ke,*id_pe,*id_stress;
```

Similarly, compute objects are declared to evaluate the computes that are entered (*line 36*):

```
class Compute *c_ke,*c_pe,*c_stress;
```

In compute_heat_flux.cpp, we start by analyzing the constructor that parses these computes.

ComputeHeatFlux::ComputeHeatFlux()

The following screenshot shows the ComputeHeatFlux() constructor method:

```
34    ComputeHeatFlux::ComputeHeatFlux(LAMMPS *lmp, int narg, char **arg) :
35      Compute(lmp, narg, arg),
36      id_ke(NULL), id_pe(NULL), id_stress(NULL)
37    {
38      if (narg != 6) error->all(FLERR,"Illegal compute heat/flux command");
39
40      vector_flag = 1;
41      size_vector = 6;
42      extvector = 1;
43
44      // store ke/atom, pe/atom, stress/atom IDs used by heat flux computation
45      // insure they are valid for these computations
46
47      int n = strlen(arg[3]) + 1;
48      id_ke = new char[n];
49      strcpy(id_ke,arg[3]);
50
51      n = strlen(arg[4]) + 1;
52      id_pe = new char[n];
53      strcpy(id_pe,arg[4]);
54
55      n = strlen(arg[5]) + 1;
56      id_stress = new char[n];
57      strcpy(id_stress,arg[5]);
58
59      int ike = modify->find_compute(id_ke);
60      int ipe = modify->find_compute(id_pe);
61      int istress = modify->find_compute(id_stress);
62      if (ike < 0 || ipe < 0 || istress < 0)
63        error->all(FLERR,"Could not find compute heat/flux compute ID");
64      if (strcmp(modify->compute[ike]->style,"ke/atom") != 0)
65        error->all(FLERR,"Compute heat/flux compute ID does not compute ke/atom");
66      if (modify->compute[ipe]->peatomflag == 0)
67        error->all(FLERR,"Compute heat/flux compute ID does not compute pe/atom");
68      if (modify->compute[istress]->pressatomflag != 1
69          && modify->compute[istress]->pressatomflag != 2)
70        error->all(FLERR,
71                   "Compute heat/flux compute ID does not compute stress/atom or
                    centroid/stress/atom");
72
73      vector = new double[size_vector];
74    }
```

Figure 6.14 – Code snippet from compute_heat_flux.cpp showing the constructor method

As you can see, the three compute names for kinetic energy (*lines 47* to *49*), potential energy (*lines 51* to *53*), and stress (*lines 55* to *57*) are parsed as character arrays; that is, `id_ke[]`, `id_pe[]`, and `id_stress[]`, respectively. The corresponding compute IDs are located by the `modify->find_compute()` methods in *lines 59* to *61*, and an error is returned if the compute IDs do not exist (*lines 62* to *63*). Then, *lines 64* to *71* check whether the computes that were entered specifically calculate the per-atom kinetic energy, per-atom potential energy, and per-atom stress. An output vector of length 6 is created (*line 73*) before closing this method.

Further error checks are performed in the `init()` method, as discussed next.

ComputeHeatFlux::init()

The `init()` method, as shown in the following screenshot, checks if the compute names that were parsed in the constructor exist (*lines 92* to *96*):

```
88    void ComputeHeatFlux::init()
89    {
90        // error checks
91
92        int ike = modify->find_compute(id_ke);
93        int ipe = modify->find_compute(id_pe);
94        int istress = modify->find_compute(id_stress);
95        if (ike < 0 || ipe < 0 || istress < 0)
96           error->all(FLERR,"Could not find compute heat/flux compute ID");
97
98        c_ke = modify->compute[ike];
99        c_pe = modify->compute[ipe];
100       c_stress = modify->compute[istress];
101   }
```

Figure 6.15 – Code snippet from compute_heat_flux.cpp showing the init() method

As you can see, the `compute` objects – that is, `c_ke`, `c_pe`, and `c_stress` (*lines 98* to *100*) – are tagged as the computes for calculating per-atom kinetic energy, per-atom potential energy, and per-atom stress, respectively.

Next, the heat flux is calculated in the `compute_vector()` method.

ComputeHeatFlux::compute_vector()

In the `compute_vector()` method, the computes are invoked if they have not been invoked yet (*lines 111* to *122*), and the `ke[]`, `pe[]`, and `stress[][]` arrays are used to extract the required values for the kinetic energy, potential energy, and stress of each atom, respectively (*lines 129* to *131*).

In *line 142*, the symmetry of the stress tensor, S, is determined by the `pressatomflag` flag, which is set to 1 for a symmetric tensor computed by `compute stress/atom` (see `compute_stress_atom.cpp`) or to 2 for an asymmetric tensor computed by `compute centroid/stress/atom` (see `compute_centroid_stress_atom.cpp`). Based on this symmetry, the tensor product, $S_i \vec{v}_i$, for atom i is computed differently, as shown in the following screenshot:

```
141     // heat flux via centroid atomic stress
142     if (c_stress->pressatomflag == 2) {
143       for (int i = 0; i < nlocal; i++) {
144         if (mask[i] & groupbit) {
145           eng = pe[i] + ke[i];
146           jc[0] += eng*v[i][0];
147           jc[1] += eng*v[i][1];
148           jc[2] += eng*v[i][2];
149           // stress[0]: rijx*fijx
150           // stress[1]: rijy*fijy
151           // stress[2]: rijz*fijz
152           // stress[3]: rijx*fijy
153           // stress[4]: rijx*fijz
154           // stress[5]: rijy*fijz
155           // stress[6]: rijy*fijx
156           // stress[7]: rijz*fijx
157           // stress[8]: rijz*fijy
158           // jv[0]  = rijx fijx vjx + rijx fijy vjy + rijx fijz vjz
159           jv[0] -= stress[i][0]*v[i][0] + stress[i][3]*v[i][1] +
160             stress[i][4]*v[i][2];
161           // jv[1]  = rijy fijx vjx + rijy fijy vjy + rijy fijz vjz
162           jv[1] -= stress[i][6]*v[i][0] + stress[i][1]*v[i][1] +
163             stress[i][5]*v[i][2];
164           // jv[2]  = rijz fijx vjx + rijz fijy vjy + rijz fijz vjz
165           jv[2] -= stress[i][7]*v[i][0] + stress[i][8]*v[i][1] +
166             stress[i][2]*v[i][2];
167         }
168       }
169     } else {
170       for (int i = 0; i < nlocal; i++) {
171         if (mask[i] & groupbit) {
172           eng = pe[i] + ke[i];
173           jc[0] += eng*v[i][0];
174           jc[1] += eng*v[i][1];
175           jc[2] += eng*v[i][2];
176           jv[0] -= stress[i][0]*v[i][0] + stress[i][3]*v[i][1] +
177             stress[i][4]*v[i][2];
178           jv[1] -= stress[i][3]*v[i][0] + stress[i][1]*v[i][1] +
179             stress[i][5]*v[i][2];
180           jv[2] -= stress[i][4]*v[i][0] + stress[i][5]*v[i][1] +
181             stress[i][2]*v[i][2];
182         }
183       }
```

Figure 6.16 – Code snippet from compute_heat_flux.cpp showing the compute_vector() method

As you can see, the case of the asymmetric S tensor (where `pressatomflag` is 2) is calculated in *lines 143* to *168*. While looping over all the atoms in the core (*line 143*) and selecting atoms belonging to the specified group (*line 144*), the sum of kinetic and potential energies for atom i (e_i) is calculated as the eng variable (*line 145*). In *lines 146* to *148*, the jc[] array calculates the three components of the convective part:

- For the x-component, we use the following equation:

$$jc[0] = \sum_i e_i v_{xi}$$

- For the y-component, we use the following equation:

$$jc[1] = \sum_i e_i v_{yi}$$

- For the z-component, we use the following equation:

$$jc[2] = \sum_i e_i v_{zi}$$

The components of the virial part of the heat flux are calculated as the jv[] array, which is calculated from the stress of each atom. In the case of asymmetric S, the array element of stress[][] accesses the following components of the stress of atom i:

- stress[i][0] = S_{xx}
- stress[i][1] = S_{yy}
- stress[i][2] = S_{zz}
- stress[i][3] = S_{xy}
- stress[i][4] = S_{xz}
- stress[i][5] = S_{yz}
- stress[i][6] = S_{yx}
- stress[i][7] = S_{zx}
- stress[i][8] = S_{zy}

Using the preceding stress components, the three components of the virial part, jv[], are calculated (*lines 159 to 166*):

- For the x-component, we use the following equation:

$$jv[0] = -\sum_i s_{xx_i} v_{xi} + s_{xy_i} v_{yi} + s_{xz_i} v_{zi}$$

- For the y-component, we use the following equation:

$$jv[1] = -\sum_i s_{yx_i} v_{xi} + s_{yy_i} v_{yi} + s_{yz_i} v_{zi}$$

- For the z-component, we use the following equation:

$$jv[2] = -\sum_i s_{zx_i} v_{xi} + s_{zy_i} v_{yi} + s_{zz_i} v_{zi}$$

Then, in the case of a symmetric tensor, S, the convective part, jc[], of the heat flux is calculated in the same way as before (*lines 172 to 175*) and the virial part, jv[], is calculated using the stress[i][0] to stress[i][5] elements, which access the stress components (s_{xx}, s_{yy}, s_{zz}, s_{xy}, s_{xz}, s_{yz}) in the given order. The components of jv[] thus look as follows (*lines 176 to 181*):

- For the x-component, we use the following equation:

$$jv[0] = -\sum_i s_{xx_i} v_{xi} + s_{xy_i} v_{yi} + s_{xz_i} v_{zi}$$

- For the y-component, we use the following equation:

$$jv[1] = -\sum_i s_{xy_i} v_{xi} + s_{yy_i} v_{yi} + s_{yz_i} v_{zi}$$

- For the z-component, we use the following equation:

$$jv[2] = -\sum_i s_{xz_i} v_{xi} + s_{yz_i} v_{yi} + s_{zz_i} v_{zi}$$

Once the convective and virial parts have been computed, the virial part, `jv[]`, is converted into the same units as the convective part, `jc[]`, by scaling by the proper units of pressure (*lines 188* to *191*). Finally, the `data[]` array is created (*line 197*) with the elements, as shown in the following code:

```
    double data[6] =
  {jc[0]+jv[0],jc[1]+jv[1],jc[2]+jv[2],jc[0],jc[1],jc[2]};
```

From the preceding code, the summations of these six elements over all cores are then retrieved by the `MPI_Allreduce()` call (*line 198*) and returned as the 1D output `vector` array declared in the `compute.h` parent class.

It should be noted that while the volume, V, is included in the equation for calculating the heat flux, J, the volume does not appear in the source code of `compute heat flux`. Therefore, the volume has to be separately incorporated (for example, in a separate compute or variable command) to calculate the correct heat flux.

This concludes this section, where we discussed a compute that accepts other computes as input parameters to calculate the heat flux.

Summary

In this chapter, we examined computes that calculate a global quantity, identify interactions between groups, tally distances over ranges and perform tensor multiplications. These computes illustrate the scope of processing and computations that can be carried out by proper implementations inside the compute style source codes.

By reading this chapter, you understand that computes can calculate and return scalar and vector quantities when properly defined, and that neighbor lists can be implemented in computes by requesting and accessing them with a pointer. In addition, combining outputs from multiple cores is facilitated by the `MPI_Allreduce()` method.

In the next chapter, we will analyze selected fix styles that can perform a variety of operations on the simulated system during a simulation run.

Questions

1. Which method is responsible for parsing beyond the third argument that's entered in a compute command in the LAMMPS input script?

2. What arguments are accepted by the MPI_Allreduce() method?

3. What is the primary purpose of the destructor method?

4. In compute reduce, the replace option can be used to find the index of the quantity, along with the maximum or minimum value of the entered quantities (see https://lammps.sandia.gov/doc/compute_reduce.html). Answer the following questions based on this information:

   a. In compute_reduce.cpp, which lines are responsible for identifying the index of the quantity with the *maximum* value out of all processors?

   b. In compute_reduce.cpp, which lines are responsible for identifying the index of the quantity with the *minimum* value out of all processors?

7
Understanding Fixes

In this chapter, we will inspect the selected fixes to elucidate the source code behind the operations performed by these fixes. **Fixes** control a large number of simulation properties during the execution of a simulation, facilitating physical factors to be incorporated into the simulation. An understanding of how fixes accomplish what we mentioned in earlier chapters allows you to modify the physics of a simulation and add timestep-dependent attributes to it.

We will cover the following topics in this chapter:

- Exploring the general structure of fixes
- Reviewing the Fix AddForce class
- Studying the Fix NVE class
- Studying the Fix NH class
- Studying the Fix Print class
- Reviewing the Fix Orient/FCC class
- Analyzing the Fix Wall and Fix Wall/LJ126 classes
- Exploring the Fix Rigid class

By the end of this chapter, you will have learned how to read the code governing fixes. This will help you exercise more customized control over a simulation run in terms of the physics and the logical flow involved.

Given the wide scope of fix styles used in LAMMPS, we will dissect several example fixes to illustrate the various facets available. Based on the features explained in each example, you can choose to study the examples that you find relevant to your purpose.

Technical requirements

To execute the instructions in this chapter, you just need a text editor (for example, **Notepad++** or **Gedit**).

> **Important Note:**
> The fix styles described in this chapter are based on LAMMPS version **3Mar20**. When analyzing fix styles in the **29Oct20** version, please refer to *Appendix D, Compatibility with Version 29Oct20*, to review compatibility.

You can find the full source code used in this book here: `https://github.com/PacktPublishing/Extending-and-Modifying-LAMMPS-Writing-Your-Own-Source-Code`

Here is the link to download LAMMPS: `https://lammps.sandia.gov/doc/Install.html`. The LAMMPS GitHub link is `https://github.com/lammps/lammps`, and is where the source code can be found as well.

Exploring the general structure of fixes

In this section, we will skim through some methods commonly found in fix child classes.

Individual fixes inherit from `fix.cpp` and `fix.h`, where the parent classes read the first three arguments (fix ID, group ID, and fix style) from the LAMMPS input script. An essential method that must be present in the child classes is `setmask()`, which dictates the place of the fix in the sequence of executing the timestep (see *Chapter 3, Source Code Structure and the Stages of Execution*). Other methods are incorporated as required in the fix and a full list of methods that can be inherited is available in the `fix.h` file.

In the following sections, we will analyze some selected fixes and describe their functionalities using their source codes.

Reviewing the Fix AddForce class

In this section, we will study the methods implemented in the `Fix AddForce` class, which applies a pre-defined force to a group of atoms.

This fix adds a force defined by its (*x*, *y*, *z*) components to every atom in a group using `fix_addforce.cpp` and `fix_addforce.h`. In a LAMMPS input script, the corresponding syntax is as follows:

```
fix  FIX_ID  GROUP_ID  addforce Fx Fy Fz
```

As you can see, the `FIX_ID` parameter is the unique ID of the fix defined, while the `GROUP_ID` parameter is the ID of the group of atoms that the fix acts on, as described in the LAMMPS manual (`https://lammps.sandia.gov/doc/fix_addforce.html`). The `Fx`, `Fy`, and `Fz` quantities represent the three force components applied to each atom. Optional keywords can be entered to specify the frequency of applying this force, the region where the atoms must reside, and the energy calculation associated with the force. First, we will look at the constructor method of this class.

FixAddForce::FixAddForce()

This constructor method ensures that a minimum of six arguments are entered (*line 43*), which are the three arguments read by the parent class and the three force components read by the `FixAddForce` constructor. These three force components (`Fx`, `Fy`, and `Fz`) can be entered as numeric values or as variables preceded by the `"v_"` string in the input script. The following screenshot illustrates how these arguments are parsed:

```
56    xstr = ystr = zstr = NULL;
57
58    if (strstr(arg[3],"v_") == arg[3]) {
59      int n = strlen(&arg[3][2]) + 1;
60      xstr = new char[n];
61      strcpy(xstr,&arg[3][2]);
62    } else {
63      xvalue = force->numeric(FLERR,arg[3]);
64      xstyle = CONSTANT;
65    }
66    if (strstr(arg[4],"v_") == arg[4]) {
67      int n = strlen(&arg[4][2]) + 1;
68      ystr = new char[n];
69      strcpy(ystr,&arg[4][2]);
70    } else {
71      yvalue = force->numeric(FLERR,arg[4]);
72      ystyle = CONSTANT;
73    }
74    if (strstr(arg[5],"v_") == arg[5]) {
75      int n = strlen(&arg[5][2]) + 1;
76      zstr = new char[n];
77      strcpy(zstr,&arg[5][2]);
78    } else {
79      zvalue = force->numeric(FLERR,arg[5]);
80      zstyle = CONSTANT;
81    }
82
83    // optional args
84
85    nevery = 1;
86    iregion = -1;
```

Figure 7.1 – Code snippet from fix_addforce.cpp showing the constructor

As you can see, *line 58* reads the Fx argument, which is listed as arg[3], by first checking if the v_ string is present. If it is present, the argument is read as a variable and the xstr string stores the variable name (*lines 59* to *61*) that will be used to locate the variable in the init() method. If it is not present, the argument is treated as a number that is read using the force->numeric() method (*lines 62* to *64*) and stored as an xvalue variable. In addition, the xstyle integer is set to CONSTANT, which has been declared by the enumerator on *line 34*. The value of xstyle will be relevant in the init() method. The Fy and Fz arguments are processed similarly in *lines 66* to *81*.

On *line 85*, the default value of nevery is set to 1 to apply the force at every iteration, as noted in the LAMMPS manual, and on *line 86*, the default value of iregion is set to -1 to disregard the region when identifying atoms to apply the force to. The optional keywords are parsed in *lines 89* to *113* by looping over all the arguments entered after the Fz parameter. The every keyword is searched and located by *line 90*. An error is returned if no entry exists after it (*line 91*) and nevery is set to the following entry, which is read as an integer (*line 92*) if it is present. Similarly, the region keyword is located (*line 95*) and iregion is set to the region ID of the succeeding entry identified using the domain->find_region() method (*line 97*). Lastly, the energy keyword is located and read as a variable in *lines 104* to *113*, and an estr string is set to the variable name.

The variables determined in this method are processed in the init() method.

FixAddForce::init()

The init() method determines the xstyle, ystyle, zstyle, and estyle variables, as shown in the following screenshot:

```
150    void FixAddForce::init()
151    {
152      // check variables
153
154      if (xstr) {
155        xvar = input->variable->find(xstr);
156        if (xvar < 0)
157          error->all(FLERR,"Variable name for fix addforce does not exist");
158        if (input->variable->equalstyle(xvar)) xstyle = EQUAL;
159        else if (input->variable->atomstyle(xvar)) xstyle = ATOM;
160        else error->all(FLERR,"Variable for fix addforce is invalid style");
161      }
162      if (ystr) {
163        yvar = input->variable->find(ystr);
164        if (yvar < 0)
165          error->all(FLERR,"Variable name for fix addforce does not exist");
166        if (input->variable->equalstyle(yvar)) ystyle = EQUAL;
167        else if (input->variable->atomstyle(yvar)) ystyle = ATOM;
168        else error->all(FLERR,"Variable for fix addforce is invalid style");
169      }
170      if (zstr) {
171        zvar = input->variable->find(zstr);
172        if (zvar < 0)
173          error->all(FLERR,"Variable name for fix addforce does not exist");
174        if (input->variable->equalstyle(zvar)) zstyle = EQUAL;
175        else if (input->variable->atomstyle(zvar)) zstyle = ATOM;
176        else error->all(FLERR,"Variable for fix addforce is invalid style");
177      }
178      if (estr) {
179        evar = input->variable->find(estr);
180        if (evar < 0)
181          error->all(FLERR,"Variable name for fix addforce does not exist");
182        if (input->variable->atomstyle(evar)) estyle = ATOM;
183        else error->all(FLERR,"Variable for fix addforce is invalid style");
184      } else estyle = NONE;
```

Figure 7.2 – Code snippet from fix_addforce.cpp showing the init() method

As you can see, in *lines 154* to *157*, the variable name is stored in xstr. If it is not null, it is retrieved using the input->variable->find() method. Then, depending on whether the variable is an equal style (*line 158*) or atom style (*line 159*) variable, the value of xstyle is set to EQUAL or ATOM, respectively (if xstr = NULL, then xstyle is set to CONSTANT, as described earlier). The values of ystyle (*lines 162* to *169*) and zstyle (*lines 170* to *177*) are determined in a similar manner. The value of the estyle integer can be either ATOM (*lines 178* to *184*), to correspond to the atom style variable that calculates the energy per atom, or NONE (*line 184*), to indicate that the energy keyword is not used.

The `xstyle`, `ystyle`, `zstyle`, and `estyle` variables will be used in the `post_force()` method when retrieving force values from variables. In addition, a `varflag` variable is defined to determine whether all entered force components are numeric only and to allocate memory for the `sforce` array, which stores the force components and energies for `atom` style variables in the `post_force()` method. If there is at least one `atom` style variable, then `varflag` is set to ATOM (*lines 194 to 195*). If there is at least one `equal` style variable in the absence of an `atom` style variable, then it is set to EQUAL (*lines 196 to 197*). If all three force components are numeric values, then it is set to CONSTANT (*lines 198*). The values of `varflag` and `estyle` are used to perform error checks (*lines 200 to 205*) that correspond to the restrictions outlined in the LAMMPS manual on the `energy` keyword.

Next, we will look at the `setmask()` method, which dictates the order of execution for this fix.

FixAddForce::setmask()

The `setmask()` method determines the points in the timestep at which `Fix AddForce` is executed. As shown in the following screenshot, the stages listed in uppercase text inside `setmask()` correspond to the stages of execution for this fix, as described in *Chapter 3, Source Code Structure and the Stages of Execution*:

```
136    int FixAddForce::setmask()
137    {
138        datamask_read = datamask_modify = 0;
139
140        int mask = 0;
141        mask |= POST_FORCE;
142        mask |= THERMO_ENERGY;
143        mask |= POST_FORCE_RESPA;
144        mask |= MIN_POST_FORCE;
145        return mask;
146    }
```

Figure 7.3 – Code snippet from fix_addforce.cpp showing the setmask() method

As you can see, *lines 141 to 144* dictate that `Fix AddForce` should be executed at the `post_force()`, `thermo_energy()`, `post_force_respa()`, and `min_post_force()` stages of execution (a full list of stages is listed in `fix.h` in *lines 252 to 276*). Since this force is applied after pairwise forces have been applied and neighbor lists have been built, it is implemented in the `post_force()` and `post_force_respa()` methods, which trail behind the `compute()` and `post_neighbor()` methods in that order, but are placed ahead of the `final_integrate()` method, which updates atom velocities.

Similarly, the output of this fix can be printed on the screen by the `thermo` command in the LAMMPS input script, which introduces the `thermo_energy()` method. Also, this fix is compatible with energy minimization algorithms, where it is applied after the other forces, and must be implemented by the `min_post_force()` method. The integer `mask` variable registers these stages by performing bitwise operations, with the bits stored in the quantities in uppercase text.

Having initiated various flags and established their order of execution, we will now move on and look at the `post_force()` method, which applies forces to atoms.

FixAddForce::post_force()

The following screenshot shows the part of the code in the `post_force()` method that's responsible for applying forces to atoms when the force components are entered as numeric values in the LAMMPS input script:

```
265    if ((varflag == ATOM || estyle == ATOM) && atom->nmax > maxatom) {
266      maxatom = atom->nmax;
267      memory->destroy(sforce);
268      memory->create(sforce,maxatom,4,"addforce:sforce");
269    }
270
271    // foriginal[0] = "potential energy" for added force
272    // foriginal[123] = force on atoms before extra force added
273
274    foriginal[0] = foriginal[1] = foriginal[2] = foriginal[3] = 0.0;
275    force_flag = 0;
276
277    // constant force
278    // potential energy = - x dot f in unwrapped coords
279
280    if (varflag == CONSTANT) {
281      double unwrap[3];
282      for (int i = 0; i < nlocal; i++)
283        if (mask[i] & groupbit) {
284          if (region && !region->match(x[i][0],x[i][1],x[i][2])) continue;
285          domain->unmap(x[i],image[i],unwrap);
286          foriginal[0] -= xvalue*unwrap[0] + yvalue*unwrap[1] + zvalue*unwrap[2];
287          foriginal[1] += f[i][0];
288          foriginal[2] += f[i][1];
289          foriginal[3] += f[i][2];
290          f[i][0] += xvalue;
291          f[i][1] += yvalue;
292          f[i][2] += zvalue;
293          if (evflag) {
294            v[0] = xvalue * unwrap[0];
295            v[1] = yvalue * unwrap[1];
296            v[2] = zvalue * unwrap[2];
297            v[3] = xvalue * unwrap[1];
298            v[4] = xvalue * unwrap[2];
299            v[5] = yvalue * unwrap[2];
300            v_tally(i,v);
301          }
302        }
```

Figure 7.4 – Code snippet from fix_addforce.cpp showing part of the post_force() method

As you can see, a 1D array, `foriginal`, is created (*line 274*) to calculate the sum of each force component over all the atoms that this fix applies to (`foriginal[1]`, `foriginal[2]`, and `foriginal[3]`), as well as the sum of energy change due to this force (`foriginal[0]`).

Then, if `varflag` is found to be set to CONSTANT (*line 280*), indicating that all three force components (`Fx`, `Fy`, and `Fz`) entered are numeric values, the code shown in the preceding screenshot loops over all the atoms in the core (*line 282*) and identifies the ones that belong to the specified group using the `groupbit` variable (*line 283*) defined in `fix.cpp`. If the `region` keyword is used, *line 284* checks if the atoms are located inside the specified region. The energy change due to the force (*line 286*) and the force components (*lines 287 to 289*) is tallied in the `foriginal` array. The force components (stored as the `xvalue`, `yvalue`, and `zvalue` variables) are applied in *lines 290* to *292* by updating the 2D force array, `f` (declared in *line 238*), which lists all three force components for every atom. If any **virial computation** is required, the six array elements of `v` are calculated in *lines 294 to 299*.

In the following screenshot, we can see the part of the code that is used when at least one of the force components is a variable style quantity:

```
313    if (xstyle == EQUAL) xvalue = input->variable->compute_equal(xvar);
314    else if (xstyle == ATOM)
315      input->variable->compute_atom(xvar,igroup,&sforce[0][0],4,0);
316    if (ystyle == EQUAL) yvalue = input->variable->compute_equal(yvar);
317    else if (ystyle == ATOM)
318      input->variable->compute_atom(yvar,igroup,&sforce[0][1],4,0);
319    if (zstyle == EQUAL) zvalue = input->variable->compute_equal(zvar);
320    else if (zstyle == ATOM)
321      input->variable->compute_atom(zvar,igroup,&sforce[0][2],4,0);
322    if (estyle == ATOM)
323      input->variable->compute_atom(evar,igroup,&sforce[0][3],4,0);
324
325    modify->addstep_compute(update->ntimestep + 1);
326
327    for (int i = 0; i < nlocal; i++) {
328      if (mask[i] & groupbit) {
329        if (region && !region->match(x[i][0],x[i][1],x[i][2])) continue;
330        domain->unmap(x[i],image[i],unwrap);
331        if (xstyle == ATOM) xvalue = sforce[i][0];
332        if (ystyle == ATOM) yvalue = sforce[i][1];
333        if (zstyle == ATOM) zvalue = sforce[i][2];
334
335        if (estyle == ATOM) {
336          foriginal[0] += sforce[i][3];
337        } else {
338          if (xstyle) foriginal[0] -= xvalue*unwrap[0];
339          if (ystyle) foriginal[0] -= yvalue*unwrap[1];
340          if (zstyle) foriginal[0] -= zvalue*unwrap[2];
341        }
342        foriginal[1] += f[i][0];
343        foriginal[2] += f[i][1];
344        foriginal[3] += f[i][2];
345
346        if (xstyle) f[i][0] += xvalue;
347        if (ystyle) f[i][1] += yvalue;
348        if (zstyle) f[i][2] += zvalue;
```

Figure 7.5 – Code snippet from fix_addforce.cpp showing part of the post_force() method

As you can see, on *line 313*, if the *x* component is an equal style variable with `xstyle == EQUAL`, then the corresponding force component, `xvalue`, is retrieved from the `Variable` class using the `input->variable->compute_equal()` method. In the case of an atom style variable (*lines 314 to 315*), the `input->variable->compute_atom()` method is used, which writes the three force components and the energy change in the 2D `sforce` array.

When looping over all the atoms in the core (*line 327*) and filtering out atoms that do not belong to the specified group (*line 328*) or region (*line 329*), the `xvalue` component is accessed from the `sforce` array if `xstyle` is ATOM (*line 331*). If `xstyle` is CONSTANT, then the `xvalue` component bypasses the previous processing steps and retains the numeric value entered in the input script. Similar steps are followed for obtaining the `yvalue` and `zvalue` force components (*lines 316 to 333*). The `foriginal` array (*lines 335 to 344*) is updated and the force components are applied (*lines 346 to 348*) for all ATOM, EQUAL, and CONSTANT styles.

The calculations that are performed over all cores can be summed up to get the total applied force components and the total energy change via the `MPI_Allreduce()` method, as used in the `compute_scalar()` and `compute_vector()` methods (*lines 377 to 405*). These methods also allow us to export these quantities when the output of `Fix AddForce` is requested in a LAMMPS input script.

In this section, we covered a sample fix and provided a detailed discussion of the `setmask()` and `post_force()` methods. In the following sections, we will analyze other fixes and focus on the methods that play the most important roles.

Studying the Fix NVE class

In this section, we will study the `Fix NVE` class, which time-integrates a system using the velocity **Verlet** algorithm we described in *Chapter 1, MD Theory and Simulation Practices*.

The first half of the algorithm updates the velocity over a half-timestep and the position over a full-timestep. How the velocity and position components are updated is shown in the following equations.

The velocity update for the *x* component is given as follows:

$$v_x\left(t + \frac{1}{2}\Delta t\right) = v_x(t) + \left(\frac{1}{2}\Delta t\right)\frac{F_{net,x}(t)}{m}$$

The position update for the *x* coordinate is given as follows:

$$x(t + \Delta t) = x(t) + v_x\left(t + \frac{1}{2}\Delta t\right)\Delta t$$

The y and z coordinates are updated similarly. The second half of the algorithm updates the three components of the velocity over the second half of the timestep.

We get the x component as follows:

$$v_x(t + \Delta t) = v_x\left(t + \frac{1}{2}\Delta t\right) + \left(\frac{1}{2}\Delta t\right)\frac{F_{net,x}(t + \Delta t)}{m}$$

The y and z components are updated in a similar fashion.

The source code for this class is provided in the `fix_nve.cpp` and `fix_nve.h` files. In a LAMMPS input script, the corresponding syntax is as follows:

```
fix  FIX_ID  GROUP_ID  nve
```

The `FIX_ID` and `GROUP_ID` parameters were discussed earlier, and they are described in the LAMMPS manual (`https://lammps.sandia.gov/doc/fix_nve.html`).

As shown in the following screenshot, the `setmask()` method in `fix_nve.cpp` indicates that this fix applies at the `initial_integrate()` and `final_integrate()` stages of execution, which correspond to the two halves of the velocity Verlet integration:

```
39    int FixNVE::setmask()
40    {
41        int mask = 0;
42        mask |= INITIAL_INTEGRATE;
43        mask |= FINAL_INTEGRATE;
44        mask |= INITIAL_INTEGRATE_RESPA;
45        mask |= FINAL_INTEGRATE_RESPA;
46        return mask;
47    }
```

Figure 7.6 – Code snippet from fix_nve.cpp showing the setmask() method

As you can see, the `init()` method defines the `dtv` variable (*line 53*) as the full timestep Δt and the `dtf` variable (*line 54*) as half the timestep $\frac{1}{2}\Delta t$, with conversion to proper units (by `force->ftm2v`) as required when calculating the velocity. The following screenshot shows these variable assignments:

```
51    void FixNVE::init()
52    {
53        dtv = update->dt;
54        dtf = 0.5 * update->dt * force->ftm2v;
55
56        if (strstr(update->integrate_style,"respa"))
57            step_respa = ((Respa *) update->integrate)->step;
58    }
```

Figure 7.7 – Code snippet from fix_nve.cpp showing the init() method

The next section explains the `initial_integrate()` method, which performs the first half of the velocity Verlet algorithm.

FixNVE::initial_integrate()

This method updates the velocity over half a timestep, $\frac{1}{2}\Delta t$, and the position over a full timestep, Δt, as shown in the following screenshot:

```cpp
64   void FixNVE::initial_integrate(int /*vflag*/)
65   {
66     double dtfm;
67
68     // update v and x of atoms in group
69
70     double **x = atom->x;
71     double **v = atom->v;
72     double **f = atom->f;
73     double *rmass = atom->rmass;
74     double *mass = atom->mass;
75     int *type = atom->type;
76     int *mask = atom->mask;
77     int nlocal = atom->nlocal;
78     if (igroup == atom->firstgroup) nlocal = atom->nfirst;
79
80     if (rmass) {
81       for (int i = 0; i < nlocal; i++)
82         if (mask[i] & groupbit) {
83           dtfm = dtf / rmass[i];
84           v[i][0] += dtfm * f[i][0];
85           v[i][1] += dtfm * f[i][1];
86           v[i][2] += dtfm * f[i][2];
87           x[i][0] += dtv * v[i][0];
88           x[i][1] += dtv * v[i][1];
89           x[i][2] += dtv * v[i][2];
90         }
91
92     } else {
93       for (int i = 0; i < nlocal; i++)
94         if (mask[i] & groupbit) {
95           dtfm = dtf / mass[type[i]];
96           v[i][0] += dtfm * f[i][0];
97           v[i][1] += dtfm * f[i][1];
98           v[i][2] += dtfm * f[i][2];
99           x[i][0] += dtv * v[i][0];
100          x[i][1] += dtv * v[i][1];
101          x[i][2] += dtv * v[i][2];
102        }
103    }
104  }
```

Figure 7.8 – Code snippet from fix_nve.cpp showing the initial_integrate() method

Before performing the velocity and position updates, the mass of the atom is read as the mass per atom (*lines 80 to 90*) or the mass per atom type (*lines 92 to 102*). In each case, the dtfm variable calculates the ratio of dtf to the mass (*lines 83 and 95*) so that the product of dtfm with the force components (f) is equivalent to the quantity, $\left(\frac{1}{2}\Delta t\right)\frac{F_{net}(t)}{m}$. This product is used to update the velocity components (*lines 84 to 86, and 96 to 98*) over a half-timestep to obtain $v(t + \frac{1}{2}\Delta t)$. In the next three lines, the position coordinates, x, are incremented by the product of the full timestep with $v(t + \frac{1}{2}\Delta t)$.

It should be noted that the force array, f, represents the net force at the beginning of the current timestep, which is the same as the net force at the end of the previous timestep, as required in the first half of the velocity Verlet algorithm. In the second half, the force at the end of the current timestep is used, as we'll see next.

FixNVE::final_integrate()

This method updates the velocity over the second half of the timestep, as shown in the following screenshot:

```cpp
108   void FixNVE::final_integrate()
109   {
110       double dtfm;
111
112       // update v of atoms in group
113
114       double **v = atom->v;
115       double **f = atom->f;
116       double *rmass = atom->rmass;
117       double *mass = atom->mass;
118       int *type = atom->type;
119       int *mask = atom->mask;
120       int nlocal = atom->nlocal;
121       if (igroup == atom->firstgroup) nlocal = atom->nfirst;
122
123       if (rmass) {
124           for (int i = 0; i < nlocal; i++)
125               if (mask[i] & groupbit) {
126                   dtfm = dtf / rmass[i];
127                   v[i][0] += dtfm * f[i][0];
128                   v[i][1] += dtfm * f[i][1];
129                   v[i][2] += dtfm * f[i][2];
130               }
131
132       } else {
133           for (int i = 0; i < nlocal; i++)
134               if (mask[i] & groupbit) {
135                   dtfm = dtf / mass[type[i]];
136                   v[i][0] += dtfm * f[i][0];
137                   v[i][1] += dtfm * f[i][1];
138                   v[i][2] += dtfm * f[i][2];
139               }
140       }
141   }
```

Figure 7.9 – Code snippet from fix_nve.cpp showing the final_integrate() method

As you can see, the dt fm variable is defined in the same way it was previously, and the per-atom (*lines 123* to *130*) and per-atom type (*lines 132* to *139*) masses are treated separately. Like before, the product of dt fm with force components is calculated, where the force is the net force, $F_{net}(t + \Delta t)$, at the end of the current timestep. Since the final_integrate() method is chronologically located after all the methods that apply forces, for example, the pre_force() and post_force() methods, the force array, f, returns the force that has accounted for all force contributions. Therefore, the quantity, $\left(\frac{1}{2}\Delta t\right)\frac{F_{net}(t + \Delta t)}{m}$, is obtained from f and is used to update the velocity in the v array (*lines 127* to *129*, and *136* to *138*) to yield $v(t + \Delta t)$.

In this section, we illustrated how the velocity Verlet algorithm is implemented by the Fix NVE class.

Next, we will look at Fix NH, which controls the NVT, NPT, and NPH integrators (**N** stands for **number**, **V** stands for **volume**, **T** stands for **temperature**, **P** stands for **pressure**, and **H** stands for **enthalpy**).

Studying the Fix NH class

In this section, we'll discuss the role of the Fix NH class, which is implemented by fix_nh.cpp and fix_nh.h. The Fix NVT, Fix NPT, and Fix NPH classes inherit from this class when employing thermostats and barostats.

In this section, we will only focus on the thermostat functionalities of Fix NH for the sake of conciseness. Fix NH applies the **Nose-Hoover thermostat**, which introduces a virtual heat bath tethered to the simulated system. This heat bath can contain a 1D chain of virtual particles where the kth particle has mass Q_k, position η_k, and momentum p_{η_k}, which gives us the following velocity:

$$\dot{\eta}_k = p_{\eta_k}/Q_i$$

The time derivative of the velocity, $\vec{v}$, of an atom, i, being *thermostatted* is given by the following formula:

$$\frac{d\vec{v}_i}{dt} = \frac{\vec{F}_{net_i}}{m_i} - \dot{\eta}_1\vec{v}_i$$

For a virtual particle, k, the $\dot{\eta}_k$ is calculated by the following formula:

$$\frac{d\dot{\eta}_k}{dt} = \frac{G_k}{Q_k} - \dot{\eta}_{k+1}\dot{\eta}_k$$

Here, G_k is the difference between double the neighboring virtual particle's kinetic energy and its targeted kinetic energy, which is determined by its thermal energy, $k_B T$:

$$G_k = Q_{k-1}\dot{\eta}_{k-1}{}^2 - k_B T$$

The value of G_1 is calculated using the KE of the total number (N) of atoms being *thermostatted*:

$$G_1 = \sum_{i=1}^{N} m_i \vec{v}_i^2 - 3Nk_B T$$

When implementing this in LAMMPS, the **Liouville operator method** is employed to numerically time-integrate the previous equations, which offers us the benefit of adjusting the timestep for slow and fast processes.

> **Tip**
>
> Please refer to `http://www.pages.drexel.edu/~cfa22/msim/node24.html` for more information on the Liouville operator method.

In this method, a series of exponential operators are utilized to update the atom and virtual particle velocities, while the position is updated by Verlet integration using these velocities (details will not be presented here as they are outside the scope of this book). These operators use fractions of *1/2*, *1/4*, and *1/8* of the timestep during the evaluation, which will appear in the source code.

In a LAMMPS input script, the syntax for implementing the Nose-Hoover thermostat is as follows:

```
fix  FIX_ID  GROUP_ID  nvt temp T_START T_STOP T_DAMP
```

The parameters listed here are defined in the LAMMPS manual (`https://lammps.sandia.gov/doc/fix_nh.html`). The `temp` keyword performs *Nose-Hoover thermostatting*, while the `T_START`, `T_STOP`, and `T_DAMP` parameters represent the starting temperature, final targeted temperature, and damping parameter of the thermostat, respectively. A full list of all permissible keywords and compatible parameters is provided in the manual.

The constructor method (FixNH::FixNH()) parses these parameters, while the setmask() method registers this fix at the initial_integrate() and final_integrate() stages of execution. The nve_v() method updates the velocity, as shown in the following screenshot:

```
2006    if (rmass) {
2007        for (int i = 0; i < nlocal; i++) {
2008            if (mask[i] & groupbit) {
2009                dtfm = dtf / rmass[i];
2010                v[i][0] += dtfm*f[i][0];
2011                v[i][1] += dtfm*f[i][1];
2012                v[i][2] += dtfm*f[i][2];
2013            }
2014        }
2015    } else {
2016        for (int i = 0; i < nlocal; i++) {
2017            if (mask[i] & groupbit) {
2018                dtfm = dtf / mass[type[i]];
2019                v[i][0] += dtfm*f[i][0];
2020                v[i][1] += dtfm*f[i][1];
2021                v[i][2] += dtfm*f[i][2];
2022            }
2023        }
2024    }
```

Figure 7.10 – Code snippet from fix_nh.cpp showing the nve_v() method

As expected from the **Verlet** algorithm, the velocity is incremented over a half-timestep (dtf) using the forces at the current timestep. The nve_x() method updates the position over a full timestep, dtv, using the current velocity, as shown in the following screenshot:

```
2041    for (int i = 0; i < nlocal; i++) {
2042        if (mask[i] & groupbit) {
2043            x[i][0] += dtv * v[i][0];
2044            x[i][1] += dtv * v[i][1];
2045            x[i][2] += dtv * v[i][2];
2046        }
2047    }
```

Figure 7.11 – Code snippet from fix_nh.cpp showing the nve_x() method

It should be noted that the nve_v() method should be executed before the nve_x() method so that the velocity is updated by half a timestep and fed into the calculation that updates the position, as dictated by the Verlet integration scheme.

Since the thermostat adjusts the temperature linearly from T_START to T_STOP over the course of the simulation run, t_{total}, the temperature, $T(t)$, at any timestep, t, in the simulation is given by the following formula:

$$T(t) = T_{start} + \left(\frac{T_{stop} - T_{start}}{t_{total}}\right) t$$

The `compute_temp_target()` method, shown in the following screenshot, returns the temperature at any timestep using the preceding formula:

```
2205  /* -------------------------------------------------------------------
2206       compute target temperature and kinetic energy
2207  ---------------------------------------------------------------------
2208
2209  void FixNH::compute_temp_target()
2210  {
2211    double delta = update->ntimestep - update->beginstep;
2212    if (delta != 0.0) delta /= update->endstep - update->beginstep;
2213
2214    t_target = t_start + delta * (t_stop-t_start);
2215    ke_target = tdof * boltz * t_target;
2216  }
```

Figure 7.12 – Code snippet from fix_nh.cpp showing the compute_temp_target() method

As you can see, the `delta` variable (*line 2211*) calculates the elapsed number of timesteps (t) by subtracting the initial timestep (`update->beginstep`) from the current timestep (`update->ntimestep`). The same variable then calculates (*line 2212*) the ratio, t/t_{total}, by dividing by the total number of timesteps in the current simulation run. The expected temperature at that particular timestep is given by the `t_target` variable (*line 2214*) and the expected KE by the `KE_target` variable (*line 2215*).

The thermostat adjusts the velocity using the **Liouville exponential operators** (refer to `http://www.pages.drexel.edu/~cfa22/msim/node24.html`) in the `nhc_temp_integrate()` method, as shown in the following screenshot:

```
1780   for (ich = mtchain-1; ich > 0; ich--) {
1781     expfac = exp(-ncfac*dt8*eta_dot[ich+1]);
1782     eta_dot[ich] *= expfac;
1783     eta_dot[ich] += eta_dotdot[ich] * ncfac*dt4;
1784     eta_dot[ich] *= tdrag_factor;
1785     eta_dot[ich] *= expfac;
1786   }
1787
1788   expfac = exp(-ncfac*dt8*eta_dot[1]);
1789   eta_dot[0] *= expfac;
1790   eta_dot[0] += eta_dotdot[0] * ncfac*dt4;
1791   eta_dot[0] *= tdrag_factor;
1792   eta_dot[0] *= expfac;
1793
1794   factor_eta = exp(-ncfac*dthalf*eta_dot[0]);
1795   nh_v_temp();
1796
1797   // rescale temperature due to velocity scaling
1798   // should not be necessary to explicitly recompute the temperature
1799
1800   t_current *= factor_eta*factor_eta;
1801   kecurrent = tdof * boltz * t_current;
1802
1803   if (eta_mass[0] > 0.0)
1804     eta_dotdot[0] = (kecurrent - ke_target)/eta_mass[0];
1805   else eta_dotdot[0] = 0.0;
1806
1807   for (ich = 0; ich < mtchain; ich++)
1808     eta[ich] += ncfac*dthalf*eta_dot[ich];
1809
1810   eta_dot[0] *= expfac;
1811   eta_dot[0] += eta_dotdot[0] * ncfac*dt4;
1812   eta_dot[0] *= expfac;
1813
1814   for (ich = 1; ich < mtchain; ich++) {
1815     expfac = exp(-ncfac*dt8*eta_dot[ich+1]);
1816     eta_dot[ich] *= expfac;
1817     eta_dotdot[ich] = (eta_mass[ich-1]*eta_dot[ich-1]*eta_dot[ich-1]
1818                        - boltz * t_target)/eta_mass[ich];
1819     eta_dot[ich] += eta_dotdot[ich] * ncfac*dt4;
1820     eta_dot[ich] *= expfac;
```

Figure 7.13 – Code snippet from fix_nh.cpp showing the nhc_temp_integrate() method

As you can see, *lines 1780* to *1786* loop over all virtual chain particles in reverse order and calculate the relevant exponential factors using *1/8* and *1/4* of the timestep, as represented by the `dt8` and `dt4` variables, respectively. The optional drag factor that's applied to the chain is also incorporated in this loop (*line 1791*). On line 1795, the atom velocities are updated over a half-timestep by the `nh_v_temp()` method, as shown in the following screenshot, by scaling with the exponential factor derived in *line 1794*:

```
2050  /* -------------------------------------------------------------
2051       perform half-step thermostat scaling of velocities
2052     ---------------------------------------------------------------- */
2053
2054  void FixNH::nh_v_temp()
2055  {
2056    double **v = atom->v;
2057    int *mask = atom->mask;
2058    int nlocal = atom->nlocal;
2059    if (igroup == atom->firstgroup) nlocal = atom->nfirst;
2060
2061    if (which == NOBIAS) {
2062      for (int i = 0; i < nlocal; i++) {
2063        if (mask[i] & groupbit) {
2064          v[i][0] *= factor_eta;
2065          v[i][1] *= factor_eta;
2066          v[i][2] *= factor_eta;
2067        }
2068      }
2069    } else if (which == BIAS) {
2070      for (int i = 0; i < nlocal; i++) {
2071        if (mask[i] & groupbit) {
2072          temperature->remove_bias(i,v[i]);
2073          v[i][0] *= factor_eta;
2074          v[i][1] *= factor_eta;
2075          v[i][2] *= factor_eta;
2076          temperature->restore_bias(i,v[i]);
2077        }
2078      }
2079    }
2080  }
```

Figure 7.14 – Code snippet from fix_nh.cpp showing the nh_v_temp() method

As you can see, velocity scaling utilizes the appropriate exponential operator (`factor_eta`) in the **Liouville exponential operators**, which employs a half-timestep (`dthalf`) increment (line 1794).

Going back to *Figure 7.13*, in *lines 1807* to *1808*, the virtual particle positions are updated over a half timestep by looping over all the virtual particles in the forward direction. Finally, *lines 1814* to *1821* loop over all the virtual particles in the forward direction to calculate the same exponential factors as in lines *1780* to *1786*.

After the thermostat has been applied by the preceding methods, the atom positions and velocities are updated in the `initial_integrate()` and `final_integrate()` methods using the quantities derived from the aforementioned methods.

In this section, we outlined the Nose-Hoover thermostat, as implemented in `Fix NH`. This fix also accommodates a barostat and a list of keywords to manipulate the temperature and pressure, which we will not discuss since they are outside the scope of this book.

The `Fix Print` class is described next, which writes outputs to disk during a simulation run.

Studying the Fix Print class

In this section, we will learn about the `Fix Print` class and its source code.

The `Fix Print` class is controlled by the source code in `fix_print.cpp` and `fix_print.h`, and it can be used to write a text string to the screen or to a specified file.

This fix accepts a string as a **Unix-like** variable from the input script and writes it every N steps. In a LAMMPS input script, the corresponding syntax is as follows:

```
fix  FIX_ID  GROUP_ID  print N STRING
```

As described in the LAMMPS manual (`https://lammps.sandia.gov/doc/fix_print.html`), for this particular fix, `GROUP_ID` serves as a placeholder and does not have any effect on the fix. The N integer represents the number of timesteps between writing the string to a file, while `STRING` is a text string that can represent the value of a variable or user-entered text. Similar to Unix-style, `STRING` should be preceded by the `$` symbol if it is a variable name; for example, `${foo}` or `$f`. Optional keywords can specify whether to write the string on the screen or to a file. Now, let's dive into the source code, starting with the constructor method.

FixPrint::FixPrint()

As usual, first, we will look at the constructor method. The constructor method ensures that a minimum of five arguments are entered (*line 34*), including the three arguments read by the parent class, N, and `STRING`. It checks whether N is entered as a variable that starts with `v_` or whether it is entered as an integer (*line 35 to 43*). Then, *lines 47 to 53* copy the string argument to a new array (`char`) and allocate two memory spaces called `work` and `copy`, which will be used later. The following screenshot illustrates how these arguments are parsed:

```
47    int n = strlen(arg[4]) + 1;
48    string = new char[n];
49    strcpy(string,arg[4]);
50
51    copy = (char *) memory->smalloc(n*sizeof(char),"fix/print:copy");
52    work = (char *) memory->smalloc(n*sizeof(char),"fix/print:work");
53    maxcopy = maxwork = n;
54
55    // parse optional args
56
57    fp = NULL;
58    screenflag = 1;
59    char *title = NULL;
60
61    int iarg = 5;
62    while (iarg < narg) {
63      if (strcmp(arg[iarg],"file") == 0 || strcmp(arg[iarg],"append") == 0) {
64        if (iarg+2 > narg) error->all(FLERR,"Illegal fix print command");
65        if (me == 0) {
66          if (strcmp(arg[iarg],"file") == 0) fp = fopen(arg[iarg+1],"w");
67          else fp = fopen(arg[iarg+1],"a");
68          if (fp == NULL) {
69            char str[128];
70            snprintf(str,128,"Cannot open fix print file %s",arg[iarg+1]);
71            error->one(FLERR,str);
72          }
73        }
```

Figure 7.15 – Code snippet from fix_print.cpp showing the constructor method

As you can see, a 1D file-type array, fp (declared in fix_print.h), is set to NULL (*line 57*) to prepare for reading any filename entered. The screenflag variable (*line 58*) is set to 1 to write the string on the screen by default if no optional keyword is entered. The filename is parsed by looping over all the optional keywords (*line 62*) and the file is opened by the fopen() command, either for writing the string to a new file (*line 66*) or for appending (*line 67*) the string to an existing file.

The rest of the constructor method (*lines 75 to 98*) reads the optional screen or title keywords. These determine whether to write the string on the screen during the simulation run and whether to write a title in the output file (see manual).

The init() method extracts the value of N if it is entered as a variable style argument, and also determines the next timestep (stored as the next_print variable) when the string will be written. It does this using the following code:

```
137    if (update->ntimestep % nevery)
138      next_print = (update->ntimestep/nevery)*nevery + nevery;
139    else
140      next_print = update->ntimestep;
141  }
```

Figure 7.16 – Code snippet from fix_print.cpp showing the init() method

As you can see, on *line 138*, the quotient (update->ntimestep/nevery) is stored as an integer. This effectively keeps count of the number of times the string has been written.

The `setmask()` method dictates that this fix is executed at the END_OF_STEP stage only. The output is written in the `end_of_step()` method, as we'll see next.

FixPrint::end_of_step()

This method is chronologically located once all the dynamics steps have been completed and it is aptly placed to write an output to the screen or a file. The following screenshot shows this method:

```cpp
159    void FixPrint::end_of_step()
160    {
161      if (update->ntimestep != next_print) return;
162
163      // make a copy of string to work on
164      // substitute for $ variables (no printing)
165      // append a newline and print final copy
166      // variable evaluation may invoke computes so wrap with clear/add
167
168      modify->clearstep_compute();
169
170      strcpy(copy,string);
171      input->substitute(copy,work,maxcopy,maxwork,0);
172
173      if (var_print) {
174        next_print = static_cast<bigint>
175          (input->variable->compute_equal(ivar_print));
176        if (next_print <= update->ntimestep)
177          error->all(FLERR,"Fix print timestep variable returned a bad timestep");
178      } else {
179        next_print = (update->ntimestep/nevery)*nevery + nevery;
180      }
181
182      modify->addstep_compute(next_print);
183
184      if (me == 0) {
185        if (screenflag && screen) fprintf(screen,"%s\n",copy);
186        if (screenflag && logfile) fprintf(logfile,"%s\n",copy);
187        if (fp) {
188          fprintf(fp,"%s\n",copy);
189          fflush(fp);
190        }
191      }
192    }
```

Figure 7.17 – Code snippet from fix_print.cpp showing the end_of_step() method

As you can see, at every iteration where the `end_of_step()` method is invoked, *line 161* checks if the fix should print an output. The `modify->clearstep_compute()` method (*line 168*) clears the invoked flags of all computes to prevent re-invoking the same compute multiple times and to flag computes that have been invoked. The $ { } and $ variables are replaced by their actual text data via the `input->substitute()` method (*line 171*), which utilizes the `work` and `copy` memory allocations. Then, *lines 173* to *180* repeat this process in the `init()` method to calculate the `next_print` variable, which schedules the next instance of writing the string.

The `modify->addstep_compute()` method (*line 182*) loops over all the computes that can register invocation times, and determines the timesteps when they will be invoked next – something that needs to be performed whenever computes are called. Finally, the string (now stored as `copy`) is written to the screen (*line 185*) or to the `fp` file (*lines 187 to 190*) using the `fprintf()` command. Note that while LAMMPS is a multicore parallel program, we only need to execute the print with just the first core that is designated by `me==0` (*line 184*).

In this section, we discussed `Fix Print`, which executes at the `end_of_step()` stage without performing any dynamics.

The next item we'll analyze is `Fix Orient/FCC`, which applies an orientation-dependent force.

Reviewing the Fix Orient/FCC class

In this section, we will discuss how the orientations of two adjoining grains are compared to determine forces that generate grain boundary migration.

This fix applies a force to atoms located at the interface of two planar grains, that is, the grain boundary, to account for a range of potential energies that may be added to these atoms based on their neighboring atom positions. It is assumed that the two grains are **face-centered cubic** (**FCC**) crystals with different orientations, with their orientation vectors defined in two separate files. Altogether, this force results in atoms being migrated from one grain to the other.

The `Fix Orient/FCC` source code files, `fix_orient_fcc.cpp` and `fix_orient_fcc.h`, are located inside the `MISC` folder and need to be compiled as a separate package. The syntax for implementing this fix in a LAMMPS input script involves several input parameters:

```
fix  FIX_ID  GROUP_ID  orient/fcc  N_PRT  DIR  A  V  CUT_LO
CUT_HI   FILE0   FILE1
```

These parameters are described in the manual (`https://lammps.sandia.gov/doc/fix_orient.html`), though we will explain some of them here, as follows:

- `N_PRT`: This parameter states the number of timesteps between printing information for this fix.

- `DIR`: This parameter states the index of grain (0 or 1). This index is used as a reference that dictates the direction of atom flow. The grain shrinks if the potential energy injected is positive and grows if the potential energy is negative.

- A: This parameter states the lattice constant of both grains.

- V: This parameter states the maximum potential energy injected per atom.

- CUT_LO: This parameter states the lower bound fraction of the order parameter at which force is activated.

- CUT_HI: This parameter states the upper bound fraction of the order parameter at which force is discontinued.

- FILE0: This parameter states the file containing the orientation lattice vectors of one of the grains.

- FILE1: This parameter states the file containing the orientation lattice vectors of the other grain.

The order parameter, ξ_i, for atom i is calculated by summing up the deviations of all its immediate (maximum of 12) neighbors, j, from a perfect crystalline structure listed in the reference grain:

$$\xi_i = \sum_{j=1}^{12} |\vec{r}_{ij} - \vec{r}_{j,0}|$$

Here, $\vec{r}_{ij} = (x_{ij}, y_{ij}, z_{ij})$ is the displacement vector pointing from atom i to atom j, and $\vec{r}_{j,0} = (x_{j,0}, y_{j,0}, z_{j,0})$ is a lattice vector in the reference crystal read from the file. In addition, the order parameter, ξ_{01}, is calculated using the lattice vectors of both crystals, $\vec{r}_{j,1}$ and $\vec{r}_{j,0}$, that were read from the two files:

$$\xi_{01} = \sum_{j=1}^{12} |\vec{r}_{j,1} - \vec{r}_{j,0}|$$

In both equations, $\vec{r}_{j,0}$ represents the lattice vector chosen from the reference crystal file that deviates the least from the other vector in the equation; that is, it makes the smallest angle and produces the largest magnitude of dot product.

ξ_{01} is used to calculate the lower and upper bounds between which the force is active. The lower bound, ξ_{low}, is calculated as follows:

$$\xi_{low} = \text{CUT\_LO} * \xi_{01}$$

Similarly, the upper bound, ξ_{high}, is calculated as follows:

$$\xi_{high} = \text{CUT\_HI} * \xi_{01}$$

The quantity, ω_i, for atom i is defined as follows:

$$\omega_i = \frac{\pi}{2}\left(\frac{\xi_i - \xi_{low}}{\xi_{high} - \xi_{low}}\right)$$

The energy, u_i, that's applied to atom i is given by the following formula:

$$u_i = \begin{cases} 0, & if\ \xi_i < \xi_{low} \\ \frac{V}{2}[1 - \cos(2\omega_i)], & if\ \xi_{low} \le \xi_i \le \xi_{high} \\ V, & if\ \xi_i > \xi_{high} \end{cases}$$

Upon calculating the force, $\vec{F_i}$, on atom i by taking the negative space derivative of u_i, we get a non-zero force, but only in the middle interval, $\xi_{low} \le \xi_i \le \xi_{high}$. The x component is given by the following formula:

$$F_{xi} = -\frac{du_i}{dx} = -\frac{du_i}{d\omega_i}\cdot\frac{d\omega_i}{d\xi_i}\cdot\frac{d\xi_i}{dx} = -V\sin(2\omega_i)\cdot\frac{\pi}{2}\left(\frac{1}{\xi_{high} - \xi_{low}}\right)\cdot\frac{x_{ij} - x_{j,0}}{|\vec{r}_{ij} - \vec{r}_{j,0}|}$$

The y and z force components are calculated similarly using the corresponding displacement components.

The source code employs various structures and multiple loops over neighbor lists to calculate the aforementioned quantities. The following screenshot shows the Nbr and Sort structures defined in the fix_orient_fcc.h header file:

```
29    struct Nbr {                      // neighbor info for each owned and ghost atom
30        int n;                        // # of closest neighbors (up to 12)
31        tagint id[12];                // IDs of each neighbor
32                                      // if center atom is owned, these are local IDs
33                                      // if center atom is ghost, these are global IDs
34        double xismooth[12];          // distance weighting factor for each neighbors
35        double dxi[12][3];            // d order-parameter / dx for each neighbor
36        double duxi;                  // d Energy / d order-parameter for atom
37    };
38
39    struct Sort {                     // data structure for sorting to find 12 closest
40        int id;                       // local ID of neighbor atom
41        double rsq;                   // distance between center and neighbor atom
42        double delta[3];              // displacement between center and neighbor atom
43        double xismooth;              // distance weighting factor
44    };
```

Figure 7.18 – Code snippet from fix_orient_fcc.h

As you can see, the Nbr structure (*line 29* to *37*) applies to individual atoms and records their neighbors, neighbor IDs, any weighting factors, values of $\frac{d\xi}{dx}$ for each neighbor, and values of $\frac{du}{d\xi}$. The Sort structure (*line 39* to *44*) holds a sorted list of neighbors to identify the immediate neighbors.

Since this fix applies a force to atoms, it is initiated at the post_force() stage of execution in the setmask() method, where these structures will be revisited to illustrate their functionalities. Also, since neighbor lists are required to identify the neighboring atoms that are the closest to each central atom, neighbor lists are requested and accessed by pointers in the init() and init_list() methods, as shown in the following screenshot:

```
211    void FixOrientFCC::init()
212    {
213        if (strstr(update->integrate_style,"respa")) {
214            ilevel_respa = ((Respa *) update->integrate)->nlevels-1;
215            if (respa_level >= 0) ilevel_respa = MIN(respa_level,ilevel_respa);
216        }
217
218        // need a full neighbor list
219        // perpetual list, built whenever re-neighboring occurs
220
221        int irequest = neighbor->request(this,instance_me);
222        neighbor->requests[irequest]->pair = 0;
223        neighbor->requests[irequest]->fix = 1;
224        neighbor->requests[irequest]->half = 0;
225        neighbor->requests[irequest]->full = 1;
226    }
227
228    /* --------------------------------------------------------------------
229
230    void FixOrientFCC::init_list(int /*id*/, NeighList *ptr)
231    {
232        list = ptr;
233    }
```

Figure 7.19 – Code snippet from fix_orient_fcc.cpp showing the init() and init_list() methods

As we can see, a neighbor list for a fix is requested on *line 222*. For pair styles, a different request would have been required. Similarly, a full neighbor list is requested on *line 225*.

Now, we will take a look at the constructor method in fix_orient_fcc.cpp.

FixOrientFCC::FixOrientFCC()

In the constructor method, the parameters are parsed (*line 76* to *81*) and the two FILE0 and FILE1 parameters are stored as string arrays, chifilename and xifilename. Using the DIR parameter, chifilename is selected as the file of the reference grain and xifilename is set as the file of the other grain (*lines 83* to *97*). The cutoff distance for locating neighbors is calculated in *lines 103* to *105* as $\frac{1}{\sqrt{2}}$ (1.57A), as described in the manual.

The lattice vectors from both files are read by only the first core me==0 (*line 110*) and broadcast to all the cores by the MPI_Bcast() command (*lines 136* to *137*). The lattice vector are also saved in the 3D half_xi_chi_vec[][][] array, as shown in the following screenshot (*lines 141* to *145*):

```
139    // make copy of the reference vectors
140
141    for (int i = 0; i < 6; i++)
142      for (int j = 0; j < 3; j++) {
143        half_xi_chi_vec[0][i][j] = Rxi[i][j];
144        half_xi_chi_vec[1][i][j] = Rchi[i][j];
145      }
146
147    // compute xiid,xi0,xi1 for all 12 neighbors
148    // xi is the favored crystal
149    // want order parameter when actual is Rchi
150
151    double xi_sq,dxi[3],rchi[3];
152
153    xiid = 0.0;
154    for (int i = 0; i < 6; i++) {
155      rchi[0] = Rchi[i][0];
156      rchi[1] = Rchi[i][1];
157      rchi[2] = Rchi[i][2];
158      find_best_ref(rchi,0,xi_sq,dxi);
159      xiid += sqrt(xi_sq);
160      for (int j = 0; j < 3; j++) rchi[j] = -rchi[j];
161      find_best_ref(rchi,0,xi_sq,dxi);
162      xiid += sqrt(xi_sq);
163    }
164
165    xiid /= 12.0;
166    xi0 = uxif_low * xiid;
167    xi1 = uxif_high * xiid;
```

Figure 7.20 – Code snippet from fix_orient_fcc.cpp showing the constructor method

As you can see, the first index of half_xi_chi_vec[][][] represents the grain of the lattice vector (the reference grain is represented by index 1, while the other grain is represented by index 0) and the next two indices represent the atom ID and coordinate axis. The order parameter, ξ_{01}, is calculated in *lines 153* to *163* as the xiid variable and averaged over all 12 neighbors (*line 165*). This is used to calculate ξ_{low} (*line 166*) and ξ_{high} (*line 167*).

The `find_best_ref()` method is used (*lines 158* and *161*) to determine the lattice vector, $\vec{r}_{j,1}$, that deviates the least from $\vec{r}_{j,0}$, as described in the next section.

FixOrientFCC::find_best_ref()

This method accepts a displacement vector (`displs`) and a grain index (`which_crystal`) as input, and outputs the square of the distance between `displs` and the lattice vector that deviates the least from it as an `xi_sq` 1D array. It outputs the vector, $(d\xi/dx, d\xi/dy, d\xi/dz)$, as a `dxi` 1D array. The method is displayed in the following screenshot:

```
546   void FixOrientFCC::find_best_ref(double *displs, int which_crystal,
547                                     double &xi_sq, double *dxi)
548   {
549       int i;
550       double dot,tmp;
551
552       double  best_dot  = -1.0;          // best is biggest (smallest angle)
553       int     best_i    = -1;
554       int     best_sign = 0;
555
556       for (i = 0; i < half_fcc_nn; i++) {
557           dot = displs[0] * half_xi_chi_vec[which_crystal][i][0] +
558                 displs[1] * half_xi_chi_vec[which_crystal][i][1] +
559                 displs[2] * half_xi_chi_vec[which_crystal][i][2];
560           if (fabs(dot) > best_dot) {
561               best_dot = fabs(dot);
562               best_i = i;
563               if (dot < 0.0) best_sign = -1;
564               else best_sign = 1;
565           }
566       }
567
568       xi_sq = 0.0;
569       for (i = 0; i < 3; i++) {
570           tmp = displs[i] - best_sign * half_xi_chi_vec[which_crystal][best_i][i];
571           xi_sq += tmp*tmp;
572       }
573
574       if (xi_sq > 0.0) {
575           double xi = sqrt(xi_sq);
576           for (i = 0; i < 3; i++)
577               dxi[i] = (best_sign * half_xi_chi_vec[which_crystal][best_i][i] -
578                         displs[i]) / xi;
579       } else dxi[0] = dxi[1] = dxi[2] = 0.0;
580   }
```

Figure 7.21 – Code snippet from fix_orient_fcc.cpp showing the find_best_ref() method

As you can see, the dot product is calculated (*lines 556* to *566*) for `displs` with each lattice vector in the specified grain (`half_xi_chi_vec[][][]`). The magnitude is used to identify the lattice vector that makes the smallest angle with the displacement vector. The distance between `displs` and the identified lattice vector is used to calculate the order parameter as the `xi` variable (*lines 568* to *572, line 575*) and also used to calculate $d\xi/dx$, $d\xi/dy$, and $d\xi/dz$ (*lines 576* to *579*).

Finally, in the next section, we will illustrate how the forces are applied in `post_force()`.

FixOrientFCC::post_force()

In this method, *lines 294* to *377* loop once over all the atoms in the core and identify the neighbors that are located within the cutoff. These neighbors are appended (*lines 322* to *331*) in the 1D sort array belonging to the Sort structure we described earlier. In *line 338*, this array is sorted to retain the closest 12 neighbors using the built-in qsort() command.

For each of these 12 nearest neighbors, the lattice vector that deviates the least is identified using the find_best_fit() method (*line 349*) and the $(d\xi/dx, d\xi/dy, d\xi/dz)$ vector is extracted as a dxi array, as shown in the following screenshot:

```
340        // copy up to 12 nearest neighbors into nbr data structure
341        // operate on delta vector via find_best_ref() to compute dxi
342
343        n = MIN(12,nsort);
344        nbr[i].n = n;
345        if (n == 0) continue;
346
347        double xi_total = 0.0;
348        for (j = 0; j < n; j++) {
349            find_best_ref(sort[j].delta,0,xi_sq,dxi);
350            xi_total += sqrt(xi_sq);
351            nbr[i].id[j] = sort[j].id;
352            nbr[i].dxi[j][0] = dxi[0]/n;
353            nbr[i].dxi[j][1] = dxi[1]/n;
354            nbr[i].dxi[j][2] = dxi[2]/n;
355            if (use_xismooth) nbr[i].xismooth[j] = sort[j].xismooth;
356        }
357        xi_total /= n;
358        order[i][0] = xi_total;
359
360        // compute potential derivative to xi
361
362        if (xi_total < xi0) {
363            nbr[i].duxi = 0.0;
364            edelta = 0.0;
365            order[i][1] = 0.0;
366        } else if (xi_total > xi1) {
367            nbr[i].duxi = 0.0;
368            edelta = Vxi;
369            order[i][1] = 1.0;
370        } else {
371            omega = MY_PI2*(xi_total-xi0) / (xi1-xi0);
372            nbr[i].duxi = MY_PI*Vxi*sin(2.0*omega) / (2.0*(xi1-xi0));
373            edelta = Vxi*(1 - cos(2.0*omega)) / 2.0;
374            order[i][1] = omega / MY_PI2;
375        }
376        added_energy += edelta;
```

Figure 7.22 – Code snippet from fix_orient_fcc.cpp showing the post_force() method

As you can see, the order parameter is also extracted and averaged over all neighboring atoms as xi_total (*line 357*). The force that's applied and the energy that's injected into the central atom are determined based on the range in which xi_total falls (*lines 362* to *375*). The force array, f, is incremented in *lines 402* to *404* by the product of $du/d\xi$ and $(d\xi/dx, d\xi/dy, d\xi/dz)$. An optional weighting factor, xismooth, can also be calculated (*line 328*, and *lines 398* to *400*) to apply a smoothening function to the force and energy that's delivered. The relevant quantities are output to the screen and the log file in the remaining part of the method (*lines 439* to *466*).

In this section, we presented `Fix Orient/FCC`, which incorporates a neighbor list and applies a force based on neighbor orientations.

In the next section, we will examine `Fix Wall`, which serves as the parent class for multiple flat wall force surfaces.

Analyzing the Fix Wall and Fix Wall/LJ126 classes

In molecular dynamics, a wall serves as a boundary condition that exerts a force on an atom that approaches its interaction range. Unlike forces exerted by typical atoms, the wall force is not radially symmetric and is usually perpendicular to the wall. The `Fix Wall` class creates such planar walls that are perpendicular to the x, y, or z axis and can exert forces according to pre-defined potential functions in its child classes.

In a LAMMPS input script, the corresponding syntax for implementing a wall is as follows:

```
fix  FIX_ID  GROUP_ID  WALL_STYLE  FACE  COORDS  …
```

The parameters described in the manual (`https://lammps.sandia.gov/doc/fix_wall.html`) include `WALL_STYLE`, which is the type of potential between the wall and an atom, such as **Lennard-Jones (LJ)**, **Morse**, and **Harmonic**; `FACE`, which is the direction that the wall is facing in, and can be one of $\pm x, \pm y,$ or $\pm z$; and `COORDS`, which is the coordinate of the wall on the axis that it is facing.

Depending on the choice of `WALL_STYLE`, three or four potential parameters need to be entered after `COORDS`; for example, `epsilon`, `sigma`, and `cutoff` for LJ and `D0`, `alpha`, `r0`, and `cutoff` for Morse. Multiple walls can be implemented using the same fix, as long as the walls are not on the same axis and facing the same direction.

The different `WALL_STYLE` choices are implemented using individual child classes, such as `Fix Wall/LJ` and `Fix Wall/Morse`. The parent class in `fix_wall.cpp` invokes these child classes to compute the force and energy at the appropriate stage of execution. The `fix_wall.h` header file declares the two essential methods in each child class, `precompute()` and `wall_particle()`, as shown in the following screenshot:

```
44    virtual void precompute(int) = 0;
45    virtual void wall_particle(int, int, double) = 0;
```

Figure 7.23 – Code snippet from fix_wall.h

As you can see, these two methods are virtual methods that are intended to be overridden in the child classes. Both virtual methods are assigned values of 0 in accordance with C++ convention. This indicates that they are pure virtual functions that only need to be declared and do not need any function definition at this point.

The precompute() method calculates the coefficients of the potential and force function, and the wall_particle() method calculates the force to apply to atoms. Since a wall surface must be perpendicular to either the x, y, or z axis, the force component is only non-zero along that axis. These two methods will be illustrated later in this section with a specific potential style example.

In fix_wall.cpp, the constructor method parses all input parameters and loops over all parameters (*lines 58* to *149*) to identify all the walls that have been implemented. Each wall is checked for direction (*lines 64* to *70*) by comparing them with the enumerated list on *line 31*, as shown in the following code:

```
enum{XLO=0, XHI=1, YLO=2, YHI=3, ZLO=4, ZHI=5};
```

The integers are read from this list as a face index array (wallwhich) that will be used to determine the dimension and facing direction of each wall in the wall_particle() method, as will be shown later in this section. Each wall is also assigned a wall index (nwall) that is incremented at each loop (*line 127*), and a new wall is checked for conflict with an existing wall in the same direction on *lines 72* to *74*. In addition, the extra potential parameter required by the Morse style wall potential is accommodated by *lines 103* to *114*.

The setmask() method dictates that these wall forces are applied at the post_force() stage of execution, but by activating the FLD keyword in the input script, the force can be applied at the pre_force() stage instead, before the pairwise forces have been applied (see manual).

The init() method extracts the wall coordinates, epsilon, and sigma values. This only happens if they are entered as variables and the precompute() method is called to assign coefficients in the appropriate wall style child class.

The `post_force()` method loops over all the wall indices, m (*lines 329 to 351*), and calls the `precompute()` method again (*line 347*) to account for the variable style parameters that might need to be updated before force is calculated, as shown in the following screenshot:

```
328    double coord;
329    for (int m = 0; m < nwall; m++) {
330        if (xstyle[m] == VARIABLE) {
331            coord = input->variable->compute_equal(xindex[m]);
332            if (wallwhich[m] < YLO) coord *= xscale;
333            else if (wallwhich[m] < ZLO) coord *= yscale;
334            else coord *= zscale;
335        } else coord = coord0[m];
336        if (wstyle[m] == VARIABLE) {
337            if (estyle[m] == VARIABLE) {
338                epsilon[m] = input->variable->compute_equal(eindex[m]);
339                if (epsilon[m] < 0.0)
340                    error->all(FLERR,"Variable evaluation in fix wall gave bad value");
341            }
342            if (sstyle[m] == VARIABLE) {
343                sigma[m] = input->variable->compute_equal(sindex[m]);
344                if (sigma[m] < 0.0)
345                    error->all(FLERR,"Variable evaluation in fix wall gave bad value");
346            }
347            precompute(m);
348        }
349
350        wall_particle(m,wallwhich[m],coord);
351    }
```

Figure 7.24 – Code snippet from fix_wall.cpp showing the post_force() method

As you can see, this method also calls the `wall_particle()` method (*line 350*) and passes the wall index (m), face index (`wallwhich`), and the wall coordinate (`coord`) as arguments to apply force to eligible atoms.

To illustrate the `precompute()` and `wall_particle()` methods, we will look at the **LJ 12-6 potential wall** example in the `Fix Wall/LJ126` child class.

Fix wall/lj126

The LJ 12-6 wall potential applies a potential energy, $V_{LJ}(r)$, of the following form:

$$V_{LJ}(r) = 4\varepsilon\frac{\sigma^{12}}{r^{12}} - 4\varepsilon\frac{\sigma^6}{r^6}$$

Here, ε is the wall potential-well depth, σ is the wall potential-well width, and r is the perpendicular distance from the wall to an atom that experiences the potential. The corresponding LJ force, $F_{LJ}(r)$, is given by the following formula:

$$F_{LJ}(r) = -\frac{dV_{LJ}(r)}{dr} = 48\varepsilon\frac{\sigma^{12}}{r^{13}} - 24\varepsilon\frac{\sigma^6}{r^7}$$

The `precompute()` method in `fix_wall_lj126.cpp` defines the LJ coefficients for the interaction between the wall and an atom using the parameters entered in the LAMMPS input script, as shown in the following screenshot:

```
32    void FixWallLJ126::precompute(int m)
33  □{
34        coeff1[m] = 48.0 * epsilon[m] * pow(sigma[m],12.0);
35        coeff2[m] = 24.0 * epsilon[m] * pow(sigma[m],6.0);
36        coeff3[m] = 4.0 * epsilon[m] * pow(sigma[m],12.0);
37        coeff4[m] = 4.0 * epsilon[m] * pow(sigma[m],6.0);
38
39        double r2inv = 1.0/(cutoff[m]*cutoff[m]);
40        double r6inv = r2inv*r2inv*r2inv;
41        offset[m] = r6inv*(coeff3[m]*r6inv - coeff4[m]);
42  └}
```

Figure 7.25 – Code snippet from fix_wall_lj126.cpp showing the precompute() method

As you can see, the epsilon[m], sigma[m], and cutoff[m] parameters are parsed from the input script by fix_wall.cpp, where the m index represents the wall index. The coeff1 and coeff2 quantities will be used to calculate the force, while the coeff3 and coeff4 quantities will be used to calculate the potential in the wall_particle() method.

The wall_particle() method accepts three parameters: the wall index (m), the face index (which), and the wall coordinate on the specified axis (coord), as shown in the following screenshot:

```
51    void FixWallLJ126::wall_particle(int m, int which, double coord)
52  □{
53        double delta,rinv,r2inv,r6inv,fwall;
54        double vn;
55
56        double **x = atom->x;
57        double **f = atom->f;
58        int *mask = atom->mask;
59        int nlocal = atom->nlocal;
60
61        int dim = which / 2;
62        int side = which % 2;
63        if (side == 0) side = -1;
64
65        int onflag = 0;
66
67        for (int i = 0; i < nlocal; i++)
68  □     if (mask[i] & groupbit) {
69            if (side < 0) delta = x[i][dim] - coord;
70            else delta = coord - x[i][dim];
71            if (delta >= cutoff[m]) continue;
72  □         if (delta <= 0.0) {
73              onflag = 1;
74              continue;
75            }
76            rinv = 1.0/delta;
77            r2inv = rinv*rinv;
78            r6inv = r2inv*r2inv*r2inv;
79            fwall = side * r6inv*(coeff1[m]*r6inv - coeff2[m]) * rinv;
80            f[i][dim] -= fwall;
81            ewall[0] += r6inv*(coeff3[m]*r6inv - coeff4[m]) - offset[m];
82            ewall[m+1] += fwall;
83
84  □         if (evflag) {
85              if (side < 0) vn = -fwall*delta;
86              else vn = fwall*delta;
87              v_tally(dim, i, vn);
88            }
89          }
90
91        if (onflag) error->one(FLERR,"Particle on or inside fix wall surface");
```

Figure 7.26 – Code snippet from fix_wall_lj126.cpp showing the wall_particle() method

As you can see, *line 61* identifies the dimension (x -> 0, y -> 1, z -> 2), while *line 62* identifies the face (0 -> facing positive direction, 1 -> facing negative direction). *Line 63* assigns a -1 value to a positive-facing side for convenience in force calculations. *Lines 67* to *89* loop over all the atoms in the core and identify the atoms belonging to the specified group, after which they calculate the displacement vector between the wall and the atom that points along the positive direction on the axis (*lines 69* to *70*).

If the atom is located outside the wall interaction cutoff (*line 71*) or behind the wall (*line 72* to *75*), then no force is applied. Otherwise, the force component on the atom along the axis is calculated in *line 79* and the LJ potential is calculated on *line 81*. The direction of this force component is adjusted using the side variable, which adds a negative sign for a wall that is facing in the positive direction.

By calling these methods in the FixWall::post_force() method, the wall force is calculated accordingly and applied to the correct atoms.

Before concluding this section, we will point out that Fix Wall serves as a parent class for *soft* walls that apply distance-dependent forces to atoms that move inside their interaction cutoff distances. Therefore, the forces from these soft walls are incorporated in the atom dynamics using the post_force() method and time-integrated accordingly. However, for reflective walls in the Fix Wall/Reflect class, the velocity of a reflecting particle is directly reversed without the forces involved needing to be altered. Therefore, reflective walls are not *soft* and employ the post_integrate() method instead to adjust their velocity. Subsequently, Fix Wall/Reflect does not inherit from Fix Wall.

This section described the implementation of walls in LAMMPS simulations and the method structure in the child classes, which allows for wall potentials to be included in a flexible manner.

As our final example, next, we will study how rigid-body dynamics is performed in the Fix Rigid class.

Exploring the Fix Rigid class

The Fix Rigid class can treat a set of atoms as an independent rigid body. Its dynamics is described in terms of the net force on its **center-of-mass** (**COM**) and torque around the COM.

As described in *Chapter 1, MD Theory and Simulation Practices*, the net force, $\overrightarrow{F_{tot}}$, on a rigid body is calculated by summing up all the forces on all its constituent atoms (N), while the torque, $\vec{\tau}$, about its COM is calculated from the sum of the cross products of the displacement vector, $\overrightarrow{r_{Di}} = (x_{Di}, y_{Di}, z_{Di})$, of each atom from the COM with the force, $\vec{F_i} = (F_{xi}, F_{yi}, F_{zi})$, acting on that atom:

$$\vec{\tau} = \sum_{i=1}^{N} (\overrightarrow{r_{Di}} \times \vec{F_i}) = \sum_{i=1}^{N} (y_{Di}F_{zi} - z_{Di}F_{yi}, z_{Di}F_{xi} - x_{Di}F_{zi}, x_{Di}F_{yi} - y_{Di}F_{xi})$$

The torque is used to update the rigid-body angular momentum, $\vec{L}$, through the velocity Verlet algorithm for rotational motion:

$$\vec{L}(t + \Delta t) = \vec{L}(t) + \frac{1}{2}[\vec{\tau}(t) + \vec{\tau}(t + \Delta t)]\Delta t$$

Using the moment of inertia tensor, I, the angular velocity, $\vec{\omega} = (\omega_x, \omega_y, \omega_z)$, of the rigid body can be obtained as follows:

$$\vec{L} = I\,\vec{\omega}$$

The angular velocity and the distance from the COM can be used to find the individual atom linear velocities, $\vec{v}_i'$, with respect to the COM frame of reference:

$$\vec{v}'_i = \vec{\omega}_i \times \vec{r}_i = (\omega_{yi}z_i - \omega_{zi}y_i, \omega_{zi}x_i - \omega_{xi}z_i, \omega_{xi}y_i - \omega_{yi}x_i)$$

The individual atom positions, $\vec{r}_i' = (x_i', y_i', z_i')$, with respect to the COM frame of reference are calculated using the product of the matrix of the three rigid-body principal axes, Q, with the displacement vector, $\vec{r}_{Di}$:

$$\vec{r}_i' = Q\,\vec{r}_{Di} \quad \Rightarrow \quad \begin{bmatrix} x_i' \\ y_i' \\ z_i' \end{bmatrix} = \begin{bmatrix} Q_{xx} & Q_{xy} & Q_{xz} \\ Q_{yx} & Q_{yy} & Q_{yz} \\ Q_{zx} & Q_{zy} & Q_{zz} \end{bmatrix} \begin{bmatrix} x_{Di} \\ y_{Di} \\ z_{Di} \end{bmatrix}$$

In every iteration, the rigid body orientation is updated through **quaternion operations**. The Q matrix is updated accordingly to reflect the change in orientation, which implicitly updates the atom positions in the COM frame of reference. The absolute positions and velocities of the atoms are obtained by adding the absolute position ($\vec{r}_{COM}$) and velocity ($\vec{v}_{COM}$) of the COM to the relative positions and velocities in the COM frame of reference. The absolute position, $\vec{r}_i = (x_i, y_i, z_i)$, is given by the following formula:

$$\vec{r}_i = \vec{r}_i' + \vec{r}_{COM}$$

The absolute velocity, $\vec{v}_i = (v_{xi}, v_{yi}, v_{zi})$, is given by the following formula:

$$\vec{v}_i = \vec{v}'_i + \vec{v}_{COM}$$

$\vec{r}_{COM}$ and $\vec{v}_{COM}$ are updated by the velocity Verlet algorithm for linear motion, as explained earlier in this chapter (see the *Studying the Fix NVE* section).

The LAMMPS input script syntax for implementing `Fix Rigid` is as follows:

```
fix  FIX_ID  GROUP_ID  rigid  BODY_STYLE
```

The `FIX_ID` and `GROUP_ID` parameters are described in the LAMMPS manual (`https://lammps.sandia.gov/doc/fix_rigid.html`). The `BODY_STYLE` parameter represents how atoms are bracketed into rigid bodies, for example, according to their molecule ID's or groups. Optional parameters can be used to implement a **Nose-Hoover** or a **Langevin thermostat**, along with controls of the torque and force values.

The constructor method in `fix_rigid.cpp` parses these parameters and keeps track of the number of rigid bodies (`nbody`), the index of each rigid body (`ibody`), and the rigid body index that each atom belongs to (`body[]`). Memory is allocated to several arrays (*lines 268 to 288*) of `nbody` length to record information for each rigid body. The `MPI_Allreduce()` method (*lines 198 and 606*) is used to find the total number of atoms (`ncount`) in all the rigid bodies in the simulation by summing over all cores. A 2D `sum[][]` array is also defined in the `fix_rigid.h` header file. This is used as a temporary placeholder for vector calculation results regarding each rigid body in the rest of the class.

The `init()` method calls the `setup_bodies_static()` method to perform one-time setup of the static properties of the rigid bodies, such as COM position and diagonalization of the moment of inertia tensor, and also calls the `setup_bodies_dynamic()` method to perform one-time setup of the dynamics properties of the rigid bodies, such as COM velocity and angular momentum.

The `setup()` method calculates the torque and the COM force on each rigid body as 2D arrays called `torque[][]` and `fcm[][]`, respectively. For each rigid body, the angular momentum calculated in the `init()` method is used to derive the angular velocity (*lines 912 to 914*):

```
MathExtra::angmom_to_omega(angmom[ibody],ex_space[ibody],ey_
space[ibody],ez_space[ibody],inertia[ibody],omega[ibody]);
```

In the preceding code, the first argument is the angular momentum array and the next three arguments – the ex_space, ey_space, and ez_space arrays – are the three principal axes of the rigid body. The moment of inertia array, inertia[], is constructed in the setup_bodies_static() method. The angular velocity is returned as an omega[] array. The calculation is performed using the MathExtra::angmom_to_omega() method in the MathExtra class, as shown in the following screenshot:

```
290  void angmom_to_omega(double *m, double *ex, double *ey, double *ez,
291                       double *idiag, double *w)
292  {
293      double wbody[3];
294
295      if (idiag[0] == 0.0) wbody[0] = 0.0;
296      else wbody[0] = (m[0]*ex[0] + m[1]*ex[1] + m[2]*ex[2]) / idiag[0];
297      if (idiag[1] == 0.0) wbody[1] = 0.0;
298      else wbody[1] = (m[0]*ey[0] + m[1]*ey[1] + m[2]*ey[2]) / idiag[1];
299      if (idiag[2] == 0.0) wbody[2] = 0.0;
300      else wbody[2] = (m[0]*ez[0] + m[1]*ez[1] + m[2]*ez[2]) / idiag[2];
301
302      w[0] = wbody[0]*ex[0] + wbody[1]*ey[0] + wbody[2]*ez[0];
303      w[1] = wbody[0]*ex[1] + wbody[1]*ey[1] + wbody[2]*ez[1];
304      w[2] = wbody[0]*ex[2] + wbody[1]*ey[2] + wbody[2]*ez[2];
305  }
```

Figure 7.27 – Code snippet from math_extra.cpp showing the angmom_to_omega() method

The preceding code extracts the angular momentum from the angular velocity using the moment of inertia array. The setup() method also assigns velocities to the individual atoms using the set_v() method, as described later.

The setmask() method places the execution of the dynamics at the initial_integrate() and final_integrate() stages. This allows for neighboring at the pre_neighbor() stage and adding external forces such Langevin forces at the post_force() stage. In the rest of this section, we will focus on the dynamics of rigid bodies, as carried out by this class according to the theory described earlier.

FixRigid::initial_integrate()

This method performs the first half of the velocity Verlet algorithm to update the COM velocity (vcm) in *lines 940 to 942*, the COM position (xcm) in *lines 946 to 948*, and the angular momentum (angmom) in *lines 952 to 954* of each rigid body over half a timestep, as shown in the following screenshot:

```
931    void FixRigid::initial_integrate(int vflag)
932    {
933      double dtfm;
934
935      for (int ibody = 0; ibody < nbody; ibody++) {
936
937        // update vcm by 1/2 step
938
939        dtfm = dtf / masstotal[ibody];
940        vcm[ibody][0] += dtfm * fcm[ibody][0] * fflag[ibody][0];
941        vcm[ibody][1] += dtfm * fcm[ibody][1] * fflag[ibody][1];
942        vcm[ibody][2] += dtfm * fcm[ibody][2] * fflag[ibody][2];
943
944        // update xcm by full step
945
946        xcm[ibody][0] += dtv * vcm[ibody][0];
947        xcm[ibody][1] += dtv * vcm[ibody][1];
948        xcm[ibody][2] += dtv * vcm[ibody][2];
949
950        // update angular momentum by 1/2 step
951
952        angmom[ibody][0] += dtf * torque[ibody][0] * tflag[ibody][0];
953        angmom[ibody][1] += dtf * torque[ibody][1] * tflag[ibody][1];
954        angmom[ibody][2] += dtf * torque[ibody][2] * tflag[ibody][2];
955
956        // compute omega at 1/2 step from angmom at 1/2 step and current q
957        // update quaternion a full step via Richardson iteration
958        // returns new normalized quaternion, also updated omega at 1/2 step
959        // update ex,ey,ez to reflect new quaternion
960
961        MathExtra::angmom_to_omega(angmom[ibody],ex_space[ibody],ey_space[ibody],
962                                   ez_space[ibody],inertia[ibody],omega[ibody]);
963        MathExtra::richardson(quat[ibody],angmom[ibody],omega[ibody],
964                              inertia[ibody],dtq);
965        MathExtra::q_to_exyz(quat[ibody],
966                             ex_space[ibody],ey_space[ibody],ez_space[ibody]);
967      }
```

Figure 7.28 – Code snippet from fix_rigid.cpp showing the initial_integrate() method

As you can see, the fflag values in *lines 940 to 942* and the tflag values in *lines 952 to 954* are set to 1 or 0 for each dimension of each rigid body in the constructor method (*lines 299 to 303*). This activates or deactivates that particular degree of freedom when simulating a 2D or a 3D system.

The three MathExtra methods in *lines 961 to 966* are used to compute the angular velocity from the updated angular momentum, update the quaternion, and update the principal axes vectors accordingly. Finally, the atom positions and velocities are calculated from the updated COM positions, COM velocities, and angular velocities by the set_xv() method in *line 977*, as discussed in the following section.

FixRigid::set_xv()

This method calculates the positions and velocities of constituent atoms from their rigid body properties using the equations provided at the beginning of this section, as shown in the following screenshot:

```
1413        // x = displacement from center-of-mass, based on body orientation
1414        // v = vcm + omega around center-of-mass
1415
1416        MathExtra::matvec(ex_space[ibody],ey_space[ibody],
1417                          ez_space[ibody],displace[i],x[i]);
1418
1419        v[i][0] = omega[ibody][1]*x[i][2] - omega[ibody][2]*x[i][1] +
1420          vcm[ibody][0];
1421        v[i][1] = omega[ibody][2]*x[i][0] - omega[ibody][0]*x[i][2] +
1422          vcm[ibody][1];
1423        v[i][2] = omega[ibody][0]*x[i][1] - omega[ibody][1]*x[i][0] +
1424          vcm[ibody][2];
1425
1426        // add center of mass to displacement
1427        // map back into periodic box via xbox,ybox,zbox
1428        // for triclinic, add in box tilt factors as well
1429
1430        if (triclinic == 0) {
1431          x[i][0] += xcm[ibody][0] - xbox*xprd;
1432          x[i][1] += xcm[ibody][1] - ybox*yprd;
1433          x[i][2] += xcm[ibody][2] - zbox*zprd;
1434        } else {
1435          x[i][0] += xcm[ibody][0] - xbox*xprd - ybox*xy - zbox*xz;
1436          x[i][1] += xcm[ibody][1] - ybox*yprd - zbox*yz;
1437          x[i][2] += xcm[ibody][2] - zbox*zprd;
1438        }
```

Figure 7.29 – Code snippet from fix_rigid.cpp showing the set_xv() method

As you can see, the displacement vector between each atom, i, in the rigid body to the rigid-body COM is represented by the `displace[i]` array, which is fed (*lines 1416 to 1417*) into the `MathExtra::matvec()` method along with the three principal axis vectors known as `ex_space[]`, `ey_space[]`, and `ez_space[]`, as shown in the following screenshot of the `MathExtra::matvec()` method:

```
481   /* ----------------------------------------------------------------------
482      matrix times vector
483   ------------------------------------------------------------------------- */
484
485   inline void MathExtra::matvec(const double *ex, const double *ey,
486                                 const double *ez, const double *v, double *ans)
487   {
488     ans[0] = ex[0]*v[0] + ey[0]*v[1] + ez[0]*v[2];
489     ans[1] = ex[1]*v[0] + ey[1]*v[1] + ez[1]*v[2];
490     ans[2] = ex[2]*v[0] + ey[2]*v[1] + ez[2]*v[2];
491   }
```

Figure 7.30 – Code snippet from math_extra.h showing the matvec() method

As shown in the preceding screenshot, the matrix product of the principal axis matrix, Q, and displace[i] is returned as an array, x[i], which represents the relative positions of the atoms with respect to the COM. Going back to *Figure 7.27*, the absolute atom velocities, v, are calculated in *lines 1419* to *1424* by adding the COM velocity to the cross-product of the angular velocity (omega) with the position (x). Similarly, the absolute atom positions are calculated in *lines 1430* to *1438* by adding the COM coordinates to the relative positions, x.

By calling the set_xv() method during initial_integrate(), the position of each atom in a rigid body is time-integrated over a full timestep and the velocity is time-integrated over the first half-timestep. The second half of the time integration is carried out by the final_integrate() method.

FixRigid::final_integrate()

This method performs the second half of the velocity Verlet algorithm by updating the COM velocity (*lines 1151* to *1153*) and the angular momentum (*lines 1157* to *1159*) of the rigid-bodies by another half-timestep, as shown in the following screenshot:

```
1136    void FixRigid::final_integrate()
1137    {
1138      int ibody;
1139      double dtfm;
1140
1141      if (!earlyflag) compute_forces_and_torques();
1142
1143      // update vcm and angmom
1144      // fflag,tflag = 0 for some dimensions in 2d
1145
1146      for (ibody = 0; ibody < nbody; ibody++) {
1147
1148        // update vcm by 1/2 step
1149
1150        dtfm = dtf / masstotal[ibody];
1151        vcm[ibody][0] += dtfm * fcm[ibody][0] * fflag[ibody][0];
1152        vcm[ibody][1] += dtfm * fcm[ibody][1] * fflag[ibody][1];
1153        vcm[ibody][2] += dtfm * fcm[ibody][2] * fflag[ibody][2];
1154
1155        // update angular momentum by 1/2 step
1156
1157        angmom[ibody][0] += dtf * torque[ibody][0] * tflag[ibody][0];
1158        angmom[ibody][1] += dtf * torque[ibody][1] * tflag[ibody][1];
1159        angmom[ibody][2] += dtf * torque[ibody][2] * tflag[ibody][2];
1160
1161        MathExtra::angmom_to_omega(angmom[ibody],ex_space[ibody],ey_space[ibody],
1162                                    ez_space[ibody],inertia[ibody],omega[ibody]);
1163      }
1164
1165      // set velocity/rotation of atoms in rigid bodies
1166      // virial is already setup from initial_integrate
1167
1168      set_v();
1169    }
```

Figure 7.31 – Code snippet from fix_rigid.cpp showing the final_integrate() method

As you can see, the angular velocity is calculated using the updated angular momentum (*lines 1161* to *1162*), while the individual atom velocities are calculated by the set_v() method, as shown in the following screenshot:

```
1566    MathExtra::matvec(ex_space[ibody],ey_space[ibody],
1567                      ez_space[ibody],displace[i],delta);
1568
1569    // save old velocities for virial
1570
1571    if (evflag) {
1572      v0 = v[i][0];
1573      v1 = v[i][1];
1574      v2 = v[i][2];
1575    }
1576
1577    v[i][0] = omega[ibody][1]*delta[2] - omega[ibody][2]*delta[1] +
1578      vcm[ibody][0];
1579    v[i][1] = omega[ibody][2]*delta[0] - omega[ibody][0]*delta[2] +
1580      vcm[ibody][1];
1581    v[i][2] = omega[ibody][0]*delta[1] - omega[ibody][1]*delta[0] +
1582      vcm[ibody][2];
```

Figure 7.32 - Code snippet from fix_rigid.cpp showing the set_v() method

As you can see, in the set_v() method, similar to the set_xv() method, the relative atom positions with respect to the COM are calculated (*lines 1566* to *1567*), and the atom velocities are calculated using the COM velocities and the cross-products of angular velocities with the relative atom positions (*lines 1577* to *1582*). Altogether, the final_integrate() method completes the second half of the velocity Verlet algorithm.

The Fix Rigid command permits variants such as rigid/npt, rigid/nve, and rigid/nvt, all of which incorporate other forms of the time integrator. These variants add their own features to the time-integration process, but they inherit the Fix Rigid class and use it to realize the rigid body dynamics calculations.

Summary

In this chapter, we described several fixes and illustrated the various data structures, methods, and operations that you can use to control simulation behavior and incorporate features to model a desired system. Fixes are responsible for implementing dynamics, thermostats, and other physical properties that allow for realistic modeling. Judicious modifications made in the source code at the correct stages of execution empower the user to exercise greater control over a simulation. When writing your own source code, you can use the examples presented in this chapter to implement similar features.

In the previous three chapters, we analyzed pair styles, compute styles, and fix styles, and a large variety of custom simulation features can be created from modifying these styles. In the next chapter, we will outline some supporting classes that may be helpful when writing a new feature into LAMMPS.

Questions

1. Which method is responsible for determining the stage of execution for a fix?

2. What quantities are represented by the `dtv`, `dtf`, and `dtfm` variables?

3. What is the primary purpose of the `fflag` and `tflag` quantities in the `Fix Rigid` class?

8
Exploring Supporting Classes

In this chapter, we will outline some supporting classes that are often imported and invoked by pair potentials, computes, and fixes. These classes play vital roles in facilitating the simulation flow, but often do not need to be modified when creating custom LAMMPS features.

We will cover the following topics in this chapter:

- Discovering the Group class
- Exploring the Variable class
- Studying the Error class
- Reviewing the Memory class
- Discussing the Angle and angle/harmonic classes

By the end of this chapter, you will have learned how these supporting classes execute their duties and how they are invoked during simulation runs.

Technical requirements

To execute the instructions in this chapter, you just need a text editor (for example, **Notepad++** or **Gedit**). You can find the full source used in this chapter here: `https://github.com/PacktPublishing/Extending-and-Modifying-LAMMPS-Writing-Your-Own-Source-Code`

You can download LAMMPS from `https://lammps.sandia.gov/doc/Install.html`. The LAMMPS GitHub link is `https://github.com/lammps/lammps`. This is also where the necessary source code can be found.

Discovering the Group class

In this section, we will discuss the source code in `group.cpp` that's responsible for controlling groups of atoms via the `Group` class (see `https://lammps.sandia.gov/doc/group.html`).

Using groups, a set of atoms can be combined as one collective group, which facilitates uniform treatment of the group members when applying fixes. It also allows mathematical operations to be performed on the group.

Groups can be defined based on criteria such as the type and region of atoms, and atoms are registered to groups using the `assign()` method. The following code snippet illustrates grouping atoms by region occupied:

```
178   if (strcmp(arg[1],"region") == 0) {
179
180       if (narg != 3) error->all(FLERR,"Illegal group command");
181
182       int iregion = domain->find_region(arg[2]);
183       if (iregion == -1) error->all(FLERR,"Group region ID does not exist");
184       domain->regions[iregion]->init();
185       domain->regions[iregion]->prematch();
186
187       for (i = 0; i < nlocal; i++)
188         if (domain->regions[iregion]->match(x[i][0],x[i][1],x[i][2]))
189           mask[i] |= bit;
```

Figure 8.1 – Code snippet from the Group:assign() method showing atom selection by region

By looping over all the atoms in the core (*line 187*), the atoms located in a given region with a region ID, `iregion`, are selected via bitwise operation (*line 189*).

The following screenshot shows the union of multiple groups:

```
419    } else if (strcmp(arg[ ],"union") ==  ) {
420
421      if (narg <  ) error->all(FLERR,"Illegal group command");
422
423      int length = narg- ;
424      int *list = new int[length];
425
426      int jgroup;
427      for (int iarg =  ; iarg < narg; iarg++) {
428        jgroup = find(arg[iarg]);
429        if (jgroup == - ) error->all(FLERR,"Group ID does not exist");
430        if (dynamic[jgroup])
431          error->all(FLERR,"Cannot union groups using a dynamic group");
432        list[iarg- ] = jgroup;
433      }
434
435      // add to group if in any other group in list
436
437      int otherbit;
438
439      for (int ilist =  ; ilist < length; ilist++) {
440        otherbit = bitmask[list[ilist]];
441        for (i =  ; i < nlocal; i++)
442          if (mask[i] & otherbit) mask[i] |= bit;
443      }
444
445      delete [] list;
```

Figure 8.2 – Code snippet from the Group:assign() method showing the union of groups

As you can see, the code loops over all the entered arguments (*line 427*), identifies the corresponding groups (*line 428*), and appends them to the 1D `list` array (*line 432*). By looping over all the atoms in the core and all the groups in `list`, the atoms belonging to the identified groups are tagged by bit operations (*lines 439 to 443*).

The `assign` method sums group assignments over all cores toward the end (*line 546*) using the `MPI_Allreduce()` method.

Group commands also accommodate computations and mathematical operations. The following code snippet shows the `count()` method, which counts the number of atoms in a group:

```
778  /* --------------------------------------------------------
779       count atoms in group
780  --------------------------------------------------------
781
782  bigint Group::count(int igroup)
783  {
784    int groupbit = bitmask[igroup];
785
786    int *mask = atom->mask;
787    int nlocal = atom->nlocal;
788
789    int n =  ;
790    for (int i =  ; i < nlocal; i++)
791      if (mask[i] & groupbit) n++;
792
793    bigint nsingle = n;
794    bigint nall;
795    MPI_Allreduce(&nsingle,&nall, ,MPI_LMP_BIGINT,MPI_SUM,world);
796    return nall;
797  }
```

Figure 8.3 – Code snippet from group.cpp showing the count() method

Atoms belonging to the specified group are identified by looping over all the atoms in the core (*lines 789* to *791*) and summing them up over all cores (*line 795*).

The upper and lower position bounds of the atoms in a group that are within a given region in each dimension are calculated by the bounds() method:

```
977  /* -------------------------------------------------------------------
978     compute the coordinate bounds of the group of atoms in region
979     periodic images are not considered, so atoms are NOT unwrapped
980  ------------------------------------------------------------------- */
981
982  void Group::bounds(int igroup, double *minmax, int iregion)
983  {
984    int groupbit = bitmask[igroup];
985    Region *region = domain->regions[iregion];
986    region->prematch();
987
988    double extent[6];
989    extent[0] = extent[2] = extent[4] = BIG;
990    extent[1] = extent[3] = extent[5] = -BIG;
991
992    double **x = atom->x;
993    int *mask = atom->mask;
994    int nlocal = atom->nlocal;
995
996    for (int i = 0; i < nlocal; i++) {
997      if (mask[i] & groupbit && region->match(x[i][0],x[i][1],x[i][2])) {
998        extent[0] = MIN(extent[0],x[i][0]);
999        extent[1] = MAX(extent[1],x[i][0]);
1000       extent[2] = MIN(extent[2],x[i][1]);
1001       extent[3] = MAX(extent[3],x[i][1]);
1002       extent[4] = MIN(extent[4],x[i][2]);
1003       extent[5] = MAX(extent[5],x[i][2]);
1004     }
1005   }
1006
1007   // compute extent across all procs
1008   // flip sign of MIN to do it in one Allreduce MAX
1009   // set box by extent in shrink-wrapped dims
1010
1011   extent[0] = -extent[0];
1012   extent[2] = -extent[2];
1013   extent[4] = -extent[4];
1014
1015   MPI_Allreduce(extent,minmax,6,MPI_DOUBLE,MPI_MAX,world);
1016
1017   minmax[0] = -minmax[0];
1018   minmax[2] = -minmax[2];
1019   minmax[4] = -minmax[4];
```

Figure 8.4 – Code snippet from group.cpp showing the bounds() method

As you can see, in the `bounds ()` method, the initial negative bounds (`extent [0]`, `extend [2]`, and `extend [4]`) are set as large values, `BIG` (`=1.0e20`), while the initial positive bounds (`extent [1]`, `extend [3]`, and `extend [5]`) are set as `-BIG` in *lines 989* to *990*. While looping over all the atoms in the core (*line 996*), the atoms that satisfy group and region criteria are identified (*line 997*) and their (*x, y, z*) coordinates are compared to the six bound values in the `extent []` array using the `MIN` and `MAX` built-in functions (*lines 998* to *1003*). For each bound, the `extent []` value is updated at every iteration. This is because the atom coordinates are compared to the existing `extent []` value, thereby locating the extreme atom coordinates when all the atoms have been compared.

Having located the atom bounds for the local atoms, the atom bounds across the global atoms in all the cores are located by using the `MPI_Allreduce ()` method with the `MPI_MAX` option (*line 1015*), which returns the maximum value among all cores. In order to process all six bounds in one invocation, the signs of the negative bounds (`extent [0]`, `extend [2]`, and `extend [4]`) are switched (*lines 1011* to *1013*) so that returning the maximum value for them effectively returns the minimum value. Once the maximum bounds have been retrieved and stored as a 1D `minmax []` array, the signs of the negative bounds are switched back accordingly (*lines 1017* to *1019*).

In this section, we provided an outline of the `Group` class and some of its methods. The `Variable` class, which we will discuss in the next section, invokes some of these methods to calculate various group properties.

Exploring the Variable class

In this section, we will outline the `Variable` class and its source code in the `variable.cpp` and `variable.h` files. This class can assign variables in order to store constants or calculate atom and group properties, among other functionalities (see `https://lammps.sandia.gov/doc/variable.html`).

A variable can return scalar values or arrays of values that are useful for conveying information from one part of the script to another during a simulation run. An equal style variable sets the variable to a provided constant value or to a formula that performs a mathematical calculation or extracts a group, atom, region, compute, fix property, and more. The following screenshot from the set() method shows the relevant code:

```
396    // EQUAL
397    // replace pre-existing var if also style EQUAL (allows it to be reset)
398    // num = 2, which = 1st value
399    // data = 2 values, 1st is string to eval, 2nd is filled on retrieval
400
401    } else if (strcmp(arg[1],"equal") == 0) {
402      if (narg != 3) error->all(FLERR,"Illegal variable command");
403      int ivar = find(arg[0]);
404      if (ivar >= 0) {
405        if (style[ivar] != EQUAL)
406          error->all(FLERR,"Cannot redefine variable as a different style");
407        delete [] data[ivar][0];
408        copy(1,&arg[2],data[ivar]);
409        replaceflag = 1;
410      } else {
411        if (nvar == maxvar) grow();
412        style[nvar] = EQUAL;
413        num[nvar] = 2;
414        which[nvar] = 0;
415        pad[nvar] = 0;
416        data[nvar] = new char*[num[nvar]];
417        copy(1,&arg[2],data[nvar]);
418        data[nvar][1] = new char[VALUELENGTH];
419        strcpy(data[nvar][1],"(undefined)");
420      }
```

Figure 8.5 – Code snippet from the Variable::set() method showing the equal style variables

As you can see, upon detecting the equal keyword (*line 401*), the find() method is used to locate the name of the variable that was entered in the preceding term (*line 403*), as shown in the following screenshot:

```
723    /* ----------------------------------------
724       search for name in list of variables names
725       return index or -1 if not found
726    ----------------------------------------- */
727
728    int Variable::find(char *name)
729    {
730      if(name==NULL) return -1;
731      for (int i = 0; i < nvar; i++)
732        if (strcmp(name,names[i]) == 0) return i;
733      return -1;
734    }
```

Figure 8.6 – Code snippet from variable.cpp showing the find() method

As you can see, by looping over all the defined variables (*line 731*), the index of the variable name is identified (*line 732*), and -1 is returned if the variable name does not exist.

Back in the set () method from *Figure 8.5*, the variable that was identified is replaced with the value represented by the argument that was entered after the equal keyword using the copy () function (*line 408*). If the variable name does not exist (*lines 410 to 420*), a new variable is created using the grow () method (*line 411*) to copy the required value into the new variable.

As seen in *lines 410 to 420*, the maxvar, which[], pad[], num[], style[], and data[][][] structures are used to assign variable values. These structures are described in variable.h, as shown in the following screenshot:

```
51     private:
52       int me;
53       int nvar;                    // # of defined variables
54       int maxvar;                  // max # of variables following lists can hold
55       char **names;                // name of each variable
56       int *style;                  // style of each variable
57       int *num;                    // # of values for each variable
58       int *which;                  // next available value for each variable
59       int *pad;                    // 1 = pad loop/uloop variables with 0s, 0 = no pad
60       class VarReader **reader;    // variable that reads from file
61       char ***data;                // str value of each variable's values
62       double *dvalue;              // single numeric value for internal variables
```

Figure 8.7 – Code snippet from variable.h

The data[][][] structure stores the value of the variable and can use its other dimensions to facilitate evaluation and retrieval. The other keywords that are used in the LAMMPS input script (for example, format, atom, and vector) utilize one or more dimensions of this structure, as can be seen from the rest of the set () method.

When reading values obtained from computes or fixes that are preceded by c_ or f_, the evaluate () method checks for these clues and processes accordingly. In the case of computes, the corresponding compute is identified by the modify->compute[] method and depending on the data type, the compute_scalar (), compute_vector (), or compute_array () method is called from the identified compute. Fixes are evaluated by a similar procedure.

Both computes and fixes use a `Tree` structure to keep track of the attributes of the variable. This structure is described in `variable.h`, as shown in the following screenshot:

```
80    struct Tree {                    // parse tree for atom-style or vector-style vars
81        double value;                // single scalar
82        double *array;               // per-atom or per-type list of doubles
83        int *iarray;                 // per-atom list of ints
84        bigint *barray;              // per-atom list of bigints
85        int type;                    // operation, see enum{} in variable.cpp
86        int nvector;                 // length of array for vector-style variable
87        int nstride;                 // stride between atoms if array is a 2d array
88        int selfalloc;               // 1 if array is allocated here, else 0
89        int ivalue1,ivalue2;         // extra values needed for gmask,rmask,grmask
90        int nextra;                  // # of additional args beyond first 2
91        Tree *first,*second;         // ptrs further down tree for first 2 args
92        Tree **extra;                // ptrs further down tree for nextra args
```

Figure 8.8 – Code snippet from variable.h showing the Tree structure

The `Tree` structures are collapsed using the `collapse_tree()` method in the `compute_atom()` and `compute_vector()` methods to retrieve the output for the atom style or vector style variables, respectively.

Group-specific calculations, such as those described in the *Discovering the Group class* section, are accommodated by the `group_function()` method, which reads keywords from the input script and calls the corresponding method in `group.cpp` (for example, `group->xcm()`, or `group->mass()`) in order to return the function outputs.

Mathematical functions are listed in the `math_function()` method. A `Tree` structure is generated for mathematical functions, which is collapsed in the `collapse_tree()` method and evaluated in the `eval_tree()` method to return the output.

The `Variable` class is vast and, in this section, we provided a gist of its functionalities. In the next section, we'll review the `Error` class, which prints out error messages during simulation runs.

Studying the Error class

In this section, we will analyze the `Error` class and its source code, which can be found in the `error.cpp` and `error.h` files.

Before we begin, we will introduce the concepts of **Universe** and **World** with regard to parallel processing – a universe consists of all the tasks in the simulation, whereas a world refers to the number of cores dedicated to each task. Subsequently, the world and universe IDs differ only if the simulation runs on more than one partition via `-partition command-line switch` (see `https://lammps.sandia.gov/doc/Run_options.html`). Once a set of cores finish a task, the cores execute the next task immediately after, and each task is considered a universe that is executed by a world of constituent cores.

The `Error` class is used when we intend to display an error message or print information in order to debug. Several types of error messages are offered:

- The `Error::all()` method
- The `Error::one()` method
- The `Error::warning()` method
- The `Error::message()` method

We will look at the aforementioned methods in brief in the following sections.

Error::all()

This method is called by all the cores in the world and prints an error message on the screen and the log file, before terminating the simulation:

```
131  /* -----------------------------------------------------------
132      called by all procs in one world
133      close all output, screen, and log files in world
134      insure all procs in world call, else will hang
135      force MPI_Abort if running in multi-partition mode
136  ------------------------------------------------------------- */
137
138  void Error::all(const char *file, int line, const char *str)
139  {
140    MPI_Barrier(world);
141
142    int me;
143    const char *lastcmd = (const char*)"(unknown)";
144
145    MPI_Comm_rank(world,&me);
146
147    if (me == 0) {
148      if (input && input->line) lastcmd = input->line;
149      if (screen) fprintf(screen,"ERROR: %s (%s:%d)\n"
150                          "Last command: %s\n",
151                          str,truncpath(file),line,lastcmd);
152      if (logfile) fprintf(logfile,"ERROR: %s (%s:%d)\n"
153                          "Last command: %s\n",
154                          str,truncpath(file),line,lastcmd);
155    }
```

Figure 8.9 – Code snippet from error.cpp showing the all() method

As you can see, the `MPI_Barrier()` method (*line 140*) synchronizes all the cores in the world by preventing them from proceeding beyond this method until all the cores have called this method. The error message is printed only by the core with index `me==0` (*lines 147* to *155*) instead of all the cores individually. The `MPI_Abort()` method (*line 177*) terminates the execution environment if multiple partitions are active, while the `MPI_Finalize()` (*line 179*) method cleans up all MPI processes and states before terminating.

Error::one()

This method is called by one core in the world and prints an error message on the screen, as well as the log file, before terminating the simulation:

```
184  /*  --------------------------------------------------------------
185       called by one proc in world
186       write to world screen only if non-NULL on this proc
187       always write to universe screen
188       forces abort of entire world (and universe) if any proc in world calls
189  --------------------------------------------------------------  */
190
191  void Error::one(const char *file, int line, const char *str)
192  {
193      int me;
194      const char *lastcmd = (const char*)"(unknown)";
195      MPI_Comm_rank(world,&me);
196
197      if (input && input->line) lastcmd = input->line;
198      if (screen) fprintf(screen,"ERROR on proc %d: %s (%s:%d)\n"
199                       "Last command: %s\n",
200                       me,str,truncpath(file),line,lastcmd);
201      if (logfile) fprintf(logfile,"ERROR on proc %d: %s (%s:%d)\n"
202                        "Last command: %s\n",
203                        me,str,truncpath(file),line,lastcmd);
204
205      if (universe->nworlds > 1)
206        if (universe->uscreen)
207          fprintf(universe->uscreen,"ERROR on proc %d: %s (%s:%d)\n",
208                universe->me,str,truncpath(file),line);
```

Figure 8.10 – Code snippet from error.cpp showing the one() method

In this method, the MPI_Barrier() method is not required since core synchronization is not attempted. An additional error message is printed out (*lines 205 to 208*) to indicate the core ID that called this method.

Error::warning() and message()

These methods are called by one core in the world and prints an error message on the screen and the log file, but do not terminate the simulation:

```
227  /* -----------------------------------------------------------------
228       called by one proc in world
229       only write to screen if non-NULL on this proc since could be file
230  ---------------------------------------------------------------- */
231
232  void Error::warning(const char *file, int line, const char *str, int logflag)
233  {
234    if (screen) fprintf(screen,"WARNING: %s (%s:%d)\n",str,truncpath(file),line);
235    if (logflag && logfile) fprintf(logfile,"WARNING: %s (%s:%d)\n",
236                                str,truncpath(file),line);
237  }
238
239  /* -----------------------------------------------------------------
240       called by one proc in world, typically proc 0
241       write message to screen and logfile (if logflag is set)
242  ---------------------------------------------------------------- */
243
244  void Error::message(const char *file, int line, const char *str, int logflag)
245  {
246    if (screen) fprintf(screen,"%s (%s:%d)\n",str,truncpath(file),line);
247    if (logflag && logfile) fprintf(logfile,"%s (%s:%d)\n",str,truncpath(file),line);
248  }
```

Figure 8.11 – Code snippet from error.cpp showing the warning() and message() methods

The difference between the `Error::warning()` and `Error::message()` methods is that the `warning()` method prints the text **WARNING**, along with the error message (*line 234*). These messages are useful for debugging purposes when printed information on the screen is desired without terminating the simulation.

In this section, we described some of the error messages in the `Error` class that help alert users to errors during a simulation run. Next, we will discuss memory allocation using the `Memory` class.

Reviewing the Memory class

In this section, we will demonstrate how the `Memory` class (`memory.cpp` and `memory.h`) in LAMMPS allocates and deallocates memory blocks as requested.

The `Memory` class is widely used in the LAMMPS source code, and it is often encountered in relation to data structure creation. Its three main methods – `create()`, `grow()`, and `destroy()` – provide handles to create, extend/shrink, and release primitive data structures, respectively. By using template overrides, these methods can accommodate 1D, 2D, and 3D arrays that serve the same function.

In `memory.h`, various template functions are defined for the `create()`, `grow()`, and `destroy()` methods in different dimensions. The following screenshot shows these template functions in 1D:

```
40        create a 1d array
41    ---------------------------------------------------------------
42
43        template <typename TYPE>
44        TYPE *create(TYPE *&array, int n, const char *name)
45        {
46          bigint nbytes = ((bigint) sizeof(TYPE)) * n;
47          array = (TYPE *) smalloc(nbytes,name);
48          return array;
49        }
50
51        template <typename TYPE>
52        TYPE **create(TYPE **& /*array*/, int /*n*/, const char *name)
53        {fail(name); return NULL;}
54
55    /* ---------------------------------------------------------------
56        grow or shrink 1d array
57    ---------------------------------------------------------------
58
59        template <typename TYPE>
60        TYPE *grow(TYPE *&array, int n, const char *name)
61        {
62          if (array == NULL) return create(array,n,name);
63
64          bigint nbytes = ((bigint) sizeof(TYPE)) * n;
65          array = (TYPE *) srealloc(array,nbytes,name);
66          return array;
67        }
68
69        template <typename TYPE>
70        TYPE **grow(TYPE **& /*array*/, int /*n*/, const char *name)
71        {fail(name); return NULL;}
72
73    /* ---------------------------------------------------------------
74        destroy a 1d array
75    ---------------------------------------------------------------
76
77        template <typename TYPE>
78        void destroy(TYPE *&array) {
79          sfree(array);
80          array = NULL;
81        }
```

Figure 8.12 – The create(), grow(), and destroy() methods for 1D arrays (from memory.h)

As you can see, in the create() method, TYPE (*line 44*) is initially an undefined data type that is automatically inferred from the arguments that are passed in when the method is invoked. There are three arguments that we need here: the pointer reference to the array (*&array), the length of the array (n), and the name of the array (name).

The *&array indicator is interpreted as a pointer to the array, according to the convention in C++ that groups from right to left. Then, in *line 46*, the required memory size allocation is calculated by multiplying the number of bytes associated with TYPE by the array length, n. In the next line (*line 47*), the smalloc() method (discussed later) is invoked to request a memory block called name, and it is returned in *line 48*.

To comply with this trick of passing in a pointer reference as an argument and assigning the memory to the reference itself, we can employ a couple of techniques. First, we can create a space directly, as shown in the following example, where an ntypes reference of (n+1) 1D array size is returned as the pair:ntypes structure:

```
memory->create(ntypes,n+1,"pair:ntypes");
```

Alternatively, we can assign the memory block to a NULL pointer:

```
ntypes = NULL;
ntypes = memory->create(ntypes,n+1,n+1,"pair:ntypes");
```

This array can be utilized like a regular array in C++:

```
itypes = ntypes[i];
```

Once the purpose of this array has been fulfilled, it must be released before exiting. This is accomplished by simply calling the destroy() method (*lines 77 to 81*), with the pointer passed in as an argument:

```
memory->destroy(ntypes);
```

The length of the array can be changed during a simulation run using the grow() method (*lines 60 to 67*). The syntax is similar to that of the create() method, where the pointer reference, the array length, and the array name are fed as input arguments. If this pointer is NULL, then a new memory block is allocated by the create() method (*line 62*).

As shown in the code in *Figure 8.12*, these template functions invoke the `smalloc()`, `srealloc()`, and `sfree()` methods from `memory.cpp`. The `smalloc()` method, shown in the following screenshot, uses the built-in `malloc()` function to allocate the required memory to the specified data structure:

```
38  /* ------------------------------------------------------------------
39       safe malloc
40  ------------------------------------------------------------------
41
42  void *Memory::smalloc(bigint nbytes, const char *name)
43  {
44    if (nbytes == 0) return NULL;
45
46  #if defined(LAMMPS_MEMALIGN)
47    void *ptr;
48
49  #if defined(LMP_USE_TBB_ALLOCATOR)
50    ptr = scalable_aligned_malloc(nbytes, LAMMPS_MEMALIGN);
51  #else
52    int retval = posix_memalign(&ptr, LAMMPS_MEMALIGN, nbytes);
53    if (retval) ptr = NULL;
54  #endif
55
56  #else
57    void *ptr = malloc(nbytes);
58  #endif
59    if (ptr == NULL) {
60      char str[128];
61      sprintf(str,"Failed to allocate " BIGINT_FORMAT " bytes for array %s",
62              nbytes,name);
63      error->one(FLERR,str);
64    }
65    return ptr;
66  }
```

Figure 8.13 – Code snippet from memory.cpp showing the smalloc() method

The `srealloc()` method uses the built-in `realloc()` function to resize the memory chunk that's been allocated to the specified structure, as shown in the following screenshot:

```
68    /* ------------------------------------------------------------
69        safe realloc
70    ------------------------------------------------------------ */
71
72    void *Memory::srealloc(void *ptr, bigint nbytes, const char *name)
73    {
74      if (nbytes == 0) {
75        destroy(ptr);
76        return NULL;
77      }
78
79    #if defined(LMP_USE_TBB_ALLOCATOR)
80      ptr = scalable_aligned_realloc(ptr, nbytes, LAMMPS_MEMALIGN);
81    #elif defined(LMP_INTEL_NO_TBB) && defined(LAMMPS_MEMALIGN) && \
82          defined(__INTEL_COMPILER)
83
84      ptr = realloc(ptr, nbytes);
85      uintptr_t offset = ((uintptr_t)(const void *)(ptr)) % LAMMPS_MEMALIGN;
86      if (offset) {
87        void *optr = ptr;
88        ptr = smalloc(nbytes, name);
89        memcpy(ptr, optr, MIN(nbytes,malloc_usable_size(optr)));
90        free(optr);
91      }
92    #else
93      ptr = realloc(ptr,nbytes);
94    #endif
95      if (ptr == NULL) {
96        char str[128];
97        sprintf(str,"Failed to reallocate " BIGINT_FORMAT " bytes for array %s",
98                nbytes,name);
99        error->one(FLERR,str);
100     }
101     return ptr;
102   }
```

Figure 8.14 – Code snippet from memory.cpp showing the srealloc() method

Finally, we will present a screenshot of the `sfree()` method, which uses the built-in `free()` function to deallocate memory that has been previously assigned to the specified data structure:

```
104   /* ------------------------------------------------
105       safe free
106   ------------------------------------------------
107
108   void Memory::sfree(void *ptr)
109   {
110     if (ptr == NULL) return;
111     #if defined(LMP_USE_TBB_ALLOCATOR)
112     scalable_aligned_free(ptr);
113     #else
114     free(ptr);
115     #endif
116   }
```

Figure 8.15 – Code snippet from memory.cpp showing the sfree() method

For higher dimensional arrays, the procedures are similar to those of 1D arrays, as illustrated in the following screenshot regarding 2D arrays:

```
112  /* --------------------------------------------------------------
113        create a 2d array
114     -------------------------------------------------------------- */
115
116     template <typename TYPE>
117     TYPE **create(TYPE **&array, int n1, int n2, const char *name)
118     {
119        bigint nbytes = ((bigint) sizeof(TYPE)) * n1*n2;
120        TYPE *data = (TYPE *) smalloc(nbytes,name);
121        nbytes = ((bigint) sizeof(TYPE *)) * n1;
122        array = (TYPE **) smalloc(nbytes,name);
123
124        bigint n = 0;
125        for (int i = 0; i < n1; i++) {
126           array[i] = &data[n];
127           n += n2;
128        }
129        return array;
130     }
131
132     template <typename TYPE>
133     TYPE ***create(TYPE ***& /*array*/, int /*n1*/, int /*n2*/, const char *name)
134     {fail(name); return NULL;}
```

Figure 8.16 – Code snippet from memory.h showing the create() method for 2D arrays

As you can see, `template` needs four arguments: the pointer reference array, the number of rows (n1), the number of columns (n2), and the array's name. A 1D memory allocation of length **n1** is created (*line 121*) and a 1D memory chain of length **n2** is added to each of its elements (*lines 124 to 128*). The following diagram illustrates the architecture of the 2D data structure we've just described:

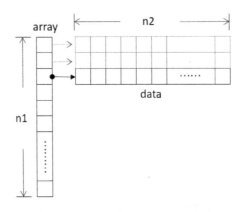

Figure 8.17 – 2D array architecture

In this section, we discussed how memory allocation in the LAMMPS source code works by looking at the `Memory` class.

In the next section, we will explain how the forces and energies associated with angles in a chain of atoms are accommodated in the `Angle` class. While the `Angle` class does not sit alongside the supporting classes discussed in this chapter, its code and physics may be relevant to users who intend to implement custom angle styles. Due to this, we have provided a section that describes how the `Angle` class implements intra-molecular forces and potentials. Similar analyses can be extended to other intra-molecular interactions, such as bonds and dihedrals.

Discussing the Angle and angle/harmonic classes

In this section, we will study the `Angle` class and demonstrate a typical angle-dependent potential, as implemented by the `angle/harmonic` child class.

An **angle-dependent potential** is a form of intramolecular potential present among bonded atoms. An angle that's formed by a chain of three bonded atoms can exert forces on those three atoms based on the deviation of this angle from an equilibrium value.

Given an angle-dependent potential, $U(\theta)$, we can calculate the force on each atom using the procedure presented. The following diagram shows a chain of three bonded atoms $(1, 2, 3)$ with (x_1, y_1, z_1), (x_2, y_2, z_2), and (x_3, y_3, z_3) coordinates, respectively, that form an angle, θ:

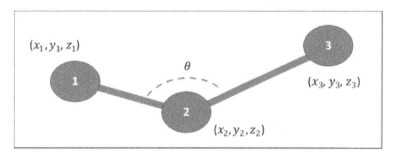

Figure 8.18 – An angle, $\boldsymbol{\theta}$, formed by three bonded atoms – 1,2,3

As you can see, the, $\vec{r}_1$ bond vector that points from atom **2** to atom **1** is formulated as follows:

$$\vec{r}_1 = (x_1 - x_2, y_1 - y_2, z_1 - z_2)$$

Similarly, the $\vec{r}_2$ bond vector that points from atom **2** to atom **3** is formulated as follows:

$$\vec{r}_2 = (x_3 - x_2, y_3 - y_2, z_3 - z_2)$$

The cosine of angle θ can be calculated using the dot product of $\vec{r}_1$ and $\vec{r}_2$:

$$\vec{r}_1 \cdot \vec{r}_2 = |\vec{r}_1||\vec{r}_2| \cos\theta \Rightarrow \cos\theta$$
$$= \frac{(x_1 - x_2)(x_3 - x_2) + (y_1 - y_2)(y_3 - y_2) + (z_1 - z_2)(z_3 - z_2)}{|\vec{r}_1||\vec{r}_2|}$$

In order to find the force, $\vec{F}$, on an atom, we need to find the gradient of $U(\theta)$:

$$\vec{F} = -\nabla U = \left(-\frac{\partial U}{\partial x}, -\frac{\partial U}{\partial y}, -\frac{\partial U}{\partial z}\right)$$

Each derivative can be converted into a derivative of $\cos\theta$ and then to a derivative of θ using the chain rule; for example:

$$\frac{\partial U}{\partial x} = \frac{\partial U}{\partial(\cos\theta)} \cdot \frac{\partial(\cos\theta)}{\partial x} = \left[\frac{\partial\theta}{\partial(\cos\theta)} \cdot \frac{\partial U}{\partial\theta}\right] \cdot \frac{\partial(\cos\theta)}{\partial x} = \left[-\frac{1}{\sin\theta} \cdot \frac{\partial U}{\partial\theta}\right] \cdot \frac{\partial(\cos\theta)}{\partial x}$$

The derivative with respect to x in the preceding equation can be evaluated for each atom from the expression of $\cos\theta$ we derived earlier. For atom **1**, the derivative with respect to x_1 is calculated as follows:

$$\frac{\partial(\cos\theta)}{\partial x_1} = \frac{x_3 - x_2}{|\vec{r}_1||\vec{r}_2|} - \frac{(x_1 - x_2)\cos\theta}{|\vec{r}_1|^2}$$

Therefore, the force components acting on atom **1** are as follows:

- The x-component, F_{1x}, which is given as follows:

$$F_{1x} = \frac{1}{\sin\theta} \cdot \frac{\partial U}{\partial\theta} \cdot \left[\frac{x_3 - x_2}{|\vec{r}_1||\vec{r}_2|} - \cos\theta\frac{(x_1 - x_2)}{|\vec{r}_1|^2}\right]$$

- The y-component, F_{1y}, which is given as follows:

$$F_{1y} = \frac{1}{\sin\theta} \cdot \frac{\partial U}{\partial\theta} \cdot \left[\frac{y_3 - y_2}{|\vec{r}_1||\vec{r}_2|} - \cos\theta\frac{(y_1 - y_2)}{|\vec{r}_1|^2}\right]$$

- The z-component, F_{1z}, which is given as follows:

$$F_{1z} = \frac{1}{\sin\theta} \cdot \frac{\partial U}{\partial\theta} \cdot \left[\frac{z_3 - z_2}{|\vec{r}_1||\vec{r}_2|} - \cos\theta \frac{(z_1 - z_2)}{|\vec{r}_1|^2}\right]$$

The force components on atom **3** are identical to the components on atom **1**, with indices *1* and *3* switched. These are as follows:

- The x-component, F_{3x}, as follows:

$$F_{3x} = \frac{1}{\sin\theta} \cdot \frac{\partial U}{\partial\theta} \cdot \left[\frac{x_1 - x_2}{|\vec{r}_1||\vec{r}_2|} - \cos\theta \frac{(x_3 - x_2)}{|\vec{r}_2|^2}\right]$$

- The y-component, F_{3y}, as follows:

$$F_{3y} = \frac{1}{\sin\theta} \cdot \frac{\partial U}{\partial\theta} \cdot \left[\frac{y_1 - y_2}{|\vec{r}_1||\vec{r}_2|} - \cos\theta \frac{(y_3 - y_2)}{|\vec{r}_2|^2}\right]$$

- The z-component, F_{3z}, as follows:

$$F_{3z} = \frac{1}{\sin\theta} \cdot \frac{\partial U}{\partial\theta} \cdot \left[\frac{z_1 - z_2}{|\vec{r}_1||\vec{r}_2|} - \cos\theta \frac{(z_3 - z_2)}{|\vec{r}_2|^2}\right]$$

The force components on atom **2** are calculated similarly, except that the derivative, $\partial U / \partial x_2$, of $\cos\theta$ with respect to x_2 is used in the calculation:

- The x-component, F_{2x}:

$$F_{2x} = \frac{1}{\sin\theta} \cdot \frac{\partial U}{\partial\theta} \cdot \left[\cos\theta\left(\frac{x_1 - x_2}{|\vec{r}_1|^2} + \frac{x_3 - x_2}{|\vec{r}_2|^2}\right) - \frac{(x_1 - x_2) + (x_3 - x_2)}{|\vec{r}_1||\vec{r}_2|}\right]$$

- The y-component, F_{2y}:

$$F_{2y} = \frac{1}{\sin\theta} \cdot \frac{\partial U}{\partial\theta} \cdot \left[\cos\theta\left(\frac{y_1 - y_2}{|\vec{r}_1|^2} + \frac{y_3 - y_2}{|\vec{r}_2|^2}\right) - \frac{(y_1 - y_2) + (y_3 - y_2)}{|\vec{r}_1||\vec{r}_2|}\right]$$

- The z-component, F_{2z}:

$$F_{2z} = \frac{1}{\sin\theta} \cdot \frac{\partial U}{\partial\theta} \cdot \left[\cos\theta\left(\frac{z_1 - z_2}{|\vec{r}_1|^2} + \frac{z_3 - z_2}{|\vec{r}_2|^2}\right) - \frac{(z_1 - z_2) + (z_3 - z_2)}{|\vec{r}_1||\vec{r}_2|}\right]$$

This also yields the following relationship between the force on atom **2** ($\vec{F}_2$) and the forces on atom **1** ($\vec{F}_1$) and atom **3** ($\vec{F}_3$):

$$\vec{F}_2 = -\vec{F}_1 - \vec{F}_3$$

These equations are implemented for various angle styles with different $U(\theta)$ in the angle child classes, as we will discuss next.

The Angle class

The `Angle` class, which is implemented in `angle.cpp` and `angle.h`, checks if all the coefficients for angle potentials have been set in the `init()` method, as shown in the following screenshot:

```
61   /* ----------------------------------------------------------------------
62       check if all coeffs are set
63   ---------------------------------------------------------------------- */
64
65   void Angle::init()
66   {
67     if (!allocated && atom->nangletypes)
68       error->all(FLERR,"Angle coeffs are not set");
69     for (int i = 1; i <= atom->nangletypes; i++)
70       if (setflag[i] == 0) error->all(FLERR,"All angle coeffs are not set");
71
72     init_style();
73   }
```

Figure 8.19 – Code snippet from angle.cpp showing the init() method

As you can see, the `angle.h` header file introduces the 1D `setflag[]` array to keep track of any angle coefficients that have been assigned, similar to the procedure in pair styles.

Child angle styles inherit from the `Angle` parent class and implement their angle potentials. The **harmonic angle potential** is commonly used to model angles that have been generated by covalent bonds. We will discuss this in more detail next.

The angle/harmonic class

This class inherits from the `Angle` class and implements a harmonic potential, $U(\theta)$, that depends on a pre-factor, K, and on the square of the deviation of the angle, θ, from an equilibrium angle, θ_0, according to the following equation:

$$U(\theta) = K(\theta - \theta_0)^2$$

In the LAMMPS input script, the command that's used to implement this angle style has the following form (see `https://lammps.sandia.gov/doc/angle_harmonic.html`):

```
angle_style harmonic
angle_coeff  ID K θ₀
```

Here, `ID` refers to the angle type that this angle style applies to. The input script parameters are parsed by `angle_harmonic.cpp` (located in the `MOLECULE` package) in the `coeff()` method, as shown in the following screenshot:

```
165  /* ----------------------------------------------------------
166     set coeffs for one or more types
167  ---------------------------------------------------------- */
168
169  void AngleHarmonic::coeff(int narg, char **arg)
170  {
171    if (narg != 3) error->all(FLERR,"Incorrect args for angle coefficients");
172    if (!allocated) allocate();
173
174    int ilo,ihi;
175    force->bounds(FLERR,arg[0],atom->nangletypes,ilo,ihi);
176
177    double k_one = force->numeric(FLERR,arg[1]);
178    double theta0_one = force->numeric(FLERR,arg[2]);
179
180    // convert theta0 from degrees to radians
181
182    int count = 0;
183    for (int i = ilo; i <= ihi; i++) {
184      k[i] = k_one;
185      theta0[i] = theta0_one/180.0 * MY_PI;
186      setflag[i] = 1;
187      count++;
188    }
189
190    if (count == 0) error->all(FLERR,"Incorrect args for angle coefficients");
191  }
```

Figure 8.20 – Code snippet from angle_harmonic.cpp showing the coeff() method

As you can see, the `coeff()` method permits exactly three arguments (*line 171*), including the angle type ID (*line 175*), K (*line 177*), and θ_0 (*line 178*). Since θ_0 is accepted in the input script in degrees, it is converted into radians (*line 185*) for calculation convenience.

The force calculations are performed in the `compute ()` method, as shown here:

```
71   for (n = 0; n < nanglelist; n++) {
72       i1 = anglelist[n][0];
73       i2 = anglelist[n][1];
74       i3 = anglelist[n][2];
75       type = anglelist[n][3];
76
77       // 1st bond
78
79       delx1 = x[i1][0] - x[i2][0];
80       dely1 = x[i1][1] - x[i2][1];
81       delz1 = x[i1][2] - x[i2][2];
82
83       rsq1 = delx1*delx1 + dely1*dely1 + delz1*delz1;
84       r1 = sqrt(rsq1);
85
86       // 2nd bond
87
88       delx2 = x[i3][0] - x[i2][0];
89       dely2 = x[i3][1] - x[i2][1];
90       delz2 = x[i3][2] - x[i2][2];
91
92       rsq2 = delx2*delx2 + dely2*dely2 + delz2*delz2;
93       r2 = sqrt(rsq2);
94
95       // angle (cos and sin)
96
97       c = delx1*delx2 + dely1*dely2 + delz1*delz2;
98       c /= r1*r2;
99
100      if (c > 1.0) c = 1.0;
101      if (c < -1.0) c = -1.0;
102
103      s = sqrt(1.0 - c*c);
104      if (s < SMALL) s = SMALL;
105      s = 1.0/s;

109      dtheta = acos(c) - theta0[type];
110      tk = k[type] * dtheta;
111
112      if (eflag) eangle = tk*dtheta;
113
114      a = -2.0 * tk * s;
115      a11 = a*c / rsq1;
116      a12 = -a / (r1*r2);
117      a22 = a*c / rsq2;
118
119      f1[0] = a11*delx1 + a12*delx2;
120      f1[1] = a11*dely1 + a12*dely2;
121      f1[2] = a11*delz1 + a12*delz2;
122      f3[0] = a22*delx2 + a12*delx1;
123      f3[1] = a22*dely2 + a12*dely1;
124      f3[2] = a22*delz2 + a12*delz1;
125
126      // apply force to each of 3 atoms
127
128      if (newton_bond || i1 < nlocal) {
129          f[i1][0] += f1[0];
130          f[i1][1] += f1[1];
131          f[i1][2] += f1[2];
132      }
133
134      if (newton_bond || i2 < nlocal) {
135          f[i2][0] -= f1[0] + f3[0];
136          f[i2][1] -= f1[1] + f3[1];
137          f[i2][2] -= f1[2] + f3[2];
138      }
139
140      if (newton_bond || i3 < nlocal) {
141          f[i3][0] += f3[0];
142          f[i3][1] += f3[1];
143          f[i3][2] += f3[2];
144      }
```

Figure 8.21 – Code snippet from angle_harmonic.cpp showing the compute() method

As you can see, the `neighbor->anglelist` method (*line 66*) is used to access all the angles in the system. By looping over all the angles (*line 71*), the three constituent atoms in the atom chain for each angle (i1,i2,i3) are identified (*lines 72 to 74*), as well as the angle type (*line 75*). Since i2 corresponds to the atom at the center of the chain, the bond vector components from i2 to i1 are calculated in *lines 79 to 81*, and those from i2 to i3 are calculated in *lines 88 to 90*. The corresponding bond lengths, r1 and r2, are found in *lines 84 and 93*, respectively.

The cosine of the angle (c) is calculated from the dot product of the bond vectors using the equation we derived earlier, as implemented in *lines 97 and 98*, and checked for domain compatibility (for example, if it's contained in the range [-1,1]) in *lines 100 and 101*. The sine of the angle is calculated with $\sqrt{1 - c^2}$ in *line 103* and is approximated as the value of the angle (in radians) if the angle is small (less than 0.001 rad) in *line 104*. The reciprocal of this sine ($1/\sin\theta$) is stored as a variable, s (*line 105*), in order to reduce computational overhead when you're finding reciprocals in the rest of the calculations.

The angle deviation, $(\theta - \theta_0)$, is calculated in *line 109* and is stored as the dtheta variable, which calculates θ using arccos(c) and subtracts θ_0. In *line 110*, the tk variable effectively stores the quantity, $K(\theta - \theta_0)$, which is half of $\partial U / \partial \theta$ for this harmonic potential.

In *lines 114 to 117*, the following variables and their corresponding quantities are calculated:

- The a variable is calculated as follows, which is the equivalent to the $-\dfrac{1}{\sin \theta} \cdot \dfrac{\partial U}{\partial \theta}$ quantity for this potential:

$$a = -\frac{2K(\theta - \theta_0)}{\sin \theta}$$

- The a11 variable is given as follows:

$$a11 = -\frac{2K(\theta - \theta_0)}{\sin \theta} \frac{\cos \theta}{r1^2}$$

- The a12 variable is given as follows:

$$a12 = -\frac{2K(\theta - \theta_0)}{\sin \theta} \frac{1}{r1 \, r2}$$

- The a22 variable is given as follows:

$$a22 = -\frac{2K(\theta - \theta_0)}{\sin \theta} \frac{\cos \theta}{r2^2}$$

Then, in *lines 119 to 124*, the force components generated by the angle potential acting on i1 and i3 are calculated using the force equations we derived earlier (see the components of $\vec{F}_1$ and $\vec{F}_3$). These forces are applied to i1 in *lines 128 to 132* and to i3 in *lines 140 to 144*. Finally, the force components on i2 are applied using the negative sum of the corresponding force components of i1 and i3 in *lines 134 to 138*, as shown in the preceding screenshot.

The angle potential, $U(\theta) = K(\theta - \theta_0)^2$, can be returned by the `single()` function, as shown in the following screenshot:

```
240    double AngleHarmonic::single(int type, int i1, int i2, int i3)
241    {
242        double **x = atom->x;
243
244        double delx1 = x[i1][0] - x[i2][0];
245        double dely1 = x[i1][1] - x[i2][1];
246        double delz1 = x[i1][2] - x[i2][2];
247        domain->minimum_image(delx1,dely1,delz1);
248        double r1 = sqrt(delx1*delx1 + dely1*dely1 + delz1*delz1);
249
250        double delx2 = x[i3][0] - x[i2][0];
251        double dely2 = x[i3][1] - x[i2][1];
252        double delz2 = x[i3][2] - x[i2][2];
253        domain->minimum_image(delx2,dely2,delz2);
254        double r2 = sqrt(delx2*delx2 + dely2*dely2 + delz2*delz2);
255
256        double c = delx1*delx2 + dely1*dely2 + delz1*delz2;
257        c /= r1*r2;
258        if (c > 1.0) c = 1.0;
259        if (c < -1.0) c = -1.0;
260
261        double dtheta = acos(c) - theta0[type];
262        double tk = k[type] * dtheta;
263        return tk*dtheta;
264    }
```

Figure 8.22 – Code snippet from angle_harmonic.cpp showing the single() method

In this method, the `tk` variable, which effectively stores the quantity, $K(\theta - \theta_0)$, is multiplied by the `dtheta` variable to return the potential as $K(\theta - \theta_0)^2$.

In this section, the mechanism behind angle styles has been described and illustrated using the harmonic angle potential. Other angle potentials follow a similar implementation, but with differing variables to account for differing derivatives, $\partial U / \partial \theta$.

Summary

This chapter outlined some of the supporting classes that complement the fixes, computes, and pair potentials that control simulation dynamics. In this chapter, we discussed groups, variables, errors, memory, and angle styles, all of which will help you understand their supporting roles in the simulation execution and enable you to implement them in your own custom LAMMPS code.

This was also the last chapter that focuses on explicating existing LAMMPS features in terms of their source code. In the next chapter, we will write custom features into LAMMPS, starting with custom pair potentials, to provide you with some hands-on practice of modifying and extending the LAMMPS source code.

Questions

1. Which methods in `variable.cpp` need to be modified to incorporate new mathematical functions that can be evaluated using the `variable equal` command in the LAMMPS input script?

2. How should multi-dimensional arrays be declared before they are fed into a `memory->create()` method?

3. For a quartic angle potential, $U(\theta) = K(\theta - \theta_0)^4$, what form should the a variable be in, in the corresponding angle style's `.cpp` file?

Section 3:
Modifying the
Source Code

You have understood the LAMMPS source code and the programming logic, which is encoded. Now it is time to make your own modifications to it and to implement custom features in your simulations.

In this section, you will learn how to modify and extend the LAMMPS source code by writing and implementing custom features in the source code. Examples are provided to illustrate the process of adding modifications according to desired simulation goals.

This section comprises the following chapters:

- *Chapter 09, Modifying Pair Potentials*
- *Chapter 10, Modifying Force Applications*
- *Chapter 11, Modifying Thermostats*

9
Modifying Pair Potentials

In the previous chapters, we discussed various classes that implement MD features and LAMMPS tools, such as **pair styles**, **fixes**, **computes**, **variables**, and **groups**. From this chapter onward, we will write custom features into LAMMPS, starting with **custom pair potentials**.

In this chapter, we will construct custom pair potentials to describe the process of writing and incorporating them in a LAMMPS input script. In the process, we will use the content covered in the previous chapters to program LAMMPS according to our requirements.

We will cover the following pair potentials in this chapter:

- Writing a harmonic potential
- Writing a height-dependent pair potential
- Writing a tangential friction-based pair style for spherical atoms

By the end of this chapter, you will have learned how to write your own pair styles and how to connect information from previous chapters to custom pair styles.

Technical requirements

To execute the instructions in this chapter, you need a text editor (for example, **Notepad++** or **Gedit**) and a platform to compile LAMMPS (for example, a **Linux Terminal**).

You can find the full source code used in this chapter here: `https://github.com/PacktPublishing/Extending-and-Modifying-LAMMPS-Writing-Your-Own-Source-Code`

This is the link to download LAMMPS: `https://lammps.sandia.gov/doc/Install.html`. The LAMMPS GitHub link is `https://github.com/lammps/lammps`, where the source code can be found as well.

Writing a harmonic potential

In this section, we will write a simple pairwise potential, that is, a **harmonic potential**, between two atoms.

A *radially-symmetric* harmonic potential tries to exert a force upon an atom pointed in the direction of the minimum energy location. The functional form of the harmonic potential, $V_H(r)$, is given by the following:

$$V_H(r) = \frac{1}{2}k_{sp}(r - r_0)^2 - \varepsilon_0$$

From the preceding equation, k_{sp} is the spring constant, r_0 is the equilibrium distance, and ε_0 is the well-depth of this harmonic potential. The radial force from this potential, $F_H(r)$, is, therefore, given as follows:

$$F_H(r) = -\frac{dV_H(r)}{dr} = -k_{sp}(r - r_0)$$

Accordingly, the *x*, *y*, *z* force components (F_{Hx}, F_{Hy}, F_{Hz}) of F_H are calculated as follows:

- x-component, $F_{Hx}(x)$:

$$F_{Hx}(x) = -k_{sp}(r - r_0)\frac{x}{r}$$

- y-component, $F_{Hy}(y)$:

$$F_{Hy}(y) = -k_{sp}(r - r_0)\frac{y}{r}$$

- z-component, $F_{Hz}(z)$:

$$F_{Hz}(z) = -k_{sp}(r - r_0)\frac{z}{r}$$

To implement this harmonic pair style, we choose a similar pair style and make modifications. Among the many choices available, we will choose `Pair Morse`, which we analyzed earlier in *Chapter 5, Understanding Pair Styles*.

The following sections will describe the required changes to convert `Pair Morse` into a harmonic pair potential.

Changing class names

To change the class names, we will follow these steps:

1. First, we make copies of `pair_morse.cpp` and `pair_morse.h`, and rename them `pair_harmonic.cpp` and `pair_harmonic.h`, respectively. If the filenames start with *pair*, then they are automatically appended into `style_pair.h` during compilation. If not, they have to be manually added to it before compilation.

2. Then, in the newly created `pair_harmonic.h` file, we change the class names from `Morse` to `Harmonic`, as shown in the following screenshot:

```
14  #ifdef PAIR_CLASS
15
16    PairStyle(morse,PairMorse)
17
18    #else
19
20  #ifndef LMP_PAIR_MORSE_H
21    #define LMP_PAIR_MORSE_H
22
23    #include "pair.h"
24
25  namespace LAMMPS_NS {
26
27  class PairMorse : public Pair {
28    public:
29      PairMorse(class LAMMPS *);
30      virtual ~PairMorse();
31      virtual void compute(int, int);
```

```
14  #ifdef PAIR_CLASS
15
16    PairStyle(harmonic,PairHarmonic)
17
18    #else
19
20  #ifndef LMP_PAIR_HARMONIC_H
21    #define LMP_PAIR_HARMONIC_H
22
23    #include "pair.h"
24
25  namespace LAMMPS_NS {
26
27  class PairHarmonic : public Pair {
28    public:
29      PairHarmonic(class LAMMPS *);
30      virtual ~PairHarmonic();
31      virtual void compute(int, int);
```

Figure 9.1 – Changes in class names between pair_morse.h (left) and pair_harmonic.h (right)

On *line 16*, the pair style name (`PairHarmonic`) and the name of the pair in the LAMMPS input script (`harmonic`) are defined. The class name is changed to `PairHarmonic` in *line 27* and *lines 29 to 30*.

3. Variables defined in `pair_morse.h` include D_0, α, r_0, which need to be changed to $k_{sp}, \varepsilon_0, r_0$ in `pair_harmonic.h`, as shown in the following screenshot:

```
45    protected:
46      double cut_global;
47      double **cut;
48      double **d0,**alpha,**r0;
49      double **morse1;
50      double **offset;
```

```
45    protected:
46      double cut_global;
47      double **cut;
48      double **ksp, **e0, **r0; // SM
49      double **offset;
```

Figure 9.2 – Variable changes between pair_morse.h (left) and pair_harmonic.h (right)

The variable for global cutoff (`cut_global`), the arrays for local cutoff (`cut []
[]`), and the offset in potential (`offset [] []`) are kept unchanged while the array to facilitate Morse potential calculation (`morse1 [] []`) is removed in `pair_
harmonic.h`. As you can see in the preceding screenshot, on *line 48*, the quantity $D_0$ (`d0 [] []`) is changed to $k_{sp}$ (`ksp [] []`), and the quantity $\alpha$ (`alpha [] []`) is changed to $\varepsilon_0$ (`e0 [] []`) whereas the cutoff (`r0 [] []`) is unchanged (I have placed my initials, `SM`, next to the line to indicate the modification made):

In `pair_harmonic.cpp`, the list of name changes made are shown in the following table:

Line Number	Change in pair_harmonic.cpp	Original code in pair_morse.cpp
14	`#include "pair_harmonic.h"`	`#include "pair_morse.h"`
30	`PairHarmonic::PairHarmonic(LAMMPS *lmp) : Pair(lmp)`	`PairMorse::PairMorse(LAMMPS *lmp) : Pair(lmp)`
38	`PairHarmonic::~PairHarmonic()`	`PairMorse::~PairMorse()`
53	`void PairHarmonic::compute()`	`void PairMorse::compute()`
130	`void PairHarmonic::allocate()`	`void PairMorse::allocate()`
154	`void PairHarmonic::settings()`	`void PairMorse::settings()`
174	`void PairHarmonic::coeff()`	`void PairMorse::coeff()`
211	`double PairHarmonic::init_one()`	`double PairMorse::init_one()`
232	`void PairHarmonic::write_restart()`	`void PairMorse::write_restart()`
253	`void PairHarmonic::read_restart()`	`void PairMorse::read_restart()`
284	`void PairHarmonic::write_restart_settings()`	`void PairMorse::write_restart_settings()`
295	`void PairHarmonic::read_restart_settings()`	`void PairMorse::read_restart_settings()`
311	`void PairHarmonic::write_data()`	`void PairMorse::write_data()`
321	`void PairHarmonic::write_data_all()`	`void PairMorse::write_data_all()`
331	`double PairHarmonic::single()`	`double PairMorse::single()`
347	`void *PairHarmonic::extract()`	`void *PairMorse::extract()`

Table 9.1 – A list of changes made to names from pair_morse.cpp to pair_harmonic.cpp

The changes listed in the preceding table effectively create a new pair style called `Pair Harmonic` that can be compiled successfully.

Having changed names and importing the proper header file, we next look at implementing proper quantities and equations at the proper places in `pair_harmonic.cpp`.

Changing variables and equations

The following variable changes are made from `pair_morse.cpp` to `pair_harmonic.cpp`: all `d0` instances are changed to `ksp` and `alpha` to `e0`. Also, all references to `morse1` are removed, either by deleting them in the destructor, `init_one()` and `allocate()` methods, or by replacing them with a different quantity as in the `compute()` and `single()` methods.

In the `compute()` method, the `fpair` variable is replaced to represent the quantity $-k_{sp}(r - r_0)/r$ multiplied by the scaling factor, `factor_lj`, as shown in the following screenshot:

```
97    if (rsq < cutsq[itype][jtype]) {
98        r = sqrt(rsq);
99        dr = r - r0[itype][jtype];
100       fpair = -factor_lj * ksp[itype][jtype] * dr / r;    // SM
101
102       f[i][0] += delx*fpair;
103       f[i][1] += dely*fpair;
104       f[i][2] += delz*fpair;
105       if (newton_pair || j < nlocal) {
106           f[j][0] -= delx*fpair;
107           f[j][1] -= dely*fpair;
108           f[j][2] -= delz*fpair;
109       }
110
111       if (eflag) {
112           evdwl = 0.5 * ksp[itype][jtype] * (dr*dr) - e0[itype][jtype] -
113               offset[itype][jtype];    // SM
114           evdwl *= factor_lj;
115       }
```

Figure 9.3 – Code snippet from the pair_harmonic.cpp showing the compute() method

As you can see in the preceding screenshot, on *line 100*, `fpair` is effectively defined as follows:

$$fpair = -factor\_lj * \frac{k_{sp}(r - r_0)}{r}$$

The assignments of the (x, y, z) force components (`fx`, `fy`, `fz`) are unchanged from `pair_morse.cpp` and are performed in *lines 102* to *109* where `fpair` is multiplied with the displacement vector components (`delx`, `dely`, `delz`).

Then, in *line 112* to *113*, the potential (`evdwl`) is defined with an offset value:

$$evdwl = \frac{1}{2}k_{sp}(r - r_0)^2 - \varepsilon_0 - offset$$

The preceding changes, in the `compute()` method, calculate the harmonic force and potential when this pair style is called during a run. When the `single()` method is called during a compute, the force and potential function need to be redefined, as shown in the following screenshot:

```
331  double PairHarmonic::single(int /*i*/, int /*j*/, int itype, int jtype, double rsq,
332                              double /*factor_coul*/, double factor_lj,
333                              double &fforce)
334  {
335      double r,dr,phi;
336
337      r = sqrt(rsq);
338      dr = r - r0[itype][jtype];
339      fforce = -factor_lj * ksp[itype][jtype] * dr / r; // SM
340
341      phi = 0.5 * ksp[itype][jtype] * (dr*dr) - e0[itype][jtype] - offset[itype][jtype];    // SM
342      return factor_lj*phi;
343  }
```

Figure 9.4 – Code snippet from the pair_harmonic.cpp showing the single() method

As you can see, similar to the compute () method, the pairwise force is defined as the fforce variable (*line 339*) and the potential including the offset is defined as the phi variable (*line 341*).

The equation to calculate the offset is modified in the init_one () method, as shown next:

```
207  /* ----------------------------------------------------------------
208      init for one type pair i,j and corresponding j,i
209  ----------------------------------------------------------------- */
210
211  double PairHarmonic::init_one(int i, int j)
212  {
213      if (setflag[i][j] == 0) error->all(FLERR,"All pair coeffs are not set");
214
215      if (offset_flag) {
216          double dr = cut[i][j] - r0[i][j];                          // SM
217          offset[i][j] = 0.5 * ksp[i][j] * (dr*dr) - e0[i][j];       // SM
218      } else offset[i][j] = 0.0;
219
220      ksp[j][i] = ksp[i][j];     // SM
221      e0[j][i] = e0[i][j];       // SM
222      r0[j][i] = r0[i][j];
223      offset[j][i] = offset[i][j];
224
225      return cut[i][j];
226  }
```

Figure 9.5 – Code snippet from the pair_harmonic.cpp showing the init_one() method

As you can see, on *line 217*, the offset is calculated as the value of the potential at the cutoff distance, $r = r_{cut}$:

$$\text{offset} = \frac{1}{2}k_{sp}(r_{cut} - r_0)^2 - \varepsilon_0$$

This offset is calculated for the (itype, jtype) pair and is copied to the (jtype, itype) pair in *line 223* to maintain symmetry when calling the offset in other methods (see *Chapter 5, Understanding Pair Styles*).

Now, that we have implemented the force and potential, the input parameters will be parsed next.

Parsing input parameters for Pair Harmonic

In the LAMMPS input script, the Morse pair style and the global cutoff are defined using the pair_style command, which can be reused without any change for the pair harmonic style. Therefore, the contents of the settings() method in pair_harmonic.cpp is left identical to that of pair_morse.cpp.

When defining the potential parameters, $k_{sp}, r_0, \varepsilon_0$, the appropriate changes are made in the coeff() method, as depicted in the following screenshot:

```
187  double d0_one = force->numeric(FLERR,arg[ ]);
188  double alpha_one = force->numeric(FLERR,arg[ ]);
189  double r0_one = force->numeric(FLERR,arg[ ]);
190
191  double cut_one = cut_global;
192  if (narg ==  ) cut_one = force->numeric(FLERR,arg[ ]);
193
194  int count = 0;
195  for (int i = ilo; i <= ihi; i++) {
196      for (int j = MAX(jlo,i); j <= jhi; j++) {
197          d0[i][j] = d0_one;
198          alpha[i][j] = alpha_one;
199          r0[i][j] = r0_one;
200          cut[i][j] = cut_one;
201          setflag[i][j] = 1;
202          count++;
203      }
```

```
184  double ksp_one = force->numeric(FLERR,arg[ ]);   // SM
185  double r0_one = force->numeric(FLERR,arg[ ]);    // SM
186  double e0_one = force->numeric(FLERR,arg[ ]);    // SM
187
188  double cut_one = cut_global;
189  if (narg ==  ) cut_one = force->numeric(FLERR,arg[ ]);
190
191  int count = 0;
192  for (int i = ilo; i <= ihi; i++) {
193      for (int j = MAX(jlo,i); j <= jhi; j++) {
194          ksp[i][j] = ksp_one;  // SM
195          e0[i][j] = e0_one;    // SM
196          r0[i][j] = r0_one;
197          cut[i][j] = cut_one;
198          setflag[i][j] = 1;
199          count++;
200      }
```

Figure 9.6 – Changes in coeff() methods of pair_morse.cpp (left) and pair_harmonic.cpp (right)

As you can see, in both pair_morse.cpp and pair_harmonic.cpp, exactly five or six input parameters are required, where the first two input parameters represent the atom types on which the potential applies. Then, the next three parameters in pair_morse.cpp represent the D_0, α, r_0, which are changed to $k_{sp}, r_0, \varepsilon_0$ in pair_harmonic.cpp. In *lines 184* to *186* of pair_harmonic.cpp, temporary placeholder variables, ksp_one, r0_one, and e0_one, are used to parse the values of $k_{sp}, r_0, \varepsilon_0$, respectively from the input script. Then, the ksp[][], r0[][], and e0[][] arrays are populated with the parsed values matched to the correct atom pairs in *lines 194* to *196*.

Altogether, the input script syntax for this harmonic potential becomes as follows:

```
pair_style  harmonic GLOBAL_CUTOFF
pair_coeff  TYPE1    TYPE2    ksp  r0  e0  LOCAL_CUTOFF
```

From the preceding code, `TYPE1` and `TYPE2` are the atom types concerned and the other parameters are self-explanatory. This pair style is tested with a trial LAMMPS input script in the next section.

Trial run (in.Test_PairHarmonic)

A simple LAMMPS script is created to test the forces and potential of the harmonic pair potential between two atoms. One atom is kept stationary and the other atom is allowed to oscillate along the x-direction under its interaction with the stationary atom. The force on the oscillating atom and the **Potential Energy** (**PE**) between the two atoms are written to disk at fixed intervals.

The simple LAMMPS script is presented next. The simulation is initialized, and two atoms are created:

```
# -------------------------------------
# INITIALIZE SIMULATION
# -------------------------------------
units metal
dimension 3
boundary p p p
atom_style atomic
atom_modify map array
# -------------------------------------
# DEFINE REGION
# -------------------------------------
region r0  block  0 20  0 20  0 20 units box
# -------------------------------------
# CREATE ATOMS
# -------------------------------------
create_box 1 r0
mass    1 10.0
create_atoms 1 single  10 10 10 units box
group G1 id 1
create_atoms 1 single  13 10 10 units box
group G2 id 2
```

The `Pair Harmonic` style is assigned to the atoms and G2 is time-integrated:

```
# ----------------------
# PAIR STYLES
# ----------------------
pair_style  harmonic 5.0
pair_coeff  1 1  1.0   2.0    2.0
# ----------------------
# FIXES
# ----------------------
compute SPRING_PE G1 group/group G2
variable SPRING_PE equal c_SPRING_PE
variable x2 equal x[2]
variable fx equal fx[2]
velocity G2 set 50.0 0 0


fix FREEZE G1 setforce 0 0 0
fix NVE G2 nve
fix PRINT_PE all print 10 "${x2} ${fx} ${SPRING_PE}" file
outputHARMONIC.dat


run 10000
```

As you can see, the harmonic pair potential is implemented in bold text, which assigns a global cutoff of 5.0 Å, k_{sp} value of 1.0 eV/Å^2, r_0 value of 2.0 Å, and ε_0 value of 2.0 eV. This potential acts between two atoms grouped as G1 and G2 that are initially located at coordinates of (10,0,0) Å and (13,0,0) Å, as defined under the CREATE ATOMS header.

While G1 is immobilized using the `fix setforce` command, G2 is assigned an initial velocity vector of (50,0,0) Å/ps and time-integrated via the `fix NVE` command. This way, G2 is confined to move only along the *x*-axis, and according to the parameters designated, G2 should perform sinusoidal motion centered at x=12.0 Å with a minimum energy of -2.0 eV.

The *x*-coordinate of G2, *x*-component of force (F_x) on G2, and the PE between the atoms are written to disk using the `fix print` command. The data written to disk is used to create plots of the trajectory of G2, the position-dependence of F_x, and the position-dependence of PE, as shown in the following diagram:

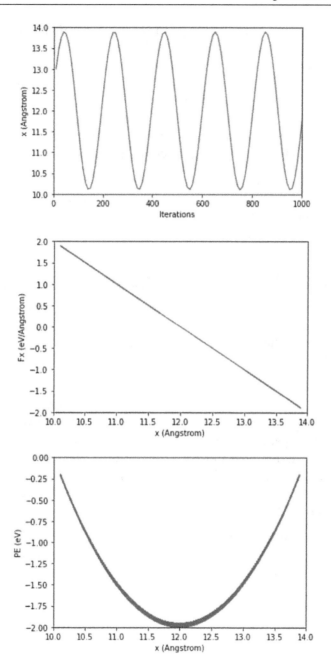

Figure 9.7 – Plots of x versus time (top), $\mathbf{F_x}$ versus x (middle), and PE versus x (bottom) for pair_harmonic.cpp

As you can see, this diagram shows that G2 performs simple harmonic oscillations under this setup as demonstrated by the sinusoidal trajectory (*top graph*), linear position-dependence of F_x (*middle graph*), and quadratic position-dependence of PE (*bottom graph*). Therefore, this trial run generates the output expected from theory and serves as a simple validation of this pair potential. As with all custom-written codes, users are advised to validate their codes against reliable expected outputs, and in the case of pair potentials, the `pair_write` command (`https://lammps.sandia.gov/doc/pair_write.html`) in the LAMMPS input script can often be used to help to validate.

In this section, we implemented a radially-symmetric pair potential defined by a simple function into the LAMMPS source code by modifying an existing pair style. In the next section, we will describe a potential that decays with height and therefore applies height-dependent forces on the paired atoms.

Writing a height-dependent pair potential

In this section, we will create a pair style that represents a potential between two atoms, which decays as the height increases from a reference level, so that both the distance between the atoms and the heights of the atoms above the reference determine the potential between them.

A height-dependent potential is relevant when simulating the interaction between atoms that are *adsorbed* on a substrate, where forces mediated by the substrate vary with the height. As a result, along with the usual inter-molecular interactions, two adsorbed atoms on the substrate experience additional interaction by virtue of their proximity to the substrate. At a certain threshold above the substrate, the interaction decays to zero. An example of such an interaction is the **McLachlan interaction** (`https://doi.org/10.1016/0039-6028(94)91259-9`) based on repulsion between dipoles of adsorbed atoms and the substrate.

A model is established where $z = z_1$ represents the reference height in the simulation box and the z-displacements of two atoms above the reference determine the additional interaction between them, as illustrated in the following diagram:

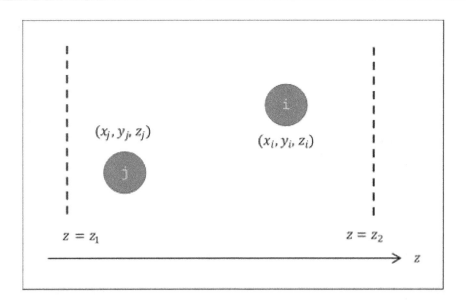

Figure 9.8 – Simulation setup showing the z-axis and z_1 and z_2, along with two atoms i and j

As you can see, in this setup, the height-dependent potential (V_{height}) applies between the dashed lines at $z = z_1$ and $z = z_2$. The two atoms, i and j, depicted have coordinates (x_i, y_i, z_i) and (x_j, y_j, z_j) respectively, and they experience the $V_{height}(x, y, z)$ if they are both located below z_2 and at least one atom is located above z_1. If both atoms are located below z_1 or at least one atom is located above z_2, then height-dependence is not considered.

The functional form of $V_{height}(x, y, z)$ consists of the usual radially symmetric potential, $V_0(x, y, z)$, and a height-dependent decay function, $f_{decay}(z)$. The decay function must start from 1 at $z = z_1$, that is, $f_{decay}(z_1) = 1$, and gradually reach 0 at $z = z_2$, that is, $f_{decay}(z_2) = 0$. For simplicity, a quadratic decay function is chosen:

$$f_{decay}(z) = a_0 + a_1(z - z_1)^2$$

From the preceding equation, $a_0 = 1$ and a_1 is a negative constant chosen to satisfy the condition, $f_{decay}(z_2) = 0$. The following diagram portrays the decay function, $f_{decay}(z)$:

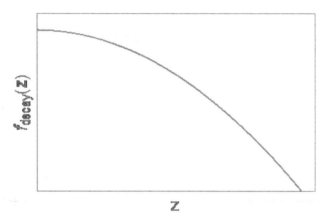

Figure 9.9 – Quadratic decay function $f_{decay} = a_0 + a_1(z - z_1)^2$ that satisfies $f_{decay}(z_1) = 1$ and $f_{decay}(z_2) = 0$

Therefore, we have the following equation for $V_{height}(x, y, z)$:

$$V_{height}(x, y, z) = V_0(x, y, z)\, f_{decay}(z)$$

Using the force vector, $\vec{F_0} = \left(-\dfrac{\partial V_0}{\partial x}, -\dfrac{\partial V_0}{\partial y}, -\dfrac{\partial V_0}{\partial z}\right)$, from the potential, $V_0(x, y, z)$, the overall force $\vec{F} = (F_x, F_y, F_z)$ components are calculated as follows:

- x-component F_x:

$$F_x = -\frac{\partial V_{height}}{\partial x} = f_{decay}(z)\left[-\frac{\partial V_0}{\partial x}\right] = f_{decay}(z)\, F_{x0}$$

- y-component F_y:

$$F_y = -\frac{\partial V_{height}}{\partial y} = f_{decay}(z)\left[-\frac{\partial V_0}{\partial y}\right] = f_{decay}(z)\, F_{y0}$$

- z-component F_z:

$$F_z = -\frac{\partial V_{height}}{\partial z} = f_{decay}(z)\left[-\frac{\partial V_0}{\partial z}\right] - V_0\frac{\partial f_{decay}}{\partial z} = f_{decay}(z)\, F_{z0} - V_0\frac{\partial f_{decay}}{\partial z}$$

From the preceding equations, (F_{x0}, F_{y0}, F_{z0}) are the (x, y, z) components of $\vec{F_0}$, which are scaled by $f_{decay}(z)$ in the overall force components. For F_z, an additional term of $V_0 \dfrac{\partial f_{decay}}{\partial z}$ has to be subtracted to account for the slope of $f_{decay}(z)$.

When calculating (F_x, F_y, F_z) for a pair of atoms that qualify for height-dependent interaction, the larger value between z_i and z_j is plugged into the corresponding force equations. That way, both the i and j atoms will experience equal and opposite F_z in accordance with Newton's third law, which would not have been guaranteed if z_i and z_j were separately used to calculate F_z for the two atoms. Therefore, the maximum z-coordinate (z_m) is calculated by comparing z_i and z_j:

$$z_m = MAX(z_i, z_j)$$

Then, z_m and $f_{decay}(z_m))$ are used to find the force components, (F_x, F_y, F_z), according to the equations presented. In the case of F_z, the directions have to be assigned based on the z-coordinates:

- Atom with *higher* z-coordinate: $F_z = f_{decay}(z_m) F_{z0} - V_0 \left.\dfrac{\partial f_{decay}}{\partial z}\right|_{z=z_m}$

- Atom with *lower* z-coordinate: $F_z = -\left(f_{decay}(z_m) F_{z0} - V_0 \left.\dfrac{\partial f_{decay}}{\partial z}\right|_{z=z_m}\right)$

To implement this height-dependent potential in LAMMPS, we will modify the `Pair Table` class since it will allow us to incorporate the decay function for any potential accommodated by `Pair Table`.

Changing the header file, pair_table.h

Copies of `pair_table.cpp` and `pair_table.h` are renamed `pair_table_z.cpp` and `pair_table_z.h`, respectively, to incorporate the height-dependence. The class names in both files are changed to `PairTableZ` and the name to be used in input scripts is changed to `tableZ` in the header file.

In addition, we introduce the `a0`, `a1`, `threshold1` and `threshold2` variables to represent the quantities $a_0, a_1, z_1,$ and z_2 in `pair_table_z.h`. The following screenshot from `pair_table_z.h` shows some of these changes:

```
16   PairStyle(tableZ,PairTableZ)
17
18   #else
19
20   #ifndef LMP_PAIR_TABLEZ_H
21   #define LMP_PAIR_TABLEZ_H
22
23   #include "pair.h"
24
25   namespace LAMMPS_NS {
26
27   class PairTableZ : public Pair {
28    public:
29      PairTableZ(class LAMMPS *);
30      virtual ~PairTableZ();
31
32      virtual void compute(int, int);
33      virtual void settings(int, char **);
34      void coeff(int, char **);
35      virtual double init_one(int, int);
36      void write_restart(FILE *);
37      void read_restart(FILE *);
38      void write_restart_settings(FILE *);
39      void read_restart_settings(FILE *);
40      virtual double single(int, int, int, int, double, double, double, double &);
41      void *extract(const char *, int &);
42
43      double a0, a1;                 // SM
44      double threshold1, threshold2;  // SM
```

Figure 9.10 – Code snippet from the pair_table_z.h

The `a0`, `a1`, `threshold1`, and `threshold2` parameters defined in *lines 43* to *44* have to be parsed from the LAMMPS input script, as discussed in the next section.

Parsing input parameters for Pair TableZ

The `Table` pair style and the global cutoff are defined using the `pair_style` command described in the `settings()` method, which can be left unchanged. In the `coeff()` method, four additional parameters need to be parsed compared to the original `Pair Table`, which is accommodated by changing the number of permitted arguments (`narg`) on *line 321*, as shown in the following screenshot:

```
319    void PairTableZ::coeff(int narg, char **arg)
320 ☐{
321      if (narg != 8 && narg != 9) error->all(FLERR,"Illegal pair_coeff command"); // SM
322      if (!allocated) allocate();
323
324      int ilo,ihi,jlo,jhi;
325      force->bounds(FLERR,arg[0],atom->ntypes,ilo,ihi);
326      force->bounds(FLERR,arg[1],atom->ntypes,jlo,jhi);
327
328      int me;
329      MPI_Comm_rank(world,&me);
330      tables = (Table *)
331        memory->srealloc(tables,(ntables+1)*sizeof(Table),"pair:tables");
332      Table *tb = &tables[ntables];
333      null_table(tb);
334      if (me == 0) read_table(tb,arg[2],arg[3]);
335      bcast_table(tb);
336
337      // set table cutoff
338
339      if (narg == 9) tb->cut = force->numeric(FLERR,arg[8]);     // SM
340      else if (tb->rflag) tb->cut = tb->rhi;
341      else tb->cut = tb->rfile[tb->ninput-1];
342
343      // SM: set threshold1, threshold2, a0, a1 for decay
344      threshold1 = force->numeric(FLERR,arg[4]);
345      threshold2 = force->numeric(FLERR,arg[5]);
346      a0 = force->numeric(FLERR,arg[6]);
347      a1 = force->numeric(FLERR,arg[7]);
```

Figure 9.11 – Code snippet from the pair_table_z.cpp showing the coeff() method

As you can see, the code now accepts eight or nine parameters and this way, the two atom types, filename, keyword, optional local cutoff, and four parameters will be parsed after the pair_coeff command in the LAMMPS input script. The changes in *lines 344* to *347* are made to parse a0, a1, threshold1, and threshold2. Also, the position of the cutoff is moved to the end as the ninth argument so that it can be kept optional (*line 339*).

Therefore, the pair_style syntax for this custom potential in the LAMMPS input script remains unchanged but the pair_coeff syntax requires four additional entries. Altogether, the input script syntax for this height-dependent Pair TableZ becomes the following:

```
pair_style tableZ TABLE_STYLE N KEYWORD

pair_coeff  TYPE1 TYPE2 FILE_NAME  VARIABLE  CUTOFF threshold1
threshold2 a0 a1
```

The quantities here have the same meaning as for Pair Table (see *Chapter 5, Understanding Pair Styles*), except for the four additional parameters specific to this potential that have been explained earlier.

Next, we analyze how the forces and potentials need to be modified in the compute() method.

Implementing height-dependence

In the `compute()` method, a few other variables are introduced (*line 87*) to facilitate calculation of height-dependent forces and potentials:

```
double maxZ, zz, dfdz, deltaFz, scalingZ;
```

These variables represent the following:

- maxZ: The value of the highest z-coordinate among the two atoms considered

- zz: The height difference between maxZ and threshold1 used to calculate $f_{decay}(z)$

- df/dz: The value of $\dfrac{\partial f_{decay}}{\partial z}$

- deltaFz: The additional force $V_0 \dfrac{\partial f_{decay}}{\partial z}$ included in F_z

- scalingZ: The value of $f_{decay}(z)$

The code that calculates these quantities is shown in the following screenshot:

```
116     if (rsq < cutsq[itype][jtype]) {
117
118         // ------------------------------------------------------------
119         // SM: define polynomial decay for particle(s) within thresholds
120
121         // no decay interaction if both atoms are below threshold1
122         if (x[j][2]<=threshold1 && ztmp<=threshold1) {
123             scalingZ = a0;
124             deltaFz = 0.0;
125         }
126
127         // if atleast one atom is above threshold2:
128         // - no decay force
129         // - set decay potential to the value at the upper threshold
130         else if (x[j][2]>=threshold2 || ztmp>=threshold2) {
131             zz = threshold2 - threshold1;    // 28Mar15
132             scalingZ = a0 + a1*zz*zz;
133             deltaFz = 0.0;
134         }
135
136         // if atleast one atom is located in between thresholds (and not above threshold2):
137         // - decay force  = -df/dz
138         // - decay potential = a0 + a1*zz^2
139         else {
140             if (ztmp >= x[j][2]) maxZ = ztmp;
141             if (ztmp < x[j][2]) maxZ = x[j][2];
142
143             zz = maxZ - threshold1;
144             scalingZ = a0 + a1*zz*zz;    // f(z)
145             dfdz = 2*a1*zz;              // df/dz
146
147             // force_z = -df/dz for molecule located farther from surface
148             // force_z = +df/dz for molecule located closer to surface
149             if (ztmp >= x[j][2]) deltaFz = -dfdz;
150             if (ztmp < x[j][2]) deltaFz = dfdz;
151         }
```

Figure 9.12 – Code snippet from the pair_table_z.cpp showing the compute() method

From this screenshot, we see that the code loops over every central atom, i, in the core and its neighbors, j. It compares the heights of i (ztmp) and each j (x[j][2]) with the thresholds, Z_1 and Z_2. The following conditions are implemented:

- *Lines 122 to 125*: If both atoms are located below Z_1, that is, x[j] [2]<=threshold1 and ztmp<=threshold1, we set $f_{decay} = a_0$ and $\frac{\partial f_{decay}}{\partial z} = 0$, so that the interaction represented by $V_0(x, y, z)$ and $\overrightarrow{F_0}$ is unchanged and the height-dependence does not contribute to the force or potential.

- *Lines 130 to 134*: If at least one atom is located above Z_2, that is, x[j] [2]>=threshold2 or ztmp>=threshold2, we set $f_{decay} = 0$ and $\frac{\partial f_{decay}}{\partial z} = 0$, so that the interaction represented by $V_0(x, y, z)$ and $\overrightarrow{F_0}$ is nullified.

- *Lines 139 to 151*: If at least one atom is located between Z_1 and Z_2 and the other is located below Z_2, then choose Z_m as the larger z-coordinate of the two atoms and calculate $(z_m - z_1)$ as zz.

  Then, calculate $f_{decay} = a_0 + a_1(z_m - z_1)^2$ and $\frac{\partial f_{decay}}{\partial z} = 2a_1(z_m - z_1)$ so that the interaction represented by $V_0(x, y, z)$ and $\overrightarrow{F_0}$ is scaled according to the height of the atom located farther from Z_1. To apply F_z in the correct directions, the deltaFz variable is assigned a positive or negative sign depending on whether the i atom is located farther or closer to Z_1 compared to the j atom.

For each of the three conditions described precedingly, the scalingZ variable stores the value of $f_{decay}(z_m)$ (*line 123, line 132*, and *line 144*) and the deltaFz variable stores $\left(-\frac{\partial f_{decay}}{\partial z}\right)$ (*line 124, line 135*, and *line 145*). To find $\left(-V_0 \frac{\partial f_{decay}}{\partial z}\right)$, deltaFz is multiplied by the potential $V_0(r)$ extracted from the table at the separation between the atoms. It is accomplished for each table type by the following lines of codes:

- LOOKUP table type (*line 170*):

```
deltaFz *= (tb->e[itable]);
```

- LINEAR table type (*line 182*):

```
deltaFz *= (tb->e[itable] + fraction*tb->de[itable]);
```

- SPLINE table type (*line 197* to *198*):

```
deltaFz *= (a * tb->e[itable] + b * tb->e[itable+1] +
          ((a*a*a-a)*tb->e2[itable] + (b*b*b-b)*tb-
>e2[itable+1]) * tb->deltasq6);
```

- BITMAP table type (*line 207*):

```
deltaFz *= (tb->e[itable] + fraction*tb->de[itable]);
```

Having established `deltaFz`, the forces and potential on the atoms are modified as shown in the following screenshot:

```
210    // SM: modify fx,fy,fz to incorporate scalingZ and deltaFz
211    f[i][0] += scalingZ*delx*fpair;
212    f[i][1] += scalingZ*dely*fpair;
213    f[i][2] += scalingZ*delz*fpair + deltaFz;
214    if (newton_pair || j < nlocal) {
215      f[j][0] -= scalingZ*delx*fpair;
216      f[j][1] -= scalingZ*dely*fpair;
217      f[j][2] -= scalingZ*delz*fpair + deltaFz;
218    }
219
220    if (eflag) {
221      if (tabstyle == LOOKUP)
222        evdwl = tb->e[itable];
223      else if (tabstyle == LINEAR || tabstyle == BITMAP)
224        evdwl = tb->e[itable] + fraction*tb->de[itable];
225      else
226        evdwl = a * tb->e[itable] + b * tb->e[itable+1] +
227          ((a*a*a-a)*tb->e2[itable] + (b*b*b-b)*tb->e2[itable+1]) *
228          tb->deltasq6;
229      evdwl *= factor_lj;
230      evdwl *= scalingZ;    // SM
231    }
232
233    if (evflag) ev_tally(i,j,nlocal,newton_pair,
234                         evdwl,0.0,fpair,delx,dely,delz);
235  }
```

Figure 9.13 – Code snippet from the pair_table_z.cpp showing force and potential modifications in the compute() method

As you can see, the F_x and F_y are multiplied by `scalingZ` to scale by $f_{decay}(z_m)$ in *lines 211* to *212* and *lines 215* to *216*. The F_z is scaled by `scalingZ` and added or subtracted by `deltaFz` to account for the $-V_0 \dfrac{\partial f_{decay}}{\partial z}$. Similarly, the potential is scaled by `scalingZ` on *line 230*.

In the `single()` method, the `scalingZ` variable is calculated and used to scale the potential before it is returned. The force is not returned and the `deltaFz` variable is not considered. The following screenshot shows this method:

```
1065    // ---------------------------------------------------------------
1066    // SM: define polynomial decay for particle(s) within thresholds
1067    double **x = atom->x;
1068    double maxZ, zz, scalingZ;
1069
1070    // no decay interaction if both atoms are below threshold1
1071    if (x[j][2]<=threshold1 && x[i][2]<=threshold1) {
1072      scalingZ = a0;
1073    }
1074
1075    // if atleast one atom is above threshold2:
1076    //   - set decay potential to the value at the upper threshold
1077    else if (x[j][2]>=threshold2 || x[i][2]>=threshold2) {
1078      zz = threshold2 - threshold1;
1079      scalingZ = a0 + a1*zz*zz;
1080    }
1081
1082    // if atleast one atom is located in between thresholds (and not above threshold2):
1083    //   - decay potential = a0 + a1*zz^2
1084    else {
1085      if (x[i][2] >= x[j][2]) maxZ = x[i][2];
1086      if (x[i][2] < x[j][2]) maxZ = x[j][2];
1087      zz = maxZ - threshold1;
1088      scalingZ = a0 + a1*zz*zz;
1089    }
```

Figure 9.14 – Code snippet from the pair_table_z.cpp showing the single() method

As you can see, the same criterion from the `compute()` method is applied to determine `scalingZ` in *lines 1066* to *1089*, that is, `scalingZ` = a_0 if both atoms are below Z_1, `scalingZ` = 0 if at least one atom is above Z_2, and `scalingZ` = $a_0 + a_1(z_m - z_1)^2$ if both atoms are located below `threshold2` and at least one is located above `threshold1`. The `phi` variable is multiplied by `scalingZ` before returning in *line 1129*:

```
return factor_lj*scalingZ*phi;
```

Altogether, the `pair_style` syntax for `Pair TableZ` in the LAMMPS inputs script remains the same as for `Pair Table`, and the syntax for `pair_coeff` becomes as follows:

```
pair_coeff   TYPE1 TYPE2   FILENAME VARIABLE threshold1
threshold2 a0 a1 LOCAL_CUTOFF
```

From the preceding code, TYPE1, TYPE2, FILENAME, and VARIABLE carry the same meaning as for Pair Table, and the other parameters are self-explanatory. This pair style is tested with a trial LAMMPS input script in the next section.

The Pair TableZ potential is tested with a trial LAMMPS input script in the next section.

Trial run (in.Test_PairTableZ)

A trial run is performed using two atoms, grouped as G1 and G2, where G1 located at coordinates (10, 10, 10) Å and G2 is initially located at coordinates (10, 10, 11) Å. The following code is used for the trial run, where the first part initializes the system and creates two atoms at the locations specified:

```
# ------------------------------------
# INITIALIZE SIMULATION
# ------------------------------------
units metal
dimension 3
boundary p p p
atom_style        atomic
atom_modify map array
# ------------------------------------
# DEFINE REGIONS
# ------------------------------------
region r0  block 0 20 0 20 0 40 units box
# ------------------------------------
# CREATE ATOMS
# ------------------------------------
create_box 1 r0
mass    1 10.0
create_atoms 1 single  10 10 10 units box
group G1 id 1
create_atoms 1 single  10 10 11 units box
group G2 id 2
```

The `Pair TableZ` style is assigned to the atoms and G2 is time-integrated:

```
# -----------------------------------
# PAIR STYLES
# -----------------------------------
pair_style   tableZ linear 10000
pair_coeff  1 1   Table_Potential.table V_Table 12.0 17.0 1.0
-0.04 10.0
# -----------------------------------
# FIXES
# -----------------------------------
compute TABLE_PE G1 group/group G2
variable TABLE_PE equal c_TABLE_PE
variable z2 equal z[2]
variable fz equal fz[2]

velocity G2 set 0 0 2.0
fix FREEZE G1 setforce 0 0 0
fix NVE  G2 nve
fix PRINT_PE all print 10 "${z2} ${fz} ${TABLE_PE}" file
outputTABLE.dat

run 1000
```

In the preceding code, a `Pair TableZ` potential is applied with
$f_{decay}(z) = 1 - 0.04(z - z_1)^2$, where $z_1 = 12.0$ Å and $z_2 = 17.0$ Å, and a cutoff of
10.0 Å is applied. A constant potential $V_0(r) = 1$ and $\overrightarrow{F_0} = (0,0,0)$ is created by the table
potential in the file titled `Table_Potential.table`. The G1 atom is frozen in place
at (10,10,10) Å, while the G2 atom is provided an initial velocity vector of (0,0,2) Å/ps
and time-integrated by `fix nve`, allowing it to continue traveling along the +z direction
under the influence of its height-dependent interaction with G1.

During the motion of G2, the z-coordinate of G2, z-component of force (F_z) on G2, and the PE between the atoms are recorded and used to create plots of the position-dependence of F_z and the position-dependence of PE, as shown in the following diagram:

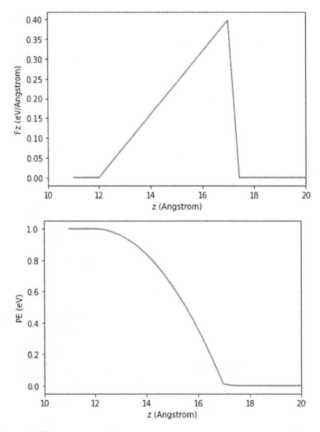

Figure 9.15 – Plots of $\mathbf{F_z}$ versus z (top), and PE versus z (bottom) for pair_table_z.cpp applied on a constant potential

As you can see, the *top* plot shows the following trend of F_z:

- $F_z = 0$, when G2 is located below the lower threshold $z_1 = 12.0$ Å
- F_z increases linearly as $F_z(z) = 0.08(z - 12)$ when G2 is located between the two thresholds $z_1 = 12.0$ Å and $z_2 = 17.0$ Å
- F_z drops to zero when G2 travels beyond the upper threshold $z_2 = 17.0$ Å

Given that the other atom, G1, is placed at a fixed location below the lower threshold $z_1 = 12.0$ Å, this force pattern agrees with expectation.

The *bottom* plot shows that $V_{height}(z)$ stays at $V_0 = 1$ while G2 is located below $z_1 = 12.0$ Å, and decays quadratically by $V_{height}(z) = 1 - 0.04(z - 12)^2$ to zero as G2 travels from $z_1 = 12.0$ Å to $z_2 = 17.0$ Å, where it remains for the rest of the plot. This potential matches expectations as well provided that G1 is located below $z_1 = 12.0$ Å.

In this section, a height-dependent, decaying potential was implemented along with proper adjustment of forces brought about by the height-dependence. For purposes of flexibility, the Pair Table class was modified to accommodate the height-dependence.

In the next section, we will describe a potential that produces tangential frictional force on spherical atoms to change their rotational motion.

Writing a friction-based pair style

In this section, a frictional force is implemented on spherical atoms that depends on the tangential time of contact and the tangential velocity difference of two interacting atoms, via the **Cundall-Strack scheme** (https://doi.org/10.1007/978-94-017-2653-5_22).

In the Cundall-Strack scheme, also known as **Coulomb friction**, a tangential frictional force, $\vec{F_t}$, acts on two spheres in contact that increases with the relative tangential velocities of the spheres up to an upper bound value. It is assumed that, during prolonged contact between the spheres, an imaginary spring of spring constant K_t is extended by a length $\Delta\vec{s}$ owing to the relative tangential velocity ($\vec{v_r}$) and it exerts an opposing force on the spheres to mimic the frictional force. In addition, a drag force is exerted based on a drag coefficient (A) and $\vec{v_r}$ that also acts tangentially to impede rotational motion.

The frictional and drag forces are pegged at an upper limit defined by $\mu_k|\vec{F_n}|$, where μ_k is the coefficient of kinetic friction and $\vec{F_n}$ is the normal force acting between the spheres, and this upper limit applies when the friction exceeds the value defined by $\mu_s|\vec{F_n}|$, where μ_s is the coefficient of static friction. Altogether, $\vec{F_t}$ acts opposite to tangential velocity and its magnitude is defined as follows:

$$|\vec{F_t}| = \begin{cases} \mu_k|\vec{F_n}| & \text{if} \quad (K_t|\Delta\vec{s}| + A|\vec{v_r}|) > \mu_s|\vec{F_n}| \\ |K_t\,\Delta\vec{s} + A\,\vec{v_r}| \;, & \text{otherwise} \end{cases}$$

When the upper limit is reached, the magnitude of $\Delta \vec{s}$ is set to $\mu_k |\vec{F_n}|/K_t$ and its direction is set to the opposite to the direction of $\vec{F_t}$:

$$\Delta \vec{s} = -\text{sign}(\vec{F_t})\frac{\mu_k |\vec{F_n}|}{K_t} \text{ , if } (K_t |\Delta \vec{s}| + A|\vec{v_r}|) > \mu_s |\vec{F_n}|$$

Since this Cundall-Strack potential acts on a spherical atom, we will modify `pair_gran_hooke_history.cpp` and `pair_gran_hooke_history.h` to implement it as `pair_CundallStrack.cpp` and `pair_CundallStrack.h`, respectively. The class names are changed from `PairGranHookeHistory` to `PairCundallStrack`.

The changes in `pair_CundallStrack.cpp` are described in detail next.

Modifying the compute() method

Throughout `pair_CundallStrack.cpp` and `pair_CundallStrack.h`, the input parameters are changed from the original files to the new files as listed:

- kn is changed to FN: FN is a constant magnitude of normal force F_n between spheres that are interacting.

- kt: kt is the spring constant of tangential spring K_t.

- gamman is changed to MuS: MuS is the coefficient of static friction μ_s.

- gammat is changed to A: A is the drag coefficient.

- xmu is changed to MuK: MuK is the coefficient of kinetic friction, μ_k.

The `dampflag` parameter is kept unchanged and is used to deactivate or activate tangential forces by entering 0 or 1.

The bulk of the change has to be made in the `compute()` method, where three new variables are introduced (*lines 99* to *100*):

```
double fsmax, shrmaginv;
int sgn;
```

The fsmax variable will be used to store the upper limit of the frictional force, $\mu_k|\vec{F_n}|$, the shrmaginv variable will represent the inverse of $|\Delta\vec{s}|$, and the sgn integer will determine the sign of the components of $\vec{F_t}$.

Next, the code loops over each atom and its neighbors, and *line 173* is modified to include neighbors that are touching:

```
if (rsq > radsum*radsum) {
```

Here, radsum is the sum of the radii, radi and radj, of the atoms, i and j. Atom pairs that are not in contact satisfy the preceding condition and are excluded while the atom pairs that are in contact are processed as follows.

Lines 179 to *181* set up the 1D array shear[] to represent the three components of $\Delta\vec{s} = (\Delta s_x, \Delta s_y, \Delta s_z)$, where firsttouch (*line 146* and *line 157*) and firstshear (*line 147* and *line 158*) determine whether the shear[] values need to be reset after every separate contact between the spheres, i and j.

After that, in *lines 188* to *219*, the code calculates the relative normal velocities and the relative tangential velocities by taking into account the *center-of-mass velocities* (v[][]) and the relative rotational velocity components (wr1, wr2, wr3). The *relative tangential velocity* components at the point of contact (vtr1, vtr2, vtr3) are calculated (*lines 215* to *217*) by subtracting the cross-product components of the center-of-mass displacement unit vector ($\Delta\hat{r}$) and relative angular velocity vectors ($\vec{\omega_r}$) from the relative tangential velocity components of the center-of-mass (vt1, vt2, vt3):

$$(\text{vtr1}, \text{vtr2}, \text{vtr3}) = (\text{vt1}, \text{vt2}, \text{vt3}) - \Delta\hat{r} \times \vec{\omega_r}$$

When the spheres are in contact (*line 226*), the shear[] quantities are incremented by multiplying (vtr1, vtr2, and vtr3) by the dt timestep (*lines 227* to *229*) to account for extension of $\Delta\vec{s}$ by relative tangential velocities at the point of contact of the spheres:

$$\Delta\vec{s} \mathrel{+}= (\text{vtr1}, \text{vtr2}, \text{vtr3}) * \text{dt}$$

Having completed velocity and shear calculations, the tangential force components (fs1, fs2, and fs3) are calculated by finding the sum of the spring force components ($K_t\Delta\vec{s}$) with the drag force components ($A\vec{v_r}$) in *lines 247* to *249*, preceded by negative signs to indicate opposite direction to (vtr1, vtr2, and vtr3), as shown in the following screenshot:

```
247         fs1 = - (kt*shear[0] + A*vtr1);
248         fs2 = - (kt*shear[1] + A*vtr2);
249         fs3 = - (kt*shear[2] + A*vtr3);
250
251         // rescale frictional displacements and forces if needed
252
253         fs = sqrt(fs1*fs1 + fs2*fs2 + fs3*fs3);
254         fsmax = MuK*FN;       // SM
255
256         if (fs > MuS*FN) {            // SM
257           if (shrmag != 0.0) {
258
259             shrmaginv = 1.0/shrmag; // SM
260
261             sgn = 1;
262             if (fs1<0) sgn=-1;
263             shear[0] = -(fabs(shear[0])*shrmaginv) * fsmax/kt * sgn;        // SM
264
265             sgn = 1;
266             if (fs2<0) sgn=-1;
267             shear[1] = -(fabs(shear[1])*shrmaginv) * fsmax/kt * sgn;        // SM
268
269             sgn = 1;
270             if (fs3<0) sgn=-1;
271             shear[2] = -(fabs(shear[2])*shrmaginv) * fsmax/kt * sgn;        // SM
272
273             fs1 *= fsmax/fs;     // SM
274             fs2 *= fsmax/fs;     // SM
275             fs3 *= fsmax/fs;     // SM
276
277           } else fs1 = fs2 = fs3 = 0.0;
278         }
279
280         fprintf(screen,"%f %f %f \n", vtr2, fs2, shear[1]); // SM
281
282         // forces & torques
283
284         fx = delx*rinv*FN + fs1;    // SM
285         fy = dely*rinv*FN + fs2;    // SM
286         fz = delz*rinv*FN + fs3;    // SM
287         f[i][0] += fx;
288         f[i][1] += fy;
289         f[i][2] += fz;
```

Figure 9.16 – Code snippet from pair_CundallStrack.cpp showing the compute() method

As you can see, the magnitude of the tangential force, fs (*line 253*), is compared with the upper limit, fsmax $= \mu_k|\vec{F_n}|$ (*line 254*), to determine whether the tangential force components should be pegged at the maximum value, fsmax.

If so, then the $\Delta\vec{s}$ components are assigned accordingly (*lines 261 to 271*) and the tangential force components (fs1, fs2, and fs3) are set to corresponding components of fsmax (*lines 273 to 275*). When assigning the signs of $\Delta\vec{s}$, the sgn variable is used to multiply each component by *+1* or *-1* based on the sign of the corresponding tangential force component.

A fprintf statement is also introduced on *lines 280* to display the *y*-components of the tangential velocity (vtr2), tangential force (fs2), and the spring extension (shear[1]) on the screen during a simulation run for testing purposes (an example is provided in the *Trial run (in.Test_PairCundallStrack)* section). Once the code has been validated, this line can be deleted or commented out without any impact on the rest of the code.

Finally, the **Center-Of-Mass (COM)** forces are assigned to the atoms in *lines 284 to 289* by adding the normal and tangential force components of each atom. The components (fs1, fs2, and fs3) represent the tangential force components whereas the normal force components are calculated by multiplying the user-entered normal force, FN, with the ratio of the corresponding displacement vector components (Δx, Δy, or Δz) to the separation (r):

- x-component of COM force fx:

$$fx = \frac{\Delta x}{r} * FN + fs1$$

- y-component of COM force fy:

$$fy = \frac{\Delta y}{r} * FN + fs2$$

- z-component of COM force fz:

$$fz = \frac{\Delta z}{r} * FN + fs3$$

The torques on the atoms in concern are assigned using the cross-product of the tangential forces with the radii vectors (*lines 291 to 296*), as has been discussed for rigid bodies in *Chapter 7, Understanding Fixes*.

Similar changes are made to the single() method (*lines 686 to 700*) to account for the tangential frictional force components.

Altogether, the input script syntax for Pair CundallStrack becomes the following:

```
pair_style  CundallStrack FN Kt MuS A MuK DAMPFLAG
pair_coeff  TYPE1 TYPE2
```

The parameters in the preceding code have been explained earlier.

Now a trial run is performed with a simple LAMMPS input script consisting of two spherical atoms, as described in the next section.

Trial run (in.Test_PairCundallStrack)

To test `Pair CundallStrack`, a 2D system in LAMMPS is created consisting of two spherical atoms of radius 0.5 Å and mass 1 amu. These atoms are placed side by side at locations (*10, 10, 0*) and (*11, 10, 0*) so that they intersect at the midpoint (*10.5, 10, 0*). The atoms are grouped as G1 and G2 respectively, and both atoms are prohibited from translating by using a `fix setforce` command. The following diagram illustrates the setup:

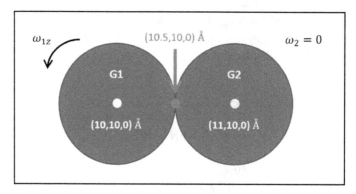

Figure 9.17 – Diagram of simulation setup showing the centers of the two atoms and their point of intersection

As you can see, while both atoms are prevented from translating, G1 is allowed to rotate in a counter-clockwise direction with an angular speed ω_{1z} viewed from above, as shown in the preceding diagram. Since G2 does not rotate ($\omega_2 = 0$), at the point of intersection, G1 is effectively travelling along the +*y* direction relative to G2. The frictional force will be calculated based on the relative velocity in this setup.

The first part of the LAMMPS input script is provided here, where the simulation is initialized, and two atom spheres are placed next to each other in contact:

```
# ----------------------
# INITIALIZE SIMULATION
# ----------------------
units            metal
```

```
atom_style sphere
dimension  2
boundary   p p p
comm_modify vel yes
timestep 0.00001
# ---------------------
# DEFINE REGIONS
# ---------------------
region r0  block 0 20 0 20 0 20 units box
# ---------------------
# CREATE ATOMS
# ---------------------
create_box 1 r0
create_atoms 1 single  10 10 0 units box
group G1 id 1
create_atoms 1 single  11 10 0 units box
group G2 id 2
set  group all mass 1
set  group all diameter 1
```

In the second part of the input script, the Pair CundallStrack style is assigned to the atoms and only G1 is time-integrated:

```
# ---------------------
# PAIR STYLES
# ---------------------
pair_style CundallStrack 10 20 0.1 0.01 0.1 1
pair_coeff 1 1
# ---------------------
# FIXES
# ---------------------
set group G1 omega 0 0 100
fix FREEZE all setforce 0 0 0
fix NVE G1 nve/sphere disc

run 1000
```

As you can see, atom G1 is assigned an angular velocity vector of $\overrightarrow{\omega_1} = (0,0,100)$ rad/ps, which makes it rotate in a counter-clockwise direction when viewed from above the *xy-plane*. A time-integrator, `fix nve/sphere disc`, is applied only on the G1 atom to allow it to rotate while no time-integration applies on the G2 atom to prevent its rotation. Therefore, the relative tangential velocity, $\overrightarrow{v_r}$, of G1 relative to G2 at the intersection point (*10.5, 10, 0*) is effectively the linear velocity of G1 at that point:

$$\overrightarrow{v_r} = \overrightarrow{\omega_1} \times \overrightarrow{\Delta r_1} = (\omega_{1z} \Delta x_1)\hat{y}$$

Here, $\overrightarrow{\Delta r_1} = (\Delta x_1, \Delta y_1, \Delta z_1) = (0.5, 0, 0)$ represents the radius vector pointing from the center of the G1 atom (*10, 10, 0*) to the intersection point (*10.5, 10, 0*). Altogether, at the intersection point (*10.5, 10, 0*), since atom G1 has a velocity along the +*y* direction and the G2 atom is stationary, the relative velocity $\overrightarrow{v_r}$ of G1 relative to G2 points along the +*y* direction at the intersection point (and the relative velocity of G2 relative to G1 points along the –*y* direction).

The Cundall-Strack interaction is applied via the `pair_style CundallStrack` command with the following parameters:

- F_n = 10 eV/Å
- K_t = 20 eV/Å²
- μ_s = 0.1
- A = 0.01 eV ps/Å²
- μ_k = 0.1
- `dampflag` = 1

Since motion in the *y*-direction is relevant for this particular system, the *y*-component of $\overrightarrow{v_r}$, the *y*-component of $\overrightarrow{F_t}$, and the *y*-component of $\overrightarrow{\Delta s}$ are printed out (using the `fprintf` statement in the source code described earlier) and plotted to observe the evolution of the system. The following diagram shows these time-evolutions for G1:

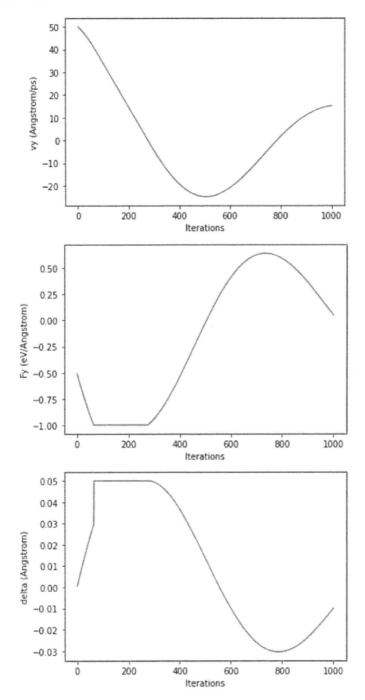

Figure 9.18 – Plots of $\mathbf{v_{ry}}$ versus time (top), $\mathbf{F_{ty}}$ versus time (middle), and $\mathbf{\Delta s_y}$ versus time (bottom)

As you can see, the plot of V_{ry} versus time at the *top* shows that the V_{ry} starts at **50 Å/ ps** (obtained by multiplying radius of the atom with ω_{1z}) and drops to -20 Å/ps before increasing to 10 Å/ps, indicating that the G1 atom switches from counter-clockwise to clockwise and back to counter-clockwise rotation at decreasing angular speeds in the duration of this simulation.

The plot of F_{ty} versus time, in the *middle*, shows that the frictional force is initially negative to oppose the positive v_{ry}, and increases almost linearly up to the magnitude of its upper limit, $\mu_k F_n = 1$ eV/Å. The friction remains constant at that value as indicated by the horizontal stretch in the preceding plot, before becoming more positive and forming a smooth peak at a positive value. As the preceding plot shows, F_{ty} switches direction as V_{ry} does, but in a gradual, smooth progression instead of an immediate jump.

The *bottom* plot of Δs_y versus time shows almost an inverse of the plot of F_{ty} versus time where Δs_y increases almost linearly until F_{ty} reaches an upper limit, at which point Δs_y jumps to its maximum extension of $\mu_k F_n / K_t = 0.05$ Å. It maintains this extension as long as F_{ty} is constant and decreases to form a trough shortly after F_{ty} forms a peak.

The corresponding plots for G2 would be flipped because of reversed relative velocity, equal, and opposite forces acting on G2 compared to G1.

In this section, we implemented a Cundall-Strack scheme of frictional forces between two rotating spherical atoms. In the context of the LAMMPS source code, it involves modifying an existing pair style that applies to spherical atoms and calculating the tangential velocities and forces.

Summary

In this chapter, we saw some examples of custom-written pair styles that illustrate the process of selecting an appropriate pair style and making modifications at the correct sections to generate the required forces and potentials. In addition, the mathematical background behind these pair styles have been provided to help you to see the connection from theory to source code implementation.

In this chapter, you have learned to choose existing pair styles and to create new pair styles by adding proper modifications. Other than modifying input parameters to parse, the force and potential functions usually need to be modified when creating a new pairwise potential. You have also seen examples of non-pairwise potentials being modified to implement location-dependence and frictional forces.

In the next chapter, we will write custom fixes that can perform user-defined maneuvers during a simulation run to suit user requirements.

Questions

1. When writing a new radially-symmetric pair potential for $V(r)$, which quantity in the compute () method should be set equal to $-\dfrac{1}{r}\dfrac{dV}{dr}$ multiplied by factor*lj?

2. If it is desired that Pair TableZ described in this chapter should not be applied to atoms belonging to the same molecule (assuming that atom_style in the input script is defined as molecular), how should pair_table_z.cpp be modified?

3. In Pair CundallStrack, if the drag force is assumed to depend on $|\vec{v_r}|^2$ instead of $|\vec{v_r}|$, what changes are required in the compute () method to implement this drag force?

10
Modifying Force Applications

In this chapter, we will write custom fixes that are able to apply non-pairwise forces on selected groups of atoms during a simulation run. Starting with existing fixes, we will make modifications that produce new fixes to exert custom forces to the atoms in the system. These forces generally represent agents that are not adequately incorporated into the MD simulation by atoms or potentials, such as self-propelling active forces.

We will cover the following topics in this chapter:

- Writing a fix to apply a 2D spring force
- Writing a fix to apply an active force in a molecular chain
- Writing a fix to apply a custom wall force
- Writing a fix to apply a bond-boost potential

By the end of this chapter, you will have learned how to write your own fix that can manipulate your MD simulation by modifying forces as programmed in the source code.

Technical requirements

To execute the instructions in this chapter, you will need a text editor (for example, **Notepad++** or **Gedit**) and a platform to compile LAMMPS (for example, **Linux Terminal**).

You can find the full source code used in this chapter here: `https://github.com/PacktPublishing/Extending-and-Modifying-LAMMPS-Writing-Your-Own-Source-Code`

You can download LAMMPS at `https://lammps.sandia.gov/doc/Install.html`. The LAMMPS GitHub link is `https://github.com/lammps/lammps`, where you can also find the source code.

Writing a fix to apply a 2D spring force

This is the list of changes that are made to the source code:

- The new files that are created are `fix_addforceXY.cpp` and `fix_addforceXY.h`.
- The existing files that have been modified are `fix_addforce.cpp` and `fix_addforce.h`.
- The methods that are modified are constructor, `init()`, and `post_force()`.
- The input parameters are x0, y0, kx, and ky.
- Other quantities that are introduced are `kxstr[]`, `kystr[]`, `kxstyle`, `kystyle`, `kxvar`, `kyvar`, and `ework[]`.
- The LAMMPS syntax is `fix FIX_NAME GROUP addforceXY x0 y0 zvalue kx ky` (we will look at this syntax shortly in this section).

In this section, we will write a fix that applies a 2D, non-radially symmetric spring force on an atom directed toward a specified point.

Theory (2D spring force)

In this setup, we have an atom in a 2D system at location (x, y) that experiences a force pointing toward a point (x_0, y_0) that depends on the spring constants k_x and k_y in the x and y directions:

- The force F_x in the x direction is given as:

$$F_x = -k_x(x - x_0)$$

- The force F_y in the y direction is given as:

$$F_y = -k_y(y - y_0)$$

There is no force contribution in the z direction, and these forces produce a *2D harmonic oscillator motion* that can produce linear, circular, elliptical, or **Lissajous** trajectories.

> **Important Note:**
> While we will modify an existing fix to implement this feature, it can conceivably be implemented by a custom pair style where the radial symmetry is altered to incorporate the x and y dependent forces.

The Fix Addforce class is able to apply additional forces to atoms, so this class was selected as the starting point for our purpose. Copies of `fix_addforce.cpp` and `fix_addforce.h` are renamed to `fix_addforceXY.cpp` and `fix_addforceXY.h`, and the method names are changed accordingly. Next, we will review the modifications for the relevant sections of these renamed files, starting with the header file.

Modifying the header file – addforceXY.h

This new Fix AddforceXY style is assigned a new fix style name `addforceXY` by making the appropriate changes in `fix_addforceXY.h` (*line 16*):

```
FixStyle(addforceXY,FixAddForceXY)
```

In a LAMMPS input script, this fix can be implemented with the `addforceXY` command.

The following quantities are declared in *lines 52 to 55*:

```
double x0,y0;
double kx,ky;
char *kxstr,*kystr;
int kxstyle,kystyle,kxvar,kyvar;
double *ework;
```

From the preceding code, `x0` and `y0` represent the coordinates (x_0, y_0), and `kx` and `ky` represent the spring constants k_x and k_y. The character arrays `kxstr` and `kystr` store the variable names that are used as the inputs of `kx` and `ky` and the `kxstyle`, `kystyle`, `kxvar`, and `kyvar` integers are used to accommodate the inputs of these parameters as constants or variables—similar quantities were used to read force components as constant values or variables in Fix Addforce (see *Chapter 7, Understanding Fixes*). The 1D array `ework []` is introduced to store the work done by the added force.

In the original `Fix Addforce` class, a 2D array `sforce[][]` was used to store the (x, y, z) force components and the work done, but in this modified `Fix AddforceXY` class, x0 and y0 cannot be entered as atom style variables, so `sforce[][]` cannot be used and is replaced with the 1D `ework[]` array.

Next, we will discuss the changes that should be made to the constructor method so that it can parse input parameters.

Modifying the constructor in fix_addforceXY.cpp

In the constructor method, *line 44* is changed to accommodate two additional input parameters from `narg < 6` to `narg < 8`:

```
if (narg < 8) error->all(FLERR,"Illegal fix AddForceXY
command");
```

In `fix_addforce.cpp`, arrays `xstr` and `ystr` are set to NULL in the original fix (*line 57*) while `kxstr`, `kystr`, and `ework` are initially set to NULL (*line 41* and *line 58*). These variables, x0, kx, y0, and ky, are parsed from the LAMMPS input script in *lines 60 to 99*, as shown in the following screenshot:

```
58      kxstr = kystr = NULL;      // SM
59
60      if (strstr(arg[3],"v_") == arg[3]) {
61          int n = strlen(&arg[3][2]) + 1;
62          xstr = new char[n];
63          strcpy(xstr,&arg[3][2]);
64      } else {
65          x0 = force->numeric(FLERR,arg[3]);   // SM
66          xstyle = CONSTANT;
67      }
68      if (strstr(arg[4],"v_") == arg[4]) {
69          int n = strlen(&arg[4][2]) + 1;
70          ystr = new char[n];
71          strcpy(ystr,&arg[4][2]);
72      } else {
73          y0 = force->numeric(FLERR,arg[4]);   // SM
74          ystyle = CONSTANT;
75      }
76      if (strstr(arg[5],"v_") == arg[5]) {
77          int n = strlen(&arg[5][2]) + 1;
78          zstr = new char[n];
79          strcpy(zstr,&arg[5][2]);
80      } else {
81          zvalue = force->numeric(FLERR,arg[5]);
82          zstyle = CONSTANT;
83      }
84      if (strstr(arg[6],"v_") == arg[6]) {  // SM
85          int n = strlen(&arg[6][2]) + 1;
86          kxstr = new char[n];
87          strcpy(kxstr,&arg[6][2]);
88      } else {
89          kx = force->numeric(FLERR,arg[6]);
90          kxstyle = CONSTANT;
91      }
92      if (strstr(arg[7],"v_") == arg[7]) {  // SM
93          int n = strlen(&arg[7][2]) + 1;
94          kystr = new char[n];
95          strcpy(kystr,&arg[7][2]);
96      } else {
97          ky = force->numeric(FLERR,arg[7]);
98          kystyle = CONSTANT;
99      }
```

Figure 10.1 – Screenshot from fix_addforceXY.cpp showing the constructor method

As you can see, if the input parameters x0, kx, y0, and ky are entered as numeric values, then the integers xstyle (*line 66*), kxstyle (*line 90*), ystyle (*line 74*), and kystyle (*line 98*) are set to the integer corresponding to CONSTANT in the enumeration list (*line 34*), and the values are read and stored in the corresponding variables using the force->numeric() method (*lines 65, 73, 89, and 97*). If any of these input parameters is a variable (of either equal or atom style), then it must be preceded by the characters v_ in the input script, and the corresponding character string (xstr, ystr, kxstr, or kystr) copies the variable name entered after the characters v_ (*lines 60 to 63, 68 to 71, 76 to 79, 84 to 87, and 92 to 95*).

It should be pointed out that the quantities zstr, zstyle, and zvalue are retained from the original fix_addforce.cpp (*lines 76 to 83*), but they do not contribute to the calculations or force assignments in the fix, and the *z* component of force is unchanged by this fix. Also, memory is assigned to ework[] on *line 138*:

```
memory->create(ework,1,"addforceXY::ework");
```

Accordingly, in the destructor method, memory is deallocated from ework[] (*line 151*):

```
memory->destroy(ework);
```

This way, numeric and non-numeric inputs are segregated: the character arrays are used to store the variable names for non-numeric values and these arrays store NULL for numeric values. These character arrays are then employed in the init() method to extract the appropriate variables.

Modifying the init() method in fix_addforceXY.cpp

In the init() method, the character arrays xstr and ystr are used to locate the IDs of the variable names that they contain, and these IDs are stored as the integers xvar (*line 175*) and yvar (*line 182*), respectively. The integers xvar and yvar are then used to extract the variable values that correspond to equal style (*line 178* and *line 185*).

In *lines 205* to *219*, the `kxstr` and `kystr` character arrays are similarly validated, with the exception being that only equal style variables are permitted, as shown in the following screenshot:

```
204     // SM
205     if (kxstr) {
206        kxvar = input->variable->find(kxstr);
207        if (kxvar < 0)
208          error->all(FLERR,"Variable name for fix AddForceXY does not exist");
209        if (input->variable->equalstyle(kxvar)) kxstyle = EQUAL;
210        else error->all(FLERR,"Variable kxvar for fix AddForceXY is invalid style");
211     } else kxstyle = NONE;
212
213     if (kystr) {
214        kyvar = input->variable->find(kystr);
215        if (kyvar < 0)
216          error->all(FLERR,"Variable name for fix AddForceXY does not exist");
217        if (input->variable->equalstyle(kyvar)) kystyle = EQUAL;
218        else error->all(FLERR,"Variable kyvar for fix AddForceXY is invalid style");
219     } else kystyle = NONE;
```

Figure 10.2 – Screenshot from fix_addforceXY.cpp showing the init() method

The validation process is similar to the one described earlier. The variable ID is checked against equal style variables (*line 209* and *line 217*) and an error is generated if there is no match (*line 210* and *line 218*). Since kx and ky are assumed to be properties of the spring that pulls the atom towards point (x0, y0), they are not permitted to be atom style variables.

Then, the condition to update the flag `varflag` is modified in *lines 229* to *232* to include the conditions involving `kxstyle` and `kystyle`, as shown in the following code:

```
if (zstyle == ATOM)
    varflag = ATOM;
else if (xstyle == EQUAL || ystyle == EQUAL || zstyle == EQUAL
|| kxstyle == EQUAL || kystyle == EQUAL)
    varflag = EQUAL;
```

As you can see in the preceding code, this way, the `varflag` is set to EQUAL if any one of the input parameters is an equal style variable. Similarly, `varflag` can be set to ATOM if there is at least one atom style variable (*lines 229* to *230*) or CONSTANT if all input parameters are numeric values (*line 233*).

Next, the force is applied to the relevant atoms in the `post_force()` method.

Modifying the post_force() method in fix_addforceXY.cpp

In the `post_force()` method, memory is allocated for `ework[]` in *lines 300 to 306*:

```
if ((varflag == ATOM || estyle == ATOM) && atom->nmax >
maxatom) {
    maxatom = atom->nmax;
    memory->destroy(sforce);
    memory->destroy(ework);
    memory->create(sforce,maxatom,4,"addforceXY:sforce");
    memory->create(ework,1,"addforceXY::ework");
}
```

As you can see in the preceding code, the `memory->create()` method is used to allocate a 2D array of size 4 by `maxatoms` to `sforce` and a 1D array of length 1 is allocated to `ework`.

When calculating forces to apply to the designated atoms, the cases of numeric and variable input parameters are separately analyzed. The following screenshot shows the case of all input parameters being numeric, where `varflag` is equal to CONSTANT:

```
317    if (varflag == CONSTANT) {
318        double unwrap[3];
319        for (int i = 0; i < nlocal; i++)
320          if (mask[i] & groupbit) {
321              if (region && !region->match(x[i][0],x[i][1],x[i][2])) continue;
322              domain->unmap(x[i],image[i],unwrap);
323              foriginal[0] -= -kx*(x[i][0] - x0)*unwrap[0] - ky*(x[i][1] - y0)*unwrap[1]; // SM
324              foriginal[1] += f[i][0];
325              foriginal[2] += f[i][1];
326              foriginal[3] += f[i][2];
327
328              // SM
329              f[i][0] += -kx*(x[i][0] - x0);
330              f[i][1] += -ky*(x[i][1] - y0);
331              f[i][2] += 0.0;
332
333              // SM
334              if (evflag) {
335                  v[0] = -kx*(x[i][0] - x0) * unwrap[0];
336                  v[1] = -ky*(x[i][1] - y0) * unwrap[1];
337                  v[2] = 0.0 * unwrap[2];
338                  v[3] = -kx*(x[i][0] - x0) * unwrap[1];
339                  v[4] = -kx*(x[i][0] - x0) * unwrap[2];
340                  v[5] = -ky*(x[i][1] - y0) * unwrap[2];
341                  v_tally(i,v);
342              }
343          }
```

Figure 10.3 – Screenshot from the FixAddForceXY::post_force() method that handles numeric input parameters

As you can see, on *line 323*, the work done by the added force is calculated by taking the dot product of the spring force with the displacement vector, and the cumulative work done on all atoms is stored as `foriginal[0]`.

Similarly, the other array components `foriginal[1]`, `foriginal[2]`, and `foriginal[3]` in *lines 324* to *326* are used to calculate cumulative (*x*, *y*, *z*) force components, respectively, and are applied to all atoms. Then *lines 329* to *331* are modified to provide additional spring forces in the *x* and *y* directions, and zero force in the *z* direction. The virial elements v[0] to v[5] are also modified in *lines 335* to *340* by replacing the previous *x* and *y* force components with the spring force components, and the *z* component of the force is replaced with zero.

Then, in the case where there is at least one non-numeric input parameter, the code in the screenshot that follows is applied:

```
354     if (xstyle == EQUAL) x0 = input->variable->compute_equal(xvar);
355     if (ystyle == EQUAL) y0 = input->variable->compute_equal(yvar);
356     if (zstyle == EQUAL) zvalue = input->variable->compute_equal(zvar);
357     if (estyle == ATOM)
358       input->variable->compute_atom(evar,igroup,&ework[0],1,0);
359
360     // SM
361     if (kxstyle == EQUAL) kx = input->variable->compute_equal(kxvar);
362     if (kystyle == EQUAL) ky = input->variable->compute_equal(kyvar);
363
364     modify->addstep_compute(update->ntimestep + 1);
365
366     for (int i = 0; i < nlocal; i++) {
367       if (mask[i] & groupbit) {
368         if (region && !region->match(x[i][0],x[i][1],x[i][2])) continue;
369         domain->unmap(x[i],image[i],unwrap);
370
371         if (estyle == ATOM) {
372           foriginal[0] += ework[0]; // SM
373         } else {
374           // SM
375           if (xstyle) foriginal[0] -= -kx*(x[i][0] - x0)*unwrap[0];
376           if (ystyle) foriginal[0] -= -ky*(x[i][1] - y0)*unwrap[1];
377           if (zstyle) foriginal[0] -= 0.0;
378         }
379         foriginal[1] += f[i][0];
380         foriginal[2] += f[i][1];
381         foriginal[3] += f[i][2];
382
383         // SM
384         if (xstyle) f[i][0] += -kx*(x[i][0] - x0);
385         if (ystyle) f[i][1] += -ky*(x[i][1] - y0);
386         if (zstyle) f[i][2] += 0.0;
387         if (evflag) {
388           v[0] = xstyle ? (-kx*(x[i][0] - x0))*unwrap[0] : 0.0;
389           v[1] = ystyle ? (-ky*(x[i][1] - y0))*unwrap[1] : 0.0;
390           v[2] = zstyle ? 0.0*unwrap[2] : 0.0;
391           v[3] = xstyle ? (-kx*(x[i][0] - x0))*unwrap[1] : 0.0;
392           v[4] = xstyle ? (-kx*(x[i][0] - x0))*unwrap[2] : 0.0;
393           v[5] = ystyle ? (-ky*(x[i][1] - y0))*unwrap[2] : 0.0;
394           v_tally(i, v);
```

Figure 10.4 – Screenshot from the FixAddForceXY::post_force() method
that handles non-numeric input parameters

As you can see, the values of x0 and y0 are extracted in *lines 354* to *355* if they are input as variables. If not, then they retain their numeric values that were parsed in the constructor method. Similarly, kx and ky are extracted in *lines 361* to *362* if they are input as equal style variables. In *lines 357* to *358*, the estyle is extracted as an atom style variable, which is the only variable style permitted for estyle, and stored as ework[].

Then, foriginal[0] is stored as ework (*line 372*) and foriginal[1], forginal[2], and foriginal[3] (*lines 375* to *377*) are set to the spring force in the *x* and *y* directions and zero in the *z* direction. The force components are assigned to the spring forces in *lines 384* to *386*, and the virial elements are adjusted in *lines 388* to *393*.

Altogether, the input script syntax for this fix addforceXY becomes the following:

```
fix FIX_NAME GROUP addforceXY x0 y0 zvalue kx ky
```

Here, FIX_NAME is the name of the fix, GROUP is the group on which the fix acts, and the parameters x0, y0, kx, and ky correspond to the position coordinates and spring constants described earlier. The quantity zvalue is a placeholder that does not affect the fix in 2D. Other optional keywords relevant to Fix Addforce are permitted as well.

The contents of the other methods, such as setmask(), compute_scalar(), and compute_vector(), are left unchanged.

The fix is then tested using a trial input script, which we will look at in the next section.

Trial run (in.Test_FixAddforceXY)

A test LAMMPS input script is created to test the forces created by the spring force. A 2D simulation box containing a single atom is created, where the point **(x0,y0)** is chosen at the center. A spring force with equal kx and ky values is provided on the atom pointing towards **(x0,y0)** using the fix addforceXY command in the input script. This atom is also assigned an initial velocity along the +*y* direction and is time-integrated using fix nve to observe its trajectory.

The following diagram shows the simulation setup consisting of the simulation box, atom, and the point **(x0,y0)**, along with a velocity vector $\vec{v}$ and force spring force vector $\vec{F}$:

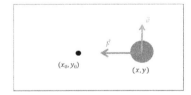

Figure 10.5 – Diagram of the simulation setup

The LAMMPS script is presented here:

```
units metal
dimension 2
boundary p p p
atom_style atomic
atom_modify map array

region r0  block 0 20 0 20 0 20 units box

create_box 1 r0
mass    1 10.0
create_atoms 1 single  15 10 0 units box
group G1 id 1

pair_style  lj/cut 1.0
pair_coeff  1 1 0.0   1.0

variable x1 equal x[1]
variable fx equal fx[1]
variable y1 equal y[1]
variable fy equal fy[1]

variable X0 equal 10
variable Y0 equal 10
variable KX equal 0.5
variable KY equal 0.5

velocity G1 set 0 10 0
fix ADDFORCEXY   G1 addforceXY v_X0 v_Y0 0 v_KX v_KY
fix NVE          G1 nve
fix PRINT_PE all print 10 "${x1} ${y1} ${fx} ${fy}" file
outputADDFORCEXY.dat screen no

run 400
```

As shown in the preceding code, a single atom in a 2D simulation is placed at an initial location and provided an initial velocity. The `Fix AddforceXY` command applies to this atom and is directed toward a given point. The input parameters x0, y0, kx, and ky are entered as variables within `fix addforceXY` to verify that the code reads variables correctly.

The 2D trajectory of the atom is plotted in the following diagram:

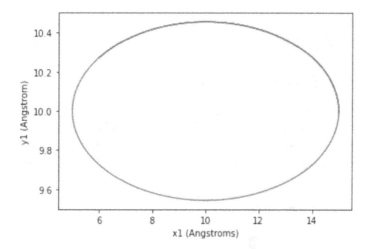

Figure 10.6 – Plot of the trajectory of an atom experiencing a spring force via Fix AddForceXY

As you can see, given the direction of the spring force and the direction of the initial velocity, the atom trajectory forms an ellipse centered around **(x0,y0)** as expected from classical mechanics. For other combinations of force magnitudes and initial velocities, the trajectories can take other forms, such as circles and straight lines.

In this section, we implemented a custom nonpairwise force and applied it to atoms by modifying the `Fix Addforce` class and including additional input parameters. In the next section, we will write a fix to exert an external, nonpairwise active force on connected atoms in a polymer chain.

Writing a fix to apply an active force

The following is a list of changes that should be made to the source code:

- The new files that should be created are `fix_activeforce.cpp` and `fix_activeforce.h`.
- The existing files that are modified are `fix_addforce.cpp`, `fix_addforce.h`, and `compute_bond_local.cpp`.

- The methods that are modified are constructor, `post_force()`.
- The input parameters are `fMagnitude`, and `direction`.
- The other quantities introduced in this section can be seen in a full list in *Figure 10.9* under `post_force()`.
- The LAMMPS syntax is `fix FIX_NAME GROUP activeforce FMAGNITUDE DIRECTION` (we'll review the syntax in this section).

In this section, we will create an active force in `Fix Activeforce` that applies a specified magnitude of force along the direction defined by two bonded atoms.

Theory (active force on bonded atoms)

An active force is generated by an atom and acts on the same atom. In this example, the active force acts on an atom in the direction along which it is bonded to another atom. This force can be used to model a self-propelling polymer where the propulsion force on each monomer acts towards the next bonded monomer. The following diagram illustrates this force:

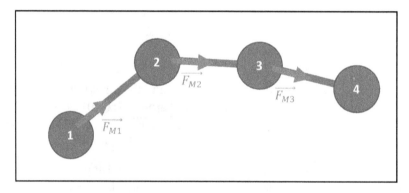

Figure 10.7 – Diagram of four bonded atoms with an active force on atoms 1, 2, and 3 respectively

In the preceding diagram, four bonded atoms form a chain consisting of three bonds **1–2**, **2–3**, and **3–4**. The active force $\overrightarrow{F_M}$ on each of atoms **1**, **2**, and **3** acts along the directions of the bonds as shown. No active force acts on atom **4** since it is located at the end of the chain as defined by the bond sequence. The direction of the active force can be reversed, in which case, there will be active forces acting on atoms **4**, **3**, and **2** in the directions opposite to the bonds **3–4**, **2–3**, and **1–2**, respectively, with no active force applied on atom **1**.

The active force $\overrightarrow{F_M}$ acts along the displacement vector $(\Delta x, \Delta y, \Delta z)$ pointing from the atom in question to the bonded atom. Its components are calculated as follows:

- The x component F_{Mx} can be derived by:

$$F_{Mx} = |\overrightarrow{F_M}| \frac{\Delta x}{\sqrt{\Delta x^2 + \Delta y^2 + \Delta z^2}}$$

- The y-component F_{My} can be derived as follows:

$$F_{My} = |\overrightarrow{F_M}| \frac{\Delta y}{\sqrt{\Delta x^2 + \Delta y^2 + \Delta z^2}}$$

- The z component F_{Mz} can be calculated by:

$$F_{Mz} = |\overrightarrow{F_M}| \frac{\Delta z}{\sqrt{\Delta x^2 + \Delta y^2 + \Delta z^2}}$$

As with the example of `Fix AddforceXY` in the previous section, we choose to modify the `Fix Addforce` class to implement this active force. Copies of `fix_addforce.cpp` and `fix_addforce.h` are renamed to `fix_activeforce.cpp` and `fix_activeforce.h`.

Modifying the header file – fix_activeforce.h

The fix style name is changed to `activeforce` in `fix_activeforce.h` (*line 16*):

```
FixStyle(activeforce,FixActiveForce)
```

The following quantities are declared (*line 56* and *line 59*):

```
int direction;
double fMagnitude;
```

From the preceding code, the integer `direction` determines the direction of the active force on each atom as either pointing in the direction of the bond or in the opposite direction, indicated by *+1* or *-1*. The magnitude of the active force is parsed as `fMagnitude`, which will be used to calculate the components.

In `fix_activeforce.cpp`, in addition to the existing header files, the `atom_vec.h` and `molecule.h` header files are imported (*lines 32 to 33*):

```
#include "atom_vec.h"
#include "molecule.h"
```

As you can see from the preceding code, these header files will be used to identify bonded atoms and molecule IDs of atoms during force assignment. In the constructor method, changes are made to accommodate the input of the magnitude of the force and the direction, as described in the next section.

Modifying the constructor in fix_activeforce.cpp

In the constructor method of `fix_activeforce.cpp`, the number of input arguments is changed from a minimum of 6 to 5 (*line 47*):

```
if (narg < 5) error->all(FLERR,"Illegal fix activeforce
command");
```

As you can see from the preceding code, the 5 mandatory input parameters include the three default parameters read by `fix.h`, the magnitude of the force, and the direction of the force.

To accommodate the input of the magnitude of the force as a numerical value or a variable (either equal or atom style), we reuse the scheme used in `Fix Addforce` (or `Fix AddforceXY`) to parse input parameters, as shown in the following screenshot:

```
62    if (strstr(arg[3],"v_") == arg[3]) {
63        int n = strlen(&arg[3][2]) + 1;
64        xstr = new char[n];
65        strcpy(xstr,&arg[3][2]);
66    } else {
67        fMagnitude = fabs( force->numeric(FLERR,arg[3]) );    // SM: changed xvalue to fMagnitude
68        xstyle = CONSTANT;
69    }
70
71    // SM: Removed fy and fz entries
72
73    // SM: choose forward or reverse direction of active force
74    if (strcmp(arg[4],"forward") == 0) {
75        direction = 1;
76    }
77    else if (strcmp(arg[4],"reverse") == 0) {
78        direction = -1;
79    }
80    else error->all(FLERR,"Illegal fix activeforce direction: must be forward or reverse");
81
82
83    // optional args
```

Figure 10.8 – Screenshot from fix_activeforce.cpp showing the constructor method

As you can see, on *lines 62 to 69*, `xstr` is used to read the variable name if the force magnitude is input as a variable, and `xstyle` is used identify a numerical versus non-numerical input, similar to the process used to parse input parameters in `fix_addforceXY.cpp` (see previous section).

Since the magnitude is required, the absolute value of a numerical input is calculated (*line 67*) as the variable `fMagnitude`. For non-numerical inputs in the form of variables, the absolute value is determined after extracting the numerical value in the `post_force()` method.

The original codes for parsing `fy` and `fz` in `Fix Addforce` have been removed since only one force needs to be parsed (see note on *line 71*).

In *lines 74 to 80*, the direction of the force is parsed as `forward` or `reverse`, where an input of `forward` sets `direction=1`, and `reverse` sets `direction=-1`. Here, the forward and reverse directions indicate the same or opposite directions with respect to the direction of the bond from one atom to another, as defined in the LAMMPS input script or data file.

The only other method where modifications are required is the `post_force()` method, which we will discuss next.

Modifying the post_force() method in fix_activeforce.cpp

In order to identify bonded atoms, part of the code from `compute_bond_local.cpp` is reused in the `post_force()` method. In order to facilitate the `post_force()` procedure, certain quantities are first introduced in *lines 281 to 292*:

```
278    // ------------------------------------------------
279    // SM: introduce atom pointer to read bonded atoms
280    // ------------------------------------------------
281    tagint **bond_atom = atom->bond_atom;
282    tagint *tag = atom->tag;
283    tagint tagprev;
284    Molecule **onemols = atom->avec->onemols;
285    int molecular = atom->molecular;
286    int *molindex = atom->molindex;
287    int *molatom = atom->molatom;
288    int *num_bond = atom->num_bond;
289    int atom1, atom2;
290    int jmol,jatom,nb;
291    double rsq,delx,dely,delz;
292    int atomIndexI;
```

Figure 10.9 – Screenshot from FixActiveForce::post_force() showing the quantities that were introduced

A brief explanation of these quantities is provided in the following list:

- `bond_atom[][]`: This is the 2D array that accesses the global IDs of bonded atoms for each atom, where the first index in the array corresponds to the central atom ID and the second index corresponds to the IDs of the bonded atoms.
- `tag[]`: This is the 1D array that converts the information from a local atom index in the processor to the corresponding global atom ID used in the LAMMPS input script or data file.
- `tagprev`: This is the variable that adjusts atom indices between global ID (listed in LAMMPS inputs script or data file) and template atom ID within a template molecule index (in molecule templates, if used).
- `onemols[][]`: This is the 2D array that accesses a list of molecule templates belonging to a molecular template system in the first index, as well as their various properties, such as the number of bonds and the list of bonded atoms in the second index.
- `molecular`: This is the integer that returns 0 if the system is atomic, 1 if the system is molecular, and 2 if the system is a molecular template.
- `molindex[]`: This is a 1D array that assigns a template molecule index to an atom belonging to a molecular template system.
- `molatom[]`: This is a 1D array that assigns a template atom ID within a template molecule index to an atom belonging to a molecular template system.
- `num_bond[]`: This is a 1D array that accesses the number of bonds linked to an atom.
- `atom1` and `atom2`: These are the local atom indices of the two bonded atoms that are used to determine the direction vector of the active force.
- `jmol` and `jatom`: These are the variables to store a template molecule index and the corresponding template atom ID within the template molecule index that are assigned to an atom belonging to a molecular template system.
- `nb`: This is a variable to store the number of bonds linked to an atom.
- `rsq`: This is the square of the distance between two bonded atoms.
- `delx`, `dely`, and `delz`: These are the (x, y, z) components of the displacement vector pointing from `atom1` to `atom2`.
- `atomIndexI`: This is the index of the atom on which the active force is applied, which can be `atom1` or `atom2` depending on the direction specified.

Both `molindex` and `molatom` are parsed from a template by `atom_vec_template.cpp` located in the `MOLECULE` folder, and are relevant only if a molecule template is used in the LAMMPS script to generate molecules (see `https://lammps.sandia.gov/doc/atom_style.html`).

These molecules have their own template indices and each atom in a template carries an atom ID within the template, which is not necessarily the same as its global atom ID. Similarly, `tagprev` is also only relevant in the case of a molecule template system, and it is used to adjust the difference between template atom ID and global atom ID in an index sequence, which is essential when identifying bonded atoms and extracting the corresponding local processor index for force assignment. This special treatment for molecule templates will be illustrated in the following section.

Assigning the active force

Having declared the quantities, as you have seen earlier, the cases of numerical versus variable input parameters are considered separately, as has been done for `Fix Addforce`. In the case that `fMagnitude` is entered as a numerical value, the following screenshot demonstrates the calculations performed:

```
305    // ---------------------------------------------------------------
306    // SM: Identifying bonds and direction of active force
307    // (from compute_bond_local.cpp)
308    // ---------------------------------------------------------------
309    atom1 = i;
310
311    if (molecular == ) {
312        nb = num_bond[atom1];
313        //fprintf(screen,"atom1 = %d \n", atom1);
314    }
315    else {
316        if (molindex[atom1] < ) continue;
317        jmol = molindex[atom1];
318        jatom = molatom[atom1];
319        nb = onemols[jmol]->num_bond[jatom];
320    }
321
322    for (int j = ; j < nb; j++) {
323        if (molecular == ) {
324            atom2 = atom->map(bond_atom[atom1][j]);
325            //fprintf(screen,"      atom2 = %d \n", atom2);
326        } else {
327            tagprev = tag[atom1] - jatom - ;
328            atom2 = atom->map(onemols[jmol]->bond_atom[jatom][j]+tagprev);
329        }
330
331        if (atom2 <  || !(mask[atom2] & groupbit)) continue;
332
333        //fprintf(screen,"tag[atom1] = %d \n", tag[atom1]);
334        //fprintf(screen,"tag[atom2] = %d \n", tag[atom2]);
335
336        delx = x[atom2][ ]-x[atom1][ ];
337        dely = x[atom2][ ]-x[atom1][ ];
338        delz = x[atom2][ ]-x[atom1][ ];
339        domain->minimum_image(delx,dely,delz);
340        rsq = delx*delx + dely*dely + delz*delz;
341
342        xvalue = fMagnitude * delx/sqrt(rsq) * direction;
343        yvalue = fMagnitude * dely/sqrt(rsq) * direction;
344        zvalue = fMagnitude * delz/sqrt(rsq) * direction;
345
346        if (direction == ) atomIndexI = atom1;
347        if (direction == - ) atomIndexI = atom2;
```

Figure 10.10 – Screenshot from FixActiveForce::post_force()
showing the treatment of the numerical fMagnitude

As you can see, `atom1` is set as equal to the integer `i` that loops over all atoms in the core (*line 309*), and if the atom style used in the LAMMPS input script is a standard molecular system (indicated by `molecular == 1`), then the number of bonds `nb` assigned to `atom1` is read directly using the `num_bond[]` array (*lines 311 to 314*).

If the atom style used is a molecule template system, then `jmol` and `jatom` parse the molecule template index and molecule template atom ID of `atom1` respectively, and the number of bonds `nb` of `atom1` are accessed through the `onemols[jmol]->num_bond[jatom]` command in *lines 315 to 320*.

Having obtained the number of bonds `nb`, the code loops over all of these bonds (*line 322*) to identify every bonded atom of `atom1`. In the case of a standard molecular system (*lines 323*), the global atom IDs of the atoms bonded to `atom1` are accessed via `bond_atom[][]`, which are then converted to the local atom index in the processor by the `atom->map()` method and assigned to variable `atom2` (*lines 324*).

In the case of a molecule template system (*line 326*), `tagprev` is calculated as the difference between the global atom ID of `atom1` (accessed as `tag[atom1]`) and the template atom ID `jatom` of `atom1` to account for the shifted indices between the global and template atom IDs (*line 327*).

Furthermore, `-1` is included in the same line to account for local atom indices starting from `0` as opposed to global and template atom ID starting from `1`. This value of `tagprev` is added to the template atom IDs of the atoms bonded to `jatom` (extracted by the `onemols[jmol]->bond_atom[jatom][j]` command), and the result is converted to the local atom index using the `atom->map()` method before being assigned to `atom2` (*line 328*).

This way, the local atom indices of the atoms forming the bond `atom1-atom2` are established, and their coordinates can be subtracted to find the displacement vector (`delx dely, delz`) pointing from `atom1` to `atom2` (*lines 336 to 338*), as well as the square of the distance (`rsq`) between the atoms (*line 340*). In between, the `domain->minimum()` method is called from `domain.cpp` to check for the minimum image convention consistency of the atoms and to ensure that the correct distance is calculated within periodic boundary conditions if the atom separation exceeds half the box length in any dimension (*line 339*).

The (x, y, and z) force components of the active force are then calculated as variables (`xvalue`, `yvalue`, and `zvalue`) that either point along (`delx`, `dely`, and `delz`) or point against (`-delx`, `-dely`, `-delz`) the direction of the force depending on the `+1` or `-1` value of the `direction` parameter (*lines 342 to 344*), which correspond to a forward and reverse force respectively. Also, the `direction` parameter determines whether to apply the active force on `atom1` (`forward`) or `atom2` (`reverse`) in *lines 346 to 347*, where `atomIndexI` is defined as the atom on which the force acts. The force is finally applied on `atomIndexI` in *lines 357 to 359*.

> **Important Note:**
>
> In *Figure 10.10*, a few `printf` commands that write the contents of `atom1` and `atom2`, as well as their global IDs, are commented out. These lines were used for testing purposes and are not required once testing has been completed.

In the next case, where `fMagnitude` is entered as a variable in the LAMMPS input script, the value of the variable is extracted in *lines 382 to 384*, and the same steps as in the preceding case are employed to identify `atom1` and `atom2` for each bond (*lines 398 to 433*). However, there is an important inclusion in *line 426*:

```
fMagnitude = fabs(fMagnitude);
```

This line ensures that the `fMagnitude` extracted from its variable is changed to its absolute value, since it is possible for the variable to contain a negative value.

Having identified the bonded atom indices and the `atomIndexI` on which to apply the active force, the changes displayed in the following screenshot are implemented for proper force assignments:

```
438         // SM: removed ystyle and zstyle
439         if (estyle == ATOM) {
440             foriginal[0] += sforce[atomIndexI][3];
441         } else {
442             if (xstyle) {
443                 foriginal[0] -= xvalue*unwrap[0];
444                 foriginal[0] -= yvalue*unwrap[1];
445                 foriginal[0] -= zvalue*unwrap[2];
446             }
447         }
448
449         foriginal[1] += f[atomIndexI][0];
450         foriginal[2] += f[atomIndexI][1];
451         foriginal[3] += f[atomIndexI][2];
452
453         // SM: removed ystyle and zstyle
454         if (xstyle) {
455             f[atomIndexI][0] += xvalue;
456             f[atomIndexI][1] += yvalue;
457             f[atomIndexI][2] += zvalue;
458         }
459
460         if (evflag) {
461             // SM: changed ystyle (v[1],v[5]) and zstyle (v[2]) to xstyle
462             v[0] = xstyle ? xvalue*unwrap[0] : 0.0;
463             v[1] = xstyle ? yvalue*unwrap[1] : 0.0;
464             v[2] = xstyle ? zvalue*unwrap[2] : 0.0;
465             v[3] = xstyle ? xvalue*unwrap[1] : 0.0;
466             v[4] = xstyle ? xvalue*unwrap[2] : 0.0;
467             v[5] = xstyle ? yvalue*unwrap[2] : 0.0;
468             v_tally(atomIndexI, v);
469         }
```

Figure 10.11 – Screenshot from FixActiveForce::post_force() showing force assignments if fMagnitude is entered as a variable

As you can see, this part of the code from `fix_addforce.cpp` is modified to remove all references to `ystyle` and `zstyle` that are inconsequential for this fix. The force components on `atomIndexI` are assigned in *lines 455 to 457*, and the `ystyle` and `zstyle` parameters in the virial parameters in *lines 462 to 467* are replaced by `xstyle`.

Altogether, the LAMMPS input script syntax for `Fix Activeforce` becomes:

```
fix FIX_NAME GROUP activeforce FMAGNITUDE DIRECTION
```

The `FIX_NAME` and `GROUP` carry their usual meanings, and `FMAGNITUDE` and `DIRECTION` refer to the parameters described in the preceding sections. As explained earlier, the entry for `DIRECTION` must be either `forward` or `reverse`.

This fix is now tested with a trial LAMMPS script, which we will look at in the next section.

Trial run (in.Test_ActiveForce)

A bead-spring model of a polymer is constructed consisting of 10 atoms with 9 identical bonds and no angles or dihedrals in data file `Polymer_10.data`:

```
# LAMMPS data file
10 atoms
9 bonds
1 atom types
1 bond types
-150 150 xlo xhi
-150 150 ylo yhi
-150 150 zlo zhi


Masses
1    1.0


Atoms
1 1 1 0 0 0
2 1 2 1 0 0
3 1 1 2 0 0
4 1 2 3 0 0
5 1 1 4 0 0
6 1 2 5 0 0
7 1 1 6 0 0
```

```
8 1 2 7 0 0
9 1 1 8 0 0
10 1 2 9 0 0

Bonds
1 1 1 2
2 1 2 3
3 1 3 4
4 1 4 5
5 1 5 6
6 1 6 7
7 1 7 8
8 1 8 9
9 1 9 10
```

As you can see, a linear chain of 10 identical atoms is built with 9 identical bonds connecting the atoms. The chain is placed in a large simulation box with the dimensions listed, and a mass of 1.0 amu is assigned to each atom.

The LAMMPS input script that reads the data file and performs the simulation is shown here:

```
# ------------------------------------
# INITIALIZE SIMULATION
# ------------------------------------
units metal
dimension 3
boundary p p p
atom_style bond
atom_modify map array


# ------------------------------------
# CREATE ATOMS
# ------------------------------------
read_data Polymer_10.data
bond_style harmonic
bond_coeff 1 0 1
```

```
# ---------------------------------------
# GROUPS
# ---------------------------------------
group       POLYMER      type 1


# ---------------------------------------
# PAIR STYLES
# ---------------------------------------
pair_style  lj/cut 1
pair_coeff  1 1   0.0   1.0


# ---------------------------------------
# FIXES
# ---------------------------------------
velocity POLYMER create 1.0 54321 dist gaussian
variable FMAGNITUDE equal 0.01
fix 1 POLYMER activeforce  ${FMAGNITUDE}   forward
fix 2 all nve
dump DUMP all custom 1000 outputAll.lammpstrj id type x y z fx
fy fz


run 200
```

From the preceding code, the bonds are designed as harmonic bond styles with an equilibrium length of 1 Å and spring constant of zero to remove any bond interaction, while identifying atoms that are bonded. Also, there is zero nonbonded pairwise interaction between the atoms.

A constant active force of 0.01 eV/Å acts on the atoms in a forward direction. This way, the only force on the atoms is applied by the active force and therefore the force-per-atom dumped during the simulation run will represent the active force.

The polymer is initially oriented perfectly linearly along the +x-axis and the atoms are assigned velocities from a **Maxwell–Boltzmann velocity distribution** using the velocity create command. The polymer is time-integrated by fix nve and the position and the forces acting on the atoms are dumped.

The atom positions and forces at the final iteration of the simulation run are extracted from the dump file. The active forces acting on the atoms are visualized in the following figure:

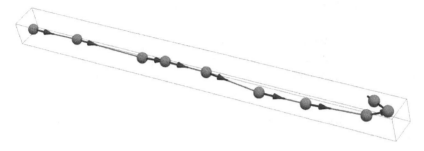

Figure 10.12 – Visualization of the polymer showing atoms (spheres),
bonds (tubes), and active forces (arrows)

It can be observed from the preceding figure that the polymer chain has been deformed because of the initial velocity, the active forces, and the absence of any bond interactions. The active force arrow on each atom is pointing to its bonded atom, except for the last atom in the chain, which does not have any active force.

In this section, an active force directed towards a bonded atom was implemented by modifying the `Fix Addforce` class and copying code from `compute_bond_local.cpp` to identify the bonds of each atom. In the next section, a custom wall force will be written that applies a user-defined force to an atom interacting with a designated wall.

Writing a fix to apply a custom wall force

Here is a list of changes that are made to the source code:

- The existing files that have been modified are `fix_wall_region.cpp` and `fix_wall_region.h`.
- The methods that have been modified are constructor, `init()`, and `post_force()`.
- The new method added is `lj126Expanded()`.
- The new input parameter introduced is `deltaLJ`.
- The LAMMPS syntax is `fix FIX_NAME GROUP wall/region REGION lj126Expanded EPSILON SIGMA DELTALJ CUTOFF` (we'll review this syntax in this section).

In this section, we will add a custom wall potential to the inventory of existing ones in the `Fix Wall/Region` class.

Theory (expanded Lennard–Jones wall force)

The Fix Wall/Region class (https://lammps.sandia.gov/doc/fix_wall_region.html) defines the surface of a region as a wall that can apply forces to an atom that interacts with it. This force of interaction can be defined in terms of a potential function (for example, **Lennard–Jones**) and its negative derivative, such that the atom experiences the potential described during its interaction period. The standard version of LAMMPS includes wall potentials of the forms harmonic, Lennard–Jones, and **Morse**, and we will add to it the option of expanding the Lennard–Jones wall potential.

The expanded Lennard–Jones potential $V(r)$ as a function of the atom-to-wall separation r has the following functional form:

$$V(r) = 4\varepsilon \left[\left(\frac{\sigma}{r - \Delta} \right)^{12} - \left(\frac{\sigma}{r - \Delta} \right)^{6} \right]$$

In this equation, ε represents the potential well depth, σ represents the separation at which the potential becomes zero for a regular Lennard–Jones potential, and Δ represents the distance by which the potential function is shifted horizontally along the axis of r. This $V(r)$ resembles a regular Lennard–Jones potential that has been translated by Δ.

Subsequently, the force function $F(r)$ is calculated from the negative derivative of $V(r)$:

$$F(r) = -\frac{dV}{dr} = \frac{48\varepsilon\sigma^{12}}{(r - \Delta)^{13}} - \frac{24\varepsilon\sigma^{6}}{(r - \Delta)^{7}}$$

This potential and force can be added directly to fix_wall_region.cpp and fix_wall_region.h without altering the existing potentials and without having to rename new copies of these files.

Modifying the header file

In fix_wall_region.h, the quantity deltaLJ and the method lj126Expanded() are declared in *lines 61 to 62*:

```
double deltaLJ;
void lj126Expanded(double);
```

From the preceding code, the variable deltaLJ will be used to parse Δ and the method lj126Expanded() will be used to calculate the wall force and potential energy.

In fix_wall_region.cpp, the LJ126Expanded item is appended to the list of enumerators in *line 31*:

```
enum{LJ93,LJ126,LJ1043,COLLOID,HARMONIC,MORSE,LJ126Expanded};
```

By appending this `LJ126Expanded` item, an enumerator is created for the expanded Lennard–Jones potential that can be used to identify this potential type throughout the class. These enumerators are used to assign a sequential integer value to each form of potential used, which is then used to parse input parameters and calculate coefficients accordingly for the potential type specified, as will be described in the following sections.

Modifying the constructor in fix_wall_region.cpp

The syntax for `Fix Wall/Region` in the LAMMPS input script is as follows:

```
fix  FIX_NAME  GROUP  wall/region  REGION  STYLE …
```

Other than the usual first three parameters, the region that defines the wall surface (`REGION`) and the form of the wall potential (`STYLE`) need to be parsed, along with a list of arguments specific to each type of potential that are represented by the dots after `STYLE`. The region specified in the input script by the parameter `REGION` is identified first in the constructor (*lines 53 to 58*), as shown in the following screenshot:

```
51   // parse args
52
53   iregion = domain->find_region(arg[3]);
54   if (iregion == -1)
55     error->all(FLERR,"Region ID for fix wall/region does not exist");
56   int n = strlen(arg[3]) + 1;
57   idregion = new char[n];
58   strcpy(idregion,arg[3]);
59
60   if (strcmp(arg[4],"lj93") == 0) style = LJ93;
61   else if (strcmp(arg[4],"lj126") == 0) style = LJ126;
62   else if (strcmp(arg[4],"lj126Expanded") == 0) style = LJ126Expanded;  // SM
63   else if (strcmp(arg[4],"lj1043") == 0) style = LJ1043;
64   else if (strcmp(arg[4],"colloid") == 0) style = COLLOID;
65   else if (strcmp(arg[4],"harmonic") == 0) style = HARMONIC;
66   else if (strcmp(arg[4],"morse") == 0) style = MORSE;
67   else error->all(FLERR,"Illegal fix wall/region command");
68
69   if (style != COLLOID) dynamic_group_allow = 1;
70
71   if (style == MORSE) {
72     if (narg != 9)
73       error->all(FLERR,"Illegal fix wall/region command");
74
75     epsilon = force->numeric(FLERR,arg[5]);
76     alpha = force->numeric(FLERR,arg[6]);
77     sigma = force->numeric(FLERR,arg[7]);
78     cutoff = force->numeric(FLERR,arg[8]);
79   }
80
81   // SM
82   else if (style == LJ126Expanded) {
83     if (narg != 9)
84       error->all(FLERR,"Illegal fix wall/region command");
85     epsilon = force->numeric(FLERR,arg[5]);
86     sigma = force->numeric(FLERR,arg[6]);
87     deltaLJ = force->numeric(FLERR,arg[7]);
88     cutoff = force->numeric(FLERR,arg[8]);
89   }
```

Figure 10.13 – Screenshot from fix_wall_region.cpp showing the constructor method

As you can see, the wall surface region entered in the input script (REGION) is searched among existing defined regions using the domain->find_region() method (*line 53*), and if the region exists, the region ID is stored as an integer iregion, which will be used in the post_force() method to extract the relevant region properties.

Next, the potential form entered by STYLE is compared against the permissible styles in *lines 60* to *67*, which include the styles corresponding to the enumerators in *line 31*. To maintain consistency, a new line (*line 62*) is created for the expanded Lennard–Jones potential style.

This line specifies that the expanded Lennard–Jones wall potential can be implemented by the style name lj126Expanded in the fix wall/region command in the LAMMPS input script, and it sets the variable style to the corresponding enumerator for the same potential.

Once the variable style has been determined based on the form of the potential entered, it is used to parse the style-specific arguments that follow. In *lines 82* to *89*, a block is added to sequentially parse the variables epsilon, sigma, deltaLJ, and cutoff for the LJ126Expanded style. The first three variables have the same meaning as described in the expanded Lennard–Jones equation earlier, and the variable cutoff is self-explanatory.

These modifications enable the constructor method to parse the wall potential form and the corresponding input parameters, which are then used in the init() method to calculate the relevant coefficients.

Modifying the init() method in fix_wall_region.cpp

A new block is added in the init() method to calculate the coefficients that will be used to find the expanded Lennard–Jones potential and force, as shown in the following screenshot:

```
179   else if (style == LJ126Expanded) {
180       coeff1 = 48.0 * epsilon * pow(sigma,12.0);
181       coeff2 = 24.0 * epsilon * pow(sigma,6.0);
182       coeff3 = 4.0 * epsilon * pow(sigma,12.0);
183       coeff4 = 4.0 * epsilon * pow(sigma,6.0);
184       double r2inv = 1.0/((cutoff-deltaLJ)*(cutoff-deltaLJ));
185       double r6inv = r2inv*r2inv*r2inv;
186       offset = r6inv*(coeff3*r6inv - coeff4);
187   }
```

Figure 10.14 – Screenshot from fix_wall_region.cpp showing the init() method

As you can see, if the `style` variable matches the expanded Lennard–Jones potential enumerator (*line 179*), then the following quantities are calculated in *lines 180* to *186*:

- coeff1 = $48\varepsilon\sigma^{12}$

- coeff2 = $24\varepsilon\sigma^{6}$

- coeff3 = $4\varepsilon\sigma^{12}$

- coeff4 = $4\varepsilon\sigma^{6}$

- r2inv = $\dfrac{1}{(\text{cutoff} - \Delta)^2}$

- r6inv = $\dfrac{1}{(\text{cutoff} - \Delta)^6}$

- offset = $\dfrac{1}{(\text{cutoff} - \Delta)^6}\left[\dfrac{\text{coeff3}}{(\text{cutoff} - \Delta)^6} - \text{coeff4}\right] = 4\varepsilon\left[\left(\dfrac{\sigma}{\text{cutoff} - \Delta}\right)^{12} - \left(\dfrac{\sigma}{\text{cutoff} - \Delta}\right)^{6}\right]$

The coefficients `coeff1`, `coeff2`, `coeff3`, and `coeff4` are calculated, and the `offset` is also calculated as the value of the potential at the cutoff. These quantities will be used in the `lj126Expanded()` method to calculate the force and potential.

Adding the lj126Expanded() method

In the `Fix Wall/Region` class, each potential form is assigned a method to calculate its force and potential. The corresponding method for the expanded Lennard–Jones potential is added to this class as `lj126Expanded()`, as shown in the following screenshot:

```
403  /* ----------------------------------------------------------
404     SM: LJ 12/6 Expanded interaction for particle with wall
405     compute eng and fwall = magnitude of wall force
406  ---------------------------------------------------------- */
407
408  void FixWallRegion::lj126Expanded(double r)
409  {
410    double rinv = 1.0/(r-deltaLJ);
411    double r2inv = rinv*rinv;
412    double r6inv = r2inv*r2inv*r2inv;
413    fwall = r6inv*(coeff1*r6inv - coeff2) * rinv;
414    eng = r6inv*(coeff3*r6inv - coeff4) - offset;
415  }
```

Figure 10.15 – Screenshot from fix_wall_region.cpp showing the lj126Expanded() method

As you can see, this method accepts the distance of an atom from the wall as argument `r` (*line 408*) and uses it to calculate `rinv`, `r2inv`, and `r6inv` (*lines 410* to *412*), which are then used in the calculation of the force of the wall `fwall` (*line 413*) and the potential of the wall `eng` (*line 414*). The coefficients `coeff1` and `coeff2` are used in the `fwall` calculation, and `coeff3` and `coeff4` are used in the `eng` calculation.

This method is called in the `post_force()` method to assign forces.

Modifying the post_force() method

In the `post_force()` method, the code loops over all of the atoms in the processor and identifies the atoms that belong to the appropriate group and are not located inside the region specified as the wall (*lines 276* to *281*), as shown in the following screenshot:

```
276     for (i = 0; i < nlocal; i++)
277       if (mask[i] & groupbit) {
278         if (!region->match(x[i][0],x[i][1],x[i][2])) {
279           onflag = 1;
280           continue;
281         }
282         if (style == COLLOID) tooclose = radius[i];
283         else tooclose = 0.0;
284
285         n = region->surface(x[i][0],x[i][1],x[i][2],cutoff);
286
287         for (m = 0; m < n; m++) {
288           if (region->contact[m].r <= tooclose) {
289             onflag = 1;
290             continue;
291           } else rinv = 1.0/region->contact[m].r;
292
293           if (style == LJ93) lj93(region->contact[m].r);
294           else if (style == LJ126) lj126(region->contact[m].r);
295           else if (style == LJ126Expanded) lj126Expanded(region->contact[m].r);    // SM
296           else if (style == LJ1043) lj1043(region->contact[m].r);
297           else if (style == MORSE) morse(region->contact[m].r);
298           else if (style == COLLOID) colloid(region->contact[m].r,radius[i]);
299           else harmonic(region->contact[m].r);
300
301           delx = region->contact[m].delx;
302           dely = region->contact[m].dely;
303           delz = region->contact[m].delz;
304           fx = fwall * delx * rinv;
305           fy = fwall * dely * rinv;
306           fz = fwall * delz * rinv;
307           f[i][0] += fx;
308           f[i][1] += fy;
309           f[i][2] += fz;
```

Figure 10.16 – Screenshot from fix_wall_region.cpp showing the post_force() method

As you can see, the variable n in *line 285* calls the `region->surface()` method from `region.cpp` to determine the number of wall surfaces that are located within the cutoff distance of the atom `i`. By looping over every surface (*line 287*), the shortest atom distance from the surface is determined using the `region->contact[]` structure defined in `region.h` (*lines 288* to *291*).

The structure returns the shortest distance r from a surface to the atom when called as a member from the object with the dot symbol. If the atom is not located on the surface (*lines 288* to *290*), then this distance is used to calculate the inverse distance `rinv` (*line 291*) that will be used to find the force components (*lines 304* to *306*).

In *lines 293* to *299*, the variable `style` that was based on the potential form is used to call the appropriate method to feed the atom distance and calculate the wall force and potential. *Line 295* is added to account for the expanded Lennard–Jones potential and to call the `lj126Expanded()` method when required.

As has been illustrated previously, the `lj126Expanded()` method yields the wall force `fwall` and wall potential eng. Together with the displacement vector components (`delx`, `dely`, and `delz`) extracted from the `region->contact[]` structure (*lines 301* to *303*), the `fwall` is used to calculate the force components exerted by the atom (*lines 304* to *306*). Similarly, eng is added to the potential of the atom in *line 313*.

The LAMMPS input syntax to apply this fix is as follows:

```
fix FIX_NAME GROUP wall/region REGION lj126Expanded EPSILON
SIGMA DELTALJ CUTOFF
```

The parameters `EPSILON`, `SIGMA`, and `DELTALJ` refer to the quantities ε, σ, and Δ, respectively.

The modified `Fix Wall/Region` class is now ready to be tested with a LAMMPS test script.

Trial run (in.Test_WallRegion)

A LAMMPS test script creates a cubic simulation box of sides 20 Å, where the sides of the box serve as walls with which to apply wall forces. A single atom is created in the middle of the box and assigned a velocity along the *x* direction, so that it travels perpendicular to the walls, which apply an expanded Lennard–Jones wall potential on the atom with a cutoff of 5 Å.

This way, the force on the atom is zero, except when the separation between the atom and the wall is less than the cutoff, in which case the only force acting on the atom is the wall force pointing along the *x* direction.

The following diagram shows the simulation setup consisting of the wall (dashed line) and the atom with a velocity vector $\vec{v}$ pointing along the x direction:

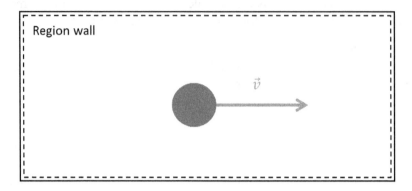

Figure 10.17 – Diagram of simulation setup

The input script is provided here, where the first part performs system initialization and creates the single atom:

```
# ---------------------
# INITIALIZE SIMULATION
# ---------------------
units metal
dimension 3
boundary p p p
atom_style atomic
atom_modify map array


# ---------------------
# DEFINE REGION
# ---------------------
region R0  block 0 20 0 20 0 20 units box


# ---------------------
# CREATE ATOMS
# ---------------------
create_box 1 R0
mass    1 10.0
create_atoms 1 single  10 10 10 units box
```

The second part assigns a zero pair potential to the atom, assigns a velocity along the x direction to it, implements the expanded Lennard–Jones wall force, and time-integrates the atom by `fix nve`:

```
# ---------------------
# PAIR STYLES
# ---------------------
pair_style  lj/cut 1
pair_coeff  1 1   0.0   1.0


# ---------------------
# FIXES
# ---------------------
velocity all set 10.0 0 0

variable x equal x[1]
variable fx equal fx[1]

variable EPSILON equal 0.1
variable SIGMA equal 2.0
variable DELTALJ equal 2.5
variable CUTOFF equal 5.0

fix WALL all wall/region R0 lj126Expanded ${EPSILON} ${SIGMA}
${DELTALJ} ${CUTOFF}
fix NVE all nve
fix PRINT all print 1 "${x} ${fx}" file outputWALL.dat screen
no

run 10000
```

When this code is executed, the atom travels along the x-axis and flips its direction by rebounding off the walls. It experiences a nonzero force only when it is located within the cutoff distance of the wall force. The x coordinate and the x component of the force on the atom are collected for plotting since the y and z coordinates and force components are necessarily zero.

The plot of force (**Fx**) versus position (**x**) is provided in the following graph:

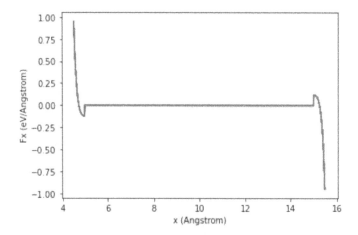

Figure 10.18 – Plot of force versus position of an atom traveling along the x direction

This preceding graph shows that the force is zero except when x ≤ 5 Å or x ≥ 15 Å, where the separation between the atom and wall drops below the cutoff. In these intervals, the force follows the expected shifted Lennard–Jones form, with switched positive or negative signs at opposite walls to indicate opposite directions of force.

In this section, we incorporated a new potential form to the existing `Fix Wall/Region` class so that the existing potentials are still supported without any change in syntax. By identifying the correct code sections to modify, the new potential is streamlined to follow the same syntax as the existing ones.

In the next section, we will construct a fix that reads the ID of the atom with the maximum height and applies a force to this atom and the neighboring atoms with which it interacts.

Writing a fix to apply a bond-boost potential

This is a list of the changes that are made to the source code:

- The new files that are created are `fix_addboost.cpp` and `fix_addboost.h`.
- The existing files that have been modified at `fix_addforce.cpp`, `fix_addforce.h`, and `fix_orient_fcc.cpp`.
- The methods that have been modified are constructor, destructor, `init()`, and `post_force()`.

- The new method that is added is `init_list()`.

- The input parameters are `jgroup`, `potentialType`, `atomID`, `param1`, `param2`, `param3`, and `cutoff`.

- The other quantities that are introduced can be seen in a full list in *Figure 10.19* in the header file.

- The LAMMPS syntax is `fix FIX_NAME GROUP addboost GROUP2 ATOMID POTENTIAL P1 P2 P3 CUTOFF` (we will reviews this syntax in this section).

In this section, we will create a fix that applies a boost potential and boost force to the atom located farthest from a surface along the *z* direction, while ensuring that the neighboring atoms that interact with it receive an equal and opposite force.

Theory (the bond-boost method)

MD simulations sometimes need to address rare events that cannot be sufficiently sampled over computationally tractable simulation time by conventional MD, such as desorption and diffusion (see `https://doi.org/10.1016/j.commatsci.2014.12.008`). These events occur rarely in regular MD particle dynamics, but they can be accelerated by applying a boost potential to the atom with the maximally stretched bond that is most likely to perform the rare event.

This way, the boost potential allows the atom to perform the rare event by separating from its neighbors in considerably less time, and altogether, a greater number of rare events can be sampled within the same simulation time duration by using this method. This technique is broadly known as **hyperdynamics**, and the downloadable version of LAMMPS comes with an implementation for it (see `fix hyper/local` `https://lammps.sandia.gov/doc/fix_hyper_local.html` and `fix hyper/global` in the manual `https://lammps.sandia.gov/doc/fix_hyper_global.html`).

The method implemented in this section accelerates the rare event of the desorption of adsorbed atoms from a surface, via the **bond-boost** technique. Among a collection of adsorbed atoms, the atom located farthest from the surface with the greatest *z* coordinate is provided a repulsive boost potential $V_b(r)$ to accelerate its desorption.

The boost potential can be an arbitrary function that must approach zero smoothly at a certain height where the atom is considered to have desorbed. In effect, the potential $V(r)$ experienced by the boosted atom is the sum of its potential with its neighbors $V_0(r)$ and the repulsive boost potential $V_b(z)$:

$$V(r) = V_0(r) + V_b(r)$$

The fix implemented in this section will accept the atom ID of the atom to be boosted as an input parameter and will allow the user to choose one of three boost potentials to apply—**Lennard–Jones (LJ)**, Morse, or harmonic—with the following functional forms:

- The LJ potential $V_{LJ}(r)$ can be calculated by:

$$V_{LJ}(r) = 4\varepsilon\left[\left(\frac{\sigma}{r}\right)^{12} - \left(\frac{\sigma}{r}\right)^{6}\right]$$

- The Morse potential $V_{Morse}(r)$ can be given by:

$$V_{Morse}(r) = D_0\left[e^{-2\alpha(r-r_0)} - 2e^{-\alpha(r-r_0)}\right]$$

- The harmonic potential $V_H(r)$ can be given by:

$$V_H(r) = \frac{1}{2}k_{sp}r^2 - \varepsilon_0$$

The parameters used in the preceding potentials have been explained in earlier chapters and will be parsed from the input script, along with a cutoff distance.

Each of these potentials will be made to generate repulsive forces, which will exert a force with a positive z component on the boosted atom and generate an equal and opposite force on its neighbors to sustain the consistency of force and not introduce external energy.

To implement this boost, we will choose to modify the `Fix Addforce` class, where copies of `fix_addforce.cpp` and `fix_addforce.h` were renamed to `fix_addboost.cpp` and `fix_addboost.h`.

Modifying the header file – fix_addboost.h

The fix style name is changed to `addboost` in `fix_addboost.h` (*line 16*):

```
FixStyle(addboost,FixAddBoost)
```

Several quantities are declared, as shown in the following screenshot:

```
41    void init_list(int, class NeighList *);    // SM
42    class NeighList *list;                      // SM
43
44    double param1, param2, param3, cutoff;      // SM
45    int jgroup, jgroupbit;                      // SM
46    int potentialType;                          // SM
47    int atomID, atomvar, atomstyle;             // SM
48    double boostV;                              // SM
49    char *jgroupstr, *atomstr;                  // SM
```

Figure 10.19 – Screenshot from fix_addboost.h showing additional declared quantities

As you can see, *lines 41* to *42* introduce a new method, init_list(), and invoke a NeighList class to access the neighbor list of the boosted atom. The other parameters are explained in the following list:

- param1, param2, param3, and cutoff: These are the required potential parameters for each of the three potentials permitted. In the case of the LJ and harmonic potentials, param3 is a placeholder, which is ignored.

- jgroup and jgroupbit: These are integers that are used to identify the group of neighboring atoms of the boosted atom that will experience an equal and opposite force because of the boost.

- potentialType: This is an integer between 1–3 that is used to identify the form of the boost potential chosen.

- atomID, atomvar, atomstyle: These are the integers that are used to read the atom ID as a numerical value or extract it from an equal style variable.

- boostV: This is the value of the boost potential applied to the boosted atom.

- jgroupstr[]: This is the character array that is used to parse a group name of a group of neighboring atoms.

- atomstr[]: This is the character array that is used to parse the name of a variable representing the atom ID of a boosted atom.

In `fix_activeforce.cpp`, several header files are imported to access the group and neighbor list properties (*lines 30 to 33*):

```
#include "group.h"
#include "neighbor.h"
#include "neigh_list.h"
#include "neigh_request.h"
```

In the constructor method, the input parameters are parsed with changes made to accommodate them as required, as described in the next section.

Modifying the constructor in fix_addboost.cpp

In the constructor, the neighboring group, atom ID, boost potential, and the potential parameters are parsed, as shown in the following screenshot:

```
55    // -------------------------
56    // SM: Parse new parameters
57    // -------------------------
58
59    jgroupstr = atomstr = NULL;
60
61    // SM: Set second group for interaction
62    int n = strlen(arg[3]) + 1;
63    jgroupstr = new char[n];
64    strcpy(jgroupstr,arg[3]);
65    jgroup = group->find(jgroupstr);
66    if (jgroup == -1)
67      error->all(FLERR,"FixAddboost second group ID does not exist");
68    jgroupbit = group->bitmask[jgroup];
69
70    // SM: Read atom ID
71    if (strstr(arg[4],"v_") == arg[4]) {
72      int n = strlen(&arg[4][2]) + 1;
73      atomstr = new char[n];
74      strcpy(atomstr,&arg[4][2]);
75    } else {
76      atomID = force->inumeric(FLERR,arg[4]);
77      atomstyle = CONSTANT;
78    }
79
80    // SM: Set type of boost potential (LJ, Morse, harmonic)
81    if (strstr(arg[5],"LJ") == arg[5]) potentialType = 1;
82    else if (strstr(arg[5],"morse") == arg[5]) potentialType = 2;
83    else if (strstr(arg[5],"harmonic") == arg[5]) potentialType = 3;
84    else error->all(FLERR,"Invalid potential type for fix addboost");
85
86    // SM: Read parameters and cutoff
87    param1 = force->numeric(FLERR,arg[6]);
88    param2 = force->numeric(FLERR,arg[7]);
89    param3 = force->numeric(FLERR,arg[8]);
90    cutoff = force->numeric(FLERR,arg[9]);
```

Figure 10.20 – Screenshot from fix_addboost.cpp showing the constructor method

As you can see, the first argument (*lines 62* to *68*) represents the group of neighboring atoms of the boosted atom and is parsed as a group name that is located from existing groups using the `group->find()` method.

The atom ID is parsed (*lines 71* to *78*) either as an integer value or as a variable name, similar to parsing input force components in `fix_addforce.cpp`. The permitted potential types are entered as `LJ`, `morse`, or `harmonic` and the variable `potentialType` is set accordingly to 1, 2, or 3 respectively for these potentials (*lines 81* to *84*). Then the three potential parameters and the cutoff are parsed in *lines 87* to *90*.

Also, the character arrays `jgroupstr` and `atomstr` are set to NULL before parsing begins (*line 59*), so these arrays are deleted in the destructor method (*lines 100* to *101*). Next, in the `init()` method, the atom ID is identified if it is entered as a variable and the neighbor list is requested.

Modifying the init() method in fix_addboost.cpp

In the `init()` method, `atomvar` extracts the variable ID if any a variable name is used to enter the atom ID, as shown in *lines 123* to *130* in the following screenshot:

```
118     void FixAddBoost::init()
119     {
120         // SM: deleted region check
121
122         // SM: check variable for atomID
123         if (atomstr) {
124             atomvar = input->variable->find(atomstr);
125             if (atomvar < 0)
126                 error->all(FLERR,"Atom ID for fix addboost does not exist");
127             if (input->variable->equalstyle(atomvar))
128                 atomstyle = EQUAL;
129             else error->all(FLERR,"Atom ID for fix addboost is invalid style");
130         }
131
132         // SM: need a full neighbor list, built whenever re-neighboring occurs
133         // (see fix_orient_fcc.cpp)
134         int irequest = neighbor->request((void *) this);
135         neighbor->requests[irequest]->pair = 0; // not called by pair
136         neighbor->requests[irequest]->fix = 1;  // called by fix
137         neighbor->requests[irequest]->half = 0; // half-list not requested
138         neighbor->requests[irequest]->full = 1; // full-list requested
139     }
```

Figure 10.21– Screenshot from fix_addboost.cpp showing the init() method

As you can see, the neighbor list is requested in *lines 134* to *138*, similar to how it is done in `fix_orient_fcc.cpp`, which we discussed in *Chapter 7, Understanding Fixes*. In addition, a new method `init_list()` is created to access the neighbor list with a pointer `list`, as shown in the following screenshot:

```
143    // SM: init_list() method to get hold of the neighbour list pointer
144    void FixAddBoost::init_list(int id, NeighList *ptr)
145    {
146        list = ptr;
147    }
```

Figure 10.22 – Screenshot from fix_addboost.cpp showing the init_list() method

Having established access to the neighbor list, the neighbors of the boosted atom are ready to be identified in the `post_force()` method.

Modifying the post_force() method in fix_addboost.cpp

In the `post_force()` method, the boosted atom ID is read from the entered integer value or extracted from the entered variable name in *lines 192* to *194*, as shown in the following screenshot:

```
184    // SM: declare variables
185    int i,maxZID;
186    int j,jj,jnum;
187    double xtmp,ytmp,ztmp,delx,dely,delz;
188    double rsq,fpair;
189    int *jlist,*numneigh,**firstneigh;
190
191    // SM: read atom ID to apply boost
192    if (atomstyle == CONSTANT) maxZID = atomID;
193    else if (atomstyle == EQUAL)
194        maxZID = (int) input->variable->compute_equal(atomvar);
195    i = atom->map(maxZID);
196
197    // SM: check if atom belongs to core and is not a ghost atom
198    if ((i >= 0) && (i < nlocal)) {
199        xtmp = x[i][0];
200        ytmp = x[i][1];
201        ztmp = x[i][2];
202
203        // SM: read neighbors of boosted atom
204        numneigh = list->numneigh;
205        firstneigh = list->firstneigh;
206        jlist = firstneigh[i];
207        jnum = numneigh[i];
```

Figure 10.23 – Screenshot from FixAddBoost::post_force() showing
the atom ID extraction and neighbor list access

As you can see, the atom ID is stored as integer `maxZID`. It represents the global ID as it appears in the LAMMPS input script or data file. It is converted to the local processor index i using the `atom->map()` method in *line 195*.

The index i is set as -1 if the atom does not belong to the current core or is a ghost atom. Since replication of the boost over multiple cores is not desired, only local atoms will be considered when applying boost potentials, while ghost atoms will be discarded. The filtering process is performed by verifying that i lies in the range of local atoms indexed from 0 to nlocal-1 (*line 198*). If satisfied, the local index i is used to locate the coordinates (xtmp, ytmp, and ztmp) of the boosted atom (*lines 199* to *201*), and subsequently access its neighbor list (*lines 204* to *207*).

In the next screenshot, the neighbor list is used to identify neighboring atoms to apply equal and opposite boost forces:

```
209      // SM: loop over all neighbors of boosted atom
210      for (jj = 0; jj < jnum; jj++) {
211        j = jlist[jj];
212        j &= NEIGHMASK;
213
214        if (mask[j] & jgroupbit) {
215          delx = xtmp - x[j][0];
216          dely = ytmp - x[j][1];
217          delz = ztmp - x[j][2];
218          rsq = delx*delx + dely*dely + delz*delz;
219
220          if (rsq <= cutoff*cutoff) {
221            // SM: apply boost pair potential
222            if (potentialType == 1) {
223              // LJ: param1 = epsilon; param2 = sigma
224              double r2inv = 1.0/rsq;
225              double r6inv = r2inv*r2inv*r2inv;
226              double sigma6 = param2*param2*param2*param2*param2*param2;
227              double sigma12 = sigma6*sigma6;
228              boostV += 4.0 * param1 * r6inv * (sigma12*r6inv - sigma6);
229              double forcelj = 24.0 * param1 * r6inv * (2.0*sigma12*r6inv - sigma6);
230              fpair = forcelj*r2inv;
231            }
232            else if (potentialType == 2) {
233              // MORSE: param1 = D0; param2 = alpha; param3 = R0
234              double r = sqrt(rsq);
235              double dr = r - param3;
236              double dexp = exp(-param2 * dr);
237              boostV += param1 * (dexp*dexp - 2.0*dexp);
238              fpair = 2.0 * param1 * param2 * (dexp*dexp - dexp) / r;
239            }
240            else if (potentialType == 3) {
241              // HARMONIC: param1 = k; param2 = well_depth
242              boostV += 0.5*param1*rsq - param2;
243              fpair = -1.0*param1;
244            }
245
246            fpair *= -1.0;  // SM: repulsive force
247
248            f[i][0] += delx*fpair;
249            f[i][1] += dely*fpair;
250            f[i][2] += delz*fpair;
```

Figure 10.24 – Screenshot from FixAddBoost::post_force() showing
the neighbor list loop and boost application

As you can see, by looping over the neighbor list of atom i, the neighboring atoms j that belong to the group entered in the input script are identified (*line 214*) and the displacement vector (delx, dely, delz) pointing from j to i is calculated (*lines 215* to *217*). If the distance between the atoms is less than the cutoff associated with the boost potential (*line 220*), then a boost is calculated in *lines 222* to *244*.

When calculating the boost, the variable `potentialType` is used to select the correct type of potential among `LJ`, `Morse`, and `harmonic`. For the LJ potential (*lines 222 to 231*), the parameters `param1` and `param2` represent the ε and σ respectively, while `param3` is disregarded.

These parameters are then used to calculate the quantity `fpair` and the cumulative boost potential `boostV` over all neighboring atoms. For the Morse potential (*lines 232 to 239*), the three parameters `param1`, `param2`, and `param3` represent D_0, α, and r_0; and for the harmonic potential, `param1` and `param2` represent k_{sp} and ε_0 (`param3` is disregarded).

The sign of `fpair` calculated for each potential is switched (*line 246*) to account for repulsive forces exerted on the participating atoms `i` and `j`, since the potentials provided would otherwise generate attractive forces. The force components are then assigned to `i` and `j` in *lines 248 to 254*. Similarly, the sign of `boostV` is switched before the final tally in *line 263*.

Finally, the computes performed in the timestep are cleared and prepared for the next iteration by *lines 264 to 265*:

```
modify->addstep_compute(update->ntimestep + 1);
modify->addstep_compute_all(update->ntimestep + 1);
```

Here, the current timestep is accessed by the `update->ntimestep` command.

The LAMMPS input syntax to apply this fix is given by:

```
fix FIX_NAME GROUP addboost GROUP2 ATOMID POTENTIALTYPE P1 P2
P3 CUTOFF
```

The `GROUP` ID is disregarded and `GROUP2` represents the group of neighboring atoms. The `ATOMID` can be an integer value or a variable. The parameter `POTENTIALTYPE` must be one of `LJ`, `morse`, or `harmonic`, and `P1`, `P2`, `P3`, and `cutoff` are the potential parameters and cutoff.

A test run with a LAMMPS input script is then performed using `Fix AddBoost`, as described in the next section.

Trial run (in.Test_FixAddboost)

A simulation box is created containing three identical atoms labeled **1**, **2**, and **3**, initially located at (8,8,100) Å, (10,10,102) Å, and (10,10,105) Å, respectively. The atoms are initially at rest and there is zero pair potential between them.

An LJ boost potential is applied to the atom with the largest z coordinate (that is, atom **3**) with coefficients $\varepsilon = 0.25$ eV and $\sigma = 2.0$ Å and cutoff 7 Å. In this setup, atom **3** should experience repulsion from the other atoms, whereas atom **1** and **2** should experience repulsion from only atom **3**.

The following diagram shows the simulation setup containing the three atoms and the repulsive forces between them indicated by force arrows labeled $\overrightarrow{F_{13}}$ and $\overrightarrow{F_{23}}$ to represent the forces between atoms **1–3** and atoms **2–3**, respectively:

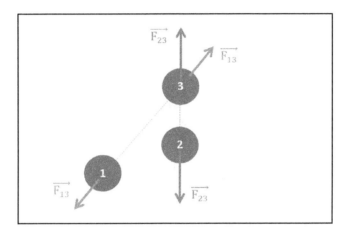

Figure 10.25 – Diagram of simulation setup

The corresponding LAMMPS input script is provided, where the first part performs system initialization and creates the three atoms:

```
# ----------------------
# INITIALIZE SIMULATION
# ----------------------
units metal
dimension 3
boundary p p p
atom_style atomic
atom_modify map array
region R0  block 0 20 0 20 0 200 units box


# ----------------------
# CREATE ATOMS
# ----------------------
```

```
create_box 1 R0
mass    1 10.0
create_atoms 1 single  8 8 100 units box
create_atoms 1 single  10 10 102 units box
create_atoms 1 single  10 10 105 units box
```

The second part assigns a zero pair potential to the atoms, identifies the atom to boost through a number of computes, applies the boost potential to the identified atom by fix addboost, and time-integrates the atoms by fix nve:

```
# --------------------
# PAIR STYLES
# --------------------
pair_style  lj/cut 10
pair_coeff  1 1  0.0   1.0


# --------------------
# FIXES
# --------------------
variable EPSILON equal 0.25
variable SIGMA equal 2.0
variable CUTOFF equal 7.0

compute C1 all property/atom id
compute C2 all property/atom z
compute C3 all reduce max c_C1 c_C2 replace 1 2
variable zID equal c_C3[1]

fix NVE all nve
fix BOOST all addboost all v_zID  LJ  ${EPSILON} ${SIGMA}  0
${CUTOFF}
dump DUMP all custom 1 outputAll.lammpstrj id x y z fx fy fz


run 500
```

When identifying the atom to boost in the preceding code, the required atom ID is determined using the computes C1, C2, and C3. The computes C1 and C2 extract the global atom IDs and z coordinates of all atoms in the system, respectively. The compute C3 finds the atom with the maximum z coordinate using the features built in compute reduce (see https://lammps.sandia.gov/doc/compute_reduce.html) and uses the replace option to retrieve the corresponding atom ID. This atom ID is stored as variable zID, which is then fed as the ATOMID input parameter in the fix addboost command.

The fix addboost command implements an LJ potential that accepts the variables EPSILON and SIGMA (defined in the input script) as the first two parameters. The third parameter is disregarded in the calculation, so a placeholder value (0) is entered, followed by the cutoff as the final parameter. Altogether, in this setup, atom **3** is retrieved as variable zID and is fed as parameter ATOMID to fix addboost. It is then provided an upwards boost force, while the other two atoms experience equal and opposite forces.

Upon executing the input script, the directions and relative magnitudes of the initial repulsive boost forces experienced by the three atoms are illustrated in the following diagram:

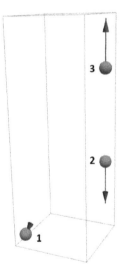

Figure 10.26 – Relative magnitudes and directions of the initial boost repulsions on the three atoms

As expected from the preceding diagram, atoms **2** and **3** experience large repulsions from each other, and atom **1** experiences a considerably smaller repulsion owing to its larger distance from atom **3**. Therefore, the direction of repulsion on atom **3** is dominated by the repulsion from atom **2**—the repulsive force on atom **2** points in the $-z$ direction and the repulsive force on atom **3** is almost perfectly opposite. On atom **1**, the force directed is the opposite of the vector pointing from atom **1** to atom **3**.

The magnitudes of the repulsive forces on each atom are plotted against time in the following graph:

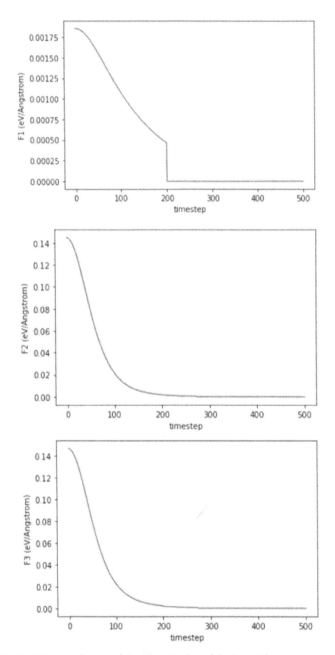

Figure 10.27 – Time evolution of the magnitudes of the boost forces on atoms 1 (top), 2 (middle), and 3 (bottom)

As you can see, the *top* plot of the magnitude of the repulsive force on atom **1** shows that the force starts at a small magnitude and drops gradually, followed by a sharp drop to zero when the cutoff is exceeded. The plots for atoms **2** and **3** in the *middle* and *bottom* show almost identical gradual drops in force, indicating that these two atoms generate the dominant share of the repulsive force. The functional forms of all three plots are consistent with the repulsive LJ functional form of the force.

It should be noted that the neighbor list in this fix is generated using the pair potential cutoff, and not the cutoff entered in the fix. Therefore, if the entered cutoff is longer than the pair potential cutoff, then the neighbor list will consist only of neighbors located within the pair cutoff and it effectively negates the entered cutoff. In the example presented for this fix, the pair potential cutoff is set at 10 Å, even though the pair potential is zero so that the entered cutoff of 7 Å does not exceed the pair cutoff.

While this fix was used to apply the boost to the atom with the largest z coordinate value, it can also be used to apply the boost to any atom that is entered as input parameter ATOMID. With the appropriate computes, atoms with other properties can be fed in as ATOMID, such as the atom with a maximum potential energy or a minimum stress component.

In this section, we described a new fix that implements a neighbor list to apply forces to atoms located within a relevant cutoff.

Summary

In this chapter, we have illustrated some custom fixes to apply user-defined forces, including a directed force on individual atoms, a force dependent on bonded atoms, a wall force, and a force applied to atoms that satisfy criteria regarding energy that is obtained from a separate compute. Altogether, these examples provide guidelines to help you write your own fixes that can manipulate forces exerted on a system.

In the next and last chapter, we will create custom fixes to perform a variety of simulation manipulations that may be required for user-specified applications.

Questions

1. In the example of the `Fix AddforceXY` class, what changes are required to add a z coordinate z_0 to the point (x_0, y_0) so that the z component of the spring force is $F_z = -k_z(z - z_0)$ with a spring constant k_z?

2. In `Fix ActiveForce`, if the active force must only be applied to an atom that is bonded to another atom of type `ATYPE` along the direction of that bond, what changes are needed in the `post_force()` method (assuming `ATYPE` has been parsed correctly)?

3. In the LAMMPS input script used in the example of `Fix Addboost`, how should the compute `C2` be changed so that the boost potential is applied to the atom with the maximum pair potential energy?

11
Modifying Thermostats

In this chapter, we will provide examples of writing custom fixes to modify the thermostat controlling the system temperature, along with an example of modifying `Fix Print` to aid in custom simulation designs. We will create new fixes that are able to thermostat the system by adjusting atom velocities and temperature increments per iteration.

We will cover the following topics in this chapter:

- Writing a fix to apply the Andersen thermostat
- Writing a fix to apply a non-linear temperature increment
- Writing a fix to print the output at evaporation

By the end of this chapter, you will learn to modify the source code relating to the *thermostatting* of a system. It will enable you to design systems that require non-conventional thermostats or related features not available in a standard LAMMPS download.

Technical requirements

To execute the instructions in this chapter, you need a text editor (for example, **Notepad++, Gedit**) and a platform to compile LAMMPS (for example, **Linux terminal**).

You can find the full source code used in this chapter here: `https://github.com/PacktPublishing/Extending-and-Modifying-LAMMPS-Writing-Your-Own-Source-Code`

This is the link to download LAMMPS: `https://lammps.sandia.gov/doc/Install.html`. The LAMMPS GitHub link is `https://github.com/lammps/lammps`, where the source code can be found as well.

Writing a fix to apply the Andersen thermostat

Here is a list of changes made to the source code directory:

- These are the new files that have been created: `fix_temp_andersen.cpp` and `fix_temp_andersen.h`
- These are the existing files that have been modified: `fix_temp_berendsen.cpp` and `fix_temp_berendsen.h`.
- These are the methods that have been modified: constructor, and `end_of_step()`
- These are the input parameters: `andFreq`, `seedMB`, `sigmaMB`
- These are the other quantities introduced: `random`, `me`
- LAMMPS syntax: `fix FIX_NAME GROUP temp/andersen FREQUENCY SEED SIGMA` (we'll review this syntax later in this section)

In this section, we will write a fix to apply the **Andersen thermostat** that adjusts the temperature of particles by assigning random velocities to them at specified intervals.

Theory – Andersen thermostat

Based on the concept of velocity and momentum adjustments upon stochastic collisions in an atomistic system, the Andersen thermostat randomly updates atom velocities at regular intervals in accordance with the expected velocity distribution. The Andersen thermostat is relatively uncomplicated and guarantees that the thermostatted system will obey the **Maxwell-Boltzmann velocity distribution**, but it can also produce drastic changes in velocities.

In a simulation, the velocities are selected at random from a Maxwell-Boltzmann velocity distribution which is constructed based on the particle mass, m, and the system temperature, T, and are assigned after every specified number of iterations. Each of the velocity components (v_x, v_y, v_z) is chosen from the 1D velocity distribution, $f(v)$:

$$f(v) = \sqrt{\frac{m}{2\pi k_B T}} \exp\left[-\frac{mv^2}{2k_B T}\right]$$

In this equation, k_B is the **Boltzmann constant**. This distribution is effectively a **Gaussian distribution** with a mean $\mu = 0$, and a standard deviation, $\sigma = \sqrt{\frac{k_B T}{m}}$, which converts $f(v)$ to the following:

$$f(v) = \frac{1}{\sigma\sqrt{2\pi}} \exp\left[-\frac{v^2}{2\sigma^2}\right]$$

As input, a fix that implements the Andersen thermostat requires the number of iterations between successive velocity adjustments and the standard deviation σ to create the 1D Maxwell-Boltzmann velocity distribution. In addition, an input seed integer is required to generate random numbers using the **Marsaglia random number generator (RNG)** built into LAMMPS in `random_mars.cpp` and `random_mars.h` (see *Chapter 5, Understanding Pair Styles*).

In order to implement this fix, the Berendsen thermostat source code is modified. Copies of `fix_temp_berendsen.cpp` and `fix_temp_berendsen.h` are renamed to `fix_temp_andersen.cpp` and `fix_temp_andersen.h`.

Modifying the header file – fix_temp_andersen.h

The fix style name is changed to `temp/andersen` in `fix_temp_andersen.h` (*line 16*):

```
FixStyle(temp/andersen, FixTempAndersen)
```

The following quantities are declared (*lines 36 to 40*):

```
double sigmaMB;
int seedMB;
int andFreq;
class RanMars *random;
int me;
```

From the preceding code, the variables `sigmaMB`, `seedMB`, and `andFreq` represent σ, the RNG seed, and the number of iterations between velocity adjustments, respectively. The `random` object is invoked from the `RanMars` class to generate the random numbers required. The last quantity, `me`, is used to identify the processor and use it along with `seedMB` to help generate random numbers.

In `fix_temp_andersen.cpp`, the `random_mars.h` file is included on *line 28*:

```
#include "random_mars.h"
```

This header file allows the RNG methods to be imported for use in the Andersen thermostat fix.

The constructor method is modified to accommodate the parsing of the input parameters, as we'll see in the next section.

Modifying the constructor in fix_temp_andersen.cpp

In the constructor method, precisely six input parameters are permitted for the Andersen thermostat fix, including the three default parameters (fix ID, group ID, and fix style) parsed by `fix.cpp` (*line 41*):

```
if (narg != 6) error->all(FLERR,"Illegal fix temp/andersen
command");
```

The `nevery` variable is set to 1 (*line 43*) to apply the fix every iteration. The following screenshot shows the constructor method:

```
38    FixTempAndersen::FixTempAndersen(LAMMPS *lmp, int narg, char **arg) :
39      Fix(lmp, narg, arg)
40    {
41      if (narg != 6) error->all(FLERR,"Illegal fix temp/andersen command"); // SM
42
43      nevery = 1;
44
45    // SM
46      andFreq = force->inumeric(FLERR,arg[3]);
47      seedMB = force->inumeric(FLERR,arg[4]);
48      sigmaMB = force->numeric(FLERR,arg[5]);
49
50    // SM: initialize Marsaglia RNG with processor-unique seed
51      random = new RanMars(lmp,seedMB + comm->me);
52    }
```

Figure 11.1 – Screenshot from fix_temp_andersen.cpp showing the constructor method

As you can see, the three parameters andFreq, seedMB, and sigmaMB are parsed on *lines 46 to 48*, and on *line 51*, a new RNG is initialized as a random object by feeding the sum of the seed, seedMB, and the core ID, me, into the RanMars class. This way, each core will use a different seed to instantiate its RNG and generate a different sequence of random numbers.

The setmask() method (*lines 56 to 62*) specifies that the fix applies in the END_OF_STEP stage, since it adjusts the atom velocities directly without having to integrate via forces or positions of the atoms, and hence it can make these changes once the integration stages have been completed.

Accordingly, the end_of_step() method, described in the next section, implements the velocity assignments.

Modifying the end_of_step() method of fix_temp_andersen.cpp

The following screenshot shows the end_of_step() method for this fix:

```cpp
66      void FixTempAndersen::end_of_step()
67      {
68
69          double **v = atom->v;
70          double **x = atom->x;
71          int *mask = atom->mask;
72          int nlocal = atom->nlocal;
73
74      // SM:
75      // 1. adjust velocities if currentTime % andFreq == 0
76      // 2. generate vx,vy,vz from random->gaussian() and scale by sigmaMB
77
78          int currentTime = update->ntimestep;   // SM
79          if ( (currentTime > 0) && (currentTime % andFreq == 0) ) {
80              for (int i = 0; i < nlocal; i++) {
81                  if (mask[i] & groupbit) {
82                      // SM: assign vx,vy,vz
83                      v[i][0] = sigmaMB * random->gaussian();
84                      v[i][1] = sigmaMB * random->gaussian();
85                      v[i][2] = sigmaMB * random->gaussian();
86                  }
87              }
88          }
89      }
```

Figure 11.2 – Screenshot from fix_temp_andersen.cpp showing the end_of_step() method

Since the Andersen thermostat applies after every specified number of iterations (andFreq), the current timestep of the simulation is extracted using update->ntimestep (*line 78*), shown in the preceding screenshot, and applied the modulo operator (%) against andFreq to check divisibility (*line 79*).

If the current timestep is found to be a multiple of the andFreq interval, the code loops over all atoms in the core (*line 80*) and identifies the atoms belonging to the group on which the Andersen thermostat acts (*line 81*). The (x, y, z) velocity components of these atoms are adjusted by selecting velocities from a 1D Maxwell-Boltzmann velocity distribution.

Lines 83 to *85* generate the three random velocity components to assign to each atom. For each component, a number belonging to the Gaussian distribution with a mean of $\mu = 0$ and a standard deviation of $\sigma = 1$ is generated by the random->gaussian() method. The standard deviation, $\sigma = $ sigmaMB, is then incorporated by multiplying each of these random numbers by sigmaMB, which effectively converts the standard deviation of the Gaussian distribution from $\sigma = 1$ to $\sigma = $ sigmaMB. The values obtained by scaling with sigmaMB are assigned as the velocity components of the atom.

The LAMMPS input script syntax for Fix Andersen is as follows:

```
fix  FIX_NAME  GROUP  temp/andersen  FREQUENCY SEED SIGMA
```

From the preceding code, the parameters FREQUENCY, SEED, and SIGMA correspond to the quantities andFreq, seedMB, and sigmaMB, respectively.

As can be seen from its source code, Fix Andersen implements a bare minimum thermostat that accepts numerical values as input and does not permit additional modifications in the same way as other thermostats. The Andersen thermostat is often used as a preliminary model to test run simulations before employing more sophisticated thermostats, so such elaborate functions may not be warranted for the Andersen thermostat fix. If additional features are desired, methods that perform similar functionalities can be copied and modified from other thermostats available in the LAMMPS source code.

The Andersen thermostat is then tested using a trial input script in the next section.

Trial run – in.Test_Andersen

A simulation box consisting of a single atom at rest is created, and the Andersen thermostat is applied on it with an arbitrary σ and a frequency of 10 iterations between velocity adjustments. The atom motion is time-integrated by `fix nve` and its (x, y, z) velocity components are plotted to observe the changes. The input script is presented here, where the first part initializes the system:

```
# ---------------------
# INITIALIZE SIMULATION
# ---------------------
units metal
dimension 3
boundary p p p
atom_style   atomic
atom_modify map array
region r0  block 0 20 0 20 0 20 units box
# ---------------------
# CREATE ATOM
# ---------------------
create_box 1 r0
mass     1 10.0
create_atoms 1 single  10 10 10 units box
```

In the preceding code, a single atom is created at the middle of the simulation box. In the second part of the input script, the atom is thermostatted and time-integrated:

```
# ---------------------
# PAIR STYLES
# ---------------------
pair_style  lj/cut 1
pair_coeff  1 1  0.0   1.0
# ---------------------
# FIXES
# ---------------------
variable vx1 equal vx[1]
variable vy1 equal vy[1]
variable vz1 equal vz[1]
```

```
variable FREQUENCY equal 10
variable SEED equal 12345
variable SIGMA equal 0.01

fix 1 all temp/andersen ${FREQUENCY} ${SEED} ${SIGMA}
fix 2 all nve
fix PRINT all print 1 "${vx1} ${vy1} ${vz1}" file
outputANDERSEN.dat screen no
run 200
```

In the preceding input script, the Andersen thermostat (fix temp/andersen) is applied to the atom with a frequency of 10 iterations and an σ of 0.01 Å/ps, along with an arbitrary seed integer (12345). The Andersen thermostat assigns velocities to the atom every 10 iterations and its trajectory is calculated by fix nve time integration.

The following graph shows the plots of each component of the atom velocity over the simulation duration:

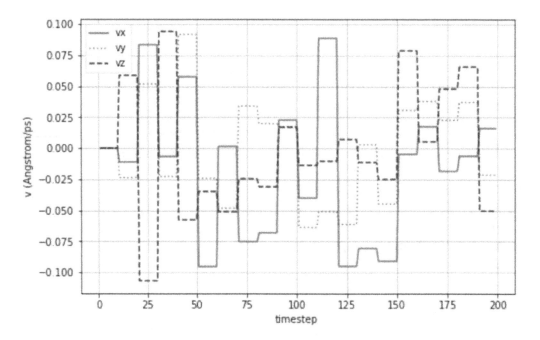

Figure 11.3 – Plots of velocity components (vx, vy, vz) versus time

As can be seen from the preceding plot, every velocity component (**vx**, **vy**, **vz**) shows a random jump after every 10 iterations, as expected by the parameters entered. The following histogram illustrates that the velocity distribution of all assigned velocities over a long simulation interval forms a Gaussian distribution:

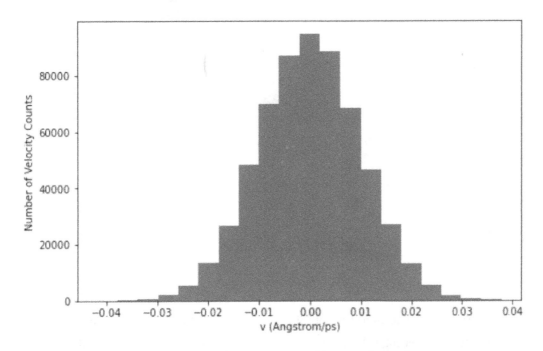

Figure 11.4 – Histogram of velocities assigned by an Andersen thermostat

The preceding histogram is centered at zero velocity and symmetrically decays on either side, as is expected of a Gaussian velocity distribution. The curvature of the histogram depends on the temperature designated by the σ value.

In the next graph, for comparison, multiple histograms are plotted for different values of $\sigma = 0.05, 0.1, 0.2$ Å/ps:

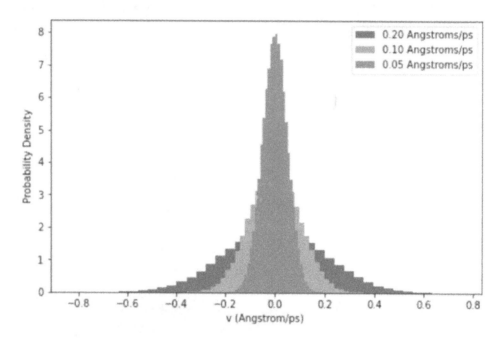

Figure 11.5 – Comparison of velocity histograms for $\sigma = 0.05, 0.10, 0.20$ Å/ps

As you can see, at increasing values of σ, which correspond to increasing temperatures for particles of the same mass, the histograms are seen to become wider, as is expected of a Maxwell-Boltzmann velocity distribution (compare with *Figure 1.2* in *Chapter 1, MD Theory and Simulation Practices*).

In this section, we created a fix to implement the Andersen thermostat using a random number generator and validated the results against expected velocity histograms. In the next section, we will modify the more sophisticated **Nose-Hoover thermostat** to implement an exponential temperature increment based on a boost potential.

Writing a fix to apply a non-linear temperature increment

Here is a list of changes made to the source code:

- These are the existing files that have been modified: `fix_nh.cpp` and `fix_nh.h`

- These are the methods that have been modified: constructor, destructor, `init()`, `compute_temp_target()`, `compute_scalar()`

- These are the input parameters: `betaTemp`, `boostV`, `tempExpScalar`

- These are the other quantities introduced: `boostStyle`, `boostVar`, `boostStr`, `tempExpFlag`

- LAMMPS syntax: `fix FIX_NAME GROUP nvt tempExp TSTART TPERIOD BETA BOOST OUTPUT_FLAG` (we'll review this syntax later in this section)

In this section, we will write a fix that increments the temperature exponentially per timestep with a Nose-Hoover thermostat in a heated system, where the exponential increment is based on the boost potential applied to the system.

Theory – Exponential temperature increment

In **hyperdynamics**, a boost potential is applied to an atom to allow it to execute a rare event in a reduced number of iterations (see *Chapter 10, Modifying Force Applications*, in the *Writing a fix to apply a bond-boost potential* section). While doing so, in this process, the boosted atom effectively transcends a long time interval within a reduced number of iterations to perform the rare event.

To account correctly for the time elapsed in this process, the time length represented by each iteration is exponentially increased using the boost potential, V_b, and the temperature, T. This way, the rare event brought about by the boost potential is simulated and sampled within a small number of iterations, but the time lapse represented by these iterations amounts to the same time as would have been required for the rare event in a conventional MD simulation.

For a regular timestep of $\Delta t = 1$ fs, the timestep Δt_b under the application of a boost potential V_b is as follows:

$$\Delta t_b = \Delta t \exp\left[\frac{V_b}{k_B T}\right]$$

Here, k_B is the Boltzmann constant.

Time acceleration by a boost potential is employed when simulating the desorption of adsorbed species from a substrate by the technique of **temperature-programmed desorption (TPD)** (see `https://doi.org/10.1103/PhysRevLett.102.046101`). In such a scenario, the desorption rate is measured, while the temperature, T, of the adsorbed system starts from an initial temperature, T_0, and increases linearly over time, t, at a heating rate of β:

$$T(t) = T_0 + \beta t$$

Therefore, in the absence of any boost, the temperature in this simulation increments by $\Delta T = \beta \Delta t$ each timestep. When a boost is applied, the temperature increments by the following:

$$\Delta T = \beta \Delta t_b = \beta\, \Delta t \exp\left[\frac{V_b}{k_B T}\right]$$

In the context of an MD simulation, the temperature increment is coded in terms of the temperature at the current timestep, $T(t)$, and at the next timestep, $T(t + \Delta t)$, as well as the boost potential applied at the current timestep $V_b(t)$:

$$T(t + \Delta t) = T(t) + \beta\, \Delta t\, \exp\left[\frac{V_b(t)}{k_B T(t)}\right]$$

In the section, we will modify `fix_nh.cpp` and `fix_nh.h` to implement this exponential increase in temperature within the Nose-Hoover thermostat scheme. The modified fix will accept the starting temperature T_0, the Nose-Hoover temperature damping factor, `TPERIOD`, the heating rate β, and the boost potential, V_b, as input parameters and compute the temperature increment while following the regular Nose-Hoover thermostat algorithm. In addition, an input parameter, `OUTPUT_FLAG`, will be used to control the scalar quantity returned by the `compute_scalar()` method.

Modifying the fix_nh.h header file

To maintain consistency, the keyword `tempExp` will be added to `Fix NH` so that it can be used by its child fixes, such as `Fix NVT`. Therefore, in `fix_nh.h`, additional parameters only need to be declared without requiring any change in the fix style name. The following quantities are declared (*lines 46 to 49*), as shown in the following screenshot:

```
46    double betaTemp, boostV;                // SM
47    int boostStyle, boostVar;               // SM
48    char *boostStr;                          // SM
49    int tempExpFlag, tempExpScalar;         // SM
```

Figure 11.6 – Screenshot from fix_nh.h showing declarations

As you can see, the variables betaTemp and boostV represent β and V_b, and the integers boostStyle and boostVar, and the character array boostStr, are used to read variable style input for the boost potential. The integer tempExpFlag will be used to keep track of whether the new keyword (tempExp) is being applied in the thermostat, and the integer tempExpScalar will be used to specify the scalar quantity returned by the compute_scalar() method.

In fix_nh.cpp, the input.h and variable.h header files are imported in *lines 37 to 38*:

```
#include "input.h"
#include "variable.h"
```

These header files allow variable style parameters to be read from the input script. In addition, enumerations are created for CONSTANT and EQUAL that will be used to distinguish between numerical and variable entries of input parameters (*line 49*):

```
enum{CONSTANT, EQUAL}
```

The constructor method is modified to accommodate the parsing of the input parameters, as described in the next section.

Modifying the constructor in fix_nh.cpp

In the constructor, the character array boostStr is initialized to NULL on *line 61* and *line 122*:

```
boostStr(NULL)
boostStr = NULL;
```

The tempExpFlag is also set to zero as its default value (*line 123*):

```
tempExpFlag = 0;
```

The appropriate code is added (*lines 138 to 164*) to accommodate the new keyword, tempExp, for parsing from the input script, as shown in the following screenshot:

```
137        // SM: tempExp option to increment timesteps exponentially
138        if (strcmp(arg[iarg],"tempExp") == 0) {
139          if (iarg+6 > narg) error->all(FLERR,"Illegal fix nvt/npt/nph command");
140          tstat_flag = 1;
141          tempExpFlag = 1;
142
143          t_start = force->numeric(FLERR,arg[iarg+1]);
144          t_period = force->numeric(FLERR,arg[iarg+2]);
145          betaTemp = force->numeric(FLERR,arg[iarg+3]);
146          t_stop = t_start;
147
148          if (strstr(arg[iarg+4],"v_") == arg[iarg+4]) {
149            int n = strlen(&arg[iarg+4][2]) + 1;
150            boostStr = new char[n];
151            strcpy(boostStr,&arg[iarg+4][2]);
152          } else {
153            boostV = force->numeric(FLERR,arg[iarg+4]);
154            boostStyle = CONSTANT;
155          }
156
157          tempExpScalar = force->inumeric(FLERR,arg[iarg+5]);
158          if ((tempExpScalar != 0) && (tempExpScalar != 1))
159            error->all(FLERR,"tempExpScalar for fix tempExp must be 0 or 1");
160
161          if (t_start <= 0.0)
162            error->all(FLERR, "Target temperature for fix nvt/npt/nph cannot be 0.0");
163          iarg += 6;
164        }
```

Figure 11.7 – Screenshot from fix_nh.h showing the constructor

As you can see, if the tempExp keyword is detected (*line 138*), a minimum of five arguments are required (*line 139*). tstat_flag is activated (*line 140*) to indicate that a Nose-Hoover thermostat has been called, and timeExpFlag is activated (*line 141*) to indicate that the tempExp keyword has been parsed.

In *lines 143 to 145*, the starting temperature (t_start), the damping period (t_period), and the heating rate, β, are parsed as the first three arguments after the keyword. While the stopping temperature (t_stop) is not required for this keyword, it is still set equal to t_start (*line 146*) to avoid errors associated with non-value assignments encountered in the rest of the code.

The boost potential, V_b, is parsed as a numerical or variable entry on *lines 148 to 155*. If a numerical value is provided (line 153), it is assigned to boostV directly. If a variable name is entered, it is stored as boostStr and will be evaluated when computing the temperature increment in the compute_temp_target() method. The last argument tempExpScalar is parsed in *line 157* as an integer 0 or 1 (*line 158 to 159*) to indicate whether compute_scalar() returns the energy (0) or target temperature, t_target (1).

In the destructor method, boostStr is deleted (*line 650*):

```
delete [] boostStr;
```

The variable name entered for the boost is validated in the init() method, which we'll see in the next section.

Modifying the init() method in fix_nh.cpp

If a variable name is entered for the boost, which is stored as boostStr, it is looked up among existing variables and boostStyle is set to EQUAL to indicate that the variable is an equal style variable, as shown in the following screenshot:

```
669   void FixNH::init()
670   {
671       // SM: check variable names
672       if (boostStr) {
673           boostVar = input->variable->find(boostStr);
674           if (boostVar < 0)
675               error->all(FLERR,"Variable name for fix tempExp does not exist");
676           if (input->variable->equalstyle(boostVar)) boostStyle = EQUAL;
677           else error->all(FLERR,"Variable for fix tempExp is invalid style");
678       }
```

Figure 11.8 – Screenshot from fix_nh.h showing the init() method

The variable is then evaluated in the compute_temp_target() method.

Modifying the compute_temp_target() method in fix_nh.cpp

The temperature increment at each iteration of the simulation is used to find the target temperature in the `compute_temp_target()` method, as seen in the following screenshot:

```
2257   /* ----------------------------------------------------------------
2258      compute target temperature and kinetic energy
2259   ----------------------------------------------------------------- */
2260
2261   void FixNH::compute_temp_target()
2262   {
2263     double delta = update->ntimestep - update->beginstep;
2264     if (delta != 0.0) delta /= update->endstep - update->beginstep;
2265
2266     // SM: calculate t_target without boost
2267     if (tempExpFlag == 0)
2268       t_target = t_start + delta * (t_stop-t_start);
2269
2270     // SM: calculate t_target with boost
2271     if (tempExpFlag == 1) {
2272       modify->clearstep_compute();
2273       if (boostStyle == EQUAL)
2274           boostV = input->variable->compute_equal(boostVar);
2275
2276       if (delta == 0) t_target = t_start;
2277       double kBT_Vb = boostV/(boltz*t_target);
2278       t_target += betaTemp * dtv * pow(M_E,kBT_Vb);
2279
2280       modify->addstep_compute(update->ntimestep + 1);
2281     }
2282
2283     ke_target = tdof * boltz * t_target;
2284   }
```

Figure 11.9 – Screenshot from fix_nh.h showing the compute_temp_target() method

As you can see, in the absence of a boost, the temperature is increased linearly at equal increments each iteration. The target temperature, t_target, at each timestep is calculated by adding the temperature increment ΔT per iteration to the current temperature:

$$\text{t\_target} \mathrel{+}= \Delta T$$

The temperature increment ΔT per iteration is calculated as follows:

$$\Delta T = \left(\frac{i_{current} - i_{begin}}{i_{end} - i_{begin}} \right) * (t\_stop - t\_start)$$

Here, $i_{current}$ represents the current timestep (accessed by `update->ntimestep`), i_{begin} represents the starting timestep of the current run (accessed by `update->beginstep`), and i_{end} represents the ending timestep of the current run (accessed by `update->endstep`). *t_start* and *t_stop* represent the starting and stopping temperatures, respectively, as already explained.

The numerator inside the parentheses in the equation for ΔT is calculated on *line 2263*, followed by division by the denominator of the same equation on *line 2264*. Then, on *lines 2267* to *2268*, the temperature is incremented linearly to find `t_target` if `tempExpFlag` is 0, indicating that the `tempExp` keyword has not been employed and therefore an exponential increment is not requested.

When `tempExpFlag` is 1 (*line 2271*), this indicates that the `tempExp` keyword has been used and therefore an exponential increment in temperature is required based on the amount of boost potential applied. The target temperature is then calculated as follows:

$$t\_target \mathrel{+}= betaTemp * \Delta t * \exp\left[\frac{boostV}{k_B * t\_target} \right]$$

In this equation, Δt is the conventional timestep (*when there is no boost*) and k_B is the Boltzmann constant. k_B has been retrieved as `boltz` from the list of built-in constants in *line 760* of the `init()` method using the `force->boltz` command:

```
boltz = force->boltz;
```

Similarly, the timestep `dtv` is retrieved on *line 721* of the `init()` method using the `update->dt` command:

```
dtv = update->dt;
```

If a variable name was entered for the boost, it is evaluated on *lines 2273* to *2274*. If a numerical value was entered, it is used directly. In the first timestep of the run, `t_target` is set equal to `t_start` since no numerical value has yet been assigned to `t_target` (*line 2276*). The variable `kBT_Vb` is created (*line 2277*) to calculate the quantity $\left(\frac{boostV}{k_B * t_{target}} \right)$ present inside the exponential term (`exp[]`) in the equation for `t_target`. Finally, `t_target` is calculated on *line 2278*. The exponential term is calculated as follows:

```
pow(M_E,kBT_Vb)
```

The pow() function raises its first argument to the power of its second argument, where the first argument is e represented by the M_E constant built into the cmath library.

On *line 2283*, the target kinetic energy *ke_target* is calculated from the standard equation:

$$ke\_target = degrees\ of\ freedom * k_B * t\_target$$

This equation yields the average kinetic energy of a particle in thermal equilibrium at a given temperature, based on its degrees of freedom, which, in turn, depends on the number of dimensions.

This method thus calculates the target temperature, *t_target*, at each timestep. *t_target* can be extracted as a variable during a simulation run using the compute_scalar() method, as described next.

Modifying the compute_scalar() method in fix_nh.cpp

The compute_scalar() method returns a scalar output that is accessed by the variable command in the LAMMPS input script. The default scalar output is the cumulative energy change brought about by the fix, but we provide an option to output t_target instead. This is accommodated by the tempExpScalar flag implemented in the compute_scalar() method, as shown in the following screenshot:

```
1566    // SM: return t_target or energy
1567    if (tempExpScalar == 1) return t_target;
1568    else return energy;
```

Figure 11.10 – Screenshot from fix_nh.h showing the compute_scalar() method

As you can see, the tempExpScalar integer can be either 0 or 1, as entered in the input script, where the default value is 0. The preceding screenshot shows that if the value of tempExpScalar is 1, then the compute_scalar() method returns t_target (*line 1567*), and otherwise it returns the energy (*line 1568*).

Altogether, the input script syntax is as follows:

```
fix FIX_NAME GROUP nvt tempExp TSTART TPERIOD BETA BOOST
OUTPUT_FLAG
```

The quantities in the script are self-explanatory based on the descriptions provided in this section. BOOST can be entered as a variable, and OUTPUT_FLAG must be either 0 or 1 to correspond to tempExpScalar.

The modified Fix NH is now tested with a LAMMPS script that applies a boost potential and increments the temperature accordingly.

Trial run – in.Test_Addboost

A LAMMPS simulation system similar to the example for `Fix Addboost` in *Chapter 10, Modifying Force Applications*, under the *Writing a fix to apply a bond-boost potential* section, is given here, consisting of three atoms at different z-coordinates, where the atom with the highest z-coordinate is provided with a boost potential:

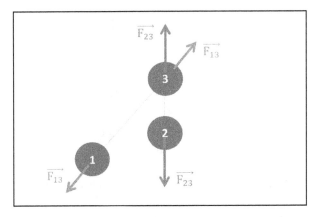

Figure 11.11 – Diagram of the simulation setup

A **Lennard-Jones (LJ)** boost potential V_b is provided in the following form:

$$V_b = 4\varepsilon \left[\left(\frac{\sigma}{r}\right)^{12} - \left(\frac{\sigma}{r}\right)^{6} \right]$$

The parameters $\varepsilon = 0.6$ eV, $\sigma = 3.0$ Å, and cutoff of 10 Å are chosen in the LJ potential in the `Fix Addboost` command. The boost potential is extracted as a variable, BOOSTV, and is fed back as input to the `fix nvt` command.

In the `fix nvt` command, a starting temperature of 45 K with a damping period of 0.1 ps is chosen. A heating rate, $\beta = 1$ K/s $= 10^{-12}$ K/ps, is applied with the default timestep of 0.001 ps.

The corresponding LAMMPS input script is provided as follows, where the first part performs system initialization and creates the three atoms:

```
# -----------------------------------------
# INITIALIZE SIMULATION
# -----------------------------------------
units metal
dimension 3
boundary p p p
```

```
atom_style atomic
atom_modify map array
region R0 block 0 20 0 20 0 200 units box


# ----------------------------------
# CREATE ATOMS
# ----------------------------------
create_box 1 R0
mass    1 10.0
create_atoms 1 single  8 8 100 units box
create_atoms 1 single  10 10 102 units box
create_atoms 1 single  10 10 107 units box
```

The second part assigns a zero pair potential to the atoms, identifies the atom to boost through a number of computes, applies the boost potential to the identified atom by fix addboost, and time integrates the atoms by fix nvt:

```
# --------------------
# PAIR STYLES
# --------------------
pair_style  lj/cut 10
pair_coeff  1 1  0  2.5


# --------------------
# FIXES
# --------------------
variable TSTART equal 45
variable TPERIOD equal 0.1
variable BETA equal 1e-12

compute C1 all property/atom id
compute C2 all property/atom z
```

```
compute C3 all reduce max c_C1 c_C2 replace 1 2
variable zID equal c_C3[1]


timestep 0.001
fix BOOST all addboost all v_zID LJ 0.6 3.0 0 10.0
variable BOOSTV equal f_BOOST
fix NVT all nvt tempExp ${TSTART} ${TPERIOD} ${BETA} v_BOOSTV 1
variable TCURRENT equal f_NVT
fix PRINT all print 1 "${BOOSTV} ${TCURRENT}" file outputBOOST.
dat


run 100
```

From the preceding code, the computes C1, C2, and C3 identify the ID of the atom to be boosted (see *Chapter 10, Modifying Force Applications*), and the boost applied by the fix addboost command is extracted by the f_BOOST command and entered as an input parameter in fix nvt.

The starting temperature (TSTART), the damping period (TPERIOD), and the heating rate (BETA) are also fed into the fix nvt command, and OUTPUT_FLAG is set to 1 to retrieve the target temperature (t_target) as output. This way, the correct atom is provided with a boost potential, which is then used to exponentially increment the target temperature in the fix nvt thermostat command.

From the preceding code, the simulation is run for 100 iterations, which would have been equal to a time interval of 0.1 ps in the absence of any boost, and the corresponding temperature increase in this interval would have been $\Delta T = 10^{-13}$ K. In the presence of the boost, the time represented by each iteration is exponentially increased and therefore the corresponding temperature also increases exponentially. The following graphs depict the boost applied and the temperature increase over time:

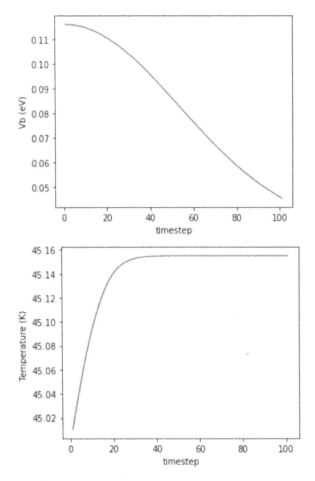

Figure 11.12 – (Top) Graph of boost potential versus time; (bottom) Graph of temperature versus time

As you can see, in this diagram, the boost potential (*top graph*) is seen to decrease as the boosted atom is repelled away from the other atoms, and the temperature (*bottom graph*) is seen to increase rapidly when the boost is large and flatten as the boost diminishes. The change in temperature is approximately 0.15 K, which is 12 orders of magnitude larger than in the case without any boost, indicating that the time interval represented by the 100 iterations is equal to about 10^{11} ps.

In this section, we modified `Fix NH` to add an option to exponentially increment the temperature at every iteration, while keeping the existing options unchanged. In the next section, we will present a fix to control the output written to disk when a certain condition is satisfied.

Writing a fix to print output at evaporation

Here is a list of changes made to the source code:

- These are the new files created: `fix_printEvaporate.cpp` and `fix_printEvaporate.h`

- These are the existing files that have been modified: `fix_print.cpp` and `fix_print.h`

- These are the methods that have been modified: constructor, destructor, `init()`, `end_of_step()`

- These are the parameters used: `iregion`, `idregion`

- LAMMPS syntax: `fix FIX_NAME GROUP printEvaporate N STRING region R` (we'll look at this syntax later in this section)

In this section, we will modify `Fix Print` to print out specified quantities when an atom enters into a particular region, as might be useful when simulating desorption.

Theory – Evaporation region

When studying the desorption of particles that are adsorbed on a surface, it is assumed that a particle has desorbed when it crosses a certain threshold or enters a certain region, usually located far from the surface where the interaction with the surface is zero. The particle at that point can be considered to have evaporated and, at that particular instant, it might be desired to print relevant quantities, such as the time of desorption and the number of particles remaining in the system, onto a file.

The modified fix that we will implement in this chapter accommodates these requirements by including an input parameter that identifies the region in the existing `Fix Print` source code. An atom that is located in this region is considered to have evaporated and the required quantities are printed when such an atom is detected. In order to implement this fix, copies of `fix_print.cpp` and `fix_print.h` are renamed to `fix_printEvaporate.cpp` and `fix_printEvaporate.h`.

Modifying the header file – fix_printEvaporate.h

The fix style name is changed to printEvaporate in fix_printEvaporate.h (*line 16*):

```
FixStyle(printEvaporate,FixPrintEvaporate)
```

The following two quantities are declared (*lines 45 to 46*) to read and identify the region entered:

```
int iregion;
char *idregion;
```

From the preceding code, the iregion integer represents the region ID and the character array idregion[], which stores the region name.

In fix_printEvaporate.cpp, the following header files are included (*lines 25 to 28*) to read atom properties, as well as group and region IDs:

```
#include "atom.h"
#include "group.h"
#include "region.h"
#include "domain.h"
```

The constructor method is modified to accommodate parsing of the region input parameters, as described next.

Modifying the constructor and init() methods in fix_printEvaporate.cpp

idregion is initialized on *line 37*:

```
idregion(NULL)
```

The value of iregion is initialized at -1 before any region is parsed (*line 66*):

```
iregion = -1;
```

Then, the code shown in the following screenshot is inserted (*line 98* to *107*) to parse the region entered:

```
97      // SM: parse region ID
98      else if (strcmp(arg[iarg],"region") == 0) {
99        if (iarg+2 > narg) error->all(FLERR,"Illegal fix printEvaporate command");
100       iregion = domain->find_region(arg[iarg+1]);
101       if (iregion == -1)
102         error->all(FLERR,"Region ID for fix printEvaporate does not exist");
103       int n = strlen(arg[iarg+1]) + 1;
104       idregion = new char[n];
105       strcpy(idregion,arg[iarg+1]);
106       iarg += 2;
107     }
```

Figure 11.13 – Screenshot from fix_printEvaporate.h showing the constructor method

As you can see, as explained in the context of other fixes (for example, see *Chapter 7, Understanding Fixes*, in the *Reviewing the fix addforce* section), if the keyword region is located (*line 98*), then the argument following this keyword is parsed as iregion (*line 100*). An error is returned if the provided region does not exist (*lines 101* to *102*). The length of the character array, idegion[], is defined as the length of the region name (*line 103*), and the name is then stored as the array (*line 105*).

In the destructor method, the idregion[] array is deleted (*line 130*):

```
    delete [] idregion;
```

In the init() method, the validity of the region is checked again, and an error is returned if the region is not found, as shown in the following screenshot:

```
165     // SM: check region validity
166     if (iregion >= 0) {
167       iregion = domain->find_region(idregion);
168       if (iregion == -1)
169         error->all(FLERR,"Region ID for fix printEvaporate does not exist");
170     }
```

Figure 11.14 – Screenshot from fix_printEvaporate.h showing the init() method

Fix Print is executed at the END_OF_STEP stage, once all the dynamics for the iteration have been completed. The modifications made in the end_of_step() method are discussed next.

Modifying the end_of_step() method in fix_printEvaporate.cpp

In the end_of_step() method, a region object is created to determine whether any atom is located inside the region (*lines 214 to 218*), as shown in the following screenshot:

```
213     // SM: update region if required
214     Region *region = NULL;
215     if (iregion >= 0) {
216        region = domain->regions[iregion];
217        region->prematch();
218     }
219
220     // SM: identify atoms located in region
221     int nlocal = atom->nlocal;
222     double **x = atom->x;
223     int *mask = atom->mask;
224     for (int i = 0; i < nlocal; i++)
225        if (mask[i] & groupbit) {
226           if (region && !region->match(x[i][0],x[i][1],x[i][2])) continue;
227           if (screenflag && screen) fprintf(screen,"%s\n",copy);
228           if (screenflag && logfile) fprintf(logfile,"%s\n",copy);
229           if (fp) {
230              fprintf(fp,"%s\n",copy);
231              fflush(fp);
232           }
233        }
```

Figure 11.15 – Screenshot from fix_printEvaporate.h showing the end_of_step() method

As you can see, the region object created on *line 214* identifies the region specified (*line 216*) and undergoes a region->prematch() check that ensures that required variables are invoked properly by all processors during the iteration.

Then, on *lines 221 to 233*, the atoms located in the region are identified. The number of local atoms in the processor (atom->nlocal), the positions of atoms (atom->x), and atom masks (atom->mask) are extracted (*lines 221 to 223*), and atoms belonging to the specified group and region are identified (*lines 224 to 226*). For each identified atom, the quantities provided are printed on the screen (*line 227*), log file (*line 228*), or file (*lines 229 to 232*).

It should be noted that, unlike the regular Fix Print, this fix is executed by every processor—the if (me==0) condition used in Fix Print has been removed in this fix. In Fix Print, only one processor is responsible for printing, whereas in this fix, each processor checks whether the atoms belonging to it are located in the region specified and prints a statement for each atom.

In this fix, the region is assumed to be the simulation box if no explicit region is entered, as established by the condition in *line 226* that disregards exclusion by region if no region is entered. In addition, the group name parsed by `fix.cpp` is disregarded in `Fix Print`, but it is used in this fix to identify the group of atoms that are checked for presence in the region provided.

Altogether, the input script syntax is as follows:

```
fix FIX_NAME GROUP printEvaporate N STRING region R
```

Similar to `Fix Print` (`https://lammps.sandia.gov/doc/fix_print.html`), the term `N` represents the number of timesteps elapsed between printing successive quantities, and `STRING` represents the quantities to be printed. The `region` keyword is followed by the region ID `R`.

This fix will now be tested on a system consisting of multiple particles traveling through an evaporation region.

Trial run – in.Test_PrintEvaporate

A LAMMPS simulation system is created consisting of three atoms and a rectangular region (**R_EVAP**) located at a certain height. The atoms are initially placed at different heights and provided with the same initial upward velocity, as shown in the following diagram:

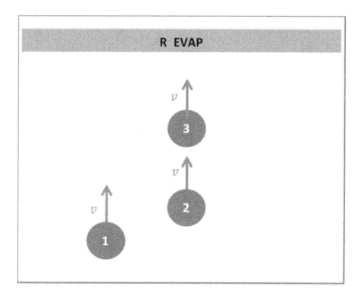

Figure 11.16 – Diagram of the simulation setup

As you can see, the atoms will cross **R_EVAP** sequentially and the `Fix PrintEvaporate` command will be able to register these crossings by printing to file. **R_EVAP** is constructed to have a thin depth (0.001 Å) so that atoms do not spend too many iterations inside it while traveling up and do not lead to too many `print` statements.

The corresponding LAMMPS input script is provided as follows, where the first part performs system initialization and creates the three atoms:

```
# ------------------------------------
# INITIALIZE SIMULATION
# ------------------------------------
units metal
dimension 3
boundary p p p
atom_style atomic


# ----------------------
# REGIONS
# ----------------------
region R0 block 0 20 0 20 0 20 units box
region R_EVAP block 0 20 0 20 13 13.001 units box


# ------------------------
# CREATE ATOMS
# ------------------------
create_box 1 R0
mass    1 10.0
create_atoms 1 single   8 8 7 units box
create_atoms 1 single   10 10 10 units box
create_atoms 1 single   10 10 12 units box
```

The region R_EVAP is defined to span over the entire xy plane and extend from $z = 13.000$ Å to $z = 13.001$ Å. The three atoms are created at the heights $z = 7$ Å, 10 Å, 12 Å.

The second part assigns a zero pair potential to the atoms and time integrates the atoms by `fix nve`, allowing the `fix printEvaporate` command to operate when the atoms cross into R_EVAP:

```
# ---------------------
# PAIR STYLES
# ---------------------
pair_style  lj/cut 5
pair_coeff  1 1   0 2.5


# ---------------------
# FIXES
# ---------------------
velocity all set 0 0 1
variable TIME equal step
fix NVE all nve
fix PRINT all printEvaporate 1 "${TIME}" file outputPRINT.dat
region R_EVAP title "Fix PrintEvaporate Timesteps"
run 7000
```

Each atom is provided with a velocity vector of (0,0,1) Å/ps to make it travel perpendicularly toward R_EVAP. The `fix printEvaporate` command writes the timestep to the `outputPRINT.dat` file when any atom enters R_EVAP.

In the event of an atom being present in R_EVAP, the timestep is printed to the `outputPRINT.dat` file, with the heading title `Fix PrintEvaporate Timesteps`. For the three atoms in this system, the following timesteps are printed:

```
Fix PrintEvaporate Timesteps
1001
3001
6001
```

As expected, the three atoms cross the region in sequence, and the timesteps of crossing correspond to their initial heights.

In this section, we provided an example of creating a custom print fix that might serve as a template for users who would like to create similar fixes to print custom output during their simulation runs.

Summary

This chapter demonstrated how to modify thermostats in LAMMPS to implement custom features, such as random velocity assignments and non-linear temperature increments. In addition, a short example of writing a fix to control the printing of quantities is provided.

Combined with the examples in the previous chapters, the content in this chapter has provided you with a platform to analyze your simulation requirements and determine an effective strategy of choosing an appropriate fix to modify or extend and implement your custom features with the proper tools and commands.

Overall, this book starts by introducing the LAMMPS source code and gradually builds up to the final chapter where custom fixes are created to apply custom thermostats to the simulated system. Using the concepts discussed in the earlier chapters, a robust framework is developed for users to refer to when writing their own modifications to the LAMMPS source code. The current version of LAMMPS includes a large and expanding library of built-in features, and users will find it more convenient to navigate and negotiate their source codes when accompanied with this book.

The remaining appendices in the book discuss the routine task of compiling customized versions of LAMMPS (*Appendix A*), debugging codes with appropriate tools (*Appendix B*), the general structure of MPI (*Appendix C*), and reviewing the differences between the LAMMPS versions 3Mar20 and 29Oct20 (*Appendix D*). While not essential to follow the content of the chapters, these appendices provide relevant information that are intended to provide a more comprehensive picture to interested users.

Questions

1. In a variation of the Andersen thermostat, a frequency, v, in the range [0,1] is provided and, in every iteration, a uniform random number in the range [0,1] is generated. If the random number is less than v, then the velocities are adjusted by a Maxwell-Boltzmann distribution. What changes are required in `fix_temp_andersen.cpp` to implement this variation (assume that the FREQUENCY input parameter is used to represent v)?

2. In the example of the exponential increase in temperature, if it is required to cap the temperature at an upper limit, `t_stop`, what changes are required in the `compute_temp_target()` method of the modified `fix_nh.cpp`?

Appendix A
Building LAMMPS
with CMake

In this appendix, we will give a brief tutorial on how to build LAMMPS with **CMake**. Unlike the traditional **Makefile**, CMake can detect available hardware, tools, features, and libraries and adjust the LAMMPS default build configuration accordingly. CMake allows customized settings with a text mode or graphical user interface, without requiring any knowledge of file formats or complex command-line syntax. In addition, CMake can automate dependency tracking for all files and configuration options.

Technical requirements

To execute the instructions in this chapter, you need a platform to compile LAMMPS (for example, a **Linux Terminal**).

Prerequisites for working with LAMMPS

Before we start working with LAMMPS, we need to get a few things up and running for hassle-free execution:

- Downloading the source code
- Installing dependencies
- Downloading MPICH

We'll look at the preceding points in the following sections.

Downloading the source code

You can download the LAMMPS source code from GitHub by entering the following command in the terminal:

```
git clone https://github.com/lammps/lammps.git
```

If, instead, the source code is downloaded from other sources (for example, the LAMMPS download page at https://lammps.sandia.gov/download.html), please make sure to unzip accordingly.

Installing the dependencies

The following commands will install the necessary components (use sudo before each apt command if required):

```
apt install build-essential
apt install cmake
apt install gfortran
apt update
apt upgrade
```

As the preceding components are being installed, progress will be displayed on the terminal screen. As for the **Fast Fourier Transform** package, if there is no third-party package detected on the machine, CMake will use the embedded KISS FFT library by default.

Downloading MPICH

To enable parallel computation of LAMMPS and communication among the cores and nodes, a framework or **Message Passing Interface** (**MPI**) is needed. **MPICH** is a high performance and widely portable implementation of the MPI standard. The required source code can be downloaded directly from the terminal by entering this:

```
sudo apt install mpich
```

Alternatively, the source code can be downloaded using the instructions provided on the official site (`www.mpich.org`) and has to be decompressed and built:

```
tar -zxvf mpich3.tar.gz
./configure -enable-shared=yes
```

In the preceding command, the `--enable-shared=yes` option is necessary to build a library. The final command is to complete the make:

```
make && make install
```

Once **MPICH** has been installed, LAMMPS can be built with parallel processing capabilities. Otherwise, LAMMPS can only be built to process in serial with a single processor.

Building LAMMPS

When building LAMMPS, an additional folder should be set up to temporarily store configuration files. In LAMMPS, `CMake` supports out-of-source compilation, and multiple configurations containing different choices of LAMMPS packages, settings, or compilers can be created in other folders outside the source.

In the folder where the LAMMPS source code has been downloaded and unzipped, enter the following command to access the relevant folder:

```
cd lammps
```

Then, a new `build` folder can be created to store different configurations:

```
mkdir build
```

This folder can then be accessed with the following command:

```
cd build
```

Once accessed, the rest of the installation process can be continued inside it.

Including packages in the build

When building LAMMPS, the source code in the src folder is automatically selected for compilation. The optional packages can be included or excluded as required. The selected packages will influence the compilation time and the size of the executable, and in general, there is no need to include a package if you do not plan to use its features. In the lammps/cmake/presets folder, CMake provides a list of pre-configuration files that are used in common simulation scenarios.

The following screenshot shows the preset file, minimal.cmake, which activates a few commonly used packages for fast compilation:

```
1   # preset that turns on just a few, frequently used packages
2   # this will be compiled quickly and handle a lot of common inputs.
3
4   set(ALL_PACKAGES KSPACE MANYBODY MOLECULE RIGID)
5
6   foreach(PKG ${ALL_PACKAGES})
7     set(PKG_${PKG} ON CACHE BOOL "" FORCE)
8   endforeach()
```

Figure 12.1 – minimal.cmake located in lammps/cmake/presets

As you can see, on *line 4*, an ALL_PACKAGES variable is created that contains four packages (KSPACE, MANYBODY, MOLECULE, and RIGID). In *lines 6 to 8*, the packages are iteratively activated via a loop. More packages can be included by adding to the set command.

Other preset files activate other combinations of packages, such as most.cmake, as shown in the next screenshot:

```
1   # preset that turns on a wide range of packages, some of which require
2   # external libraries. Compared to all_on.cmake some more unusual packages
3   # are removed. The resulting binary should be able to run most inputs.
4
5   set(ALL_PACKAGES ASPHERE CLASS2 COLLOID CORESHELL DIPOLE
6          GRANULAR KSPACE MANYBODY MC MISC MOLECULE OPT PERI
7          PYTHON QEQ REPLICA RIGID SHOCK SNAP SRD VORONOI
8          USER-CGDNA USER-CGSDK USER-COLVARS USER-DIFFRACTION USER-DPD
9          USER-DRUDE USER-FEP USER-MEAMC USER-MESO
10         USER-MISC USER-MOFFF USER-OMP USER-PHONON USER-REAXC
11         USER-SPH USER-SMD USER-UEF USER-YAFF)
12
13  foreach(PKG ${ALL_PACKAGES})
14    set(PKG_${PKG} ON CACHE BOOL "" FORCE)
15  endforeach()
```

Figure 12.2 – most.cmake located in lammps/cmake/presets

As you can see, this file lists a longer collection of packages to activate (*line 5*). Other preset files include `all_on.cmake`, which activates all existing packages, and `all_off.cmake`, which deactivates all existing packages to reset.

The required preset file can be called when compiling LAMMPS, as will be explained later in this section.

Including modified codes

CMake automatically builds the source code files that start with `pair_`, `fix_`, `compute_`, and so on. When compiling, custom-written source code files will be automatically included if they are preceded by these terms. If not, the filenames have to be added to the appropriate style header file in the `src` folder. The full list of automatically detected terms is available in `StyleHeaderUtils.cmake`, located in the `lammps/cmake/modules/` folder.

Building with CMake

By default, CMake automatically selects a compiler based on internal preferences and it will add optimization flags as appropriate. Here is a list of advanced flags that are empty by default and can be modified by the user before compilation:

- Global compiler options (set `value` to `yes` or `no`):

```
-D CMAKE_TUNE_FLAGS=value
```

- Name of the **C++** compiler:

```
-D CMAKE_CXX_COMPILER=name
```

- Name of the **C** compiler:

```
-D CMAKE_C_COMPILER=name
```

- Name of the **Fortran** compiler:

```
-D CMAKE_Fortran_COMPILER=name
```

- Flags to use with the **C++** compiler:

```
-D CMAKE_CXX_FLAGS=string
```

- Flags to use with the **C** compiler:

```
-D CMAKE_C_FLAGS=string
```

- Flags to use with the **Fortran** compiler:

```
-D CMAKE_Fortran_FLAGS=string
```

- Add an executable file to a path via the **make install** command:

```
-D CMAKE_INSTALL_PREFIX=path
```

- Control compilation options (set `value` to `Release` or `Debug`):

```
-D CMAKE_BUILD_TYPE=value
```

- Set the name of the executable file:

```
-D LAMMPS_MACHINE=string
```

More information about CMake flags can be found in the LAMMPS manual (`https://lammps.sandia.gov/doc/Howto_cmake.html`).

As an example, the following command installs the packages in the `minimal.cmake` preset file and prepares a compiled executable file called `lmp_test`:

```
cmake -C ../cmake/presets/minimal.cmake -D LAMMPS_MACHINE=test
-D CMAKE_BUILD_TYPE=Debug ../cmake
```

A summary of build configurations is provided on the screen, as shown in the following screenshot:

```
-- <<< Build configuration >>>
   Operating System: Linux
   Build type:       Debug
   Install path:     /root/.local
   Generator:        Unix Makefiles using /usr/bin/make
-- Enabled packages: KSPACE;MANYBODY;MOLECULE;RIGID
-- <<< Compilers and Flags: >>>
-- C++ Compiler:     /usr/bin/c++
      Type:          GNU
      Version:       7.5.0
      C++ Flags:      -g
      Defines:       LAMMPS_SMALLBIG;LAMMPS_MEMALIGN=64;LAMMPS_OMP_COMPAT=3;LAMMPS_JPE
G;LAMMPS_PNG;LAMMPS_GZIP;FFT_FFTW3;FFT_FFTW_THREADS
-- <<< Linker flags: >>>
-- Executable name:  lmp_test
-- Static library flags:
-- <<< MPI flags >>>
-- MPI_defines:
-- MPI includes:      /usr/lib/x86_64-linux-gnu/openmpi/include/openmpi;/usr/lib/x86_64
-linux-gnu/openmpi/include/openmpi/opal/mca/event/libevent2022/libevent;/usr/lib/x86_6
4-linux-gnu/openmpi/include/openmpi/opal/mca/event/libevent2022/libevent/include;/usr/
lib/x86_64-linux-gnu/openmpi/include
-- MPI libraries:     /usr/lib/x86_64-linux-gnu/openmpi/lib/libmpi_cxx.so;/usr/lib/libm
pi.so;
-- <<< FFT settings >>>
-- Primary FFT lib:  FFTW3
-- Using double precision FFTs
-- Using threaded FFTs
-- Configuring done
-- Generating done
```

Figure 12.3 – The build configuration

As you can see, if the settings displayed are satisfactory, the build can be commenced with the make command:

```
make
```

The preceding step creates the executable file that can be used to run LAMMPS scripts. Every time a modification is made to the source code, cleaning via the make clean command followed by recompilation are required to create a new executable that registers the modification.

> **Important Note:**
>
> It should be noted that depending on machine configurations (for example, standalone or HPC clusters) and/or the operating system used, the preceding steps may not compile LAMMPS properly. In such cases, it is advisable to web search for specific solutions or to contact the appropriate support staff.

This section describes a LAMMPS compilation in a Linux environment. In the next section, we will describe a LAMMPS compilation in Windows.

Compiling LAMMPS in Windows

This section was contributed by Abdullah Arafat, an apprentice of Dr. Shafat Mubin, and a senior year undergraduate student of Materials Science and Engineering at **Khulna University of Engineering and Technology (KUET)** *in Bangladesh. He is experienced in molecular modelling and molecular dynamics simulations, with proficiency in* **Python, LAMMPS, VESTA,** *and* **Materials Studio***. He is keenly interested in computational physics and materials science and is currently engaged in his undergraduate thesis on the growth kinetics of 2D materials.*

In this section, the procedure to build LAMMPS in **Windows** using CMake is detailed. Before beginning, please make sure to update Windows to its latest version.

First, the source code needs to be downloaded and CMake for Windows needs to be installed. The source code can be downloaded using `Git` for Windows, as described next.

Downloading Git for Windows

You can download `Git` from the link: `https://git-scm.com/downloads`.

Once downloaded and installed, `Git` for Windows can be used to download the LAMMPS source code as described in the next section.

Downloading the source code

You can download the LAMMPS source code from GitHub with the following command in Windows Command Prompt or **PowerShell**:

```
git clone https://github.com/lammps/lammps.git
```

Alternatively, you can download the zipped file from the official LAMMPS GitHub repository: `https://github.com/lammps/lammps`.

The following screenshot shows the downloaded .zip file from the aforementioned link:

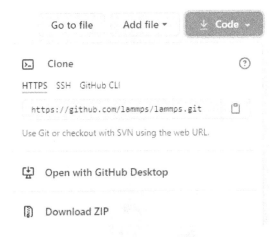

Figure 12.4 – The downloaded .zip file from the LAMMPS GitHub repository

Unzip the zipped file, lammps-master.zip, in your desired directory, which we will refer to as LAMMPS_DIR in the following instructions.

Next, we outline the installation of CMake for Windows.

Downloading CMake for Windows

You can download CMake for Windows from the following link: https://cmake.org/download

Download the installer suitable for your platform and install it, as shown in the following screenshot:

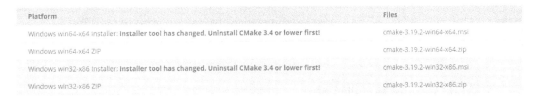

Figure 12.5 – Multiple installers of CMake

Once completed, you will have access to the source code and CMake for Windows. The instructions in the following section will describe the installation of **MPI** to facilitate parallel processing and Codeblocks to provide an **Integrated Development Environment (IDE)**.

Downloading Microsoft MPI

You can download **MS-MPI** from the following link: `https://docs.microsoft.com/en-us/message-passing-interface/microsoft-mpi`.

> **Important Note:**
> Please note that **MS-MPI** is only required if you want to run LAMMPS on multiple parallel processes (similar to `MPICH`).

The following screenshot shows the downloadable versions available:

Figure 12.6 – The latest version of MS-MPI

Download both `msmpisetup.exe` and `msmpisdk.msi`, and install them.

Downloading Code::Blocks

You can download `Codeblocks` with **MinGW** (for example, `codeblocks-20.03mingw-setup.exe`) from the following link: `http://www.codeblocks.org/downloads/binaries`

MinGW refers to **Minimalist GNU for Windows**, so installing `Codeblocks` with MinGW will include the **GCC/G++/GFortran** compiler and the **GDB debugger**, which will allow you to build LAMMPS with more convenience.

Having completed the preceding prerequisite installations, we move on to building LAMMPS using these tools.

Developing LAMMPS

We follow these steps to start building LAMMPS:

1. In the folder where the LAMMPS source code has been downloaded and unzipped (which we will call `LAMMPS_DIR`), create a new folder and rename it `build`.

2. Now run CMake (cmake-gui), enter LAMMPS_DIR/cmake in the box titled **Where is the source code**, enter LAMMPS_DIR/build in the box underneath titled **Where to build the binaries**, and click **Configure**.

3. When configuring the project for the first time, a new window will appear asking for the generator to use for this project, where the **CodeBlocks – MinGW Makefiles** option can be selected. Click **Finish**, as shown in the following screenshot:

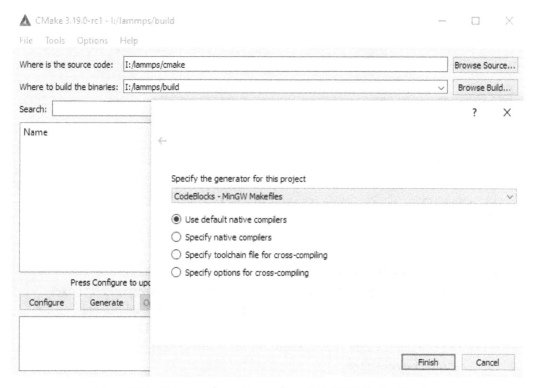

Figure 12.7 – Using cmake-gui to configure LAMMPS for the first time

In the preceding screenshot, the folder that contains the source code (that is, LAMMPS_DIR) for this particular example is the I:/lammps folder entered in the two boxes at the top.

4.   Now select the desired LAMMPS packages to include in the LAMMPS executable to be built, as seen in the following screenshot:

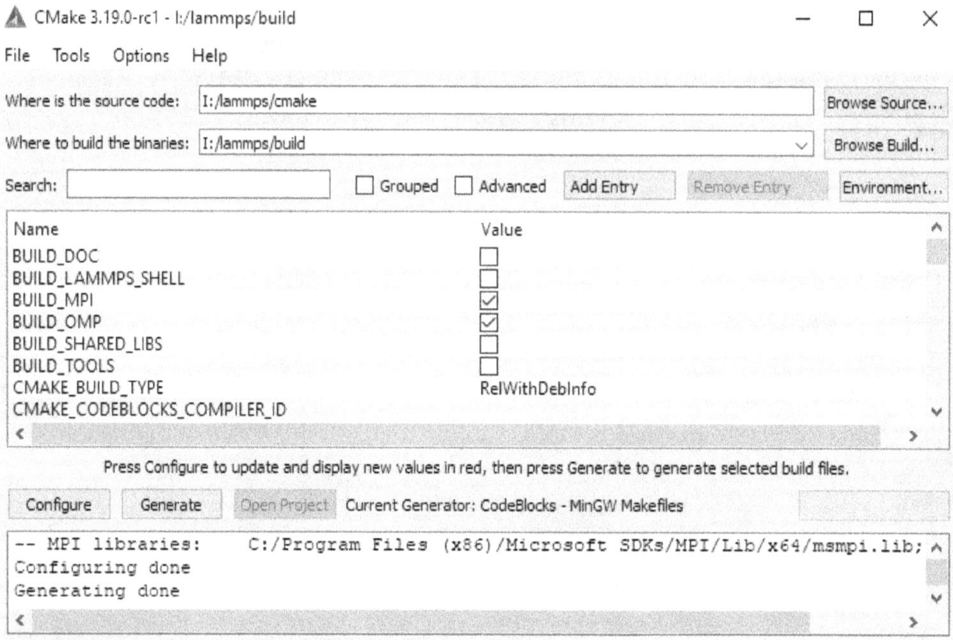

Figure 12.8 – cmake-gui after selecting the required packages and clicking Configure and Generate

As you can see, packages can be selected by checking their corresponding boxes under the **Value** column. However, some packages may require additional steps, for example, **BUILD_DOC**, **PKG_KOKKOS**, and **PKG_LATTE**, for which the LAMMPS manual (https://lammps.sandia.gov/doc/Build_extras.html) should be consulted.

> **Tip:**
> For a minimal installation, the default selection of packages can be used.

5.   After generating with CMake, a Codeblocks project called lammps.cbp will be created. Open this project with Codeblocks and press *Ctrl + F9*, or click the **Build** button, as marked in the following screenshot:

Figure 12.9 – Code::Blocks after successfully compiling LAMMPS

As demonstrated, after successful compilation you may notice the message
Process terminated with status 0 and 0 error(s) in the **Build log** at the bottom.
Concurrently, an executable file titled lmp.exe is generated in the build
directory of the LAMMPS folder, LAMMPS_DIR.

This executable can be used to run a LAMMPS script from **Command Prompt**. Also,
you can add the location of lmp.exe in the user or system path variable to access it from
anywhere in the system. To set LAMMPS as a user path variable, open Command Prompt,
and type the following:

```
setx PATH "LAMMPS_DIR\build;%PATH%"
```

To set LAMMPS as a system path variable, open Command Prompt as administrator, and
type this:

```
setx /m PATH "LAMMPS_DIR\build;%PATH%"
```

As described earlier, LAMMPS_DIR entered in both the aforementioned Command
Prompt lines should refer to the folder containing the source code.

To verify that LAMMPS has been properly built, select an existing LAMMPS input script to test run, for example, the `in.crack` script located in `examples/crack/` in the LAMMPS folder. Open Command Prompt or PowerShell to navigate to this directory and enter either of the followings commands:

- For serial execution, use this:

```
lmp -in in.crack
```

- For parallel execution (using `mpi` with 2 cores), use the following:

```
mpiexec -n 2 lmp -in in.crack
```

Successful execution of the `in.crack` script produces a screenshot similar to the following:

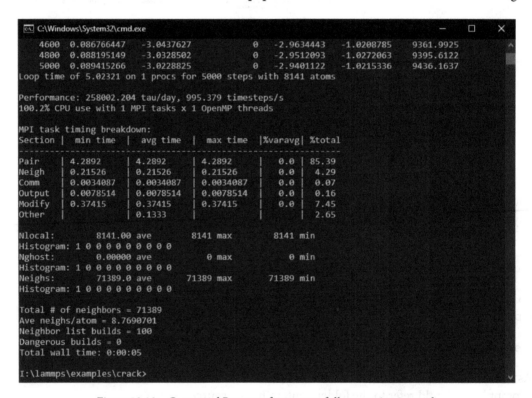

Figure 12.10 – Command Prompt after successfully executing in.crack

In this section, we learned about the LAMMPS compilation process in Windows. While Windows offers its own set of conveniences, it does not facilitate other features. Please see this webpage (`https://lammps.sandia.gov/doc/Build_windows.html`) from the LAMMPS manual for a brief overview of building LAMMPS in Windows.

Apart from using CMake, LAMMPS can be built using traditional **Make**, which offers a quicker way to compile and is discussed in the next section.

Building with Make

Make is a traditional method to build LAMMPS that uses a configuration file, called a `makefile`, to specify build options. The LAMMPS optional packages need to be included manually in this method.

First, you should change your directory to the source code folder:

```
cd src
```

Before compilation, each desired package should be included using the `make yes-<package>` command, where `<package>` is the name of the selected package. For example, you would use this if you wanted to include the `MOLECULE` package:

```
make yes-molecule
```

This operation copies all the files in `src/MOLECULE` to the `src` folder and prepares them for compilation.

In order to build LAMMPS, a customized `Makefile.<machine>` file is required based on the system used, where `<machine>` represents the type of machine setup being used (for example, `serial` or `mpi`).

The `src/MAKE` folder contains these customized files, the `OPTIONS` folder contains specific options that can be enabled, the `MACHINES` folder stores configurations for specific machines, and `MINE` usually stores your customized makefiles.

If we need to change some flags, such as for the integer data size, we open a certain `makefile` (for example, `Makefile.serial` or `Makefile.mpi`) in the `src/MAKE` folder, find the `LMP_INC` line, and add the required –D flags:

```
LMP_INC  =  -DLAMMPS_GZIP  _DLAMMPS_SMALLBIG
```

The complete list of flags can be found on the appropriate page of the LAMMPS manual (https://lammps.sandia.gov/doc/Build_settings.html).

After completing the previous steps, we can type make <machine> -jN to compile the code, where <machine> corresponds to the same text as in Makefile.<machine>. For example, entering make mpi will use Makefile.mpi as the configuration file. Additionally, the -jN flag can be used to specify the number of cores used to compile:

```
make mpi -j4
```

When LAMMPS is built for the first time, it assembles a list of dependencies. When LAMMPS is rebuilt, recompilation is necessary. If settings in the makefile are changed, then all existing objects must be deleted using the make clean-<machine> command, as here:

```
make clean-all
```

It should be noted that if this traditional Make is used in the LAMMPS source directory, CMake will generate an error if this is attempted in the same directory. In such a case, the make no-all purge command has to be used to uninstall and delete existing files before CMake can proceed.

Further reading

Build LAMMPS with CMake: https://lammps.sandia.gov/doc/Build_cmake.html

Build LAMMPS with Make: https://lammps.sandia.gov/doc/Build_make.html

Appendix B
Debugging Programs

Fred Brooks, the father of the **IBM** mainframe, wrote in his famous book, *The Mythical Man-Month*, that software development requires one-third of the time to design and half of the time to test, but only one-sixth to code. Even when written by a programmer with rich development experience, programs are almost always prone to mistakes.

Through the process of debugging the program, we can monitor every detail of the program execution, including the value of variables, the calling process of functions, the data in memory, and the scheduling of threads, just to find hidden errors or inefficient sections of code.

We will cover the following topics in this appendix:

- Debugging with **GDB**
- Debugging with **Visual Studio Code (VSCode)**
- Understanding sbmask() as a tool for debugging

Technical requirements

To execute the instructions in this chapter, you need to install GDB and/or VSCode, and have access to a **Linux terminal**.

What is debugging?

There are two types of errors in a program—**syntax errors** and **logical errors**. A syntax error is an error in code grammar or composition that can be detected by the compiler, and therefore can usually be corrected relatively easily.

A logical error refers to an error in code design in terms of its intended purpose versus actual outcome. The quintessential symptom of a logical error in the program is successful compilation followed by an erroneous output upon execution. These errors have to be detected and corrected manually.

The debugging process involves letting the code execute step by step and tracking the program's process of execution. Generally, the most efficient way to detect logical errors is to debug the program with designated debugging tools that allow the tracking of execution steps.

For example, you can make the program stop at a certain step to view the contents of variables or data in memory. You can also make the program execute one or more statements at a time to check the output of the code the program has executed.

Due to space constraints, the specific command usage will not be introduced here, but only the common operations will be outlined. More information about the debuggers described are available in the respective debugger manuals.

Prerequisites

Before starting the debugging process, a test LAMMPS executable file should be built. When building with **CMake** (see *Appendix A*, *Building LAMMPS with CMake*), adding a `-D CMAKE_BUILD_TYPE=Debug` flag assists in the debugging process since it does not optimize out any variable, that is, the compiler does not eliminate intermediate values.

After CMake configuration, it is fine if **C++** flags only show up as `-g` in the build configuration. Also, it is advisable to rename the executable from `lmp` to `lmp_test` to distinguish it accordingly. The following screenshot shows the build configuration after executing the CMake configuration:

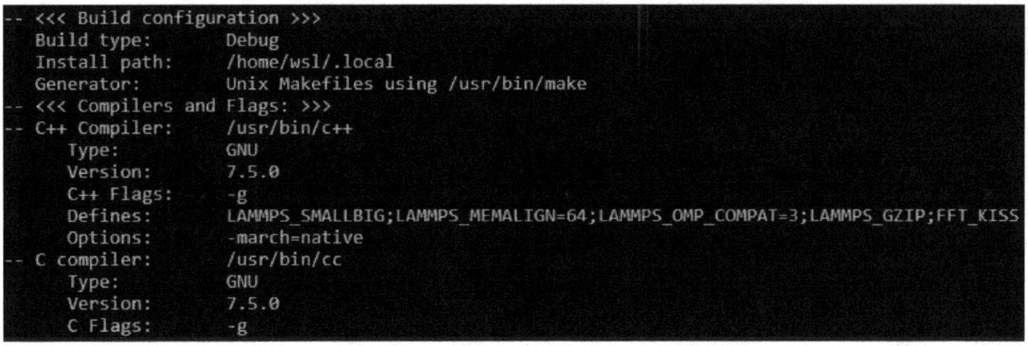

```
-- <<< Build configuration >>>
   Build type:        Debug
   Install path:      /home/wsl/.local
   Generator:         Unix Makefiles using /usr/bin/make
-- <<< Compilers and Flags: >>>
-- C++ Compiler:      /usr/bin/c++
     Type:            GNU
     Version:         7.5.0
     C++ Flags:       -g
     Defines:         LAMMPS_SMALLBIG;LAMMPS_MEMALIGN=64;LAMMPS_OMP_COMPAT=3;LAMMPS_GZIP;FFT_KISS
     Options:         -march=native
-- C compiler:        /usr/bin/cc
     Type:            GNU
     Version:         7.5.0
     C Flags:         -g
```

Figure 13.1 – Screenshot showing the build configuration by CMake

As you can see, having created an executable, we will apply debugging tools to analyze the purpose of the `sbmask()` method in `pair_lj_cut.cpp`. A data file (`test.data`) is created to construct a linear polymer chain consisting of 5 bonded atoms connected by 4 identical bonds of equilibrium length 1 unit:

```
# test.data

5 atoms

4 bonds


1 atom types

1 bond types


0 10 xlo xhi

0 10 ylo yhi

0 10 zlo zhi


Atoms


1 1 1 0.0 0.0 0.0 0.0

2 1 1 0 1.0 0.0 0.0

3 1 1 0 2.0 0.0 0.0

4 1 1 0 3.0 0.0 0.0

5 1 1 0 4.0 0.0 0.0


Bonds

```

```
1 1 1 2
2 1 2 3
3 1 3 4
4 1 4 5
```

Using a simple LAMMPS input script (test.in), pair and bond coefficients are assigned to the atoms and the system is time-integrated by fix nve. A cutoff distance of 5.5 units is assigned for pair interactions. The following test input script illustrates the process:

```
# test.in
units lj
atom_style full
read_data test.data

mass 1 1.0
special_bonds lj 0.3 0.5 0.7
pair_style lj/cut 5.5
pair_coeff 1 1 1.0 1.0 5.5

neighbor 0.3 bin
neigh_modify delay 0 every 20 check no
fix 1 all nve
run 100
```

From the preceding code, the bond type is designated as special bond LJ that assigns weights to the first (0.3), second (0.5), and third (0.7) bonded neighbors via a bonded **Lennard-Jones (LJ)** potential (see https://lammps.sandia.gov/doc/special_bonds.html). Note that in pair_lj_cut.cpp, the 1D array, special_lj, and the sbmask() function relate to the special_bonds command in the input script, and they appear as (*line 103*, *line 183*, *line 261*, and *line 341*):

```
factor_lj = special_lj[sbmask(j)];
```

The preceding line indicates that sbmask() is a function that determines whether an atom is bonded to another atom as a first, second, third, or higher neighbor, and then it applies the appropriate weighting factor corresponding to the special_lj command entry in the input script.

Having prepared the data file and the input script, we can begin the debugging process. Two methods will be illustrated—using GDB directly, and using VSCode to invoke GDB.

Method 1 – Debugging with GDB

Most cluster computers and **high-performance computing (HPC)** systems do not offer graphical user interfaces, and instead rely on command-line inputs. GDB can be installed by entering the following command in the terminal:

```
sudo apt-get install libc6-dbg gdb valgrind
```

The following commands start GDB and load the executable `lmp_test` file:

```
[in] user@user-Main:~/lammps/test$ gdb -silent
[in] (gdb) file lmp_test
```

The following output is expected:

```
[out] Reading symbols from lmp_test...done.
```

Since we are interested in analyzing `sbmask()`, a breakpoint will be added at a line where `sbmask()` is located to pause the code at that point. The following input command places a breakpoint (b) at *line 93*, right after the loop over the neighbor list begins, and the corresponding output registers the breakpoint:

```
[in] (gdb) b pair_lj_cut.cpp:93
[out] Breakpoint 1 at 0x637e12:file/home/lammps/src/pair_lj_
cut.cpp, line 93.
```

Then, the input script is run:

```
[in] (gdb) run -in test.in
[out] Starting program: /home/wsl/lammps/build/lmp_test
-in in.test Breakpoint 1, LAMMPS_NS::PairLJCut::compute
(this=0x90d4230, eflag=1, vflag=2)at /home/lammps/src/pair_lj_
cut.cpp:93
93    i = ilist[ii];
```

In the preceding command line, the b command adds a breakpoint, whereas other single-letter commands perform other tasks, for example:

- n (next): This means to execute the next line.

- s (step): This means to proceed to the next command, which may be located in a different subroutine.

- c (continue): This means to continue executing commands until the next breakpoint.

- p (print): This means to print a quantity to the screen.

A detailed instruction manual is available at `http://sourceware.org/gdb/download/onlinedocs/gdb.pdf`.

The following example inputs and outputs demonstrate the purposes served by some of these commands. In the following example, a breakpoint (b) is applied at *line 103*, where `sbmask()` appears first, and the script is then continued (c):

```
[in] (gdb) b 103
[out] Breakpoint 2 at 0x8637f3f: file /home/wsl/lammps/src/
pair_lj_cut.cpp, line 103.
[in] (gdb) c
[out] Continuing.
Breakpoint 2, LAMMPS_NS::PairLJCut::compute (this=0x90d4230,
eflag=1, vflag=2)
at /home/wsl/lammps/src/pair_lj_cut.cpp:103
103         factor_lj = special_lj[sbmask()];
```

As we saw in *Chapter 4*, *Accessing Information by Variables, Arrays, and Methods*, the quantities jlist and jnum were explained.

In the next example, the value of an array will be accessed by the print (p) command. For a scalar, we use p directly to display it, while for an array in C/C++, where the variable name is a pointer that points to the address of the first element, we use * for dereferencing it and @ to specify the number of elements in the array:

```
[in] (gdb) p *jlist@jnum
[out] $1 = {1073741825, -2147483646, -1073741821, 4}

[in] (gdb) p j
[out] $2 = 1073741825

[in] (gdb) s
[out] LAMMPS_NS::Pair::sbmask (this=0x90d4230, j=1073741825) at
/home/wsl/lammps/src/pair.h:263
263         return j >> SBBITS & 3;
```

```
[in] (gdb)p j
[out] $3 = 1
```

```
[in] (gdb) s
[out] LAMMPS_NS::PairLJCut::compute (this=0x90d4230, eflag=1,
vflag=2) at /home/wsl/lammps/src/pair_lj_cut.cpp:104
104             j &= NEIGHMASK;
```

```
[in] (gdb)
[out] 106       delx = xtmp - x[j][0];
```

```
[in] (gdb) p j
[out] $4 = 1
```

As you can see, the various single-letter commands can be used to locate and display values of variables or arrays, which are useful when debugging. In the next section, we will introduce VSCode, which provides a more user-friendly interface to debug.

Method 2 – Debugging with VSCode

For users not accustomed to command-line interfaces, VSCode offers a more convenient alternative. In essence, VSCode is based on GDB and it contains the same command format.

To successfully employ this method, you need to do the following:

1. Install Visual Studio Code (https://code.visualstudio.com/Download).

2. Install the C++ extension for VSCode (https://marketplace.visualstudio.com/items?itemName=ms-vscode.cpptools).

3. Configure launch.json (since LAMMPS has already been compiled, we do not require task.json).

VSCode automatically generates a `launch.json` with most of the required information. Before beginning the debugging process, the `program` field needs to be set to the correct path. The following screenshot shows a sample configuration:

```
1   {
2       "configurations": [
3       {
4           "name": "(gdb) debug",
5           "type": "cppdbg",
6           "request": "launch",
7           "program": "${workspaceFolder}/build/lmp_test",
8           "args": ["-in", "test.in"],
9           "stopAtEntry": false,
10          "cwd": "${workspaceFolder}/build",
11          "environment": [],
12          "externalConsole": false,
13          "MIMode": "gdb",
14          "setupCommands": [
15              {
16                  "description": "Enable pretty-printing for gdb",
17                  "text": "-enable-pretty-printing",
18                  "ignoreFailures": true
19              }
20          ],
21          "miDebuggerPath": "/usr/bin/gdb"
22      }
23      ]
24  }
```

Figure 13.2 – An example of launch.json in VSCode configuration

A full list of configuration controls can be found at https://code.visualstudio.com/docs/cpp/launch-json-reference.

To add a breakpoint, click on the left side, next to the line number desired, as shown in the following screenshot:

```
101      for (jj = 0; jj < jnum; jj++) {
102          j = jlist[jj];
103          factor_lj = special_lj[sbmask(j)];
104          j &= NEIGHMASK;
```

Figure 13.3 – Screenshot of the breakpoint at line 103

To control the flow of the program, use the bar shown in the following screenshot to implement the `continue`, `next`, `step in`, `step out`, and `stop` commands:

Figure 13.4 – Screenshot of the control bar

The value of a variable can be displayed with the mouse cursor hovering on it. For an array, an expression can be added to the `Watch` sidebar, as shown in the following screenshot:

WATCH   + ⊟ ⊡
  ∨ *special_lj@4: [4]
      [0]: 1
      [1]: 0.29999999999999999
      [2]: 0.5
      [3]: 0.69999999999999996
  ∨ *jlist@jnum: [4]
      [0]: 1073741825
      [1]: -2147483646
      [2]: -1073741821
      [3]: 4

Figure 13.5 – Screenshot of the array content displayed in the Watch sidebar

Using the tools described, we will analyze `sbmask()` and investigate the role of bits in indexing operations in the next section. The debugging tools will be used to output the relevant quantities during the simulation run and the corresponding bitwise representations will be interpreted accordingly.

Insight into sbmask()

Bitmask is a widely used technique to validate authority, often using the bitwise AND operation for fast operations. A well-known example is the **subnet mask**, which operates on IP addresses in a network and yields the routing prefix. In the context of bonded atoms in LAMMPS, `sbmask()` uses the same mechanism to identify whether a particle is linked by a special bond.

In order to analyze bitmask operations in the LAMMPS source code, we now return to the example LAMMPS script (`test.in`) and `pair_lj_cut.cpp` implemented as `pair style lj/cut`. As described in *Chapter 4, Accessing Information by Variables, Arrays, and Methods*, the `ilist` array represents a collection of central atoms to loop over, and the `jlist` array represents the corresponding neighbors of each member of `ilist`. Recall that in our example LAMMPS script, the cutoff radius is 5.5 units, so the first atom (`i=0`) has five pairwise atoms (`j`) interacting with it.

A short simulation run is performed and using the debugging tools described, the following table is generated, which lists the contents of the quantities `i`, `j`, and `sbmask()`, the output of the bitwise operation `j&=NEIGHMASK`, and the binary representations of `j` created during a loop over the neighbor list of a single atom (`i=0`) in `pair_lj_cut.cpp`:

i	j	sbmask(j)	j&=NEIGHMASK	Binary representation
0	1073741825	1	1	0100 0000 0000 0000 0000 0000 0000 0001
0	-2147483646	2	2	1000 0000 0000 0000 0000 0000 0000 0010
0	-1073741821	3	3	1100 0000 0000 0000 0000 0000 0000 0011
0	4	0	4	0000 0000 0000 0000 0000 0000 0000 0100
0	5	0	5	0000 0000 0000 0000 0000 0000 0000 0101

Table 13.1 – Table showing the values of i, j, sbmask(), j&=NEIGHMASK, and the binary representation of j

To understand the preceding table, let's analyze the fifth column first. The fifth column in the table provides the binary representation that contains the neighbor index and the special bond index. The binary representation consists of 32 bits, where the first 2 bits indicate the special bond index of the neighbor, `j`, and the next 30 bits indicate the neighbor index.

In the table, the first 2 bits of the binary representation and the corresponding `sbmask()` values are compared for every row:

```
sbmask():  1  2  3  0  0
binary 2 bits:  01  10  11  00  00
```

When converted to decimal, it is observed that the first two bits of the binary representation yield the index of the special bond, indicating that the first row is the first neighbor, the second row is the second neighbor, the third row is the third neighbor, and that the fourth and fifth rows are not bonded.

Since the two bits can only represent between 0 and 3, this convention does not permit the creation of special bonds beyond the third neighbor. When the sbmask() function is applied to neighbor j (for example, *line 103*), the first two bits are extracted to read the special bond index of j relative to the atom i. Once the index is read, the corresponding scaling factor coefficient is obtained from the special_lj[] or special_coul[] array, and stored as a variable, factor_lj.

The next 30 bits of the binary representation yield the neighbor index of j relative to i. Comparing the fourth column and the last 4 bits of the fifth column (since the first 26 bits of the index are zero) of the table, we get the following:

```
j &= NEIGHMASK: 1 2 3 4 5
 binary 30 bits: 0001 0010 0011 0100 0101
```

When converted to decimal, these bits represent the neighbor index of j, indicating that the neighbors in the 5 rows are sequentially indexed from 1 to 5 for this particular atom, i. Given the limit of 30 bits, the maximum number of possible neighbors that can be accommodated in LAMMPS is $(2^{30} - 1)$.

When performing a bitwise AND operation (&) on j and NEIGHMASK (for example, *line 104*), the first two bits of the complete binary representation are stripped away and the remaining 30 bits are used to retrieve the neighbor index of j (if the first two bits are not removed, the interpreted number can exceed the permitted upper bound and create a segmentation fault).

This section provided an example of bitwise operation used in sbmask() to identify special bonds. Another example can be found in the use of atom->mask which identifies atoms belonging to a group. We introduced two approaches to debugging code, and presented a brief description of bitmask analyzed using these tools. Although there is no direct relationship between debugging and the extension of LAMMPS, it is an essential part in the process of writing code. Using the content of this appendix, you will be able to locate and correct code problems more efficiently.

Further reading

- http://www.sourceware.org/gdb/
- https://code.visualstudio.com/docs/cpp/cpp-debug
- https://en.wikipedia.org/wiki/Mask_(computing)

Appendix C
Getting Familiar with MPI

In this appendix, we will introduce the concept of the **Message Passing Interface** (**MPI**). LAMMPS is designed to support parallel computing, and an understanding of the basic principles of MPI is helpful when modifying its source code.

We will cover the following sections in this appendix:

- Learning about the six basic APIs of the MPI
- Learning the MPI framework in LAMMPS
- Writing an example code to calculate π using the MPI

You will have learned how LAMMPS performs parallel computation, how MPI is structured, and you can apply MPI techniques based on this appendix.

Technical requirements

To execute the instructions in this chapter, you need a text editor (for example, **Notepad++**, **Gedit**) and a platform to run a .cpp file (for example, **Linux terminal**).

What is MPI?

The MPI is a standard or specification, but not a specific implementation of LAMMPS. Each device manufacturer needs to provide support according to the interface specified in the specification. Therefore, a versatile MPI program should be able to run on all machines that support it. Common MPI implementations include mhich and openmpi. The standard of writing widely used information transferring programs is not only practical and transferrable, but also flexible, and it has not changed significantly over time.

MPI names have a common prefix—MPI_. There are 287 interfaces in the mpi-2 standard, but in theory, all communication functions can be realized through six basic calls. The following description of MPI is language independent and will introduce the structure of the parameters. Each call accepts parameters that are used to read quantities passed in (IN) or produce quantities to pass to the MPI (OUT).

MPI initialization

MPI_Init is the first call of the MPI:

```
MPI_INIT()
```

MPI_Init completes all initializations of the MPI program and is the first executable statement of all MPI programs.

MPI finalization

MPI_Finalize is the last call of the MPI program:

```
MPI_FINALIZE()
```

MPI_Finalize ends the MPI program run and is the last execution statement of the MPI program. If not implemented, the program will produce unpredictable results.

MPI current process ID

`MPI_COMM_RANK` call returns the process identification number of the calling process in a given communication domain:

```
MPI_COMM_RANK(comm, rank)
IN comm [the communication domain (handle) in which the process
is located]
OUT rank [the identifier of the calling process in comm
(integer)]
```

With this identification number, a process can be distinguished from other processes and can be used to streamline parallel computation.

MPI (number of processes)

`MPI_COMM_SIZE` returns the number of processes in a given communication domain:

```
MPI_COMM_SIZE(comm, size)
IN comm [communication domain(handle)]
OUT size [the number of processes in comm (integer)]
```

`MPI_COMM_SIZE` allows other processes to determine the number of processes that are computing in parallel in a given communication domain.

MPI send message

`MPI_SEND` sends data items of the `datatype` type and of given dimensions (`count`) in a buffer to the destination process of the identification number, `dest`, and a flag, `tag`, is applied to the message. Using this flag, the message sent can be distinguished from other messages sent to the same destination process. The buffer specified in the `MPI_SEND` call is composed of consecutive data spaces of the `datatype` type and `count` dimensions, with a starting address of `buf`. The following code exemplifies this:

```
MPI_SEND(buf, count, datatype, dest, tag, comm)
IN buf [starting address of the send buffer (optional type)]
IN count [the dimensions of data items sent (non-negative
integer)]
IN datatype [type of data being sent (handle)]
IN dest [destination process ID (integer)]
IN tag [message flag (integer)]
IN comm [communication domain (handle)]
```

Note that the length of each data item is specified by the datatype (for example, `MPI_SHORT` and `MPI_INT`) instead of the `count` size, which determines the dimensions of the data items in the message.

MPI receive message

`MPI_RECV` receives the message from the specified `source`, and the `datatype` type and identifier of this message must correspond to the parameters in `MPI_RECV`. The dimensions of the message must not exceed `count`. If the buffer size of data (`buf`) is less than the buffer size received, then the received buffer size must be less than the received buffer length. The following code shows us the same:

```
MPI_RECV(buf, count, datatype, source, tag, comm, status)
OUT buf [starting address of accepted buffer (optional data
type)]
IN count [the maximum dimensions of data items that can be
received (integer)]
IN datatype [datatype of received data (handle)]
IN source [process ID of the process from which the data was
received, that is the same as the process ID of the process
that sent the data (integer)]
IN tag [message flag that matches the representation of the
corresponding send operation (integer)]
IN comm [communication domain (handle) of this process and the
sending process]
OUT status [return status (status type)]
```

If a message shorter than the receiving buffer arrives, only the addresses corresponding to the message are modified. `count` can be zero, in which case the data part of the message remains empty.

MPI message

MPI message includes two parts—*envelope* and *data*. The envelope consists of identifying information including the source/destination, tag, and communicator, while data is the content to be delivered. The envelope and data include three parts, which can be represented by a ternary array:

- **Envelope**: Source/destination, ID, communication domain
- **Data**: Start address, count, datatype

The following screenshot illustrates this structure:

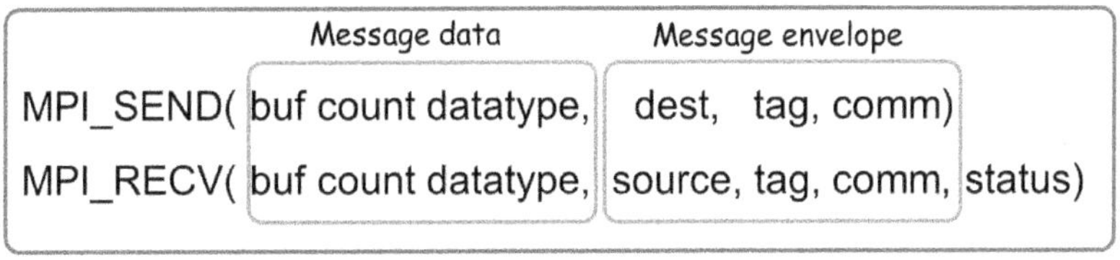

Figure 14.1 – Structure of the envelope and data

In addition to the source and destination, there are tags in the message envelope to allow the receiver to distinguish between two or more messages of the same type sent from the same sender to the same receiver, as shown in the following screenshot:

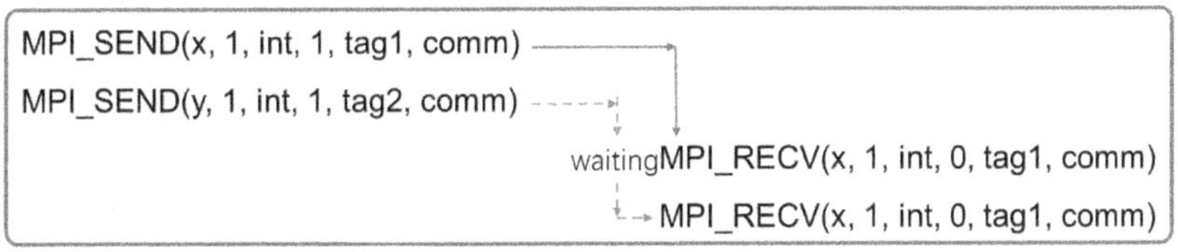

Figure 14.2 – The role of envelope tags in distinguishing between simultaneous messages

In the preceding figure, `Message 2` with **tag2** arrives without a matching receive operation. That is to say, even if `Message 2` arrives first, the data **y** of `Message 2` will not be received as **x** because the tag IDs do not match (that is, **tag2** of `Message 2` versus **tag1** of the receiver). Instead, the process that sends `Message 1` will block `Message 2` until the data **x** is received from `Message 1` with the matching tag ID (**tag1**).

MPI in LAMMPS

In this section, we will explore how LAMMPS uses the MPI in `main.cpp` to execute the input script code in the correct order. The initialization is performed by `MPI_Init` on *line 36*, as shown in the following screenshot:

```
36    int main(int argc, char **argv)
37    {
38        MPI_Init(&argc,&argv);
```

Figure 14.3 – Screenshot showing MPI_Init in main.cpp

Next, a predefined communication domain descriptor, MPI_COMM_WORLD, can be used (*line 64*), as shown in the following screenshot:

```
63   #else
64      LAMMPS *lammps = new LAMMPS(argc,argv,MPI_COMM_WORLD);
65      lammps->input->file();
66      delete lammps;
67   #endif
68      MPI_Barrier(MPI_COMM_WORLD);
69      MPI_Finalize();
```

Figure 14.4 – Screenshot showing MPI calls in main.cpp

The MPI communication domain consists of two parts: **process group** and **communication context**. The process group is the collection of all the processes participating in the communication. If n processes participate in the communication, the number is *0-n-1*. The communication context provides a relatively independent communication area. Different messages are delivered in different contexts, and messages in different contexts do not interfere with each other. The communication context can distinguish between different communications.

When instantiating a LAMMPS class, MPI_COMM_WORLD is passed to the constructor method (*line 64*). Then, the class member file() method of the Input class starts reading the input script (*line 65*). The function of the LAMMPS class is to initialize all the required classes, allocate them to memory, and provide a pointer class as an underlying class to the others for calling each other. When the initialization is complete, the LAMMPS instance is released (*line 66*).

The MPI_ Barrier call (*line 68*) synchronizes across all processors by blocking all calling processes until all participating processes are ready to make the call. Then, the call in each process is allowed to run and when all the processes have finished, the MPI_Finalize call (*line 69*) ends the program.

As soon as the program starts, MPI_Init pulls up a specified number of processes and executes the same code simultaneously. *But what if some operations only need to be operated once, such as opening and reading an input script?*

This requirement is facilitated by the MPI calls in the Input class (input.cpp), as shown in the following screenshot:

```
65   Input::Input(LAMMPS *lmp, int argc, char **argv) : Pointers(lmp)
66   {
67      MPI_Comm_rank(world,&me);
```

Figure 14.5 – Screenshot showing the MPI_Comm_rank call in input.cpp

As you can see, the `Input` class inherits from the `Pointer` class (see *Chapter 3, Source Code Structure and Stages of Execution*). When instantiated, all processes execute the same constructor, `input::input()`. In this case, the `MPI_Comm_Rank` call is used (*line 67*) to get the ID of each process in the current communication domain.

Once the process IDs have been obtained, only the process with `ID = 0` is permitted to open and read the file, as shown in the following screenshot:

```
81    if (me == 0) {
82        nfile = 1;
83        maxfile = 16;
84        infiles = new FILE *[maxfile];
85        infiles[0] = infile;
86    } else infiles = NULL;
```

Figure 14.6 – Screenshot showing file opening and reading by a single process in input.cpp

As you can see, *line 81* dictates that only the process with `me==0` is selected, and this process opens and reads the specified input file (*lines 82 to 85*). The other processes are blocked until this process finishes this step.

For a job with a large number of calculations involved, the program will decompose the job into multiple tasks that are assigned to multiple processes for simultaneous processing. After each process performs its designated calculations, it needs to communicate with the other processes to coordinate and accumulate the results. The concept of reduction is introduced here via the `MPI_Reduce` call:

`MPI_REDUCE(sendbuf, recvbuf, count, datatype, op, root, comm)`
IN sendbuf [the start address of sending buffer(optional data type)]
OUT recvbuf [address in receive message buffer (variable, for root process only)]
IN count [the count of sending data (non-negative integer)]
IN datatype [type of sending data(handle)]
IN op [reduce operator(handle)]
IN root [root process id (integer)]
IN comm [communication domain(handle)]

From the preceding code, `MPI_Reduce` accepts the data in the send buffers of all processes in the group and summarizes them based on the `op` operation specified (for example, sum, average, finding max, and finding min). The results are returned in the output buffer with the process sequence number `root`. This way, contributions from multiple processes can be synchronized to generate an overall output to the `root` process.

A similar operation is performed by the MPI_Allreduce call:

```
MPI_ALLREDUCE(sendbuf, recvbuf, count, datatype, op, comm)
IN sendbuf [the start address of sending buffer (optional data
type)]
OUT recvbuf [address in receive message buffer (variable)]
IN count [the count of sending data (non-negative integer)]
IN datatype [type of sending data (handle)]
IN op [reduce operator (handle)]
IN root [root process id (integer)]
IN comm [communication domain (handle)]
```

From the preceding code, the MPI_Allreduce call is equivalent to each process executing MPI_Reduce once and transmitting the output to every process, as opposed to outputting to a single processor.

Compute RDF can be analyzed as an example. This compute counts the number of target pair atoms around specified central atoms and involves repeated calculations on multiple atoms based on their neighbor lists (see *Chapter 6, Understanding Computes*).

The entire counting job can be divided among processes, and after each process completes its counting, the results from all processes need to be summed to generate the overall radial distribution function (RDF). At this point, the MPI_Allreduce call is executed to collect the results from all processes, calculate the summation, and distribute the results to each process, as shown in the following screenshot:

```
254    int *scratch = new int[npairs];
255    MPI_Allreduce(icount,scratch,npairs,MPI_INT,MPI_SUM,world);
256    for (i = 0; i < npairs; i++) icount[i] = scratch[i];
257    MPI_Allreduce(jcount,scratch,npairs,MPI_INT,MPI_SUM,world);
258    for (i = 0; i < npairs; i++) jcount[i] = scratch[i];
259    MPI_Allreduce(duplicates,scratch,npairs,MPI_INT,MPI_SUM,world);
260    for (i = 0; i < npairs; i++) duplicates[i] = scratch[i];
261    delete [] scratch;
```

Figure 14.7 – Screenshot showing MPI_Allreduce calls in compute_rdf.cpp

As you can see, summation over all processes is performed by the MPI_SUM option. The MPI predefines other operations, including finding the maximum (MPI_MAX), finding the minimum (MPI_MIN), the logical AND operation (MPI_LAND), and the logical OR operation (MPI_LOR).

Example of evaluating π

In this section, we demonstrate the MPI process with an example of approximating the value of π using broadcast and reduction operations of group communication. We observe that π can be calculated by evaluating the following integral:

$$\int_0^1 \frac{4}{1+x^2}\,dx = 4\arctan(x)\big|_0^1 = 4\arctan(1) - 4\arctan(0) = 4\arctan(1) = \pi$$

Substituting $f(x) = 4/(1+x^2)$, we get the following:

$$\int_0^1 f(x)\,dx = \pi$$

Therefore, the area contained between x=0 and x=1 under the f (x) curve gives the value of π, as illustrated in the following graph:

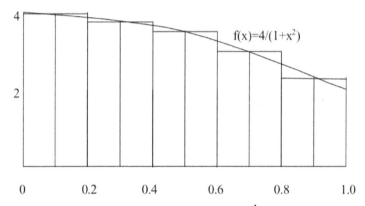

Figure 14.8 – Approximation of the area under $f(x) = \frac{4}{1+x^2}$ in the range $0 \leq x \leq 1$

As you can see, this area can be approximated by the area of N rectangular slices, as shown in the graph, with each slice occupying a width of 1/N.

The approximation for π is therefore expressed as a sum of rectangle areas, where the width of each rectangle is 1/N and the height is the value f (x) at the midpoint of each rectangle:

$$\pi \approx \frac{1}{N} \times \sum_{i=1}^{N} f\left(\frac{i-0.5}{N}\right)$$

The following screenshot shows the C++ code (`calcpi.cpp`) that calculates π by using the preceding principle, where different processors calculate the areas under different rectangles, and the total area is calculated by exchanging the results between processors:

```cpp
1   #include <mpi.h>
2   #include <stdio.h>
3   #include <math.h>
4
5   double f(double x){ return ( 4.0/ (1.0+x*x));}
6
7   int main(int argc, char *argv[]){
8
9       int done=0, myid, numprocs, i, namelen;
10      double PI = 3.141592653589793238462643;
11      double mypi, pi, h, sum, x;
12      double startwtime=0.0, endwtime;
13
14      char processor_name[MPI_MAX_PROCESSOR_NAME];
15      MPI_Init(&argc, &argv);
16      MPI_Comm_size(MPI_COMM_WORLD,&numprocs);
17      MPI_Comm_rank(MPI_COMM_WORLD,&myid);
18      MPI_Get_processor_name(processor_name,&namelen);
19      fprintf(stdout, "Process %d of %d on %s\n", myid, numprocs, processor_name);
20      int n;
21      if (myid==0){
22          printf("Please enter N=\n");
23          scanf("%d", &n);
24          startwtime = MPI_Wtime();
25      }
26      MPI_Bcast(&n, 1, MPI_INT, 0, MPI_COMM_WORLD);
27      h = 1.0 / (double) n;
28      sum = 0.0;
29      for (i = myid + 1; i <= n; i += numprocs){
30          x = h * ((double)i - 0.5);
31          sum += f(x);
32      }
33      mypi = h * sum;
34      MPI_Reduce(&mypi, &pi, 1, MPI_DOUBLE, MPI_SUM, 0, MPI_COMM_WORLD);
35      if (myid == 0) {
36          printf("pi is approximately %.16f, Error is %.16f\n", pi, fabs(pi - PI));
37          endwtime = MPI_Wtime();
38          printf("wall clock time = %f\n", endwtime-startwtime);
39          fflush( stdout );
40      }
41
42      MPI_Finalize();
43  }
```

Figure 14.9 – C++ code to calculate π by evaluating the area under f(x) using MPI processing

As you can see, the code is discussed here:

- *Lines 1 to 3* import the relevant header files.

- *Line 5* defines $f(x) = \dfrac{4}{1 + x^2}$.

- *Lines 8 to 11* define relevant quantities, including the theoretical value of π (*line 9*).

- *Lines 13 to 18* set up the MPI for calculations and print out the details of each process.

- *Lines 19* to *24* enter (input) the number of rectangles (n) to be read by process 0.

- *Line 25* broadcasts the number of rectangles (n) to all processes using MPI_Bcast, where 1 is the count, MPI_INT is the integer datatype, 0 is the transmitting process, and MPI_COMM_WORLD represents all processes that receive the broadcast. The following diagram illustrates the broadcasting process:

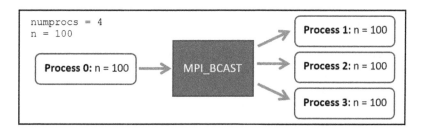

Figure 14.10 – Illustration of broadcasting n=100 from process 0 to the other processes

- *Lines 27* to *33* calculate the area of each rectangle by assigning rectangles sequentially to processes, as indicated by the step of the number of processes (numprocs). For example, if n = 100 and numprocs = 4, the first process calculates the areas of rectangles 1, 5, 9, …, 97, while the second process calculates rectangles 2, 6, 10, …, 98, and so on.

- *Line 34* accumulates all the rectangular areas from all processes and ascertains the sum of areas using the MPI_Reduce call, where mypi is the area calculated by each process and pi is the combined area that serves as the output quantity.

  Also, 1 is the count, MPI_DOUBLE indicates the floating-point datatype, MPI_SUM indicates the summation of all the mypi values received, 0 is the process that accepts the output sum, pi, and MPI_COMM_WORLD represents all processes that receive the broadcast. The following diagram illustrates the reduction process:

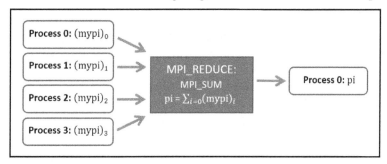

Figure 14.11 – Reduction of individual mypi values by summing across all processes to obtain pi, which is then output to process 0

- *Lines 35* to *40* allow only process 0 to print out the summed value, pi, and to calculate the difference and the processing time.

- *Line 42* ends the program with the MPI_Finalize call.

To execute the code in the command line, make sure that MPICH is installed and enter the following code:

```
mpicxx calcpi.cpp
```

The preceding code step creates the a.out file, which can be executed by means of the following command:

```
mpirun a.out
```

The command prompt will display the number of processes and ask for the number of rectangles (Please enter N=). When entered, the calculation completes and the calculated value of π, along with its deviation from the theoretical value and the processing time, will be displayed.

This appendix provides an introduction to the MPI and an overview of its implementation in LAMMPS. The MPI is used to establish parallel processing in computes, fixes, and so on, where the appropriate MPI calls are employed to exchange information properly and return the required output.

The next section briefly describes the data exchange process between owned and ghost atoms when using multiple cores in a simulation.

Data exchange between owned atoms and ghost atoms

LAMMPS is able to run on a distributed-memory machine, requiring the communication among processors to be carried out by MPI. This is implemented by the Comm class and its two child classes that implement specific functionalities:

- One of the child classes is CommBrick, described by comm_brick.h and comm_brick.cpp. In this Comm style, the simulation box is considered as a 3D grid where each block in the grid is assigned to a processor, which is responsible for communicating with its six neighboring blocks in the *(x, y, z)* directions to exchange information about neighboring atoms. This decomposition is especially suitable for uniform particle density, where every block can be expected to contain the same number of particles.

- The other child class is CommTiled, described in comm_tiled.h and comm_tiled.cpp, which can adjust the processor domains dynamically and is more effective when the system particle density is non-uniform. The desired Comm style can be selected via the comm_style command in the LAMMPS input script (https://lammps.sandia.gov/doc/comm_style.html), where the default option is CommBrick.

In *Chapter 1, MD Theory and Simulation Practices*, it is explained that interactions between atoms owned by different cores are accommodated by a shell built by each core. This accounts for atoms located at the fringes of each core domain. At every iteration, the workflow of these communications between cores depends on whether the neighbor lists need to be rebuilt. The neighbor->decide() method checks to determine whether rebuilding is required and returns a decision via the nflag quantity. If nflag is assigned a value of 1, the neighbor list needs to be rebuilt, and the following methods are invoked:

```
fix->pre_exchange()
domain->pbc()
domain->reset_box()
comm->setup()
neighbor->setup_bins()
comm->exchange()
comm->borders()
fix->pre_neighbor()
neighbor->build()
fix->post_neighbor()
```

The actual communication is facilitated by the Comm class, while the other classes perform data processing. The setup() method updates the ghost atoms' information with regards to the simulation box size, and then the exchange() method migrates atoms to new processors. The borders() method identifies ghost atoms in each processor shell (see *Figure 1.6* in *Chapter 1, MD Theory and Simulation Practices*) and copies ghost atoms' information to neighboring processors.

Else, if nflag is assigned a value of 0, then the neighbor list need not be rebuilt and it can simply exchange information between the processors. Each processor invokes the forward_comm() method to acquire the coordinates of its ghost atoms.

After calculating necessary atom interactions, LAMMPS needs to combine all contributions, including those from ghost atoms. At this stage, the reverse_comm() method is used to communicate and sum the data from ghost atoms back to their corresponding owned atoms. In effect, it is an inverse operation of the forward_comm() method.

Appendix D
Compatibility with
Version 29Oct20

In this appendix, we will discuss translating source code from the LAMMPS stable version, **29Oct20**, to the stable version, **3Mar20**. In the middle of 2020, the LAMMPS development team started using automated document generation tools to build more specific manuals that are targeted to better help us to modify their code. These tools also extract the auxiliary functions of some new classes and refactor some core classes.

Our book was started before this transition process was complete, and this book's content is based on the stable version **3Mar20**. Following the release of the stable version **29Oct20** consisting of significant changes, we illustrate some of the key differences between the current and previous versions by demonstrating the conversion of the `Fix Widom` class from the current to the previous version. More information regarding the changes is available at `https://github.com/lammps/lammps/releases/tag/stable_29Oct2020`.

After reading this appendix, you will have learned about the differences between the previous and current versions of LAMMPS and understood how to employ the knowledge gained from this book to current and future versions of LAMMPS.

Technical requirements

To execute the instructions in this chapter, you need a text editor (for example, **Notepad++** or **Gedit**) and a platform to compile LAMMPS (for example, a **Linux Terminal**). The LAMMPS version **29Oct20** can be accessed from `https://github.com/lammps/lammps/tree/stable_29Oct2020`, or downloaded from `https://lammps.sandia.gov/download.html`.

Translating Fix Widom into the 3Mar20 version

Once you download the current version (**29Oct20**) of LAMMPS, you need to copy the `fix_widom.cpp` and `fix_widom.h` files located in the `src/MC` folder to a temporary location. Use `git reset -hard b3040db1e` to revert back to the **3Mar20** version, and copy the `fix_widom.cpp` and `fix_widom.h` files back to the `src/MC` folder of this version, renamed as `fix_widom_modified.cpp` and `fix_widom_modified.h`, respectively.

Upon performing regular compilation (see *Appendix A, Building LAMMPS with CMake*) including the `MC` package, several errors are produced, some of which are shown in the following screenshot:

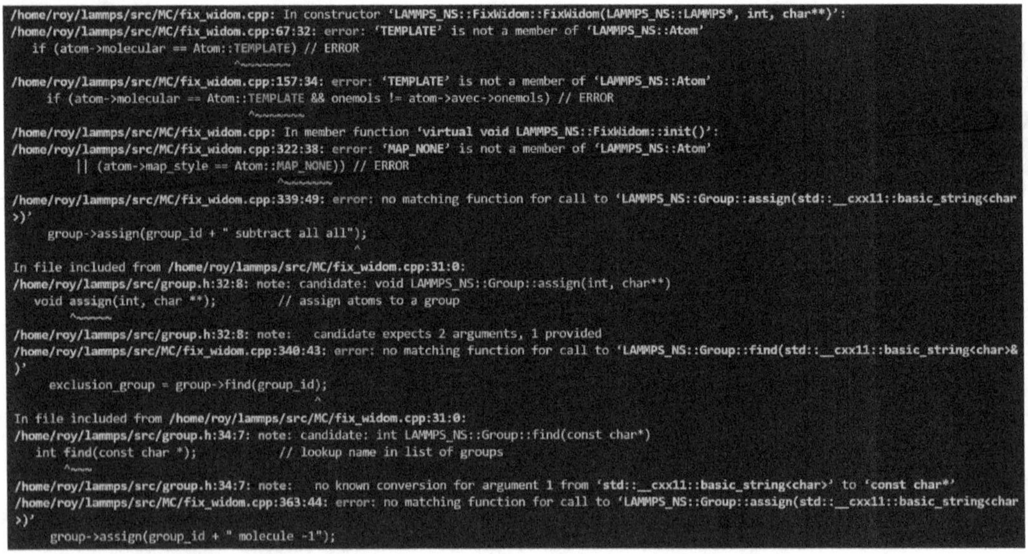

```
/home/roy/lammps/src/MC/fix_widom.cpp: In constructor 'LAMMPS_NS::FixWidom::FixWidom(LAMMPS_NS::LAMMPS*, int, char**)':
/home/roy/lammps/src/MC/fix_widom.cpp:67:32: error: 'TEMPLATE' is not a member of 'LAMMPS_NS::Atom'
   if (atom->molecular == Atom::TEMPLATE) // ERROR
                                ^~~~~~~~
/home/roy/lammps/src/MC/fix_widom.cpp:157:34: error: 'TEMPLATE' is not a member of 'LAMMPS_NS::Atom'
     if (atom->molecular == Atom::TEMPLATE && onemols != atom->avec->onemols) // ERROR
                                  ^~~~~~~~
/home/roy/lammps/src/MC/fix_widom.cpp: In member function 'virtual void LAMMPS_NS::FixWidom::init()':
/home/roy/lammps/src/MC/fix_widom.cpp:322:38: error: 'MAP_NONE' is not a member of 'LAMMPS_NS::Atom'
         || (atom->map_style == Atom::MAP_NONE)) // ERROR
                                      ^~~~~~~~
/home/roy/lammps/src/MC/fix_widom.cpp:339:49: error: no matching function for call to 'LAMMPS_NS::Group::assign(std::__cxx11::basic_string<char>)'
     group->assign(group_id + " subtract all all");
                                                 ^
In file included from /home/roy/lammps/src/MC/fix_widom.cpp:31:0:
/home/roy/lammps/src/group.h:32:8: note: candidate: void LAMMPS_NS::Group::assign(int, char**)
   void assign(int, char **);         // assign atoms to a group
        ^~~~~~
/home/roy/lammps/src/group.h:32:8: note:   candidate expects 2 arguments, 1 provided
/home/roy/lammps/src/MC/fix_widom.cpp:340:43: error: no matching function for call to 'LAMMPS_NS::Group::find(std::__cxx11::basic_string<char>&)'
     exclusion_group = group->find(group_id);
                                           ^
In file included from /home/roy/lammps/src/MC/fix_widom.cpp:31:0:
/home/roy/lammps/src/group.h:34:7: note: candidate: int LAMMPS_NS::Group::find(const char*)
   int find(const char *);            // lookup name in list of groups
       ^~~~
/home/roy/lammps/src/group.h:34:7: note:   no known conversion for argument 1 from 'std::__cxx11::basic_string<char>' to 'const char*'
/home/roy/lammps/src/MC/fix_widom.cpp:363:44: error: no matching function for call to 'LAMMPS_NS::Group::assign(std::__cxx11::basic_string<char>)'
     group->assign(group_id + " molecule -1");
```

Figure 15.1 – A partial list of errors when compiling Fix Widom in the 3Mar20 version

As you can see, the errors can be categorized into the following:

- Parsing input parameters with the Utils class
- Identifying molecular systems using the Atom class
- Additional function signatures in group.cpp

In the following sections, we will describe the preceding incompatibilities and corresponding corrections.

Incompatibility 1 – Parsing input parameters

In the **3Mar20** version, methods used in parsing such as numeric() and inumeric() are located in force.cpp, described in *Chapter 4, Accessing Information by Variables, Arrays, and Methods*. In the **29Oct20** version, these methods have been moved to utils.cpp. Therefore, to convert from the **29Oct20** into the **3Mar20** version, all parsing methods accessed by utils:: must be changed to force->, as shown in the following screenshot:

```
83    nevery = utils::inumeric(FLERR,arg[3],false,lmp);
84    ninsertions = utils::inumeric(FLERR,arg[4],false,lmp);
85    nwidom_type = utils::inumeric(FLERR,arg[5],false,lmp);
86    seed = utils::inumeric(FLERR,arg[6],false,lmp);
87    insertion_temperature = utils::numeric(FLERR,arg[7],false,lmp);
```

```
83    nevery = force->inumeric(FLERR,arg[3]);                        // JL
84    ninsertions = force->inumeric(FLERR,arg[4]);                   // JL
85    nwidom_type = force->inumeric(FLERR,arg[5]);                   // JL
86    seed = force->inumeric(FLERR,arg[6]);                          // JL
87    insertion_temperature = force->numeric(FLERR,arg[7]);  // JL
```

Figure 15.2 – (Top) 29Oct20 version using utils:: and (bottom) 3Mar20 version
using force-> to access parsing methods

As you can see, the Utils classes in the **29Oct20** version (*top*) are replaced by Force classes in the **3Mar20** version (*bottom*) in *lines 83 to 87*. Similar changes are made in *lines 234* and *242*.

Incompatibility 2 – Atom class

In the **29Oct20** version, the Atom class identifies the molecule type and map style using enumerations, as given in atom.h (*lines 34 to 35*):

```
enum{ATOMIC=0,MOLECULAR=1,TEMPLATE=2};
enum{MAP_NONE=0,MAP_ARRAY=1,MAP_HASH=2,MAP_YES=3};
```

In the **3Mar20** version, both the molecule type and map style are represented by integers, as seen in `atom.h` on *lines 35* and *203*:

```
int molecular;        // 0 = atomic, 1 = standard molecular
                      system,
                      // 2 = molecule template system
int map_style;        // style of atom map: 0=none, 1=array,
                      2=hash
```

In `fix_widom.cpp`, this incompatibility leads to multiple errors such as in *line 67*:

```
if (atom->molecular == Atom::TEMPLATE)
```

The preceding errors are corrected in the **3Mar30** version by replacing the enumerations with integers, as shown in the table here:

	Version 3Mar20	Version 29Oct20
Atom molecule type: `atom->molecular`		
Atomic	0	`Atom::ATOMIC`
Standard molecular system	1	`Atom::MOLECUAR`
Molecule template system	2	`Atom::TEMPLATE`
Atom Map_Style value: `atom->map_style`		
No request	0	`Atom::MAP_NONE`
Array	1	`Atom::MAP_ARRAY`
Hash	2	`Atom::MAP_HASH`

Table 15.1 – Conversions of atom class properties between the 3Mar20 and 29Oct20 versions

Accordingly, *line 67* in `fix_widom_modified.cpp` is changed to the following:

```
if (atom->molecular == 2)
```

In the **3Mar20** version (in `fix_widom_modified.cpp` and `fix_widom_modified.h`), similar changes are made in *lines 157, 322, 788*, and *946*.

Incompatibility 3 – Function signatures in group.cpp

In the **29Oct20** version, the Group class contains additional methods compared to the Group class in the **3Mar20** version. The following screenshot shows one such method, the convenience function, assign():

```
534  /* ------------------------------------------------------------------
535       convenience function to allow assigning to groups from a single string
536     ------------------------------------------------------------------
537
538   void Group::assign(const std::string &groupcmd)
539   {
540     auto args = utils::split_words(groupcmd);
541     char **newarg = new char*[args.size()];
542     int i=0;
543     for (const auto &arg : args) {
544       newarg[i++] = (char *)arg.c_str();
545     }
546     assign(args.size(),newarg);
547     delete[] newarg;
548   }
```

Figure 15.3 – The Group::assign() method in the 29Oct20 version

In the **3Mar20** version, the group->assign() method needed to split and compare the char array contents one character at a time. In the **29Oct20** version, using the auxiliary functions in the Utils class, the string can be passed directly to the method. Therefore, in the **3Mar20** version, appropriate changes need to be made to accommodate splitting and comparing the character array.

Another incompatible method is the group->find() method, shown in the following screenshot:

```
582  /* ------------------------------------------------------------------
583       return group index if name matches existing group, -1 if no such group
584     ------------------------------------------------------------------
585
586   int Group::find(const std::string &name)
587   {
588     for (int igroup = 0; igroup < MAX_GROUP; igroup++)
589       if (names[igroup] && (name == names[igroup])) return igroup;
590     return -1;
591   }
```

Figure 15.4 – The Group::find() method in the 29Oct20 version

Like the group->assign() method, the group->find() method in the **29Oct20** version can read a string directly, as you can see in the preceding screenshot. Therefore, the group name has to be split and entered as a character array in the **3Mar20** version for this method as well.

The Utils class in the **29Oct20** version offers other common reusable methods, such as conversion, validation, I/O, and argument processing. More information is available in the official manual at https://lammps.sandia.gov/doc/Developer_utils.html.

To correct both of these errors, we introduce the following modifications in fix_widom_modified.cpp:

- *Line 334* creates a 2D character array, group_arg[][]:

```
char **group_arg = new char*[4];
```

- *Lines 340* to *345* replace the std::string convention (which is **C++11** standard) with the **C-style** string character array convention (see fix_gcmc.cpp for an example), as shown in the following screenshot:

```
339    // JL
340    int len = strlen(id) + 29;
341    group_arg[0] = new char[len];
342    sprintf(group_arg[0], "FixWidom:widom_exclusion_group:%s", id);
343    group_arg[1] = (char *) "substract all all";
344    group->assign(2, group_arg);
345    exclusion_group = group->find(group_arg[0]);
346
347    // auto group_id = std::string("FixWidom:widom_exclusion_group:") + id;
348    // group->assign(group_id + " subtract all all");
349    // exclusion_group = group->find(group_id);
```

Figure 15.5 – The first conversion from std::string into a character array in fix_widom_modified.cpp

- *Line 362* sets arg[2] as the first element of the character array instead of using the C++11 convention, c_str, on the group ID:

```
362    arg[2] = group_arg[0];                        // JL
363    // arg[2] = (char *) group_id.c_str();  // JL
```

Figure 15.6 – The conversion from c_str in fix_widom_modified.cpp

- *Lines 374* to *379* replace the std::string convention with the C-style string character array convention, as shown in the following screenshot:

```
373    // JL
374    int len = strlen(id) + 29;
375    group_arg[0] = new char[len];
376    sprintf(group_arg[0], "FixWidom:rotation_gas_atoms:%s", id);
377    group_arg[1] = (char *) "molecule -1";
378    group->assign(2, group_arg);
379    molecule_group = group->find(group_arg[0]);
380
381    // auto group_id = std::string("FixWidom:rotation_gas_atoms:") + id;
382    // group->assign(group_id + " molecule -1");
383    // molecule_group = group->find(group_id);
```

Figure 15.7 – The second conversion from std::string into the character array
in fix_widom_modified.cpp

The preceding changes, along with importing `fix_widom_modified.h` in *line 18* of `fix_widom_modified.cpp`, allow the successful compilation of the `Fix Widom` class in the **3Mar20** version.

This appendix demonstrated some common differences in source code structure encountered in the **29Oct20** version, and possible modifications to facilitate compatibility with the **3Mar20** version. Similarly, modifications can be made in reverse to facilitate compatibility of code written in the **3Mar20** version with the **29Oct20** version.

Assessments

Chapter 1, MD Theory and Simulation Practices

Question 1

Using a simulation box that has periodic boundaries in all directions, how can a metal slab consisting of a few layers be generated so that the slab extends indefinitely in the xy-plane but accommodates a long vacuum above and below the slab?

Answer

The xy-plane of the simulation box should exactly fit the xy-plane of the slab whereas the z-dimension should be considerably larger than the slab thickness. The slab can then be placed midpoint along the z-direction.

Question 2

How should the optimum skin width compare between a solid at a low temperature versus a gas at a high temperature?

Answer

The skin width for the solid at low temperature should be smaller than for a gas at a high temperature to account for larger atomic speeds for the latter.

Question 3

In a large simulation box containing a uniform density of solute and solvent molecules, how would the pair potential energy of a solute molecule at the center of the box change with periodic or non-periodic boundaries (assuming that the pair potential cutoff is shorter than half of any of the simulation box side lengths)?

Answer

There is no change since the boundaries do not influence the interaction of the molecule at the center of the box.

Question 4

Given a uniform metal nanocrystal, how can subdomains and ghost atoms be established?

Answer

They can be established by uniform spatial decomposition by volume where every domain contains the same number of atoms and ghost atoms.

Chapter 2, LAMMPS Syntax and Source Code Repository

Question 1

In the `src` folder, what files do the folders titled in uppercase letters contain?

Answer

They contain the source code of optional packages.

Question 2

Which is the top-most level class in the source code hierarchy?

Answer

The LAMMPS class (`lammps.cpp` and `lammps.h`) is the top-most level class.

Chapter 3, Source Code Structure and Stages of Execution

Question 1

What quantities are represented by the `id`, `igroup`, and `style` variables in `fix.cpp`?

Answer

Fix ID, group ID, and fix style are represented by the `id`, `igroup`, and `style` variables in `fix.cpp`.

Question 2

Which method in `pair.h` returns the pair potential between atoms?

Answer

`single()` in `pair.h` returns the pair potential between atoms.

Question 3

Which methods in `verlet.cpp` perform the two halves of the velocity Verlet algorithm?

Answer

The `initial_integrate()` and `final_integrate()` methods in `verlet.cpp` perform the two halves of the velocity Verlet algorithm.

Chapter 4, Accessing Information by Variables, Arrays, and Methods

Question 1

What do the * and ** symbols preceding variable names imply regarding their memory allocation?

Answer

* indicates a 1D array, and ** indicates a 2D array, accessed via pointers.

Question 2

What information is contained in the `firstneigh` array as commonly created during neighbor list requests?

Answer

The neighbor list of each atom is contained in the `firstneigh` array as commonly created during neighbor list requests.

Question 3

When should the `force->inumeric()` method be used instead of the `force->numeric()` method to parse input from a script?

Answer

The `force->inumeric()` method should be used instead of the `force->numeric()` method to parse input from a script when the input parameter must be parsed as an integer instead of a floating-point number.

Chapter 5, Understanding Pair Styles

Question 1

Which methods are used to read global and local coefficients in pair styles?

Answer

For global coefficients, we use `settings()` and for local coefficients, we use the `coeff()` method.

Question 2

Why does the `fpair` variable always have the force function multiplied with the reciprocal of the separation?

Answer

The `fpair` variable always has the force function multiplied with the reciprocal of the separation so, that way, each force component can be calculated by multiplying `fpair` by the corresponding displacement vector component.

Question 3

What is the primary purpose served by the `single()` method?

Answer

The primary purpose served by the `single()` method is to return the total pairwise energy of a pair style.

Question 4

The Yukawa potential has the functional form $V(r) = \frac{A \exp(-\kappa r)}{r}$ with the radial force function, $F(r) = \frac{A \left(\kappa + \frac{1}{r} \right) \exp(-\kappa r)}{r}$, where A and κ are parameters. Based on this, answer the following:

a. In `pair_yukawa.cpp`, which line parses A?

b. In `pair_yukawa.cpp`, which line parses κ?

c. In `pair_yukawa.cpp`, what quantity does the variable `forceyukawa` (*line 100*) represent?

d. In `pair_yukawa.cpp`, what quantity does `fpair` (*line 102*) represent?

Answer

a. *Line 183* parses A:

```
double a_one = force->numeric(FLERR,arg[2]);
```

b. *Line 156* parses κ:

```
kappa = force->numeric(FLERR,arg[0]);
```

c. $A\left(\kappa + \dfrac{1}{r}\right)\exp(-\kappa r)$

d. $\dfrac{A\left(\kappa + \dfrac{1}{r}\right)\exp(-\kappa r)}{r^2}$

Chapter 6, Understanding Computes

Question 1

Which method is responsible for parsing beyond the third argument entered in a compute command in the LAMMPS input script?

Answer

The constructor method is.

Question 2

What are the arguments accepted by the `MPI_Allreduce()` method?

Answer

The `input`, `output`, `size`, `datatype`, `operation`, and `cores` arguments.

Question 3

What is the primary purpose served by the `destructor` method?

Answer

It performs the memory deallocation of quantities that have been allocated memory earlier.

Question 4

In `compute reduce`, the `replace` option can be used to find the index of the quantity with the maximum or minimum value among entered quantities (see `https://lammps.sandia.gov/doc/compute_reduce.html`). In `compute_reduce.cpp`, which lines are responsible for identifying the index of the quantity with the following:

a. The maximum value out of all processors?

b. The minimum value out of all processors?

Answer

a. *Line 433* identifies the maximum value out of all processors:

```
   MPI_Allreduce(&pairme,&pairall,1,MPI_DOUBLE_INT,MPI_
MAXLOC,world);
```

b. *Line 411* identifies the minimum value out of all processors:

```
   MPI_Allreduce(&pairme,&pairall,1,MPI_DOUBLE_INT,MPI_
MINLOC,world);
```

Chapter 7, Understanding Fixes

Question 1

Which method is responsible for determining the stage of execution of a fix?

Answer

The `setmask()` method is responsible.

Question 2

What quantities are represented by the `dtv`, `dtf`, and `dtfm` variables?

Answer

`dtv` is for a full timestep, `dtf` for a half-timestep, and `dtfm` for the ratio of `dtf` to mass.

Question 3

What is the primary purpose of the `fflag` and `tflag` quantities in the `Fix Rigid` class?

Answer

`fflag` is for activating or deactivating translational degrees of freedom; `tflag` is for activating or deactivating rotational degrees of freedom.

Chapter 8, Exploring Supporting Classes

Question 1

Which methods in `variable.cpp` need to be modified to incorporate new mathematical functions that can be evaluated using the `variable equal` command in the LAMMPS input script?

Answer

`math_function()`, `eval_tree()`, and `collapse_tree()` need to be evaluated, along with the enumeration list in *lines 65 to 71*.

Question 2

How should multi-dimensional arrays be declared before they are fed into a `memory->create()` method?

Answer

They should be declared as pointer arrays preceded by multiple * symbols to correspond to the number of dimensions.

Question 3

For a quartic angle potential, $U(\theta) = K(\theta - \theta_0)^4$, what should be the form of variable a in the corresponding angle style .cpp file?

Answer

The form is a = -4.0 * tk * dtheta * dtheta * s;.

Chapter 9, Modifying Pair Potentials

Question 1

When writing a new radially-symmetric pair potential for V(r), which quantity in the compute() method should be set equal to $-\frac{1}{r}\frac{dV}{dr}$ multiplied by factor*lj?

Answer

The quantity is fpair.

Question 2

If it is desired that Pair TableZ described in this chapter should not be applied to atoms belonging to the same molecule (assuming that atom_style in the input script is defined as molecular), how should pair_table_z.cpp be modified?

Answer

Changes in the compute() method are as follows:

- *Line 88*:

```
tagint *molecule = atom->molecule;
```

- *Line 116*:

```
if (rsq < cutsq[itype][jtype] && (molecule[i] !=
molecule[j])) {
```

Question 3

In `Pair CundallStrack`, if the drag force is assumed to depend on $|\vec{v_r}|^2$ instead of $|\vec{v_r}|$, what changes are required in the `compute()` method to implement this drag force?

Answer

Changes in the `compute()` method are as follows:

- *Line 247*:

```
fs1 = - (kt*shear[0] + A*vtr1*vtr1);
```

- *Line 248*:

```
fs2 = - (kt*shear[1] + A*vtr2*vtr2);
```

- *Line 249*:

```
fs3 = - (kt*shear[2] + A*vtr3*vtr3);
```

Chapter 10, Modifying Force Applications

Question 1

In the example of the `Fix AddforceXY` class, what changes are required to add a z-coordinate z_0 to the point (x_0, y_0) so that the z-component of the spring force is $F_z = -k_z(z - z_0)$ with a spring constant k_z?

Answer

Following is a summary of changes:

Header file: Declare `kz`, `*kzstr`, `kzstyle`, and `kzvar`.

Constructor: A code block to parse `kz`.

`init()`: A code block to check `kz` variable; delete *lines 229, 230*; insert `kzstyle` in *line 231*.

`post_force()`:

      a. *Line 331*: `f[i][2] += -kz*(x[i][2] - z0);`

      b. *Line 386*: `if (zstyle) f[i][2] += -kz*(x[i][2] - z0);`

      c. Changes in virial calculations

Question 2

In `Fix ActiveForce`, if the active force must only be applied to an atom that is bonded to another atom of the `ATYPE` type along the direction of that bond, what changes are needed in the `post_force()` method (assuming `ATYPE` has been parsed correctly)?

Answer

The changes are as follows:

- *Line 293*: `int *type = atom->type;`
- *Line 332*: `if (type[atom2] != ATYPE) continue;`
- *Line 419*: `if (type[atom2] != ATYPE) continue;`

Question 3

In the LAMMPS input script used in the example of `Fix Addboost`, how should the `C2` compute be changed so that the boost potential is applied to the atom with the maximum pair potential energy?

Answer

`compute C2` can be changed to `compute C2 all pe/atom` so that the boost potential is applied to the atom with the maximum pair potential energy.

Chapter 11, Modifying Thermostats

Question 1

In a variation of the Andersen thermostat, a frequency v in the range $[0,1]$ is provided and in every iteration, a uniform random number in the range $[0,1]$ is generated. If the random number is less than v, then the velocities are adjusted from a Maxwell-Boltzmann distribution. What changes are required in `fix_temp_andersen.cpp` to implement this variation (assume that the `FREQUENCY` input parameter is used to represent v)?

Answer

Change *line 79*: `if ( (currentTime > 0) && (random->uniform() < FREQUENCY) ) {`

Question 2

In the example of exponential increment of temperature, if it is required to cap the temperature at an upper limit, t_stop, what changes are required in the compute_temp_target() method of the modified fix_nh.cpp file?

Answer

Change *line 2279*: `if ( t_target > t_stop ) t_target = t_stop;`

Other Books You May Enjoy

If you enjoyed this book, you may be interested in these other books by Packt:

Modern C++ Programming Cookbook - Second Edition

Marius Bancila

ISBN: 978-1-80020-898-8

- Understand the new C++20 language and library features and the problems they solve
- Become skilled at using the standard support for threading and concurrency for daily tasks
- Leverage the standard library and work with containers, algorithms, and iterators
- Solve text searching and replacement problems using regular expressions
- Work with different types of strings and learn the various aspects of compilation
- Take advantage of the file system library to work with files and directories
- Implement various useful patterns and idioms
- Explore the widely used testing frameworks for C++

Windows Subsystem for Linux 2 (WSL 2) Tips, Tricks, and Techniques

Stuart Leeks

ISBN: 978-1-80056-244-8

- Install and configure Windows Subsystem for Linux and Linux distros

- Access web applications running in Linux from Windows

- Invoke Windows applications, file systems, and environment variables from bash in WSL

- Customize the appearance and behavior of the Windows Terminal to suit your preferences and workflows

- Explore various tips for enhancing the Visual Studio Code experience with WSL

- Install and work with Docker and Kubernetes within Windows Subsystem for Linux

- Discover various productivity tips for working with Command-line tools in WSL

Leave a review - let other readers know what you think

Please share your thoughts on this book with others by leaving a review on the site that you bought it from. If you purchased the book from Amazon, please leave us an honest review on this book's Amazon page. This is vital so that other potential readers can see and use your unbiased opinion to make purchasing decisions, we can understand what our customers think about our products, and our authors can see your feedback on the title that they have worked with Packt to create. It will only take a few minutes of your time, but is valuable to other potential customers, our authors, and Packt. Thank you!

Index

Symbols

π
  evaluating, example 333-336
2D spring force
  about 222, 223
  addforceXY.h file, modifying 223
  application, by writing fix 222
  constructor, modifying in fix_
    addforceXY.cpp 224, 225
  init() method, modifying in fix_
    addforceXY.cpp 225, 226
  in.Test_FixAddforceXY file,
    running 229-231
  post_force() method, modifying in
    fpost_force() method 227-29
3Mar20 version
  Fix Widom, translating into 340
12-6 Lennard-Jones potential 5

A

active force
  applying, to write fix 231
active force, on bonded atoms
  assigning 237-240
constructor in fix_activeforce.cpp,
    modifying 234, 235
  creating 232, 233
  fix_activeforce.h file, modifying 233, 234
  in.Test_ActiveForce file,
    running 240-243
  post_force() method, modifying in
    fix_activeforce.cpp 235, 236
  testing, with in.Test_ActiveForce 241
Andersen thermostat
  about 268
  applying, to write fix 268
  testing, with trail input script 273-276
  theory 268, 269
Angle class
  studying 173-176
angle-dependent potential 173
angle/harmonic class
  studying 173-180
atom indices
  mapping 51
atom properties
  accessing 48-51

B

Bitmask 321
Boltzmann constant 269
bond-boost potential
  about 253, 254
  applying, to write fix 252
  constructor in fix_addboost.
    cpp, modifying 256, 257
  fix_addboost.h file, modifying 254, 256
  init() method, modifying in
    fix_addboost.cpp 257, 258
  in.Test_FixAddboost file,
    running 260-265
  post_force() method, modifying in
    fix_addboost.cpp 258-260
boost potential
  testing, with trail input script 285-289
Buckingham potential 75

C

C++ extension, for VSCode
  URL 319
C++ flags 314
Center-Of-Mass (COM) 213
child classes 30
child pair style classes
  methods 66
CMake 314
compute group/group class
  ComputeGroupGroup() method 93, 94
  compute_vector() method 97
  init_list() method 95
  init() method 95
  pair_contribution() method 95, 96

reviewing 93
  scalar() method 97
compute heat flux class
  ComputeHeatFlux() method 109, 110
  compute_vector() method 110-114
  init() method 110
  reviewing 107-109
compute KE class
  ComputeKE() method 90
  compute_scalar() method 91, 92
  init() method 90
  reviewing 89
compute RDF class
  compute_array() method 104-107
  ComputeRDF() method 100, 101
  init_list() method 102, 103
  init() method 102, 103
  init_norm() method 103, 104
  reviewing 98, 99
computes
  structure, reviewing 88, 89
compute_scalar() method
  modifying, in fix_nh.cpp 284
compute_temp_target() method
  modifying, in fix_nh.cpp 282-284
constructor
  modifying, in fix_nh.cpp 279-281
  modifying, in
    fix_printEvaporate.cpp 290
  modifying, in fix_temp_
    andersen.cpp 270
cores 15
Coulomb friction 209
Cundall-Strack scheme 209
custom wall force
  application, by writing fix 243

D

dangerous build 15
data types
  incorporating 62, 63
debugging
  about 314
  prerequisites 314-316
  with GDB 317-319
  with VSCode 319-321
Dissipative Particle Dynamics (DPD) 80
distribution of particles
  temperature and velocity,
    examining 9, 10
DPD potential
  compute() method 83-85
  reviewing 80, 81
  settings() method 82, 83

E

end_of_step() method
  modifying, in fix_printEvaporate.
    cpp 292, 293
  modifying, in fix_temp_
    andersen.cpp 271, 272
Error class
  all() method 165
  messages() method 166, 167
  one() method 166
  studying 164, 165
  warning() method 166, 167
Euler algorithm 7
evaporation region
  output, printing to write fix 289
  testing, with trail input script 293-295
  theory 289

expanded Lennard-Jones wall force
  about 244
  constructor in fix_wall_region.
    cpp, modifying 245, 246
  header file, modifying 244, 245
  init() method, modifying in fix_
    wall_region.cpp 246, 247
  in.Test_WallRegion file,
    running 249- 252
  lj126Expanded() method, adding 247
  post_force() method,
    modifying 248, 249
exponential temperature increment
  theory 277, 278

F

face-centered cubic (FCC)
  about 137
  find_best_ref() method 142
  FixOrientFCC() method 141
  post_force() method 143, 144
Fast Fourier Transform package 298
fix
  general structure, exploring 118
  writing, to apply 2D spring force 222
  writing, to apply active force 231
  writing, to apply Andersen
    thermostat 268
  writing, to apply bondboost
    potential 252
  writing, to apply custom wall force 243
  writing, to apply non-linear
    temperature increment 277
  writing, to print output at
    evaporation region 289

Fix AddForce class
  FixAddForce() method 119, 120
  init() method 120, 121
  post_force() method 123-125
  reviewing 118
  setmask() method 122
Fix NH class
  studying 129-134
fix_nh.cpp
  compute_scalar() method,
      modifying in 284
  compute_temp_target() method,
      modifying in 282-284
  constructor, modifying in 279-281
  init() method, modifying in 281
fix_nh.h header file
  modifying 278, 279
Fix NVE class
  final_integrate() method 128, 129
  initial_integrate() method 127, 128
  studying 125, 126
Fix Orient/FCC class
  reviewing 137-140
Fix Print class
  end_of_step() method 136
  FixPrint() method 134-136
  studying 134
fix print command
  reference link 293
fix_printEvaporate.cpp
  constructor, modifying in 291
  end_of_step() method,
      modifying in 292, 293
  init() methods, modifying in 291
fix_printEvaporate.h header file
  modifying 290

Fix Rigid class
  exploring 148, 149-151
  final_integrate() method 154, 155
  initial_integrate() method 152
  set_xv() method 153, 154
fix_temp_andersen.cpp
  constructor, modifying in 270
  end_of_step() method,
      modifying in 271, 272
fix_temp_andersen.h header file
  modifying 269
Fix Wall class
  analyzing 144, 145
Fix wall/lj126 class
  analyzing 146, 147, 148
Fix Wall/LJ126 class
  analyzing 144, 146
Fix Widom, translating into
      3Mar20 version
  about 340
  Atom class 341, 342
  function signatures, in group.
      cpp 343, 344
  input parameters, parsing 341
fluctuation dissipation theorem 81
friction-based pair style
  compute() method, modifying 210-213
  in.Test_PairCundallStrack
      file, running 214-218
  writing 209, 210

G

Gaussian distribution 269
Gaussian function 9
GDB
  used, for debugging 317-319

ghost atoms
    about 16
    and owned atoms, data exchange
        between 336, 337
Group class
    discovering 158-161
    reference link 158, 161

H

harmonic angle potential 176
harmonic potential
    writing 186, 187
height-dependent pair potential
    header file, modifying 199, 200
    implementing 202- 206
    input parameters, parsing for
        Pair TableZ 200, 201
    in.Test_PairTableZ file, running 206-209
    pair_table.h, modifying 199, 200
    writing 196-199
high-performance computing (HPC) 317
hyperdynamics 253, 277

I

image flag 13
init() method
    modifying, in fix_nh.cpp 281
    modifying, in fix_printEvaporate.
        cpp 290
input.cpp
    input script commands,
        parsing by 43, 44
input script
    parameters, reading from 57-61
input script commands
    parsing, by input.cpp 43, 44

input script, LAMMPS
    structure 20, 21
Integrated Development
    Environment (IDE) 305
iterative updates
    performing, via Velocity
        Verlet algorithm 6, 7

K

kinetic energy (KE) 89

L

LAMMPS, building
    about 299
    CMake, using 301-312
    modified codes, including 301
    packages, including 300
LAMMPS code, structure and algorithms
    reference link 42
LAMMPS compilation, in Windows
    about 304
    CMake, downloading 305
    CodeBlocks, download link 306
    Git, download link 304
    Microsoft MPI, download link 306
    source code, downloading 304
LAMMPS simulation
    min.cpp class 41
    stages, executing 36
    verlet.cpp class 36, 41
LAMMPS version
    reference link 60
Large-scale Atomic/Molecular Massively
    Parallel Simulator (LAMMPS)
    about 11
    building 299, 306-310

compiling, in Windows 304
download link 298
input script structure 20, 21
MPI 329- 332
URL 20
working with, prerequisites 298
Lennard-Jones (LJ) boost potential 285
Lennard-Jones potential 75
Liouville exponential operators 132
Liouville operator method 130
Lissajous trajectories 223
logical errors 314

M

Make 311
make install command 302
Marsaglia random number generator 83
Marsaglia random number
    generator (RNG) 269
Maxwell-Boltzmann velocity
    distribution 9, 242, 268
McLachlan interaction 196
MD simulation practices
  implementing 11
  neighbor lists 14, 15
  pair-potential cutoff 11
  periodic boundary conditions 11-13
  processor communication 15, 16
  processor communication, stages 17
Memory class
  reviewing 167-172
Message Passing Interface (MPI)
  about 92, 299, 326
  current process ID 327
  finalization 326
  initializing 326
  in LAMMPS 329-332

messages, receiving 328
messages, sending 327, 328
number of processes 327
min.cpp class 41
Minimalist GNU for Windows
    (MinGW) 306
minimization 36
minimum image convention 13
molecular dynamics (MD) theory 4
Morse potential
  allocate() method 68
  coeff() method 70
  compute() method 72-74
  init_one() method 71
  reviewing 67
  settings() method 69
  single() method 74
MPICH
  URL 299
MPI communication
  context 330
  process group 330
MPI message
  about 328, 329
  data 329
  envelope 328

N

neighbor list
  about 14, 51
  elements, accessing 53
  requesting 52-55
node 15
non-linear temperature increment
    applying, to write fix 277
Nose-Hoover thermostat 129, 276

O

owned atoms
  and ghost atoms, data exchange
    between 336, 337

P

Pair Morse, converting into
  harmonic pair potential
  class names, modifying 187-89
  equations, modifying 189-191
  input parameters, parsing for
    Pair Harmonic 192, 193
  in.Test_PairHarmonic file,
    running 193-196
  variables, modifying 189-191
pair_style dpd command
  reference link 81
pair_style morse command
  reference link 67
pair styles
  general structure, reviewing 66
pair_style table command
  reference link 76
pair table potential
  coeff() method 78
  compute() method 79, 80
  reviewing 75, 76
  settings() method 76, 77
pair_write command
  reference link 196
parameters
  reading, from input script 57-61
parent classes
  about 30
  compute.cpp 35, 36
  compute.h 35, 36

  fix.cpp 30-32
  fix.h 30, 31, 32
  pair.cpp 32-35
  pair.h 32-35
periodic boundary conditions 11
physical constants
  accessing 55-57
pointers class
  role 42
point particles
  dynamics 4-6
Potential Energy (PE) 193
prerequisites, for working with LAMMPS
  about 298
  dependencies, installing 298
  MPICH, downloading 299
  source code, downloading 298

Q

quaternion operations 149

R

radial distribution function (RDF) 98
radially-symmetric harmonic
  potential 186
Rayleigh distribution 10
rotational motion 8, 9

S

sbmask() 322, 323
sequence-control methods
  min_post_force() 41
  min_pre_exchange() 41
  min_pre_force() 41
shared-memory machines 15

skin width 14

source code hierarchy
    reference link 24
    reviewing 23, 24

source code repository
    about 22
    reference link 24

spatial decomposition 16

subnet mask 321

syntax errors314

T

temperature-programmed
        desorption (TPD)
    reference link 278

V

Variable class
    exploring 161-164
    reference link 161

Velocity Verlet algorithm
    about 7
    iterative updates, performing via 6, 7

velocity Verlet integration 36

verlet.cpp class 36, 41

verlet.cpp class, methods
    about 40
    force_clear() method 37
    init() method 36
    setup() method 38, 39

virial computation 124

Visual Studio Code (VSCode)
    URL 319
    used, for debugging 319-321

W

Windows
    LAMMPS, compiling in 304